Work
Motivation

FOUNDATIONS FOR ORGANIZATIONAL SCIENCE
A Sage Publications Series
Series Editor
David Whetten, *Brigham Young University*
Editors
Anne S. Huff, *University of Colorado* and *Cranfield University* (UK)
Benjamin Schneider, *University of Maryland*
M. Susan Taylor, *University of Maryland*

The FOUNDATIONS FOR ORGANIZATIONAL SCIENCE series supports the development of students, faculty, and prospective organizational science professionals through the publication of texts authored by leading organizational scientists. Each volume provides a highly personal, hands-on introduction to a core topic or theory and challenges the reader to explore promising avenues for future theory development and empirical application.

Books in This Series

PUBLISHING IN THE ORGANIZATIONAL SCIENCES, Second Edition
Edited by L. L. Cummings and Peter J. Frost
SENSEMAKING IN ORGANIZATIONS
Karl E. Weick
INSTITUTIONS AND ORGANIZATIONS
W. Richard Scott
RHYTHMS OF ACADEMIC LIFE
Peter J. Frost and M. Susan Taylor
RESEARCHERS HOOKED ON TEACHING:
Noted Scholars Discuss the Synergies of Teaching and Research
Rae André, and Peter J. Frost
ORGANIZATIONAL JUSTICE AND HUMAN RESOURCE MANAGEMENT
Robert Folger and Russell Cropanzano
RECRUITING EMPLOYEES: Individual and Organizational Perspectives
Alison E. Barber
ATTITUDES IN AND AROUND ORGANIZATIONS
Arthur P. Brief
IDENTITY IN ORGANIZATIONS: Building Theory Through Conversations
Edited by David Whetten and Paul Godfrey
PERSONNEL SELECTION: A Theoretical Approach
Neal Schmitt and David Chan
BUILDING STRATEGY FROM THE MIDDLE: Reconceptualizing Strategy Process
Steven W. Floyd and Bill Wooldridge
MISSING ORGANIZATIONAL LINKAGES: Tools for Cross-Level Research
Paul S. Goodman
THE CONTINGENCY THEORY OF ORGANIZATIONS
Lex Donaldson
ORGANIZATIONAL STRESS: A Review and Critique of Theory, Research, and Applications
Cary L. Cooper, Philip J. Dewe, and Michael P. O'Driscoll
INSTITUTIONS AND ORGANIZATIONS, Second Edition
W. Richard Scott
ORGANIZATIONAL CULTURE: Mapping the Terrain
Joanne Martin
PERSONALITY IN WORK ORGANIZATIONS
Lawrence R. James and Michelle D. Mazerolle
CAREERS IN AND OUT OF ORGANIZATIONS
Douglas T. Hall
ORGANIZATION CHANGE: Theory and Practice
W. Warner Burke
COMPENSATION: Theory, Evidence, and Strategic Implication
Barry Gerhart and Sara L. Rynes
THE PSYCHOLOGY OF DECISION MAKING, Second Edition: People in Organizations
Lee Roy Beach and Terry Connolly
WORK MOTIVATION: History, Theory, Research, and Practice
Gary P. Latham

Gary P. Latham

Joseph L. Rotman School of Management,
University of Toronto

Work Motivation

History, Theory, Research, and Practice

Foundations for
Organizational
Science
A Sage Publications Series

SAGE Publications
Thousand Oaks ■ London ■ New Delhi

For information:

Sage Publications, Inc.
2455 Teller Road
Thousand Oaks, California 91320
E-mail: order@sagepub.com

Sage Publications Ltd.
1 Oliver's Yard
55 City Road
London EC1Y 1SP
United Kingdom

Sage Publications India Pvt. Ltd.
B-42, Panchsheel Enclave
Post Box 4109
New Delhi 110 017 India

Printed in the United States of America

Library of Congress Cataloging-in-Publication Data

Latham, Gary P.
Work motivation: History, theory, research, and practice / Gary P. Latham.
    p. cm. — (Foundations for organizational science)
Includes bibliographical references and index.
ISBN 978-0-7619-2017-5 (cloth)
ISBN 978-0-7619-2018-2 (pbk.)
    1. Employee motivation. I. Title. II. Series.
HF5549.5.M63.L385 2007
658.3'14—dc22

                                    2006006357

This book is printed on acid-free paper.

08   09   10   9   8   7   6   5   4   3   2

Acquisitions Editor:	Al Bruckner
Editorial Assistant:	MaryAnn Vail
Typesetter:	C&M Digitals (P) Ltd.
Indexer:	Pamela Van Huss

Contents

Introduction to the Series   ix
David Whetten

Editor's Comments   xi
Benjamin Schneider

Preface and Acknowledgments: Person-Environment Fit   xiii

Introduction: Thirteen Critical Incidents in
    the Life of a Scientist/Practitioner   xxiii

Part I: The 20th Century: Understanding the Past   1

Chapter 1: 1900–1925: Biology, Behavior, and Money   3
    Introduction   3
    Biology   6
    Behavior   9
    Money   11
    Concluding Comments   12

Chapter 2: 1925–1950: Dust Bowl Empiricism   13
    Introduction   13
    Attitude Surveys   15
    Laboratory Experiments   16
    Field Experiments   17
    Hawthorne Studies   18
    World War II   21
    Concluding Comments   24

Chapter 3: 1950–1975: The Emergence of Theory   27
    Introduction   27
    Job Satisfaction and Job Performance   28
    Motivation Theory   29
    Need Hierarchy Theory   30
    Theory X and Theory Y   32
    Theory-Driven Empirical Research   33
    Job Characteristics   36

Equity Theory   42
Expectancy Theory   44
Behavior Modification   48
Goal-Setting Theory   52
Concluding Comments   56

Chapter 4: 1975–2000: The Employee Is Immersed in Thought   59
Introduction   59
Goal-Setting Theory   60
   Goal Limitations   63
Social Cognitive Theory   70
Self-Regulation   76
Job Characteristics Revisited   79
A Comprehensive Framework: The High-Performance Cycle   80
   Demands Influence Performance   80
   Mediators   85
   Moderators   86
   Performance Leads to Rewards That Affect Satisfaction 92
   Satisfaction Leads to Organizational Commitment   93
Principles of Organizational Justice   95
Concluding Comments   98

Chapter 5: 20th-Century Controversies   99
Money   99
Intrinsic vs. Extrinsic Motivation   102
Performance and Satisfaction   105
Participative Decision Making   108
Seismic Events: Summary and Overview of the 20th Century   116
   From a Scientist's Viewpoint   116
   From a Practitioner's Viewpoint   121

Part II: The 21st Century: Examining the Present: 2000–2005   125

Chapter 6: Needs: The Starting Point of Motivation   127
Introduction   127
Need Hierarchy Theory   128
Socioanalytic Theory   130
Concluding Comments   131

Chapter 7: Personality Traits: Distal Predictors of Motivation   133
Introduction   133
Five Factor Model (FFM)   135
Self-Regulatory/Self-Monitoring Personality   137
Core Self-Evaluations   139

Goal Orientation	141
Self-Determination Theory	142
Concluding Comments	145
Chapter 8: Values: Trans-Situational Goals	**149**
Introduction	149
Context	150
Societal Culture	151
Job Characteristics	157
Person-Environment Fit	161
Concluding Comments	172
Chapter 9: Cognition: Goals, Feedback, and Self-Regulation	**175**
Introduction	175
Goal-Setting Theory	176
Conscious Goals	177
Contextual Conditions	180
Implementation Intentions and Subconscious Goals	190
Feedback	198
Self-Regulation	203
Chapter 10: Social Cognitive Theory	**207**
Self-Efficacy	207
Outcome Expectancies	210
Moral Disengagement	212
Pygmalion Effect	214
Action Theory	217
Concluding Comments	219
Chapter 11: Affect/Emotion: The Employee Has Feelings Too	**221**
Introduction	221
Emotions and Moods	222
Principles of Organizational Justice	229
The Psychological Contract	233
Concluding Comments	237
Part III: Future Directions and Potential Misdirections	**241**
Chapter 12: Boundaryless Psychology	**243**
Introduction	243
Social Psychology	244
Clinical Psychology	244
Life-Span Research	248
Evolutionary Psychology	249
Neuroscience	251

Time 253
Computer Models 255
Teams 256
Levels of Analysis 257
Integration 258

Part IV: Epilogue 263

Chapter 13: The Art of Practice 265

References 281

Index 321

About the Author 337

Foundations for Organizational Science

Introduction to the Series

The title of this series, **Foundations for Organizational Science** (**FOS**), denotes a distinctive focus. FOS books are educational aids for mastering the core theories, essential tools, and emerging perspectives that constitute the field of organizational science (broadly conceived to include organizational behavior, organizational theory, human resource management, and business strategy). Our ambitious goal is to assemble the "essential library" for members of our professional community.

The vision for the series emerged from conversations with several colleagues, including Peter Frost, Anne Huff, Rick Mowday, Benjamin Schneider, Susan Taylor, and Andy Van de Ven. A number of common interests emerged from these sympathetic encounters, including: enhancing the quality of doctoral education by providing broader access to the master teachers in our field, "bottling" the experience and insights of some of the founding scholars in our field before they retire, and providing professional development opportunities for colleagues seeking to broaden their understanding of the rapidly expanding subfields within organizational science.

Our unique learning objectives are reflected in an unusual set of instructions to FOS authors. They are encouraged to: (1) "write the way they teach"—framing their book as an extension of their teaching notes, rather than as the expansion of a handbook chapter, (2) pass on their "craft knowledge" to the next generation of scholars—making them wiser, not just smarter, (3) share with their "virtual students and colleagues" the insider tips and best-bets for research that are normally reserved for one-on-one mentoring sessions, and (4) make the complexity of their subject matter comprehensible to non-experts so that readers can share their puzzlement, fascination, and intrigue.

We are proud of the group of highly qualified authors who have embraced the unique educational perspective of our "Foundations" series. We encourage your suggestions for how these books can better satisfy your learning needs—as a newcomer to the field preparing for prelims or developing a dissertation proposal, or as an established scholar seeking to broaden your knowledge and proficiency.

David Whetten
Series Editor

Editor's Comments

When I ask authors to contribute a book to the Organizational Behavior Series as part of the larger Foundations of Organization Science (FOS) Series, I stress the idea that the books should be written for entry-level Ph.D. students much in the style of lectures to a class. Authors have been very good about doing this; Gary Latham has taken the suggestion to some unique and interesting places. As readers will soon discover, Gary has not only written about the theory, research, and practice of work motivation but has solicited ideas on the subject from colleagues in our field to include as part of his narrative (e.g., Bandura, Edwards, Frese, Hough, Judge, Kanfer, Kristoff-Brown, Lawler, Locke, Meyer, Pinder, Porter, Rousseau, Weiss, and Vroom). No book to my knowledge contains as many anecdotes from and about subject matter experts in the field of motivation, and these lend a very interesting perspective on the way the minds that make the field have influenced it.

A key aspect of this use of reflections and anecdotes by Gary is his emphasis on the role of mentors in the development of scholars. And this includes his own reflections on the influence of his mentors on the way he thinks, the way he conducts research, and the way he conceptualizes practice and science as part of a larger whole. On this latter issue, science and practice as part of a larger whole, Gary's book emphasizes the value of science for practice and vice versa. Drawing on his experience as a staff psychologist in industry and his years as a consultant, Gary takes an autobiographical approach to make explicit how theories can be very useful as a basis for interventions that produce lasting effects in organizations and also, of course, how such interventions can yield theoretically meaningful journal publications and books, too.

Finally, the book departs from traditional approaches to the presentation of theoretical subject matter, where a particular theory is explained in depth before discussing another. Taking a loosely chronological approach from the end of the 19th century to the beginning of the present one, Gary shows how some theories emerge in one time period only to be discarded and then re-emerge in still another point in time, while other theories capture the attention of researchers from their inception and endure across time.

You will find this book a very interesting read, one that is chock-full of personal insights and reflections as well as a comprehensive treatment of the history of work motivation theory, research, and practice.

Benjamin Schneider

Preface and Acknowledgments

Person-Environment Fit

B etween 2002 and 2005, Randy White, the current President of Division 13 (Consulting) of the American Psychological Association, and I have taught leadership and motivational principles to more than 1,000 high-level managers in Europe and North America. A former scientist-practitioner in the Center for Creative Leadership where I currently serve on the Board of Governors, Randy frequently administers personality tests to managers. This year I asked him to administer one to me. The test results suggest that I prefer small, intimate groups to large ones; I am very selective about who I include in my life; I prefer an environment where I can shut the door and work without interruptions, yet I appreciate exchanging ideas with people who are in my field of work. With regard to influence and responsibility, the test indicated that I have a strong desire to be in control, a reluctance to take a lot of direction from others, and a strong desire to pursue those things that please me. In addition, the test suggested that I strive for excellence and expect others to do likewise. Finally, the test stated that I prefer a business-like environment where I can distinguish myself, as opposed to an informal one characterized by a lot of informal chit-chat.

Because I agree so strongly with the results of this personality assessment, I later found myself engaged in introspection on my personal characteristics, the ways in which I typically behave, the environments in which I have worked, and most importantly the people with whom I have worked within them that culminated in the publication of this book in the 60th year of my life. My conclusion is that I have been blessed by a high degree of person-environment fit in terms of my vocation, job, group, and organization, and hence there are many people who I need to thank who directly or indirectly influenced me in writing this book.

With regard to vocation, I know of no greater source of excitement than figuring out what theory to draw upon and what methodology to develop or adapt in order to solve a critical problem in an organizational setting. My vocation has taught me ways of predicting, explaining, and influencing my own behavior and the behavior of those around me. My vocation is also a source of fascination for my family, friends, and clients who are constantly asking me to explain the different ways of doing this.

My first two jobs in the private sector honed my skills as a scientist-practitioner. As my ninth-grade Latin teacher said, "experientia docet." Experience is indeed a wonderfully effective teacher. My current job in academia allows me to proselytize others based on the results of my research in field and in laboratory settings. Through proselytizing MBA students, executive MBA students, and executives in our executive education programs, I am afforded opportunities to work in multiple organizational settings in both the public and private sectors.

To be sure, there are at least one or two people in most groups who can suck the energy out of the sun. No such person is in the Summit Group or the Society of Organizational Behavior (SOB) where I have been a career-long member.[1] The people who actively participate in the Society of Industrial and Organizational Psychology (SIOP), the Canadian Society of Industrial and Organizational Psychology, the Human Resource and the Organizational Behavior Divisions of the Academy of Management whom I have had the privilege of knowing throughout my career are not only intelligent, they are creative and they are helpful.

---

[1]Milton Hakel, an academic, then at Ohio State University contacted Richard Campbell, a practitioner at AT&T, to see if he would be interested in forming a group that would meet annually to discuss ways of building upon and integrating ideas from science and practice. The first meeting was held in the Summit Suite of the Summit Hotel in New York City, November 18, 1968. In addition to Milt and Dick, the invited members included Paul Banas (Ford Motor Company), John Campbell (University of Minnesota), Robert Carlson (Life Insurance Management Research Association), Bill Graham (University of California, Berkeley), John Hinrichs (IBM), Ed Lawler (Yale), Wayne Sorenson (State Farm Insurance), Bob Thompson (Bendix), and Paul Wernimont (3M). Hotel rooms were $20.00 single; the lunch and the conference room were $10.00 per person. Both Milt and Dick were subsequently elected president of Division 14 (Industrial and Organizational Psychology) of the American Psychological Association as was John Campbell.

The Society of Organizational Behavior of which I am among the founding members was instigated by Jim Naylor (Ohio State). Jim, who was dissatisfied with the de-emphasis on science in favor of advocacy by the American Psychological Association, decided to form a group of allegedly the top 50 people whose primary interest was the advancement of I/O psychology and organizational behavior. Today these two groups continue to thrive. Membership in them is by invitation.

None are more so than my career-long collaborator, Ed Locke. In a sentence, Ed Locke makes me think. And he did so regarding my writing this book. In addition to being intellectually stimulating, he is very generous with his time, and he is fun to be around. I cannot ask more of a friend.

A fellow member of the Summit Group, SOB, SIOP where he is a past president, the Human Resource Division, and the Organization Behavior Division where he is also a past president, Ben Schneider and I have laughed continuously together since meeting one another in 1976 at the American Psychological Association. I know of few people who are more creative than he. In his role as the editor of this series, he provided me a gentle yet effective hand ("I just want you to think about it; I will go with whatever you decide"). Working with Ben and with Sage, Mary Ann Vail was invaluable in finding six anonymous reviewers who provided a thorough, thoughtful critique of an earlier draft of this book.

The organizations in which I have worked provided me with environments populated with colleagues where it was difficult not to grow and mature as a scientist-practitioner. The American Pulpwood Association and the Weyerhaeuser Company gave me carte blanche to listen and respond to issues of concern for line managers on the basis of rigorous research. Both institutions actively encouraged me to maintain strong ties with universities to assist me in doing so.

The University of Washington and the University of Toronto emphasize the value of empirical research. They excel at attracting and retaining talented faculty members who can do so. How could I fail in my job when I was surrounded by colleagues at the University of Washington who included Cecil Bell, Lee Beach, Fred Fiedler, Wendell French, Marilyn Gist, Vandra Huber, Tom Lee, and Terry Mitchell? The University of Washington has had more presidents of the Academy of Management than any other institution (i.e., Monty Kast, Pres Lebreton, and Charlie Summer). My close friends and former colleagues, Tom Lee and Bill Scott, are past editors of the *Academy of Management Journal*. Jim Rosenzweig was an editor of the *Academy of Management Review*. Terry is one of three "Gold Members" of the *Academy of Management Journal's* Hall of Fame as a result of publishing 25 or more articles in that outlet. Wendell French and Cecil Bell wrote "the" book on organization development. My current colleagues at the University of Toronto include: Hugh Arnold, Jennifer Berdahl, Stephane Cote, Hugh Gunz, Geoffrey Leonardelli, Julie McCarthy, Maria Rotundo, Alan Saks, Soo Min Toh, Anil Verma, Mark Weber, Glen Whyte, Jia Lin Xie, and David Zweig.

All four institutions where I have worked provided an environment for personal growth and mastery as well as meaningful collegial relationships. What differentiates the two academic organizations from the two in industry is the rewarding opportunity in the former to nurture the next generation of scientists, practitioners, and scientist-practitioners.

Both the University of Washington and the University of Toronto attract outstanding doctoral students, many of whom I have had the honor of serving as their dissertation supervisor. In chronological order they include Lise Saari (IBM), Charles Fay (Rutgers University), Dennis Dossett (Microsoft), Colette Frayne (California Polytechnic State University), Dawn Winters (Seattle University), Daniel Skarlicki (University of British Columbia), Zeeva Millman (practitioner in private practice), Nina Cole (Ryerson University), Gerard Seijts (University of Western Ontario), Christina Sue-Chan (Hong Kong University of Science and Technology), Lucie Morin (University of Quebec, Montreal), Travor Brown (Memorial University), Peter Heslin (Southern Methodist University), Ute Klehe (University of Amsterdam), and Marie-Helene Budworth (York University). They are cited throughout this book because of their contributions to the literature. I served as a member of Neil Fassina's dissertation committee. Neil, who is now a faculty member of the University of Manitoba, performed extraordinarily well as my research assistant, as did the people whose dissertations I chaired. I am grateful to Colleen Stuart and Basak Yanar, my current research assistants, who were very helpful in finding information to fill gaps in my knowledge necessary for writing this book. In addition to my biological children, I am very very proud of my "psychological offspring." There is no greater joy for an academic than seeing one's former students advancing knowledge in our field.[2]

In addition to vocation, group, and organizational fit, I have also benefited from person-supervisor fit. All of my "bosses" recognized my

---

[2]As is evident from the following story, this does not imply that a psychologist in industry cannot have a significant influence on the subsequent career of a student.

While I was clearing out my office at the University of Washington (UW), Tom Lee came in. He surprised me with his knowledge of an incident that had occurred two years after I had received my PhD. Ken Wexley had gone to Berkeley for his sabbatical. He and Shelley Zedeck invited me to give a talk on my research at the Weyerhaeuser Company. I recalled vividly, as Tom and I chatted, Shelley's graduate students, particularly Rick Jacobs and Denise Rousseau. What Tom told me that I did not know is that he was a student in the undergraduate I/O psychology class that Ken asked me to address. It was my presentation, Tom said, that resulted in him deciding to choose the field of organizational behavior as a career. Upon graduating from Berkley he went to the University of Oregon where Rick Mowday became his mentor and lifelong friend and collaborator. I am as honored today relating this story as I was hearing it from Tom on my last day at UW.

need for autonomy, all of them "gave me my head," trusting that what I would do would turn out to be worthwhile for the attainment of the organization's goals. Dr. Tom Walbridge, a forester and head of the American Pulpwood Association's research arm, frequently dropped by my office seemingly to listen and offer an encouraging suggestion—usually in the form of a well-articulated question. Dick Siegel, the vice president of human resources at Weyerhaeuser, gave me a list of line VPs to see and hear during my first week on the job. Among the line VPs who subsequently became my champions were Peter Belluschi and Steve Conway. Without them, many of my studies I describe in this book would not have taken place.

At the urging of Cecil Bell and Terry Mitchell, my dean at the University of Washington, Nancy Jacob, persuaded me in 1983 to vacate my part-time faculty position as a lecturer and to take a tenure track position in the Business School as an assistant professor with an adjunct appointment in the Department of Psychology. In 1984, I was promoted to associate professor. Over several drinks on a pier overlooking Lake Union on a sunny afternoon in 1985, Nancy persuaded me to become the Department Chair of Management and Organization; I was promoted to full professor, too. Controversial among the faculty for her high academic standards, in my eyes she was and is a wonderful leader and motivator. She created an environment for task variety, formal and informal recognition, and opportunities for advancement. She gave me autonomy when I wasn't even aware that I required it: "Gary, there are some things that a smart department chair does not tell the dean."

In 1989 Roger Wolff, the dean of the Business School at the University of Toronto, came to the University of Washington to interview our faculty and students before inviting me to accept the Secretary of State Professorship. Very few tenured faculty leave the University of Washington's Business School. I did so because of the immense amount of freedom that comes with an endowed professorship/chair. I accepted Roger's offer on condition, in writing, that he would never ask me to consider taking an administrative position. Roger broke his promise during the first month in my new job. I stood firm, and he became saintly in my eyes shortly thereafter. My passion is conducting empirical research and disseminating my findings to all who will listen. Roger understood that. Shortly thereafter, I received joint appointments in Industrial Relations, Nursing, and the Psychology Department.

Hugh Arnold, my next dean, received his Ph.D. under the supervision of Victor Vroom. Hugh introduced himself to me in 1977 at the annual meeting of the Canadian Psychological Association in Vancouver. It was there that we began a lifelong friendship. Years later, a consultant attempted to hire Hugh. He "turned the tables" by hiring her as his assistant dean of executive education. Shortly thereafter, I chose to dislike this person when she failed to appreciate my use of humor in the classroom. Hugh then "turned the tables" on both of us by insisting that we find a way to work together effectively. Soosan and I "turned the tables" on Hugh by making him the best man at our wedding. As the subsequent VP of HR for J. P. Morgan, Canada, her ongoing arguments with me at the dinner table on integrating science and practice led to several articles that we co-authored and are now described in this book.

Dr. Joseph Rotman, for whom our business school is named (i.e., the Rotman School of Management), was influential in the selection of my current dean, Roger Martin. Roger consistently provides me with the resources to enhance my research productivity.

Unfortunately, one's environment is not always idyllic. All lives include difficult, discouraging situations. Both Joe and Roger modeled for me the interrelationship between leadership and motivation in their steadfast support of me during some "down" moments in time. I have learned much from Joe's counsel, which often begins with: "Young man, learn from my mistakes as well as my father's." Roger, coincidentally, uses a similar approach with me: "The wisest person I know is my mother. The advice I believe she would give is. . . ."[3] I have also benefited enormously from the motivational principles given to me by Joe's son, and my friend, Ken. I asked him one day the advice he would give to a father of two adult sons, a father who, hypothetically speaking might be a tad "controlling" according to a personality test that the father had taken. His answers: (1) Define success in their terms rather than your own. (2) Be there when they need you rather than when you wish to be there. (3) Most importantly, talk to them about your failures rather than the successes. I believe his three suggestions are as appropriate to leadership and motivation in the workplace as they are in one's home.

The two statements I would like to have said about me are that: (1) I am a good parent to my children and a good mentor to my doctoral

---

[3]I wish I could acknowledge my own father in this regard. Despite the fact that he has had a tremendous positive influence on me and I loved him dearly, I cannot do so. Throughout my formative years he would look me in the eye and say, "son, do your best." Now, if he had assigned me a specific high goal, I might have completed this book years earlier.

students. (2) My research and practice is worthwhile for others. This book was written with these two goals in mind. Specifically, it was written with the goal of providing countless clues for graduate students and newly minted scholars as to where they can jump into the heart of key issues in the field of motivation in the workplace. This book revises and expands upon the chapters that I wrote, respectively with Marie-Helene Budworth that appeared in L. Koppes (Ed.), *Historical perspectives in industrial-organizational psychology: The first hundred years;* and with Craig Pinder that appeared in the 2005 *Annual Review of Psychology* on work motivation; as well as my presidential address to the Canadian Psychological Association (Latham, 2000a), and articles written with my collaborator of 30-plus years, Ed Locke (Latham, Locke, & Fassina, 2002; Locke & Latham, 2004). Preparation of this book was funded in part by a grant from the Social Sciences and Humanities Research Council, Canada.

Scholarly summaries and critiques of motivation research and theory are found readily in the academic literature (e.g., Kanfer, 1990; Pinder, 1998; Mitchell & Daniels, 2003). Rather than duplicate these reviews, I have attempted to provide an "insider view" of the history of research and theory on work motivation in the 20th and 21st centuries. This book is based on my knowledge of key scholars who had a major influence, and in many instances, continue to influence the field's understanding of employee motivation. This knowledge is based on oral history as told to me by my mentors, as well as my interactions with the second and third generation of scholars who conducted research on motivation in the 20th century. To reduce criticism that this book reflects little more than reminiscences, the words of the scholars who were pioneers in the study of employee motivation are quoted frequently so as to allow the words of those scientist-practitioners to echo down through the years. Hence you the reader can see firsthand their opinion regarding a specific topic.

By the late 20th century, motivation research was dominating I/O psychology journal space, accounting for one third of the published articles (Cooper & Robertson, 1986). By the final decade, motivation had become the "most frequently researched topic in micro organizational behavior" (O'Reilly, 1991, p. 431). Yet this was not true in the early part of that century. Then the focus was on employee selection, and the topic of motivation was left to studies of laboratory animals by experimental psychologists, or to studies of tasks in the workplace conducted by engineers. As late as 1959, Cofer lamented that motivation was not one of the categories used by *Psychological Abstracts*.

Why and how did the subject of employee motivation become so important to behavioral scientists? To answer this question, this book reviews the scholarly literature over the past 110 years. In doing so, I have attempted to follow a chronological path. Thus, this book is organized into six time periods: the first (1900-1925), second (1925-1950), third (1950-1975), and fourth quarters (1975-2000) of the 20th century, the dawn of the present millennium, and a peek into the future.

In the first time period with the birth of behaviorism, experimental psychologists focused on observable behavior and the stimuli that elicited it. Inner motivational states were not studied. In this same time period, engineers argued that money is the critical incentive for work, and that employees should be assigned a specific difficult task or goal to be attained. The assumption was that a worker would *choose* to exert *effort*, to *persist* until the task goal was attained in order to obtain money. In the second time period, I/O psychologists focused on the employee's attitudes and attitude measurement. The belief in this time period was that the pathway to discovering sources of employee motivation was to identify the attitudes of the workforce. Numerous surveys revealed that money was only one of the multiple variables that people report as having an effect on their motivation. The Hawthorne studies, and studies on employee participation in decision making supported this conclusion. Studies in this time period were for the most part atheoretical.

The third quartile of the 20th century witnessed the development of theories as frameworks for predicting, explaining, and influencing employee motivation. These theories focused on employee needs, cognition, and characteristics of the job itself. In the final quarter, three scientific theories dominated the scholarly literature on motivation in the workplace.

Thus, Part I of this book emphasizes the subject's relatively unique genealogy by providing a loose chronological overview of the research on and theories of motivation in the workplace.[4] In doing so I address the strengths, contributions, and the limitations of each in terms of their advancement of our understanding of work motivation.

---

[4]For those who are prone to pedantry, the phrase "loose chronological" means that I had no hesitancy whatsoever in citing an article published in one quartile in another in order to support the logic of an argument. Thus an article published in 1949 may very well be described in the 1950-1975 time period; similarly an article published in 1996 may very well be described in the 2000-2005 time period.

Hopefully the detail here is sufficient so as to relieve you, the reader, from having to plow through every original source, but rather to use this section as a filter from which to select those original works that you want to investigate beyond this text.

Advancement in the understanding of an employee's motivation did not occur in the absence of controversy. Debates raged among scholars on (1) the importance of money, (2) whether there is a meaningful distinction between intrinsic and extrinsic motivation in the workplace, (3) the relationship between job performance and satisfaction, and (4) the effect of participation in decision making on the employee's affect and behavior. These debates conclude Part I.

At the dawn of this millennium, three shifts in the study of motivation are apparent. Affect, particularly emotion, in addition to cognition are being examined; personality, once shunned, is now overwhelming the motivation literature, and there is growing interest in the pre- or subconscious in addition to consciousness.

Thus, in Part II, I focus on where this field is currently grounded so that you are up to speed on research and theory. Consequently, the same theory is discussed in more than one place in this book in order to demonstrate how it rose to prominence in one time period, faded from view in another, only to be resurrected, in some instances, in still another. Other theories are cited in more than one place in this book because they have captured the attention of scientist/practitioners across time periods.

Part III explicitly addresses what I believe to be promising avenues for future theory development and empirical research. I bring this book to a close with a discussion, in Part IV, the Epilogue, of the art of putting into practice behavioral science principles of motivation. Together these four sections should provide "handles" for those of you who are new to this field to grab as you advance your career as scientists/practitioners.

My editor, Ben Schneider, asked me to write this book as I would speak to and teach a doctoral seminar. Specifically, he asked me to use a "mentor" voice that is highly personal and rich in examples. His requests were reemphasized by the anonymous reviewers. On the first day of a seminar, I talk about my personal involvement in human resource management and organizational behavior/psychology with the doctoral students. Consequently, I have included an autobiography for the reader that is based in part on an article that I wrote for *The Industrial/Organizational Psychologist* (TIP) and one that appeared in Locke and Latham (2005). In addition, to mitigate the fact that many history books are so boring despite the subject matter being so fascinating, I have included lots of anecdotes in order to make the major figures in our field come alive for the reader. I have done this after observing the enjoyment of my doctoral students, as well as audiences in colloquia whom I have addressed, hearing my "behind the scenes" accounts of research and the researchers who conducted it.

In closing, I wish to thank the organizations and each of the people whose names I have cited here for the motivating force they have had on me.

Gary P. Latham
June 2006
Toronto

Introduction

Thirteen Critical Incidents in
the Life of a Scientist/Practitioner

When I read a nonfiction book, particularly one on history, I appreciate knowing the lens through which it was written. Who and what shaped the author's thinking on the subject? What are the author's biases? This chapter provides answers to these questions regarding this book and me. Throughout the book I frequently refer to myself as a practitioner-scientist rather than the reverse because from the outset of my career I was interested in ways of applying behavioral science principles to issues of practical significance in the workplace.

In the 1770s, my ancestors, loyal to King George III, emigrated from Massachusetts to Nova Scotia. In 1950, my father, believing that it was now safe for him and his family to do so, became the first member of our clan to return to the United States. Before going back to Massachusetts, it was preordained by family and knowledgeable friends that I would return to Nova Scotia to attend Dalhousie University. I did so in 1963, following a critical incident that had occurred the previous year.

Another promotion for my father resulted in our family moving, in my senior year of high school, to another city. While I was washing dishes in the back of a restaurant, a 19-year-old waiter, Tom, observed that I was no longer fun to be around. After pouring out my heart to him regarding the girl I had been "forced" to leave behind, he suggested that I major in psychology when I entered university. That was the first I had heard of this discipline. In minutes, he differentiated clinical psychology from psychiatry. In seconds, I knew that this was what I wanted to pursue for the rest of my life. I have not seen Tom since fall 1962, when he resumed his studies at Boston University. I have never been able to thank him for the impact he has had on me. Sadly, I do not recall his last name.

Although I was accepted into Boston University and the University of Massachusetts, the summers I had spent with my grandparents in Nova Scotia had convinced me that Dalhousie was the right place for me to pursue my education. The psychology department at Dalhousie was the hot bed for behaviorism in Canada in 1960s. The majority of the courses included 2–3 hour laboratories. In my first laboratory course, my new girlfriend received 19/25 on her laboratory report with the comment: "Congratulations, highest grade in class." Stunned, as I had helped her prepare the report, I waited in anticipation for my grade. Imagine my chagrin when I read "21/25 minus 4 points for poor penmanship." Immediately I raced to my professor, Dr. Horace "Ace" Beach, demanding that my rightful grade be restored. After I patiently explained to him the importance of grades for gaining admission to a graduate psychology department, he patiently replied that I should improve my legibility. Exasperated, I informed him of the impossibility of me doing so at my age. This frustrating man then had the gall to ask me, a third-year student, to define psychology. In my attempt to educate him, I explained that it is the science of behavior. Without looking up at me from his chair, he then laconically requested that I tell him what psychologists do. Doubly exasperated, I informed him that psychologists predict, explain, and, and, and; damn it, Dr. Beach had just allowed me to hang myself in his presence. "Well, changing behavior is not easy," I blustered. He agreed. The grade stood.

The laboratory assignments included two research proposals, one in December, the other in April. While unimpressed by my poor attempt to improve my penmanship, Dr. Beach was nevertheless impressed by my creativity as well as my ability to entice my fraternity brothers to serve as participants in my experiments. At the end of my third year, I became, I believe, the first undergraduate student at Dal to become a research assistant. This was the second critical incident that advanced my career toward psychology.

Dr. Beach was a former Rhodes Scholar, a World War II hero, a boxer while in the military, and the director of the Clinical Psychology program. I loved him. We did research and subsequently published a paper on the importance of awareness vs. unawareness in the conditioning of the galvanic skin response. My "cool" or distant interactions with clients in his clinic, however, led to the third critical incident.

An article in the *Psychological Bulletin* mysteriously appeared on my desk in Dr. Beach's laboratory, an article on job satisfaction and performance by two people named Brayfield and Crockett. I read it.

Immediately, I raced into the office: "Dr. Beach, I want to be an industrial psychologist." He looked at me long and hard before replying that it was time for me to return to the US. Not only was there no I/O psychology program in Canada in that time-period, we students had never even heard of one.

Walking in the hallway from a psychology class, I noticed a bulletin board with a description of the I/O program at Georgia Tech. That was the fourth critical incident. Fall 1967 I was among that school's graduate students. I did not know at the time that I would remain in the US until 1990.

Georgia Tech embraced the scientist-practitioner model. The majority of the faculty had served in the military as psychologists during World War II and/or had worked as psychologists in industry. They taught us how psychology could make a difference in organizational settings. Their focus was on individual differences and on ways of measuring and then both predicting and influencing the criterion. Our heroes included Marvin Dunnette, John Flanagan, Ed Ghiselli, and Ed Webster. Since our department head's dissertation adviser was Ted Cureton, we students knew validity, reliability, and what constitutes baloney (Cureton, 1950). My mentor was Bill "Red" Ronan,[5] who had studied under John Flanagan. My thesis was based on the critical incident technique.

In 1968, The American Pulpwood Association (APA) requested Dr. Ronan's services to help them identify ways to measure and then improve the productivity of pulpwood producers in the southern United States. He agreed to be a consultant on condition that he be paid the astronomical sum of $200 a day, and that I be hired as a research assistant for $400 a month, twice the sum I received as an RA in the psychology department. I was elated, particularly when APA agreed with Dr. Ronan that my work for them should allow sufficient rigor to serve as my master's thesis. In 1969, I passed my oral defense of my thesis and then presented my findings to a panel of 12 executives from APA's sponsor companies (e.g., Georgia Kraft, International Paper, Owens-Illinois, Union Camp). When I finished my presentation, they asked me where I planned to go next. As it was 11:55 a.m., I told them I was going home for lunch. Seeing their eyes roll, I was relieved to be informed that I should leave the room. Before going very far, I was summoned back. To my astonishment, the executives offered me the position of staff

---

[5]Bill had red hair.

psychologist, in addition to lunch. This was the fifth critical incident in my now budding career.

APA was populated solely by industrial engineers who conducted time and motion studies, or mechanical engineers who designed equipment to minimize the human factors that they believed restricted productivity. Because psychology was so alien to the forest products sector, the executives who hired me stated that my acceptance in the industry might increase if it were said that my job was to examine the "nonphysical" rather than psychological factors that influence productivity. Hence the title on my business card, "Manager of Non Physical Factors." Because I would be working in the deep South, they also emphasized to company foresters that I was a Canadian not a Yankee; much to Lincoln's consternation, Canada had supported the Confederacy during the American Civil War.

1969–1971 were exhilarating years. If Dr. Beach had gotten me into the air, Dr. Ronan had given me the confidence to fly. Critical incident interviews with pulpwood workers and questionnaires completed by foresters led to the conclusion that a measure of job attendance was a much more reliable (inter-observer and test-retest) measure to predict and influence than subjectively classified measures of absenteeism. Behaviorally anchored rating scales proved not to be effective in assessing what differentiates the productive from the nonproductive pulpwood crew. Hence, behavioral observation scales (BOS) were developed for use by company foresters as a checklist for identifying independent pulpwood crews with whom a forest-products company should do business. BOS have served as dependent variables for me to assess the effectiveness of an intervention or as criteria to assess the validity of a predictor in my practice and research to the present day.

Georgia Tech had instilled in me the belief that theories are invaluable frameworks for practice. Thus, one Saturday I drove to the Tech library to peruse the *Psychological Abstracts* for ways to increase the productivity of pulpwood crews. Serendipity struck in the form of a sixth critical incident. There was a series of abstracts written by a young Ph.D. who had been at the American Institutes for Research (AIR) founded by Flanagan. This newly minted Ph.D., hired by Ed Fleishman, then the President of AIR, had recently taken a job as an assistant professor at the University of Maryland. His laboratory experiments showed that a person who has a specific high goal solves more simple arithmetic problems, makes more words out of scrambled letters, and creates more toys out of plastic bricks than do people who are merely urged to do their best. I quickly telephoned Dr. Ronan, who was still working for us as a consultant. In a factor analysis of survey data, we too had found that pulpwood crews who set specific high goals have higher productivity than those who don't. Yet that finding had not captured my attention until that day in the library. "Dr. Ronan," I said excitedly, "Locke says. . . ."

In that time period, I read the journals primarily for "practice" rather than to advance scholarship. The emphasis of both Tech and APA was on applications that "make a difference." In reading the journals, I stumbled upon two names that began appearing again and again, Drs. Yukl and Wexley. Realizing from my reading of the literature that my knowledge was limited, I decided I should return to school for a Ph.D. Together, Drs. Yukl and Wexley were applying the experimental procedures in behavior modification, procedures that I had learned at Dalhousie, to I/O psychology.

Not much older than I, Gary Yukl and Ken Wexley shared and enhanced my love of application as well as the need for empirical research. Ken, a Ph.D. from the University of Tennessee, strengthened and deepened the knowledge that I had acquired at Georgia Tech. His focus was on the selection interview and ways of minimizing rating errors. He would alternately enter a seminar in the role of a vice president of B.F. Goodrich, an HR person seeking a knowledgeable consultant, or as a critic of our field. As Dr. Wexley, he drilled into us the necessity of publishing in our journals; if we did not do so upon receipt of our Ph.D., he said, we were no longer to contact him. He inspired in us the goal to become a Fellow. My association with Yukl, however, was a seventh critical incident. A graduate of the University of California Berkeley, it was Gary who opened my eyes to the "O" in our field. Gary's research passion was leadership. Within the year, Rensis Likert and Ed Lawler were added to my list of heroes. The newly published book by Campbell, Dunnette, Lawler, and Weick (1970) that both he and Wexley assigned to us to read became my academic bible. But most of all, I wanted to continue to read everything by Ed Locke. Dr. Yukl encouraged me to write to him regarding my field studies at the American Pulpwood Association on goal setting. To my delight, Ed responded immediately to my letter with encouragement to submit my findings to a journal.

Before I could complete my Ph.D., the eighth critical incident occurred. Because of my work experience between the receipt of my masters in 1969 and entering the University of Akron in 1971, I devoured the assigned readings from Wexley and Yukl. Exams were relatively easy as

I was consistently asking myself ways that I could apply what I read in the journals to improving the performance of pulpwood crews. Both Yukl and Wexley assigned us roles to take in weekly debates on sundry issues (e.g., composite vs. multiple criteria; pro vs. con on expectancy theory). Unknown to me, since my leaving the American Pulpwood Association, Weyerhaeuser Company had been tracking my progress at the University of Akron. They telephoned me in the Fall of my second year of my doctoral program to ask me to join them as their first staff psychologist. When I explained that I could not accept the offer because I had yet to do my doctoral dissertation, they countered with the promise that they would provide me the resources to do it with them on any subject I wished. I accepted the offer without further hesitation. I did so without stating that I had yet to pass my comprehensive examinations. I passed the written examinations soon after with relative ease.

The oral examination was a different matter. "Explain how training is directly based on learning theory" commanded Wexley. I did. "Give another example." I did. "Give another example." I did. Now it occurred to me that if Wexley continued to pursue this matter, I might run out of examples. He did; I did. Yukl stared at the ceiling. Another faculty member noted that a new book had appeared on *The Greening of America*. He wanted to know how the book would affect my work when I went to Weyerhaeuser. I didn't know. Yukl continued to stare at the ceiling. Wexley jumped back in regarding an article published a year or so earlier by Abe Korman. He wanted my assessment of it. I sputtered that I did indeed recall the article as I honestly had read it. I simply could not recall at that instant what Abe had written. Yukl stared at the ceiling. Hours passed. Weyerhaeuser had informed me that I was to be there by June 15, 1973, or not to come. The reason why this date was so important to them eludes me to this day.

The day of my oral examination, the plane from Cleveland left at 5 p.m. for Seattle. With legs wobbling, I left the oral examination room. The graduate students waiting outside to wish me well remained respectfully silent when they saw me emerge around 2 p.m., crestfallen. As my career opportunity of a lifetime was passing me by, the door to the examination room flew open. Wexley strode quickly down the hall, stopped to congratulate me with a wide grin, and then kept on going. Other faculty were equally congratulatory. Yukl, the last to emerge, walked slowly toward me. Incredulous, I asked him how I could possibly have passed my orals. I can still hear his response: "I didn't know the answers to any of those questions either."

After a year and a half in Akron, I arrived at Weyerhaeuser, in Washington. I immediately put into practice what I had learned about reinforcement schedules as an undergraduate and doctoral student. Company vice presidents as well as union officials congratulated me for bringing "Las Vegas" to the forest products industry. Employees were now planting trees or trapping the mountain beavers that eat the seedlings in order to "gamble" for money that was paid on different schedules of reinforcement. We never had a single grievance over the program from an employee. A year or two later I received a letter from Pat Smith stating that only I would have the temerity to conduct such experiments in field settings.

Ed Fleishman thrilled me by accepting an invitation to speak on the subject of leadership to Weyerhaeuser. He thrilled me even more so by accepting an invitation to spend the weekend in Seattle. His visit was an eighth critical incident because of the advice he gave me in his roles as president of Division 14 and editor of the *Journal of Applied Psychology*. "Give your manuscript to your 'enemies' before you submit it to a journal; whereas your friends will tell you how good it is, your 'enemies' will gladly point out its weaknesses." The word enemy was hyperbole to make his point. To this day, I heed his advice by sending my manuscripts to those I believe will be constructively critical of them.

Henry Tosi had given me similar advice on the value of criticism. At a party that Ken Wexley held in honor of me getting my Ph.D., Henry, who was in Akron visiting Ken, tapped me on the shoulder and said, "Kid, always be the first to criticize your own work. Not only will it lead to another publication, it will drive your enemies crazy."

My ninth critical incident is related to the sixth. In 1974, Milt Blood organized a symposium at the American Psychological Association on behavior modification in the workplace. When I finished my presentation, an urbane well-dressed blond-haired individual introduced himself: "Hi, I am Ed Locke." Knowing Ed's loathing of behaviorism, the irony of the setting did not escape me. Despite the context, we immediately became close friends and colleagues, a relationship that has lasted more than a quarter of a century. Our only conflicts have been over the order of authorship. He has argued vehemently that I should be first author when I have said that he should be. We have yet to co-author an article together that failed to get published.

The tenth, eleventh, and twelfth critical incidents are the support I have received from colleagues. Dr. Beach, now in his late 80s, continues to be my mentor. In 1974, as president of the Applied Division, he invited me to present the results of my doctoral dissertation on goal setting and Likert's approach to participation in decision making to the Canadian Psychological Association (CPA). Subsequently, I became the first I/O psychologist to be elected the president of CPA (1999–2000). In 1975, Jim Naylor invited me to join his newly formed organization, the Society of Organization Behavior, a group that focuses on scholarship. That same year, Fred Fiedler was instrumental in getting me an adjunct appointment in the psychology department at the University of Washington. In 1977, Mel Sorcher was instrumental in inviting me to join the Summit Group; a group of people evenly divided between scientists and practitioners who over the years have become avid scientist-practitioners.

My lucky thirteenth incident can be traced back to Billy Hoke, a forester at International Paper Company in North Carolina. When I was with the American Pulpwood Association, he stressed to me the importance of being bilingual, that is, being able to explain theory and research in meaningful memorable ways not only to scholars but to managers and hourly employees. Embracing this advice not only has allowed me to conduct research in field settings, it propelled me into the business school. With the support of Cecil Bell and Terry Mitchell, I joined the University of Washington business school as an assistant professor in 1983. In 1985 I was department chair. 1990 found me back in Canada with an endowed chair. Bob House had left the University of Toronto for Wharton. Martin Evans asked me to be a candidate for the vacated position. Bob talked to me at SIOP in Boston and urged me to do so.[6]

Among the principles I have followed as a scientist-practitioner are the following: (1) Seek mentors. They have been and continue to be indispensable to my career. (2) Embrace their constructive feedback; set specific high goals based on their feedback. (3) Acquire the skill to speak and write to people in the workforce in addition to scholars. Doing so not only increases the likelihood that what is said will be remembered, it increases the likelihood of being invited by organizational decision makers to do field research. (4) "Give back" to our field. Contribute

---

[6]Years earlier, Gary Yukl, my mentor, introduced me to Bob at my first *Academy of Management* meeting. Bob, who thinks very highly of Gary, said that if I ever decided to leave Weyerhaeuser, I should contact him about the possibility of coming to Toronto. That was 1973. True to his word, Bob encouraged me in 1989 to take his place. Having a mentor introduce a doctoral student to key people in the field can be invaluable.

knowledge to our journals and to our scholarly societies so that our field can continue to provide as exciting a career for others as it has been and continues to be for me.

The principles that have enabled me to function as a practitioner and a scientist are described in Latham and Latham (2003). In brief, they are as follows:

1. *Set mutually interdependent goals.* Academics and organizational decision makers typically view each other as pursuing self-serving interests. I was sometimes seen by industry leaders as wanting to pursue narrowly defined interests that would affect an easily measured dependent variable and hence lead to a journal publication; I viewed the human resources manager as wanting to pursue broadly defined objectives that would affect a fuzzily conceived "bottom line" and hence will lead to a salary increase, if not a promotion. Working together could jeopardize the attainment of both of our goals—a rational reason perceived by both parties for maintaining two solitudes.

A solution for overcoming this distrust is to set mutually interdependent goals. Two facilitators for the setting of interdependent goals are for the two parties to become members of the same team, and for their effectiveness to be measured with the same yardstick. For example, I joined the American Pulpwood Association upon completing my master's thesis. The goal that the organization had of finding concrete ways to increase the productivity of logging crews coincided with my goal to do meaningful research (e.g., Latham & Kinne, 1974; Ronan, Latham, & Kinne, 1973).

2. *Stop, look, and listen: Be seen as a teamplayer.* "Are we doing this project for Gary or for the company?" This question has been asked on numerous occasions by human resource managers. Their suspicions were frequently the result of me taking the initiative to attack issues I believed needed to be resolved. Questions such as this subsided once I learned to listen first and speak second. There is an art to being "proactively reactive" to organizational needs. It is mastered by stopping to hear the concerns of organizational decision makers before offering one's suggestions. This can lead to researchers being invited to join ad hoc teams that are formed to problem solve a question of concern to one or more members of senior management. "What does one logging crew do that results in high productivity while another crew goes out of business" (Latham & Wexley, 1977)? "How can we motivate engineers/scientists to achieve excellence in

the eyes of line managers" (Latham, Mitchell, & Dossett, 1978)? "I can step on more mountain beavers than those union employees can trap (Latham & Dossett, 1978).

It is difficult to hear the question or concern of managers, see the contextual issues, know who is the primary person who is asking the question, offer suggestions, and subsequently receive an invitation to join the team unless the researcher is a member of the organization where the issues arise—a group member who is evaluated by the same senior manager by the same yardstick as every other member of the team. To this day, I have found that it was easier to conduct field experiments when I was an employee of the American Pulpwood Association and the Weyerhaeuser Company than it is now that I am a faculty member of a university. As an outsider to organizations, I now propose ideas that I hope some decision maker in some organization will find of interest; but, as an organizational insider, I was able to respond to concerns that I knew one or more key decision makers wanted/needed answered. Fortunately, universities are organizations too. They, like any organization, have difficulties with employee attendance (Frayne & Latham, 1987; Latham & Frayne, 1989) and with taking disciplinary action (Cole & Latham, 1997). As a scientist-practitioner, I capitalize on this fact.

3. *Find a champion who is an influential member of the other solitude.* The research question becomes important, the research process is seen as doable, and the results are soon implemented when there is a champion of the academic's research who is a member of the other solitude. Among my champions was a Weyerhaeuser VP, Peter Belluschi. He valued facts rather than hunches or intuition to unanswered issues. Jim Taylor, his HR manager, Bob Butler, his financial manager, and I met regularly to find ways to get answers to questions that Pete asked. His desire for hard data led to his appreciation for empirical research.

4. *Become bilingual.* As noted above, I learned from Billy Hoke, the forester at International Paper, that academics are perceived as having mastered the language of obfuscation. We are often viewed as making seemingly straightforward explanations complex. I learned from other managers that academics are frequently seen as confusing the words "quality" and "precision" with those of "hard" and "abstruse." Consequently, I found that I was making it easy for me to be ignored by business people. Adding to my self-infliction, I would buttress my conclusions with statistical techniques. I was a newly minted Ph.D. when Mike Beer

would ask teasingly: "Latham, are you still doing t-tests? When you become good, you won't have to do so. You will know when your intervention worked." My final coup de grace to my lack of credibility with managers would be hedging the most straightforward conclusions within contingencies, followed by whining for the need for "more research." People such as Billy Hoke and Mike Beer helped cure me of these ailments.

In becoming bi-lingual, in learning to speak to managers in addition to researchers, I stopped doing "research" and I started doing "projects" and "interventions." I stopped doing "statistical analyses" and I started to do "documentation." Instead of presenting the results of a statistical analysis, I showed people graphs. Rather than refer to a control group, I showed what failed to occur in a comparison group. For example, when logging crews who set specific high productivity goals had lower performance than they had prior to setting them, I showed a graph that documented how productivity was even worse among those crews who did not set goals. My graphs would also display how a hurricane or flood can be a boundary condition, a moderator variable, and a situational constraint for productivity. I consciously worked on ways to phrase and present material in memorable ways. I used language to capture the attention and imagination of organizational decision makers with little concern on my part for the precision in language required by a scholarly audience. In time, I became bilingual.

5. *Educate the other solitude.* After leaving Weyerhaeuser for the University of Washington, I seldom passed-up an opportunity to teach in a university executive program or an executive MBA course. As part of their education, I pose a question to the managers (e.g., Do you think bias can be minimized if not eliminated in a performance appraisal?), encourage strong debate (Why? Why not?), and then immediately involve them in an experiment to obtain the answer. The participants love the suspense, and I do too (e.g., Latham & Seijts, 1997).

In closing, I believe a terrific researcher can become a great teacher, and a great teacher can become a terrific researcher. In both roles, one has to have the confidence in one's intelligence to communicate in a straightforward and simple manner. Now let's examine the history of work motivation in terms of research that led to theory which in turn led to practice. Let's do so through the eyes of a scientist and a practitioner.

To my mentors who discovered my ability and motivated me to use it.

H. D. Beach

W. W. Ronan

G. A. Yukl

Part I

The 20th Century

UNDERSTANDING THE PAST

1 1900–1925

Biology, Behavior, and Money

Introduction

The term motivation, as Steers, Mowday, and Shapiro (2004) pointed out, is a derivation of the Latin word for movement, *movere*. Its importance in the workplace is captured in the equation promulgated by Victor Vroom's former mentor, N. R. F. Maier (1955), a half century ago: Job performance = ability x motivation. This equation succinctly explains why the subject of motivation is a cornerstone in the fields of Human Resource Management (HRM), Industrial and Organization Psychology (I/O), and Organization Behavior (OB).[1]

Motivation is an integral aspect of training. The time, money, and resources an organization devotes to ways of increasing a person's abilities are wasted to the extent that an employee chooses not to learn what is being taught, or chooses not to apply newly acquired knowledge and skills in the

---

[1]Division 14 of the American Psychological Association changed its name from Industrial Psychology to Industrial/Organizational Psychology (I/O) in 1973. Hence the abbreviation I/O psychology is used throughout this book. The Academy of Management was formed in 1936. Professors Clark Jamison of the University of Michigan and William Mitchell of the University of Chicago sent letters to colleagues inviting them to Chicago on December 28th to discuss the wisdom of forming an organization to advance the philosophy of management. The outcome of the meeting was agreement to formalize the Academy's name and to support research and the exchange of ideas. The constitution of the Academy was formally adopted December 27, 1947. The Human Resources Management (HRM) and the Organizational Behavior Divisions were not founded until 1971 when William Wolf was president.

The I in I/O psychology typically refers to the science and practice of recruitment, selection, socialization, performance appraisal and training of an organization's human resources. When I/O psychologists were recruited to business schools in the 1960s, the *I* became known as Human Resources Management or HRM. The *O* in I/O psychology typically refers to the science and practice of leadership, motivation, job satisfaction, decision making, organization and job design, as well as organization climate and culture. In business schools this subject matter generally falls within the domain of Organization Behavior or OB.

workplace.[2] Hence the purpose of performance appraisal/performance management is to focus not only on identifying the requisite abilities an individual requires to be able to perform effectively, it is to coach the person so as to inculcate a desire for continuous improvement (Latham & Mann, 2006). To facilitate the coaching process, researchers in the area of selection/staffing focus on the identification and development of tests that predict who is predisposed to being highly motivated in a work setting.

Motivation is a core competency of leadership. AstraZeneca, a global pharmaceutical company, headquartered in London, expects its leaders to determine the areas, which if acted upon, will generate "breakthrough performance," as well as determine the necessary actions required of people to generate a "breakthrough." They are expected to instill in the people who report to them a sense of urgency and flexibility. Leaders at Microsoft, headquartered in Redmond, a suburb of Seattle, are expected to create an environment where the very best people can do their very best work. The strategy at Manulife, a global financial services company headquartered in Toronto, includes a focus on employee commitment to values expressed in the acronym, PRIDE (professionalism, real value to our customers, integrity, demonstrated financial strength, and employer of choice).

Among the requirements for performing effectively as a leader in these organizations is the ability to galvanize and inspire individuals to exert effort, to commit to and persist in the pursuit of an organization's values or goals.[3] Hence the importance for leaders of answers to such questions as:

---

[2]All of us have encountered professors who, although loaded with ability in their area of expertise, lacked the motivation to communicate their knowledge in memorable meaningful ways in the classroom. Their performance as a teacher was dismal.

[3]I don't know of any study that has looked solely at the implementation of motivational principles on an organization's effectiveness. Inferences can be drawn, however, from existing research. Both Huselid and Beaeker (1996) and Watson Wyatt (2002), a consulting firm, concluded that HR practices are "leading indicators" of a firm's future financial performance. Similarly, Guest, Michie, Conway, and Sheehanl (2003) found that HR practices are related to high profitability in UK firms. Fulmer Gerhart and Scott (2003) studied the "100 Best Companies to Work For." Being included in the top 100 is dependent upon responses to an attitude survey that includes a multitude of motivational items. The authors found that there is indeed "a connection using firm level data between the strategy of developing an attractive workplace (the success of which is judged primarily by employees themselves) and having financial performance that is as good, and often substantially better than that of competitors. "In fact, our study demonstrates that an investment portfolio constructed on the basis of employee relations in 1998 (i.e., whether a company was on the 100 Best List) would have yielded a significantly superior cumulative investment returns over the broad market in subsequent years (82% vs. 37% over 1998–2000 in our subset of 100 Best Firms)" (p. 987). Of course, using different predictors, different criteria, and different settings can lead researchers to question the findings of others (see Wright, Gardner, Moynihan, & Anen, 2005).

1. Do the keys to unlocking motivation lie within the *personal characteristics* of an individual? If yes:

   (a) Should we focus on a person's *needs?* Should we expect people who are worried over finding adequate food and clothing for their family to be focusing on ways to attain a specific high goal with regard to increasing a company division's revenue?

   (b) The employees in a telecommunications company where I am a consultant wear a lapel pin with the word, "*attitude.*" They do so because of their belief that attitude and motivation are interrelated. Are they correct?

   (c) If a person likes the job, will the person be motivated? What is the relationship between an employee's *job satisfaction* and job performance? Are highly trained happy individuals productive employees? Is it likely that a person who is highly satisfied with multiple aspects of the job has little or no motivation to be a high performer?

   (d) What is the importance of a person's affect to job performance? Should we be concerned with a person's *moods and emotions?*

   (e) Instead of, or in addition to affect, should we examine *cognition* in terms of a person's goals, self-efficacy, and outcome expectancies? If we assign people specific high *goals,* will their performance increase? Are self set, or participatively set goals likely to lead to an even greater increase in a person's job performance? Should we be looking at ways to enable employees to see the relationship between what they do and the outcomes that they can expect? If yes, should we be seeking ways to increase their confidence that they can attain a high goal? Are there ways of inducing a "can-do" mindset among those people who perceive one or more goals as unattainable?

   (f) If the answer to the question of motivation lies within the person, are some *personality traits* likely to be more predictive of a high performer than others?

2. Peter Drucker, a highly regarded thought-leader for managers throughout much of the 20th century, argued:

   > An employer has no business with a man's personality. Employment is a specific construct calling for specific performance, and for nothing else. Any attempt of an employer to go beyond this is usurpation. It is immoral as well illegal intrusion of privacy. It is abuse of power. An employee owes no "loyalty," he owes no "love," and no "attitudes"—he owes performance and nothing else . . . Management and manager development should concern themselves with changes in behavior likely to make a man more effective. (Drucker, 1973, pp. 424–425)

   Are there effective motivational techniques for increasing the frequency of desired and decreasing the frequency of undesired behavior? Rather than focus on the person, should the focus be on a person's *behavior?*

3. Do the keys to unlocking employee motivation lie within the *environment?* Do factors external to a person act as inducements for action?

   (a) Does the environment shape one's values?

(b) Does the environment affect one's behavior?

(c) Can an environment mask or minimize personality differences among people?

(d) Are there characteristics of a job that will lead to an increase in both a person's job satisfaction and motivation?

(e) To what extent do organizational procedures, processes, and systems affect a person's feelings of trust and fairness, and hence their subsequent behavior?

(f) Can an employee's motivation be bought? If yes, when and how should money be given for performing effectively?

4. Will answers to motivation be found in *person-environment fit*? As I noted in the Foreword, they have for me. Is person-environment fit likely to prove beneficial for others? If yes, in what ways?

5. Are there reasons to believe that the keys to unlocking the secrets to motivation are to be found in "all of the above"? Is there *reciprocal determinism* among characteristics of the person, the person's behavior, and characteristics of the environment?

To answer these questions, the history of work motivation research and theory in the 20th century must be examined, as well as the progress that has been made in the present century in understanding and explaining this fascinating topic.

Few areas should be more exciting and more worthwhile reading to facilitate understanding the present than history. Yet few books are more tedious to read than those written by many historians. This is often because the subject matter is explained void of the motivation of people and the circumstances that affected them. For example, most people know that the British won Canada by defeating the French on the Plains of Abraham in 1759. But, how many know that the victory was due in part to the lack of motivation of a French Officer to rally his troops? His *choice, effort,* and *persistence*—the three pillars that define motivation in the workplace—were to remain in bed with his mistress despite being warned that the British were scaling the cliffs of Quebec City. Most people have studied the conquests of Alexander the Great. How many know that he burned the city of Persepolis in Iran the morning following the request of a woman to do so as proof of his love for her? Little wonder that, as recently as the middle of the 20th century, sex was said to be a motivator of an employee's job performance (Harrell, 1949).

Biology

At the opening of the 20th century, Freud (1913) argued that a person's motivation is a function of the unconscious, and that it is biologically, that is, sexually, based. When asked to define the capabilities of a healthy person, he responded: "To work and to love" (Kelloway & Day, 2005).[4] Trained as a physician, Freud formed his conclusions on the basis of what he heard from people who came to him because of difficulties they were experiencing in their personal lives, as opposed to those who confronted difficulties primarily in the workplace. He did not conduct empirical research to test his theory. This is because psychoanalysis is more an art, a philosophy, and a practice than it is a science.[5]

Freud believed that crucial developmental experiences with our parents affect how we later adapt to authority. The crux of his theory is Eros-Thanatos. Eros concerns the biological need to develop bonds with others. Thanatos concerns the need to dominate others. Freud argued that human relationships are ambivalent because of these two motivating needs. Thus, friendships, argued Freud, are tinged with implicit if not explicit resentment as well as competition.

A century later, in his historical review of psychotherapy, Bandura (2004a) noted that Freud's theories were discarded by behavioral scientists because they lack predictive power. Moreover, outcome studies showed that one could predict the type of insights a client gained from psychoanalysis based on knowledge of a therapist's particular orientation. Finally, these outcome studies showed that it is difficult to change a person's behavior only by talking to a therapist. These studies would lead to a paradigm shift in the 1950s–1960s from unconscious psychic dynamics to a causal analysis of the interplay among personal, behavioral, and environmental influences without reference to the unconscious.

William James (1890) published one of the earliest textbooks on psychology, *Principles of Psychology*. He was concerned with "the description and explanation of states of consciousness" (James, 1892, p. 1). Unlike Freud, he eschewed hypothetical constructs of unconsciousness (i.e., id, superego, ego) and the use of dreams as a methodology for studying behavior. Instead, he studied his own consciousness through introspection.[6] Long before the empirical findings of experimental psychologists (e.g., Hebb, 1949; Kolb, 2003), James argued the importance

---

[4]As Kelloway and Day (2005) noted, Freud's theory for the most part has not held up to empirical inquiry. But, his identification of an intimate connection between work and mental health is consistent with a vast body of scientific literature (e.g., Kornhauser, 1965; Kelloway, Francis, & Montgomery, 2005; Quick, Quick, Nelson, & Hurrell, 1997).

[5]From the outset of the 20th century, "the atmosphere at the American Psychological Association meetings was so distinctly experimental that the mere mention of Sigmund Freud . . . was occasion for either complete silence or violent debate" (Cleeton, 1962 p. 32). Nevertheless, Freud's work influenced Hogan's (2004) socio-analytic theory of personality, a theory discussed in Part II.

of biological/physiological variables on behavior. Learning, he said, leads to the formation of pathways in the nerve centers. Hence, habits, he believed, were formed early in life. By the age of 30, they were "set like plaster" (James, 1892, p. 375).

James's research interests did not include employee behavior in the workplace. This was not true of Hugo Munsterberg, the father of I/O psychology (Hothersall, 1984).[7] Rather than rely on introspection or Freud's methodology, he engaged in systematic observations as well as interviews of factory workers (Munsterberg, 1913). This work is a pre-cursor to the study of employee motivation in that it pointed to the need for overcoming "dreadful monotony" and "mental starvation" in the workplace (p. 196). His call went largely unheeded for nearly two decades. Musterberg himself was far more interested in the issue of employee selection than he was in motivation.[8] He remained fascinated by the differences he had observed as a doctoral student among the participants in the experiments conducted in Wundt's laboratory. Landy (2005) has made the argument that it was therefore in Wundt's

---

[6]To my knowledge, few people followed up on this suggestion. As Locke and I noted (Locke & Latham, 2004), Freud and his followers rejected introspection as a methodology because they believed that motivation is in the unconscious, not the subconscious or preconscious, and hence is not accessible to direct awareness. The behaviorists, as is discussed shortly, rejected the concept of consciousness as relevant to psychology. Cleeton (1962, p. 31) observed that in the 19th century "description and hypothesis in psychology was augmented by experimentation to such an extent that it became almost unprofessional to introspect or speculate. In fact, it would appear that for a time in the history of psychology, the only two men who were permitted by their professional colleagues to exercise insight in the observance of behavior were William James and G. Stanley Hall." Questionnaire studies in our field, however, implicitly rely on introspection by the respondents. Locke and I argued that the benefits of training people in introspection would likely increase understanding of the relationship between traits and underlying motives, the factors that influence choices, including one's values and organizational circumstances, and the reciprocal effects between motivation and knowledge.

[7]Munsterberg, who did his doctoral work under Wundt in Germany, followed James as director of the psychology laboratory at Harvard University. Ciske (2004) argued that it is the establishment of a laboratory that marked the transition of psychology from philosophy to science. Wundt is credited for establishing the first laboratory in psychology in 1879.

[8]Arguably, selection was a logical starting point for the emerging science of industrial psychology. One has to select people before worrying about ways to motivate them. Soon, the U.S. military would be asking for the assistance of psychologists in selecting people for service in World War I. Walter Dill Scott was also an expert on selection. Ferguson (1962, p. 16), who was credited by Gilmer (1962) as "America's important industrial psychology historian," stated that Munsterberg has erroneously been given credit for being the first industrial psychologist: "Scott preceded him by eight years at least." In 1921, Bruce Moore was the first person to receive a Ph.D. in industrial psychology. His mentor was Walter Bingham. Moore went to the Pennsylvania State University where he offered the first seminar on industrial psychology given under that title. Thurstone, upon learning of Moore's intention to do so, urged him not to limit it to selection and placement but to "bring in some material on dynamics, motivation, and group behavior" (Moore, 1962, p. 5).

laboratory that the groundwork for the field of differential psychology was laid. This is ironic because, as Landy noted, Wundt did not allow his student Munsterberg to publish the results on these individual differences. Wundt feared that doing so would undermine his search for universal laws of consciousness.

Behavior

The philosophy of behaviorism was articulated in this time period by its founder, John B. Watson. This philosophy advocated a focus on the effect of environmental stimuli on observable behavior. Disagreeing with James, Watson advocated epiphenomenalism, the argument that consciousness has no causal efficacy: "The time seems to have come when psychology must discard all reference to consciousness; when it needs no longer to delude itself into thinking that it is making mental states the object of observation" (Watson, 1913, p. 158). Consciousness "has never been seen, touched, smelled, tasted or moved" (Watson & McDougall, 1928, p. 14). Thus Watson embraced the philosophy of positivism, a philosophy that only social, directly observable knowledge is valid. Scientific data for the behaviorists in that era were restricted to muscular movements or glandular secretions in time and space that lent themselves to quantitative analyses. Thus, from the outset, systematic measurement was a cornerstone of behaviorism. An enduring legacy of behaviorism in I/O psychology is an emphasis on measurement, particularly the ability to draw causal conclusions when n = 1 (see Komaki, 1977).

Motivation, as an internal psychological concept, was of no interest to the behaviorists. They were only interested in the prediction and influencing of responses. "By response we mean anything the animal does— such as turning toward or away from a light, jumping at a sound, or more highly organized activities such as building a skyscraper, drawing plans, having babies and the like" (Watson, 1925, pp. 6–7). Behavior was viewed as automatic or reflexive to a stimulus rather than cognitive or intentional; thus the focus of the behaviorists was on learning rather than motivation. The objectives of the behaviorists were twofold: (1) predict the response knowing the stimulus; and (2) identify the stimulus, knowing the response. A belief, fundamental to the behaviorists, is that there is an immediate response of some sort to every effective stimulus. In short, they imposed a strict cause and effect determinism in behavior. For them, human choice, or "free will" is an illusion.

Watson's (1913) methodology led him to the study of affect, particularly the conditioning and reconditioning of emotional responses in infants and children, as well as the elimination of conditioned fears.[9] In 1920, Watson left the academic community for the field of advertising, where he stayed until he retired. He did not publish empirical research conducted in organizational settings. The subject of emotion was largely ignored by I/O psychologists until the end of the century.

The behaviorists acknowledged that although human behavior is more complex than that of animals, it is influenced by similar underlying principles. Thus animals, particularly rats and pigeons, were studied for reasons of cost and convenience. The behaviorists attached no importance to the reasoning capacity of a human being.

E. Thorndike, among the most famous experimental psychologists in this time period, found that by presenting a reward (e.g., food) immediately after a behavior targeted by the experimenter occurred, the frequency of the behavior increases. Thorndike (1911) labeled this discovery the law of effect:

> Of several responses made to the same situation, those which are accompanied or closely followed by satisfaction to the animal will, other things being equal, be more firmly connected with the situation, so that, when it recurs, they will be more likely to recur; those which are accompanied or closely followed by discomfort to the animal will, other things being equal, have their connections with that situation weakened, so that, when it recurs, they will be less likely to occur. The greater the satisfaction or discomfort, the greater the strengthening or weakening of the bond. (Thorndike, p. 244)

Thorndike (1917) later conducted an empirical study on satisfaction with work that was published in the first volume of the *Journal of Applied Psychology*. Specifically, he examined the productivity and satisfaction of 29 adults who graded 10 printed compositions for 2 hours on 2 days. Speed of work and quality of work as well as satisfaction were measured every 20 minutes. The results indicated that the quality and quantity of work remained the same during the 2-hour period, but "satisfyingness" decreased steadily. Thorndike concluded that lack of rest affected a person's interest, willingness, or tolerance rather than the quality and quantity of the product produced. The seeds were now planted for what was to become a major controversy throughout the 20th century, namely, the relationship between job satisfaction and performance.

With minor exceptions, little or no attention was given by psychologists in this time period to the subject of motivation in the workplace.[10] Widespread application of the methodology of behaviorism to motivation in organizational settings was ignored until the 1970s, some 50 years later.

---

[9]A film of Watson working with children can be seen in the Archives of the History of American Psychology housed at the University of Akron.

The emphasis of I/O psychologists in this time period was on selection and placement. World War I had ushered in the importance of staffing, particularly of military officers. In the decade following the war, the North American economy boomed. The research of I/O psychologists was supported by organizations where there was great demand on hiring an efficient and effective workforce (Katzell & Austin, 1992). Burtt's (1926) comprehensive textbook on *Principles of Employment Psychology* contained no mention of the concept of motivation. The focus, instead, was exclusively on such topics as job analysis, mental tests of intelligence, the criterion, and rating scales. The implicit study of motivation, as defined by efficient/effective behavior, was left to engineers.

Money

With the ongoing shift from small, independent, family-run businesses in the 19th and early 20th century to large industrial organizations, Gilbreth, an engineer, founded the Society for the Promotion of the Science of Management. He and his wife Lillian, who had a Ph.D. in psychology, advocated "the One Best Way to Do Work" (Gilbreth, 1914; Gilbreth & Gilbreth, 1923) that could be identified through time-study and motion-study. Gilbreth (1920, p. 151) believed that motion-study and time-study data would benefit "the work of the industrial engineer, the machine designer and the behavioral psychologist—that their various pieces of information, usually obtained through entirely different channels and methods of attack, may be automatically brought together to the same filing folders under the same filing subdivision." He argued that the identification of the *One Best Sequence* would lead to the greatest speed and least effort and fatigue in learning because it would result automatically in the shortest possible learning period with least habit interference.

Frederick Winslow Taylor (1911), also an engineer, developed what he called scientific management. Adopting scientific management, argued Taylor, would result in a mental revolution on the part of the workers as to their duties toward themselves and toward their employers, as well as a mental revolution in the outlook of employers whereby they would set out to do something on behalf of their members, to which the workers would respond by giving a share of their initiative. The principles of scientific management are manifold:

---

[10]McDougall (1908), a social psychologist, was among the very few in this era who rejected a stimulus-response view of behavior. He was a proponent of instincts and their effect on active strivings toward anticipated goals. He was so struck by the goal-seeking quality of behavior that he later described himself as a purposive psychologist (McDougall, 1930).

1. The systematic gathering of knowledge about work by means of time and motion study of workers

2. Foreshadowing goal-setting theory, Taylor advocated giving each employee a task, that is, a specific difficult amount of work to complete, of a certain quality, on the basis of a time and motion study

3. Scientific selection of the workers followed by training and development

4. Offering a monetary incentive to the worker

5. Redividing work completely to bring about democracy and cooperation between management and workers

The outcome of applying these four principles is a revolutionary outlook, argued Taylor, whereby both the workmen and the management come to see that a "*surplus*" (i.e., money) can be made so great that there is no occasion to quarrel. Each side can get more than ever before. In short, Taylor believed that employees should be paid substantial bonuses for goal/task attainment because compensation for work done efficiently and effectively, he believed, leads to satisfied employees. This is one of the earliest explications of the notion that performance, which leads to rewards, leads to satisfaction. This notion would be later promulgated by Lawler and Porter (1967).

Concluding Comments

The enduring discoveries from this time period are Thorndike's law of effect and the importance that engineers placed on tying money to performance. The conditions under which money affects our performance would be examined in the remaining three quarters of the 20th century. Behaviorism would not be embraced by our field until the beginning of the 1970s. The importance that Hall attached to the study of consciousness proved to be omniscient as cognitive variables would be shown in the third quarter of the 20th century to explain the findings of the behaviorists. His use of introspection to study consciousness has to this date been rejected by our field; but, as will be shown in the next chapter, from the second quarter of the 20th century to the present day introspection is used implicitly through attitude surveys of employee morale and job satisfaction. Freud's focus on the subconscious was rejected immediately by our field. Not until the opening of the present century would behavioral scientists become aware of the importance of studying nonconscious motivation for predicting, understanding, and influencing a person's behavior in organizational settings. As will be discussed in Part II of this book, we are doing so without embracing Freud's theory.

2   1925–1950

Dust Bowl Empiricism

Introduction

Three events affected I/O psychology research in the second quarter of the 20th century. First, the world's economy crashed, second I/O psychology was embraced by departments of psychology (Koppes, 2003), and the third was World War II. The first event, the worldwide collapse of the economy, decreased dramatically the need for the selection of workers. The Great Depression increased the concern of psychologists for the plight of human beings and the concomitant humanization of the workplace. With unemployment high, with access to food and shelter in danger for many people, the needs and goals of people became of paramount concern to psychologists such as Abraham Maslow.

In 1932, at the age of 34, Morris Viteles published *Industrial Psychology*.[1] Unlike Burtt (1926), Viteles included a chapter on "Motives in Industry." He argued that despite the use of financial incentive programs advocated

---

[1]From an obituary by Albert S. Thompson (on the web page of the Society for Industrial and Organizational Psychology, http://www.siop.org/):

> After several years of annual summaries of the literature on industrial psychology for the *Psychological Bulletin*, in 1932 at the age of 34, Viteles published *Industrial Psychology*. This monumental book not only established him as a leader in the field, but also helped define the growing field. So influential was the book that some people later regarded him as the founder of the field, but Viteles himself credited Hugo Munsterberg with that role. Nevertheless, *Industrial Psychology* continued to be considered the "Bible of Industrial Psychology" for many years. When Viteles planned to update it after World War II, he began by revising the original 15 pages on "Motivation in Industry" and ended up with a new 500-page volume in 1953 entitled *Motivation and Morale in Industry*. That book became another "Bible" in its subject. His own practitioner role was a model. Not only did he engage in

(Continued)

by Taylor (1911), "analyses of restriction of output reveals not only an unhealthy economic condition but a serious situation in workers' attitudes toward management" (p. 564).[2] He stressed the need for "a detailed analysis of *motives-in-work* to determine the factors that underlie attitudes and activities which promote or interfere with economic efficiency and individual satisfaction at work" (p. 565). Viteles eschewed the then popular instinct hypothesis (e.g., curiosity, acquisition, anger) that was tied to Freud's concepts of repression, rationalization, and sublimation. "The chief objection to the instinct explanation of motives is that in the final analysis instincts are nothing more than logical abstractions . . . the assumption that the instincts represent well-organized neurological or mental patterns of behavior is entirely gratuitous" (p. 567). Viteles recommended a focus on "worker feelings and experiences . . ." (p. 581). The prime element, he said, "is the wish to enjoy the feeling of worth—recognition and respect on the part of others" (p. 582).

(Continued)

careful research and application in the "real world," but he published his findings in both practitioner and scientific journals. The success of his consulting roles is evidenced by the scope and duration of his consulting relationships. For example:

- 1924–1961 Yellow Cab Company
- 1927–1964 Philadelphia Electric Company where he served as a part-time Director of Selection and Training
- 1930s & 1940s Technical Board of the U.S. Employment Service where he helped develop the USES Job Classification System
- 1942–1951 National Research Council Committee on Aviation Psychology where, among other activities, he monitored a series of studies on pilot training and helped develop the Standard Flights for pilot evaluation, as well as serving as the chairman of the committee supporting a wide range of research relevant to the war effort.
- 1942–1951 National Defense Research Committee, involving studies of training and safety in naval settings.
- 1951–1984 Bell Telephone Co. of Philadelphia, where he sponsored a management development program based on the need for "humanistic education" of managers. During the 1950's, nearly 140 members of the managerial staffs on Bell System companies spent a full year at Penn devoted entirely to the humanities, including history, science, philosophy, and the arts. As was typical of him, Viteles evaluated the program through use of control groups and follow-ups which demonstrated that the experience resulted in long-term change in attitudes and managerial effectiveness.

Viteles had an important impact not only on American psychology but also in international circles. In the 1950s, he was a leader in the founding of the International Association of Applied Psychology, serving as the first American president from 1958–1968. Michael Frese, an I/O psychologist in Germany, is the current president.

[2]Years later, Bandura (1989) would argue that a focus solely on monetary incentives neglects the affective self-evaluative rewards of performance attainments. Forethought of outcomes (e.g., loss of one's job) influences effort and performance.

The importance of "feelings," however, would not receive a great deal of research attention until the end of the 20th century. Instead, I/O psychologists shifted their emphasis to finding ways of measuring attitudes of employees in order to identify sources of motivation in the workplace. The implicit theory of these studies is that the predominant personal characteristic that affects subsequent performance is a person's attitude.[3]

Attitude Surveys

Thurstone (1929) defined attitude as affect or overall degree of favorability regarding an object. The anonymous employee-attitude survey as a method for data collection in organizational settings by I/O psychologists became popular in the 1930s. Uhrbrock (1934) was among the first I/O psychologists to use the Thurstone (1929) scale. He assessed the attitudes of 3,934 factory workers, 96 clerical workers, and 400 foremen toward the company. Rensis Likert's (1932) doctoral dissertation at Columbia University revealed that a straightforward method, subsequently known as the Likert scale, permitted the measurement of attitudes that is much simpler than Thurstone's method of scale construction.[4] Moreover, Likert's method eliminated the need for unfavorable items, items to which management frequently objected to including in a survey. It also eliminated the need for judges in scaling the statements. Most importantly, Likert showed that his method correlated highly with more complex methods of survey construction such as Thurstone's.[5] Likert's method requires nothing more than the respondent indicating on a 5-point scale the extent of agreement with or approval of a survey item.

---

[3]Both Eagly (1992) and Ajzen (2001) concluded that there is now a strong basis for the argument that attitudes are indeed important causes and strong predictors of manifest behavior. Markman and Brendl (2000) argued that people evaluate objects in relation to currently active goals. However, they do not state or imply that job satisfaction leads to or predicts job performance. Attitude surveys are nevertheless used today by many organizations, including the Center for Creative Leadership, for gauging employee satisfaction with the job, the leadership team and the organization as a whole.

[4]Likert's name is among the most mispronounced in our field. It is phonetically Lick-ert.

[5]Paul Thayer now a retired department head of psychology at North Carolina State University was formerly vice president of research from 1967–1973 and senior vice president from 1973–1977 of the Life Insurance Management Association. He stated (2003, personal communication) that "most people don't know what a Thurstone scale is, much less all the work that must go into building one. I've built one and it is a beast."

The results of these attitude surveys immediately brought into question the validity of a core principle of scientific management, namely, that employees are uniformly motivated by a desire for money; the assumption that other motives are of little consequence. Houser (1938) found that nonselling employees, including unskilled labor, of a large merchandizing company ranked money as 21st in importance. Of far greater importance were: chances to show initiative (11.5), safety (3), steady employment (2), and fair adjustment of grievances (1).

In a study that focused explicitly on job satisfaction as opposed to motivation, Hoppock (1935) reported that it is affected by many factors other than money.[6] These factors, he found, include the relative status of the person within the social and economic group with which he identifies himself, relations with superiors and associates on the job, the nature of the work, opportunities for advancement, variety, freedom from close supervision, visible results, appreciation, and security. These two studies foreshadowed theories subsequently put forth by Maslow (1943) and Herzberg (Herzberg, Mausner, Snyderman, 1959).

Comprehensive statistical studies by Kolstad (1938) showed that successful employees have higher morale than those who are struggling with their jobs. Specifically, he found that in a department store employees with low sales had morale scores that were significantly lower than the scores of employees whose sales were high. Those results suggested that employees should not be placed or kept in jobs where they are unable to perform effectively. The data also lend support to the iconoclastic conclusion that Lawler and Porter (1967) would promulgate years later—that job performance affects job satisfaction, not the reverse.

Laboratory Experiments

Few laboratory experiments on motivation were conducted in this time period. An exception is a series of experiments conducted by Mace (1935) in Great Britain. He found that the standard that was set affected a person's performance but only when the person's skill had developed to the point where there was a reasonable expectation by the individual that the standard could be reached.[7] Otherwise, urging people to do

---

[6]Employee motivation should not be equated with job satisfaction. Satisfaction with one's job is often associated with high levels of work commitment and willingness to expend effort to attain organization-related goals, but satisfaction is not a prerequisite for motivation (Franco, Bennett, & Kanfer, 2002).

[7]Mace's empirical work was a basis for Locke's doctoral dissertation on goal setting.

their best led to the highest performance. Mace's latter finding was replicated in the United States by Kanfer and Ackerman (1989) more than 50 years later in their goal-setting study involving air force cadets in an air-traffic control simulation. They, too, found that when knowledge is lacking, performance is higher when people are urged to "do their best" than it is when a specific challenging performance goal is set. Setting a standard (goal) for the performance of the worker, Mace concluded, will be most effective if it is adjusted to his level of skill and ability. This latter finding is the bedrock of the field studies on goal setting by my colleagues and me 40 years later (e.g., Latham & Kinne, 1974).

Field Experiments

By the late 1920s, the widespread use of time and motion studies by engineers led to the systemization of highly repetitive work. Each employee was, in effect, "standardized." As Dunnette and Kirchner (1965) noted years later, employees were viewed by engineers as identical elements in the production process to be studied and manipulated as any other cog in the machinery of production.

Research in Great Britain on job fatigue by Wyatt, Fraser, and Stock (1929) was a precursor to job enlargement. They found that changing jobs at specific intervals reduced monotony. With light repetitive work, employees produce their best output if their task is changed every 1.5 to 2 hours. More frequent changes interfere with the "swing" of work. In addition, they found that piece-rate pay resulted in fewer symptoms of boredom than hourly pay. This finding predates Lawler's (1965) and supports Taylor's (1911) earlier conclusion that money can indeed be an incentive for performance if job performance is the criterion for determining the person's pay.

A subsequent study by Wyatt, Frost, and Stock (1934) foreshadowed field research on goal setting. Factory workers reduced their boredom by creating "definite aims" to complete a certain number of units in a given period of time.

The application of scientific management principles in a Philadelphia textile mill in the 1920s increased employee antagonism toward management as well as labor grievances and turnover.[8] Elton Mayo,

---

[8]Locke (1982a) is highly appreciative of Taylor's work. Taylor believed, in Locke's words (2004, personal communication) in the rule of knowledge when designing work tasks and processes based on systematic studies. Taylor's work, Locke believes, has been misunderstood because so many people misused his ideas. My own reading of Taylor's original work supports Locke's view. Taylor's desire was for a highly motivated workforce. In many instances, his ideas are a forerunner of both goal setting and monetary incentive plans.

a psychologist at Harvard, concluded, based on observation, that these difficulties were due to the monotony of the work.[9] His solution was to allow the workers to take rest periods according to their own agreed-upon schedules, a forerunner to the importance psychologists would give to participation in the decision-making process. The result was a significant decrease in turnover and an increase in productivity. Mayo's solution was based on his reasoning that money is only an effective incentive when it is used in conjunction with, rather than in opposition to, man's other needs.

Hawthorne Studies

Mayo and his colleagues were subsequently asked to become involved with a series of studies of employee productivity (Homans, 1941; Mayo, 1933; Roethlisberger & Dickson, 1939) for the Committee on Work in Industry of the National Research Council. Field experiments were conducted between 1927 and 1933 in the Hawthorne (Chicago) plant of the Western Electric Company, a manufacturer of equipment for the telephone industry. They led to the "realization that the productivity, satisfaction, and motivation of workers were all interrelated" (Roethlisberger, 1977, p. 46). This research subsequently became the foundation of the Human Relations Movement.

The original purpose of the Hawthorne studies was to determine the relation between intensity of illumination and efficiency of workers, measured in output. In Homans' (1941/1977) words:

> The experiment failed to show any simple relation between experimental changes in the intensity of illumination and observed changes in the rate of output. The investigators concluded that this result was obtained, not because such a relation did not exist, but because it was in fact impossible to isolate it from the other variables entering into any determination of productive efficiency. This kind of difficulty, of course, has been encountered in experimental work in many fields. Furthermore, the investigators were in agreement as to the character of some of these other variables. They were convinced that one of the major factors which prevented their securing a satisfactory result was psychological. The employees

---

[9]Mayo was born in Adelaide, Australia. He received his BA (1910) and MA (1919) in psychology from Adelaide University. After teaching at the Universities of Queensland in Brisbane (1919–1923) and Pennsylvania in Philadelphia (1923–1926), he joined the Harvard Graduate School of Business (1926–1947).

being tested were reacting to changes in light intensity in the way in which they assumed that they were expected to react. That is, when light intensity was increased they were expected to produce more; when it was decreased they were expected to produce less. A further experiment was devised to demonstrate this point. The light bulbs were changed, as they had been changed before, and the workers were allowed to assume that as a result there would be more light. They commented favorably on the increase in illumination. As a matter of fact, the bulbs had been replaced with others of just the same power. Other experiments of the sort were made, and in each case the results could be explained as a "psychological" reaction rather than as a "physiological" one. (p. 51)

This "psychological" reaction to the increase in attention the employees received led to the coining of the term, "the Hawthorne effect" (Adair, 1984; Roethlisberger, 1977).[10]

A subsequent study in 1927 involved the selection of six "girls" who were placed in a separate Relay Assembly Test Room. Homans (1941/1977) stated:

The girls had no supervisors in the ordinary sense, such as they would have had in a regular shop department, but, a "test room observer." . . . whose duty it was to . . . secure a cooperative spirit on the part of the girls. The purpose of this study was to determine the effect of changes in working conditions such as rest periods, mid-morning breaks, and shorter working hours. Two weeks of pretest measures of each worker's output were taken prior to the study, without the person's knowledge. . . . The output of the group continued to rise until it established itself on a high plateau. . . , [yet] there was no simple correlation with the experimental changes in the working conditions. Interviews revealed that "the girls liked to work in the test room; 'it was fun.'" Secondly, the new supervisory relation or, as they put it, the absence of the old supervisory control, made it possible for them to work freely without anxiety. . . . Another factor in what occurred can only be spoken of as the social development of the group itself. Often one of the girls would have some good reason for feeling tired. Then the others would "carry" her. That is, they would agree to work especially fast to make up for the low output

---

[10]My initial experience with the Hawthorne effect occurred at a Weyerhaeuser plant. Because of low job attendance, the company, with the union's support decided to institute a "Lucky Bonus Day" whereby people who were on the job on a given day, determined by a variable-interval schedule, would receive a sizable amount of money. My first invited colloquium was at the University of Maryland in 1974. There Benjamin Schneider criticized me for failing to collect pre-measures before I had randomly assigned pulpwood crews to conditions. So, this time I did so. The result of the pre-measure was an immediate increase in employee attendance. The increase remained so high for so long that the Lucky Bonus Day program was never implemented. Interviews with the employees revealed that the attention given to the pre-measurement of attendance made them realize how much time they were missing work. As Mason Haire was fond of saying, that which gets measured gets done.

expected from her. . . . Finally, the group developed leadership and a common purpose. . . . The common purpose was an increase in the output rate. [This output rate was] related to what can only be spoken of as the development of an organized social group in a peculiar and effective relation with its supervisors. (p. 53)

Dunnette and Kirchner (1965, p. 133) commented that: "The impact of Mayo's research was heightened by the zealous manner in which he publicized it." His zeal garnered him unflattering comments within the academic community. In his autobiography, Roethlisberger (1977), Mayo's colleague, recalled:

Mayo's participation in the Hawthorne researches was unusual from the point of view of orthodox scientific methodology—so unusual that it aroused the curiosity of many social scientists. Some of them felt that some kind of skullduggery was going on. Let me try to correct this understanding. . . . Mayo had nothing to do with the design of or conduct of the original illumination experiments or of the Relay Assembly Test Room. . . . Mayo himself never collected any of the data. . . . Mayo came into the—I cannot specify the exact date—some time around Period XII in the Relay Assembly Test Room, when the persons in charge of these experiments were having trouble interpreting the findings. (pp. 48–49)

The division of labor between Mayo and me was roughly this. He interacted with the top executives of the company more than I did. I interacted with the lower levels of supervision more than he did. (p. 49)

Mayo was an adventurer in ideas. . . . Again and again Mayo performed the function of interpretation. The data were not his; the results were not his; the original hypotheses were not his; but as the researches continued, the interpretations of what the results meant and the new questions and hypotheses that emerged from them were his. Also the way of thinking which he brought to the research and which finally gave them a sense of direction and purpose was his. . . . By his behavior, Mayo escalated the positive Hawthorne effect. To his concern, interest and curiosity, the Hawthorne researchers responded with increasing vigor, just as the employees had responded with increased output to the concern, interest and curiosity of the researchers. . . . Let's bow our heads in silence for a moment, because without Mayo's contributions the results would still be in the archives of the company in the green files collecting dust. Nobody would have known what they meant. (pp. 50–51)[11]

The Hawthorne studies were attacked vigorously by Argyle (1953) for their lack of methodological rigor. In a statistical re-analysis of the data, Franke and Kaul (1978) showed that two key reasons for relay

---

[11]In 1959 Harvard University awarded Roethlisberger its Ledlie Prize as the member of the faculty "who had by research discovered or otherwise made the most valuable contribution to science or in any way for the benefit of mankind."

performance improvement were the replacement of two low-producing workers and the introduction of an incentive system. By modern standards, these and other methodological confounds render the original conclusions of the Hawthorne studies highly suspect. Where the advocates of scientific management simplistically assumed that man's most basic motive is economic, Mayo and his colleagues made an "equally oversimplified assumption that group membership and affiliation are the most fundamental and essentially the only human needs of any consequence" (Dunnette & Kirchner, 1965, p. 133).

Nevertheless, these studies are considered seminal. As Ryan and Smith (1954) noted, the Hawthorne studies showed that when people are given the opportunity to express their preferences and opinions, are free of overly strict supervision, and are given standards, that is, goals that take into account their ability, they work effectively. Years later, Blum and Naylor (1968) concluded that just as Munsterberg's work is considered the birth of industrial psychology, the Hawthorne studies can be considered its "coming of age."

World War II

In response to the War with repressive fascist regimes in Europe and in light of the findings of Mayo and his colleagues, the importance of employee participation in the decision-making process was becoming an implicit if not an explicit hypothesis of I/O psychologists as well as union leaders. Harold Ruttenberg (1941), research director of the Steel Workers Organizing Committee, stated that the urge for self-expression is present in every individual in an industrial plant, and that each person constantly seeks some way to express himself.

Following World War II, the economy boomed. Severe employee strikes designed to compensate for wage freezes during the war were now crippling industry so much so that employers were forced to listen to employee demands on sundry issues so as to restore productivity in the workplace.

Fifteen years of economic depression and a second world war led N. R. F. Maier (1946) to conclude that the most undeveloped aspect of industrial progress is management of labor power.[12] He cited an

---

[12]As noted earlier, it is Maier (1955) who proposed that job performance = motivation × ability. Wright et al. (1995) subsequently showed that need for achievement is positively related to performance among those high in ability and yet negatively related to performance among those low in ability. In short, there are few things more dysfunctional in an organization than a highly motivated incompetent running through the hallway. Hence the ongoing importance of training (Wexley & Latham, 2002).

unpublished field experiment by Alex Bavelas, a former student of Kurt Lewin's,[13] as an example of how to motivate workers. By securing employee participation in decision making, previously unattainable goals were reached by those workers. Two years later, Ghiselli and Brown (1948) argued that the new emphasis of industrial psychology should be to maximize productivity consistent with the abilities, energies, interests, and motives of the worker.

French, also a former student of Lewin's, showed that employee participation in decision making can overcome resistance to change (Coch & French, 1948).[14] Similar findings were obtained 40 years later regarding the importance of "voice," a concept central to organizational justice theory (Greenberg, 1987). Empirical research conducted by the University of Michigan's Survey Research Center (1948, p. 10) in an insurance company was also interpreted as corroborating the importance of employee participation in the decision making process:

> People are more effectively motivated when they are given some degree of freedom in the way in which they do their work than when every action is prescribed in advance. They do better when some degree of decision making about their jobs is possible than when all decisions are made for them. They respond more adequately when they are treated as personalities than as cogs in a machine. In short, if the ego motivations of self determination, of self expression, of a sense of personal worth can be tapped, the individual can be more effectively energized. The use of external sanctions, of pressuring for production, may work to some degree, but not to the extent that more internalized motives do.[15]

This research was a harbinger for the emphasis that Deci would place on self-determination.

---

[13]Lewin (1945), a renowned social psychologist, was famous for his research on level of aspiration and the variables that affect it. Among his many legacies is his dictum: "Nothing is as practical as a good theory" (p. 129).

[14]In his book, *The Practical Theorist,* Marrow (1969) also a doctoral student of Lewin's, pointed out that Lewin became interested in the applications of participation in the decision making process after experiencing and subsequently escaping from Nazi Germany. This led to the Lewin, Lippitt, and White (1939) studies on autocratic, democratic, and laissez-faire studies of leadership styles which in turn led to the studies by Coch and French as well as Bavelas. After receiving his Ph.D., Marrow became head of the Harwood Manufacturing Company where Bavelas conducted his experiment.

[15]A meta-analysis by Wagner (1994) showed that the effect of participation in the decision-making process on an employee's performance has statistical significance but lacks practical significance. Nevertheless, Erez (1997) found that participation in the decision-making process is now used across cultures as a motivational technique. This issue is discussed later in Part I.

By the end of the second quarter of the 20th century and at the beginning of the third quarter, I/O psychologists were critiquing scientific management. For example, Ryan (1947) concluded that time and motion study was inadequate because it relies upon extremely crude estimates of effort by engineers. Moreover it is based on the erroneous assumption that effort remains constant throughout comparisons of different work methods. Foreshadowing the research on job enrichment, he argued that wages are of secondary consideration because workers want a certain degree of independence and initiative, plus recognition for their work and value to the organization. In addition, people want a superior who guides and directs rather than commands.

Similar to Ryan, Harrell (1949), as did Mayo, argued that motivation does not occur through the application of money alone. Harrell called the erroneous assumption that money is the only important incentive the "rabble hypothesis" because workers are treated as a group of unorganized rabble insensitive to the social motives of approval and self-respect. Similarly, Stagner (1950) stated that the problem of industrial harmony would not be solved until there is realization that both executives and workers want democratic self-assertion. He took strong issue with what he called the "dollar fallacy," the erroneous belief that employers and employees are motivated only by dollars and cents.

Tiffin (1952) took umbrage with reference to workers as "hired hands" because it, too, reflects a mistaken viewpoint by management. A man's hands alone are never hired. The four factors that affect a worker's morale, he said, were similar to those identified in the Hawthorne studies. It is not so much the job itself, as it is how the person (1) feels about it, and (2) how the boss regards the employee that determines morale. In addition, Tiffin advised the necessity of taking into account (3) social factors, and (4) working conditions.

The concept of motivation was now being explicitly discussed in the I/O literature, so much so that Harrell (1949) concluded that as recently as 1930 we assumed that the importance of psychology in industry was largely confined to the use of tests; today we view its function as the analysis of human relations in industry. Ryan (1947) stated that motive refers to factors which raise or lower the level of effort an individual puts into the task. Shortly thereafter, with his former doctoral student, Patricia Cain Smith (Ryan & Smith, 1954), he stated that motivation is the central problem that needs to be addressed by industrial psychologists.

Harrell (1949), after reviewing the ongoing research of the behaviorists in experimental psychology (e.g., Hull, 1943; Spence, 1948), concluded that motives are based on physiological drives (i.e., food, water, rest, sleep, and sex activity) that act in combination with a learned response to gratify these drives. The most important motives in industry are the activity or the work itself, hunger, sex, social approval, and self-respect. Sex as a motive for work, he said, operates indirectly by making a person work harder and steadier in order to get married or to support his wife and family. In addition, he emphasized: "Whether or not motivation will be effective depends in part on the internal state of the organism–his level of aspiration–what a man expects of himself" (p. 269). In general, employees in either the professions, or in management, concluded Harrell, are highly motivated; this is not true, he said, of the factory worker. Such was the thinking of eminent people in our field in that era.[16]

Concluding Comments

As the first half of the 20th century came to a close, the near exclusive emphasis of I/O psychologists on employee selection had shifted to include the topic of motivation and satisfaction. A major methodological breakthrough was the development and use of surveys to measure attitudes in the workplace. The implicit theory underlying these studies is that job attitudes affect job performance. Viteles' review of the literature showed convincingly that people are motivated by a multitude of variables in addition to money. The Hawthorne studies were said to have marked the "coming of age" of I/O psychology. Despite their methodological weaknesses, they were the stimulus for literally hundreds of subsequent studies on the relationship between employee attitudes and performance.[17]

---

[16]Although Harrell's comments may sound naïve if not elitist by today's standards, 30 years later, Hofstede (1979) working with survey data on IBM employees, did in fact find striking differences in the saliency of work values among occupational groups. Whereas professionals stressed the importance of the content of their jobs, skilled workers and technicians placed greater value on job security and money, and the unskilled, he found, stressed only benefits and physical work conditions.

[17]Viteles (1932) is among the first to question this relationship. He cited a study by Kornhauser and Sharp (1932), conducted at the Kimberly-Clark Company on "the feelings and attitudes of 200–300 girls employed on routine, repetitive machine and conveyor operations. One of the most significant findings is the discovery, in contrast to the findings of the Hawthorne investigation, that efficiency ratings of employees showed no relationship to their attitudes" (p. 577). Recall that Thorndike (1917), years earlier, had also found no relationship. The controversy regarding the causal effect of job satisfaction on job performance was about to emerge.

It was in this time period that psychologists began to systematically explore the effect of participation in decision making on an employee's performance. As Harold Leavitt (1962) noted, prior to this time period, "Classical industrial psychology had been ideologically, at least, an ally of Taylorism and scientific management. Certainly our work on the measurement of abilities, on job analysis, on noise and monotony, were quite consonant with Taylor's physiological view of man" (p. 25). In contrast, the human relations movement was not only for participation, it was "unswervingly against scientific management" (p. 25).

I/O psychology research, up to this point in time, was largely atheoretical. This was about to change as a result of an essay, written by Abraham Maslow (1943), a clinical psychologist. In that essay, he specified needs, and the cues that arouse them, that energize and direct behavior. However, this essay went largely unnoticed until Maslow published his book in 1954 and McGregor argued cogently for the immediate applicability of Maslow's theory to industry. Hence, Maslow's (1943, 1954) theory is discussed in Chapter 3, "1950–1975: The Emergence of Theory."

 **3**   1950–1975

The Emergence of Theory

Introduction

Research in the early part of the 1950s did not differ appreciably from the research of the four preceding decades. Attitude surveys continued to be the primary method of data collection for I/O psychologists in their study of motivation. Behaviorism was at its zenith in experimental psychology with B. F. Skinner (1953) as its articulate champion. Research with animals continued to show the importance of antecedent stimuli and external consequences on behavior.

Ryan and Smith (1954) argued against I/O psychology adopting the prevailing motivational paradigms of experimental and clinical psychology. To translate worker goals into Watson's (1925) terms of stimuli and responses, they said, was not only useless but misleading since it implies that the laws that govern these stimuli and responses in experimental laboratory paradigms are the same as those that hold for all other stimuli and responses in everyday situations. They took issue with Hull's (1928) and Spence's (1948) research on the primary drives of animals because to postulate some simple mechanism by which new activities come to be attractive to the organism make it difficult, if not impossible, they said, to demonstrate that a particular activity in the work setting arises through biological determinism.[1] As for Freud, Ryan and Smith noted wryly that his evidence that the individual is unaware of his real wish is likely due only to the fact that the individual does not

---

[1] Hull and Spence were interested in the biological determinants that activate consummatory and protective behavior. They studied motivation largely in terms of the energizing and directive functions of physiological activators.

wish to admit or explain it to the listener.[2] Finally, they dismissed the relevance of behaviorism and psychoanalysis because neither paradigm emphasized the importance of consciousness in regulating behavior. Consequently, Ryan and Smith called for general theories of motivation by industrial psychologists that take into account the wants, wishes, desires, and experiences of the individual.[3] They argued the importance of intentions to anticipate future obligations or to avoid them.

> Whether a means activity is initiated, and the degree of effort which is devoted to it, are functions of (a) the attractiveness of the goal, (b) the attractiveness of the means activity itself and of its surrounding conditions, (c) the uniqueness of the goal (as perceived by the individual), (d) the directness of relationship between the means and the end result, also as perceived or understood by the subject, and (e) the individual's estimates of his ability to perform the means activity well enough to achieve the goal. (Ryan & Smith, 1954, pp. 387–388)[4]

Job Satisfaction and Job Performance

Viteles (1953) equated motivation with employee performance and morale. The inference drawn from attitude surveys as well as from the Hawthorne studies was that the worker who is highly productive is a worker who has positive attitudes toward the job. Thus a primary variable of interest to I/O psychologists was employee morale or satisfaction.[5]

A major breakthrough in knowledge occurred with an enumerative review of the literature by Brayfield and Crockett (1955) that forcibly and thoughtfully challenged that belief. They showed that there was little or no relationship between these two variables. Shortly thereafter, a quantitative review by Vroom (1964) showed that the median correlation between a

---

[2]In acknowledging the importance of goals, Alfred Adler split with Freud over the emphasis of sexual instincts as explanations of behavior. Adler viewed people as goal directed, motivated by their expectations of their future. "Causes, powers, instincts, impulses, and the like cannot serve as explanatory principles. The final goal alone can explain man's behavior" (Adler, 1930, p. 400).

[3]Although people in the workplace were still referred to in scholarly literature as men or girls, the use of the word worker was shifting to that of employee and the neutrally descriptive term, individual.

[4]The seeds were now planted for their future doctoral student to sow, a decade later, Edwin Locke. Note too that letter (e) is a forerunner of Bandura's concept of self-efficacy.

[5]The terms job satisfaction and morale were used interchangeably until Guion (1958) and Stagner (1958) argued for differentiation. The former refers to the individual's attitudes toward the job; the latter refers to the perception that, through cooperation with the group, one's motives or needs will be met.

person's satisfaction and performance was only 0.14. Nevertheless, these two variables remained interdependent in the eyes of many employers and I/O researchers, an issue discussed further in chapter 6.

Motivation Theory

In 1953 Viteles published his book *Motivation and Morale.*[6] This became the definitive textbook on this subject for three decades. In his review of theories in both experimental and social psychology, he commented favorably on Lewin's "insistence that without a good 'theoretical' foundation applied research follows a path of trial and error, and becomes misdirected and inefficient" (p. 121). One-shot, one-context attitude surveys in the 1930s had hampered the development of motivation theory in the workplace.

In the opening sentence of his "Annual Review of Psychology" chapter, Heron (1954), a psychologist in the United Kingdom, observed:

> It may well be that in the last five years we have experienced the end of an era in the history of industrial psychology. No startling development took place, no text appeared to establish a landmark, no new theory provoked widespread discussion and opened fresh vistas; but perhaps something less sensational may be detected. Discontent can sometimes be divine, provided that it results in thinking which ultimately issues in more appropriate activity.[7]

---

[6]Edward Webster, at McGill University, was highly skeptical of motivational concepts. He was a 'dyed in the wool' adherent to tests and measurements, selection and vocational guidance. He was shocked when one of his idols, Viteles, came out with *Motivation and Morale in Industry.* So, in the spring of 1954 he scheduled a seminar around this new book. There were at least a dozen masters students around to help Webster examine the contents of this book. They included Victor Vroom and Harry Triandis. "My best recollection is that Ed took it all as a hypothesis yet to be proven but worthy of research" (Vroom, 2003, personal communication).

[7]In his review, Heron (1954) cited approvingly Mace's observation of "the widespread provision in the United States of education for management at the university or college level using the Harvard Business School as a leading example" ... and the "need for closer collaboration between the business schools and other departments in which psychologists are engaged in research" (p. 222). A decade later, Haire (1960) commented enthusiastically on the conclusions by the Ford Foundation on the need to incorporate industrial psychology research in the curriculum of American business schools. As Vroom (2003, personal communication) noted, these conclusions resulted in a massive infusion of funds, particularly by the Ford Foundation, into building a link between the social science departments and the business schools. The net effect was the hiring of industrial psychologists into business schools. This in turn broadened the emphasis of industrial psychology from primarily selection, performance appraisal and training to motivation, leadership and organizational design.

Heron's observation proved to be remarkably prescient. Innovation and knowledge in I/O psychology were about to blossom in the form of myriad theories of work motivation. These theories would soon provide a framework for planning, conducting, and interpreting research.[8] In the interim, McGregor argued cogently for the immediate applicability of Maslow's need hierarchy theory to industry.

Need Hierarchy Theory

As was the case with Freud's theory of psychoanalysis, Maslow's (1943) theory of human motivation was based on conclusions he drew from his observations of individuals who came to him for assistance in coping with difficulties in their personal lives. The theory was written during the Great Depression. From the outset of his paper, Maslow acknowledged that:

> It is far easier to prove and to criticize the aspects of motivation theory than to remedy them. Mostly this is because of the very serious lack of sound data in this area. I conceive this lack of sound facts to be due primarily to the absence of a valid theory of motivation. The present theory then must be considered to be a suggested program or framework for future research and must stand or fall, not so much on facts available or evidence presented, as upon researches yet to be done, researches suggested perhaps, by the questions raised in this paper. (p. 371)

Rather than a focus on attitudes, Maslow posited that there is a hierarchy of five sets of goals for which people strive in seeking satisfaction of their basic needs. Needs determine the repertoire of behaviors that a person develops in order to satisfy each goal. Unlike the experimental psychologists such as Watson and Thorndike, he emphasized that:

> This theory starts with the human being rather than any lower and presumably "simpler" animal. Too many of the findings that have been made in animals have been proven true for animals but not for the human being. There is no reason whatsoever why we start with animals in order to study motivation. (p. 392)

Maslow proposed the following sequential hierarchical order of the development of five basic needs.

---

[8]Theories, argued Klein and Zedeck (2004) are invaluable because they tell us why something occurs, not simply what occurs. Good theories provide novel insights that are practical and testable. They simplify and structure what were once scattered observations.

1. Physiological needs. All other needs become simply nonexistent or are pushed into the background until physiological needs are satisfied. A peculiar characteristic of the human organism when it is dominated by a certain need, Maslow said, is that the whole philosophy of the future tends also to change. "For our chronically and extremely hungry man, utopia can be defined very simply as a place where there is plenty of food" (p. 374). When this need is met: "At once other (and 'higher') needs emerge and these, rather than physiological hungers, dominate the organism" (p. 375). Maslow's belief that this lower order need becomes stronger as deprivation increases was likely influenced by the laboratory findings of Hull and Spence with animals.

2. Safety needs. "Again, we may say of the receptors, the effectors, of the intellect and other capacities that they are primarily safety-seeking tools" (p. 376). Confronting a child with the new, unfamiliar, strange, or unmanageable stimuli frequently elicit the danger or terror reaction. The need for safety is manifested in "the common preference for a job with tenure and protection, the desire for a savings account, and for insurance of various kinds (medical, dental, unemployment, disability, old age)" (p. 379), as is "the tendency to have some religious or world-philosophy that organizes the universe and the men in it into some sort of satisfactorily coherent, meaningful whole" (p. 379).

3. Love needs. Once the two lower needs are satisfied, there will emerge the love and affection and belongingness needs. The "thwarting of these needs is the most commonly found core in cases of maladjust-ment and more severe psychopathology" (p. 381).

4. Esteem needs. Most people have a need or desire for a firmly based high evaluation of themselves, based on achievement that leads to respect from others, and inculcates confidence to face the world. Thwarting this need produces feelings of inferiority, weakness, and of helplessness.

5. Self-actualization. The clear emergence of this need rests upon man's prior satisfaction of the other four. "It refers to the desire for self-fulfillment, namely, to the tendency for him to become actualized in what he is potentially" (p. 382).

The crux of this theory is that as one need becomes fulfilled, its strength diminishes while the strength of the next need higher in the hierarchy increases. Systematic research based on Maslow's (1943) theory did not occur in organizational settings for another two decades.

Nevertheless, the theory and his subsequent book (Maslow, 1954) wherein he described the theory more fully had a tremendous influence on McGregor's (1957) formulation of "Theory X" and "Theory Y."

Theory X and Theory Y

Douglas McGregor received his Ph.D. from Harvard University where he was influenced by Gordon Allport, a social psychologist. However, McGregor did not see himself as an experimentalist (McGregor, 1960). Rather, he was, in the words of Warren Bennis (1985), a champion of the application of behavioral sciences with a flair for the right metaphor that generated and established a new idea. Of all behavioral scientists, he was in this time period the best known by managers until his death in 1964 (Boone & Bowen, 1987).[9]

McGregor (1957) believed that the time had come to apply the social sciences to make human organizations truly effective: "To a degree the social sciences today are in a position like that of the physical sciences with respect to atomic energy in the thirties. We know that the past assumptions of man are in dispute and in many ways, incorrect" (McGregor, 1957, p. 22). The subject of motivation is the best way, he said, of indicating the inappropriateness of the conventional view of employees, which he called "Theory X." The assumption underlying Theory X is that without active intervention by management, people are passive—even resistant—to organizational needs. This is because the average man is by nature indolent, lacks ambition, is inherently self-centered, and is not very bright. This behavior is not a consequence of man's inherent nature, argued McGregor, rather it is the outcome of management philosophy and practice. He then explained Maslow's theory in detail to show why Theory X is an inadequate approach to motivation: "Unless there are opportunities *at work* to satisfy these higher level needs, people will be deprived. . . . People will make insistent demands for more money under these conditions. It becomes more important than ever to buy the material goods and services which can provide limited satisfaction to the thwarted needs" (p. 28).

---

[9]Warren Bennis (2003, personal communication) wrote: "It was through Doug that I got to know Abe so well. When Abe came to Doug's memorial service at MIT with his wife Bertha, at which time I spoke, Bertha whispered to me afterwards that when Abe died, she'd like me to do the same for her husband. I did at Stanford, only a few years later."

Thus, McGregor concluded that a different theory of human motivation was needed in the workplace, a theory based on the correct assumptions about human nature—a theory that makes explicit "the human side of an enterprise." McGregor called this "Theory Y." Theory Y differs from Theory X in that the latter places exclusive reliance upon external control of behavior while Theory Y emphasizes self-control and self-direction. The essence of Theory Y is:

> The motivation, the potential for development, the capacity for assuming responsibility, the readiness to direct behavior toward organizational goals are all present in people. Management does not put them there. A responsibility of management is to make it possible for people to recognize and develop these human characteristics for themselves. (p. 6)[10]

Successful applications of Theory Y, in McGregor's view, included management by objectives at Sears, Roebuck and Company, job enlargement, pioneered by IBM and Detroit Edison, participation in the decision-making process, as well as self-appraisals whereby each employee at General Mills and General Electric set targets or objectives and subsequently does a self-evaluation semi-annually or annually.

As was the presentation by Maslow (1943), McGregor's (1957) article and subsequent book (McGregor, 1960) were void of data to support either Theory Y or Maslow's theory on which it was directly based. It was not until the 1960s that theory-driven empirical research was conducted. Lyman Porter was among the first to do so.

Theory-Driven Empirical Research

Trained as an experimental psychologist at Yale University under the supervision of Neil Miller, Lyman Porter was immediately hired upon graduation to come to Berkeley by Edwin Ghiselli, a renowned industrial psychologist who, in addition, was the department chair. Never having taken a formal I/O psychology course, Porter obtained the lecture notes of an undergraduate student, Geoffrey Keppel, to help

---

[10]This last sentence explains why McGregor would soon endorse Herzberg's emphasis on the enrichment of jobs. McGregor argued vehemently that an essential task of management is to arrange organizational conditions and methods of operation so that people can achieve their own goals best by directing their own efforts toward organizational objectives (McGregor, 1960, p. 178).

in preparation for teaching one that Ghiselli had assigned to him.[11] Immediately thereafter, Porter devoted his academic life to research in I/O psychology, particularly in regard to motivation.

Porter developed a need deficiency scale that required people to rate the importance of characteristics present in their job as well as how much of each characteristic they would prefer to have in the job. Using Maslow's theory as a framework, Porter (1961) administered a 15-item survey to 64 foremen and 75 middle level managers who worked in three different companies.[12] In that study, Porter deleted reference to physiological needs and replaced it with need for autonomy which he said fell between need for love, which he labeled esteem, and self-actualization. The data showed that the highest order need, self-actualization, is the most critical of those studied, in terms of both perceived deficiency in fulfillment and perceived importance to the individual. This was true for both bottom and middle management. Contrary to Maslow's theory, need for security, in addition to self-actualization, was seen as a more important area of need satisfaction than esteem and autonomy by individuals in both management groups. However, as one might predict from Maslow's theory, the needs for esteem, security, and autonomy were significantly more satisfied in middle than in entry-level management. Porter (1962) replicated his

---

[11]Keppel would subsequently become Department Chair at Berkeley in 1972. Porter went on to become the only I/O psychologist in the 20th century to become president (1975–1976) of both the American Psychological Association's Division 14 (I/O Psychology) and the Academy of Management (1974–1975). He was among the first to cogently argue the necessity for a marriage within the field of industrial psychology, namely "the mature personnel-differential part of the field to the younger, and seemingly more glamorous, industrial-social or organizational area" (Porter, 1965, p. 395).

[12]Porter (2005, personal communication) stated: "My intent at the time was never to 'test' Maslow's theory. Rather I was simply using it as a relevant framework for looking at the patterns of need satisfaction among managers in medium and large organizations (i.e., organizations with structures composed of at least several levels of management and different functional areas). I was interested in studying the management parts of organizations because I felt that the then-existing field of industrial psychology (not until later called industrial-organizational psychology) had always been over-focused on rank-and-file employees and had basically ignored managerial attitudes and behaviors. Maslow's theory for me at the time was simply an interesting 'vehicle' that offered potential for understanding what was going on in the management sections of organizations in terms of manager's attitudes towards the motivational aspects of their jobs. The 'organization' in this case was the American Management Association. Mason Haire provided me contact to one of their key staff members at the time who agreed to sponsor the research project because AMA was interested in undertaking more research (and, in the next few years established a non-profit off-shoot called the American Foundation for Management Research to further this aim)."

study in a nationwide survey of managers. The needs for autonomy and self-actualization were reported as the least fulfilled for them as well.

In his third study, Porter (1963a) found that higher level managers placed more emphasis on self-actualization and autonomy needs than did lower level managers. However, no significant differences due to managerial level for the other needs were found. In his fourth study, he looked at horizontal rather than vertical differences in responses of managers. Line managers reported greater need fulfillment than staff. The largest differences were fulfillment of needs for esteem and self-actualization (Porter, 1963b).

In the fifth and final study, Porter (1963c) hypothesized that:

> There are good reasons for presuming that organizational level might have an inter-action effect on size in relation to job attitudes. For example, a worker at the bottom of a large organization has a much larger superstructure of organization levels and of sheer numbers of people above him than does a similar worker in a small company. . . . However, at the other end of the hierarchy—top management—the pic-ture should be reversed. A top manager in a large company controls or "bosses" more people than a top manager in a smaller organization, and hence has (or should have) more absolute influence in the work situation. (p. 387)

The data supported this hypothesis. At the lower levels of manage-ment, managers in smaller companies were more satisfied, that is, they reported greater fulfillment of their needs than their counterparts in large companies. The reverse was true of higher levels of management.

In the next decade, with the publication of Wahba and Bridwell's (1976) critique, Maslow's need hierarchy theory was largely abandoned by the research community. None of their factor analytic studies showed clear support for Maslow's classification of needs. Using a dif-ferent methodology, namely interviews of managers at AT&T, Hall and Nougaim (1968) also failed to find support for a need hierarchy. Researchers concluded that there was no validity for Maslow's theory.

That Maslow (1965) himself was concerned by the readiness of people to accept his theory as well as Theory Y in the absence of solid research is evident in the following quote:

> After all, if we take the whole thing from McGregor's point of view of a contrast between a Theory X view of human nature, a good deal of the evidence upon which he bases his conclusions comes from my researches and my papers on moti-vations, self-actualization, et cetera. But I of all people should know just how shaky this foundation is as a final foundation. My work on motivations came from the clinic, from a study of neurotic people. The carry-over of this theory to the industrial situation has some support from industrial studies, but certainly

I would like to see a lot more studies of this kind before feeling finally convinced that this carry-over from the study of neurosis to the study of labor in factories is legitimate. The same thing is true of my studies of self-actualizing people—there is only this one study of mine available. There were many things wrong with the sampling, so many in fact that it must be considered to be, in the classical sense anyway, a bad or poor or inadequate experiment. I am quite willing to concede this—as a matter of fact, I am eager to concede it—because I'm a little worried about this stuff which I consider to be tentative being swallowed whole by all sorts of enthusiastic people, who really should be a little more tentative in the way that I am. (pp. 55–56)

In an attempt to address problems with Maslow's theory, Alderfer (1972) reformulated it based upon three related needs in an organizational setting, namely existence (e.g., pay, fringe benefits), relatedness (e.g., social interactions), and growth (e.g., esteem and self-actualization). Unlike Maslow's proposed hierarchy, Alderfer argued that these three needs can affect a person simultaneously. Much of the research on this theory, conducted by Alderfer himself, yielded mixed results (Pfeffer, 1982).[13]

Job Characteristics

"A good theory is one that holds together long enough to get you to a better theory" (Hebb, 1969). McGregor (1960, p. x) had argued that without minimizing the importance of the work that has been done to improve the selection of people, the most important problems lie elsewhere:

The reason is that we have not learned enough about the utilization of talent, about the creation of an organizational climate conducive to human growth. The blunt fact is that we are a long way from realizing the potential represented by the human resources we now recruit into industry. We have much to accomplish with respect to utilization before further improvements in selection will become important. (p. 21)

McGregor (1960) quoted approvingly from a comprehensive study published in a book a year earlier by Herzberg and his colleagues (1959) that described how to design jobs that are conducive to satisfying needs for human growth:

---

[13]An arguable flaw in Maslow's theory regarding a universal hierarchy is that individuals prioritize their needs in accordance with their values.

A recent, highly significant study of the sources of job satisfaction and dissatisfaction among managerial and professional people suggests that these opportunities for "self-actualization" are the essential requirements of both job satisfaction and high performance. The researchers find that the wants of employees divide into two groups. One group revolves around the need to develop in one's occupation as a source of personal growth. The second group operates as an essential base to the first and is associated with fair treatment in compensation, supervision, working conditions, and administrative practices. *The fulfillment of the needs of the second group does not motivate the individual to high levels of job satisfaction and . . . extra performance on the job* (Italics mine). All we can expect from satisfying [the second group of needs] is the prevention of dissatisfaction and poor job performance. (pp. 114–115)[14]

This book was the basis for what was to become known alternatively as the Two Factor Theory, Motivation-Hygiene Theory, or Job Enrichment. In reference to Herzberg's research, Vroom, with his former mentor, Maier, wrote in the *Annual Review of Psychology* that until this point in time: "The motivational effect of the nature of the tasks performed by the individual continues to be a neglected problem in psychology" (Vroom & Maier, 1961, p. 432). Characteristics of the job, Herzberg believed, facilitate or hinder satisfaction of the "growth needs" for self-esteem and self-satisfaction.

Frederick Herzberg obtained his Ph.D. under the supervision of John Flanagan at the University of Pittsburgh. Herzberg's peers as a doctoral student included George Albee, who would become a clinical psychologist, and William W. Ronan, who would become an I/O psychologist. Herzberg, torn between choosing a career in clinical or I/O psychology, decided to study the mental health of people in industry. In a doctoral seminar, he informed Flanagan that he wanted to use the critical incident technique (Flanagan, 1954) to collect data.[15] Flanagan responded dryly as to the inappropriateness of doing so because of the likelihood that people would attribute satisfying incidents to their own behavior

---

[14]The word "mine" is McGregor's.

[15]While a military officer in World War II, Flanagan was presented with the problem that many bombardiers were missing their targets. Flanagan's solution was to focus on the behaviors that are critical for hitting a target, that is, the behaviors that differentiate the effective from the ineffective bombardier. His methodology, which he labeled the critical incident technique (CIT) involved interviews of incumbent's supervisors, not the incumbents themselves. Today the CIT is among the most frequently used methods of job analysis, particularly for developing appraisal instruments. Following World War II, Flanagan founded the American Institutes for Research (AIR). Among the employees who went on to become famous in the areas of leadership and motivation are Ed Fleishman (who subsequently became president of AIR) and an employee he hired, Ed Locke.

and incidents that were dissatisfying to them to factors outside their control (Ronan, 1968, personal communication). The warning was ignored.

In the preface to their book, Herzberg and his colleagues (Herzberg, Mauser, & Snyderman, 1959) wrote that:

> We are faced by significant unemployment, by an underutilization of our industrial plants, and by a shift of interest from the problems of boredom and a surfeit of material things to the serious problems of unemployment and industrial crisis. . . . In fact, it may be during hard times the edge that will determine whether a concern will survive will be given by the level of morale within the personnel. (p. 121)

Similar to Maslow and McGregor, Herzberg (1966) believed that "the primary function of any organization, whether religious, political, or industrial, should be to implement the needs for man to enjoy a meaningful existence" (p. x). He and his colleagues (Herzberg et al., 1959) analyzed the content of the critical incidents they collected from engineers and accountants regarding when these people felt exceptionally good or exceptionally bad about their jobs in order to determine ways to increase productivity, decrease turnover and absenteeism, and smooth labor relations. Just as Flanagan had predicted, the results showed that job content factors were reported by employees to be a primary source of motivation or satisfaction while context or hygiene factors were the source of dissatisfaction, hence the label, two-factor or motivation-hygiene theory.[16]

Herzberg's most controversial conclusion was that job satisfaction and job dissatisfaction, rather than being on one continuum are two continua. That is, the opposite of dissatisfaction is not satisfaction but no dissatisfaction; similarly, the opposite of job satisfaction is not dissatisfaction but no job satisfaction. To enrich a job, Herzberg (1966) argued that attention should be given to the work itself (job content), recognition, responsibility, achievement, and opportunities for advancement. Contextual or hygiene factors such as working conditions, company policy, supervision (technical as well as interpersonal), and pay should be attended to only as ways of minimizing job dissatisfaction. Focusing on

---

[16]In this same time period, Argyris (1957) was arguing that one's personality can be stunted when confronted with an unchallenging job environment. He shared Maslow's and Herzberg's belief that needs are universal among people.

the latter, he said, will have little or no effect on a person's effort or performance.[17]

In his "Annual Review of Psychology" chapter, Dunnette (1962, p. 303) concluded that Herzberg's theory: "Offers great promise as a stimulator of future research on employee attitudes."[18] By the end of the decade, the bulk of the research on motivation was indeed concerned with considerations of Herzberg's two factor theory (Smith & Cranny, 1968).

As were Mayo and McGregor before him, Herzberg was masterful in getting the ear of the public. Reprints of his article in the *Harvard Business Review* (Herzberg, 1968) remain to this day among the most sought after papers published by that outlet. His lasting contribution to practitioners has been shifting their primary focus to the importance of the work itself rather than on what he called hygiene variables (e.g., employee benefits). He forcefully drove home the message that the job must be enriched in ways that will allow people to become motivated to perform effectively.

The two-factor aspect of Herzberg's theory was subsequently explained by Vroom (1964) in his book, and again (Vroom, 1967) to a standing-room-only symposium at APA where Herzberg was a presenter, to be a methodological artifact. Herzberg's results were replicated only when the critical incident technique was used, a technique that had been originally designed by his mentor, Flanagan, for job analysis.[19] Other psychologists agreed with Vroom's criticism (e.g., King, 1970; Schneider & Locke, 1971). The same events caused both satisfaction and dissatisfaction, but different agents were perceived by employees as responsible—the self for satisfying events, and variables other than the self for dissatisfying events (Locke, 1976).

---

[17]One can see why McGregor, who championed Maslow's theory, also endorsed Herzberg's work. Herzberg too was concerned with a person's needs. The contextual or hygiene factors were similar to Maslow's emphasis on satisfying physiological and security needs; the job content or motivators were similar conceptually to Maslow's emphasis on a person's needs for self-esteem and self-actualization. By changing characteristics of the job environment, Herzberg and his colleagues argued that an employee's needs would be satisfied. Needs impel behavior. Therefore, implicit in Maslow's and Herzberg's theories is the assumption that one does not directly motivate another person, one creates an environment where people can motivate themselves.

[18]It was during this time period Dunnette's colleagues developed the Minnesota Satisfaction Questionnaire or MSQ (Weiss, Dawis, England, & Lofquist, 1967). MSQ assesses an employee's intrinsic (e.g., the job itself, sense of achievement) and extrinsic satisfaction (e.g., pay, benefits).

[19]Despite Vroom's criticism (1964, p. 129), he agreed that: "Herzberg and his associates deserve credit for directing attention toward the psychological effects of job content, a problem of great importance in a world of rapidly changing technology."

Herzberg (1966, pp. 130–131) responded in vain to this attack:

> The supposition that people would prefer to blame hygiene factors rather than the
> motivators for their job unhappiness in order to make themselves look good is
> naïve. It does not take too much experience with job-attitude data to find that the
> opposite is more often true. Employees who wish to make themselves look good are
> much more prone to say they are unhappy because they do not have responsibility,
> are not getting ahead, have uninteresting work, and see no possibility for growth.[20]

Blood and Hulin (1967) were among the first to caution against
universal application of job enrichment/enlargement methods. An
employee's values, they said, moderate employee affective responses to
tasks. Specifically they found that the values of blue collar workers in
urban locations correlate negatively with satisfaction with enriched
jobs; for non-alienated employees, such as white collar workers as well
as blue collar workers from rural areas, the relationship is positive.

A subsequent version of job enrichment theory was formulated by
Richard Hackman and his doctoral student Gregory Oldham (1975,
1976). Hackman's colleagues and Oldham's professors at Yale, where the
authors formulated the theory, included Alderfer, Argyris, Lawler, and
Schneider. They, rather than Herzberg, influenced the authors' choice of
variables. Consequently, Herzberg viewed the theory and the authors with
disdain (Oldham, 2005, personal communication). In brief, Hackman and
Oldham developed a job diagnostic survey to assess the motivating
potential of a job, and the employee's growth needs for personal accomplishment, learning, and development. These psychological needs, they
said, are threefold: (a) experienced meaningfulness (need for job experiences "to connect" or be aligned with one's values), (b) responsibility
(need to feel accountable or responsible for the work one does), and (c)
knowledge of results (wanting knowledge for how well one is performing in one's job). The essence of this theory is that people who have high
growth needs are more satisfied and perform better than those who
have low growth needs when they are placed in an enriched job. Thus

---

[20]In 1975 Herzberg gave an address to a large audience of managers in Seattle. Upon introducing
myself to Fred as a former student of Bill Ronan's, he replied with little humor, "The trouble with
you industrial psychologists is that when you climb down into a mine you ask a miner, 'when you
have to pee, can you always do so, generally do so, sometimes do so, seldom do so, or never do so?'
I simply ask, 'what do you do when you have to pee while you are down here?'" Fred had distanced
himself from a discipline that he believed had unfairly attacked him and his work. Criticism, however, is a cornerstone of science. As difficult as criticism is to read regarding one's work, it must be
embraced in order for the field to advance, not to mention the quality of one's own work.

the theory, unlike Herzberg's, takes into account individual differences among employees.[21] An enriched job is one that scores high on skill variety, task identity, task significance, autonomy, and task feedback. The likelihood that an employee with high growth needs will experience meaningfulness increases to the extent that a job provides skill variety, task identity, and task significance. Responsibility is likely to be experienced if the job allows for autonomy. Knowledge of results, as the name implies, occurs to the extent that feedback regarding one's performance is relatively direct and immediate. This version of job enrichment, embraced by many academics (e.g., Korman, Greenhaus, & Badin, 1977), never received the applause of the public that was given to Herzberg's theory of job enrichment.[22] The relationship between job characteristics to an employee's absenteeism and performance was not found to be as strong as expected. They did correlate highly with a person's job satisfaction and motivation, that is, experienced meaningfulness and responsibility (Hackman & Oldham, 1976).

In his *Annual Review of Psychology* chapter, Mitchell (1979) concluded that few significant results with regard to job performance were obtained with Hackman and Oldham's theory, and there was little or no consistency in the interpretation of the results. Roberts and Glick (1981) attacked the theory for its lack of discriminant validity with other attitudinal measures as well as halo error among perceived characteristics of jobs. Fried and Ferris (1987) showed that the formula for calculating a

---

[21]Dawis (1996) noted that: "The psychology of individual differences (also called *differential psychology* or *correlational psychology*) originated from two intellectually revolutionary achievements of Francis Galton, both occurring before the beginning of this century: The discovery that statistical models (initially, the normal curve) provided a robust rationale for psychological measurement, and the invention of correlation as a powerful technique for data analysis (see Dawis, 1992, for more detail). The contributions of individual differences psychology to the science of psychology have been enormous and pervasive, especially in the assessment of human psychological attributes (particularly intelligence, abilities, interests, values, and personality traits)" (pp. 231–232).

[22]Both Blood and Hulin's (1967) study and Hackman and Oldham's theory ushered in the concept of moderators in research on motivation. Conceptually a moderator is a conditional variable or boundary condition. Why does a job enrichment intervention work under some conditions but not under others? Some people believe that its effectiveness is moderated (enhanced) by a person's higher order need strength. In those conditions where employees have high needs for esteem and self actualization, introducing job enrichment is likely to prove to be effective. A boundary condition or limitation of the effectiveness of this intervention is where the majority of employees have a low need "to grow" in their job. Knowing the moderator variable(s) enhances the likelihood that an intervention will be effective; it will not be introduced under inappropriate conditions. Interestingly, Herzberg believed there were no boundary variables affecting a job enrichment intervention. Hackman and Oldham disagreed with him.

Motivating Potential Score is no more predictive of outcomes than a simple index that is computed by merely adding up the scores given to the five core job characteristics. Subsequent studies showed that moderating effects of individual differences on task or job design were not significant. "Enriched jobs seem to exert positive affective and behavior effects regardless of an incumbent's desire for higher order need satisfaction, need for achievement, need for autonomy, etc." (Cummings, 1982, p. 546). Yankelovich's (1974) surveys of job-related attitudes among American youth revealed a strong preference for careers involving self-control over one's job activities and a desire for interesting work as well as material rewards, regardless of education level. The surveys also revealed that people in general define success in terms of self-fulfillment. Moreover, consistent with what Maslow would have predicted in this economic time period, the respondents indicated little or no fear of financial hardship and thus were free to explore ways to satisfy "higher needs." These findings tended to eliminate studies in which demographic variables such as age, sex, or race are examined as moderator variables because they usually did not correlate with anything (Schneider, 1985).

Working independently of Herzberg and Hackman and Oldham, Eric Trist and his colleagues at the Tavistock Institute in the United Kingdom developed a theory of socio-technical systems as a way of enriching jobs.[23] As the name implies, the emphasis is on the integration of the technical aspects of the job with the social needs of the worker (Emery & Trist, 1965; Trist & Bamworth, 1951). Similar to both Herzberg and Hackman and Oldham's theories, socio-technical systems theory views people as resources to be developed; it emphasizes the importance of autonomous work teams, responsibility for production process, and feedback (Trist, 1981). Socio-technical systems is used widely by industry (e.g., Weyerhaeuser Company) to the present day. Interestingly, it has been relatively ignored by motivation researchers in North America, possibly because the unit of analysis is the group rather than the individual.

Equity Theory

Herzberg's theory of job enrichment states that money, or the lack thereof, can be a major source of dissatisfaction. The theory says little about what the person will do as a result of this dissatisfaction. Equity

---

[23]Trist later took a faculty position at York University in Toronto.

theory, developed by Jean "Stacy" Adams, filled in the blank. Adams, born in Belgium, received his Ph.D. at the University of North Carolina, Chapel Hill. His theory was developed as a result of his association at Stanford University with Leon Festinger as well as his own work at the General Electric Company.

Adams was influenced by Festinger's (1957) cognitive dissonance theory which states that to the extent that a person perceives there is a discrepancy between one's belief and one's behavior, the person is motivated to reduce it; the greater the perceived discrepancy, the greater the motivation. In addition, the theory states that people evaluate information sources in terms of personal relevance, using similar others for comparison.

Equity theory deals primarily with money. In brief, the theory (Adams, 1963, 1965) states that people examine the ratio of their "outcomes" (denominator) relative to their "inputs" (numerator) relative to those of a comparison other.[24] Inputs include the person's effort, education, and experience. Outcomes include money, recognition, and working conditions. Equity theory states that unequal ratios produce tension within the person. This tension can be alleviated by cognitively distorting one's inputs or outcomes, leaving/quitting the situation, changing the inputs (e.g., increase/decrease effort or quality of one's performance) or outcomes, or changing one's comparison other (e.g., for me personally it would be focusing on my peers in universities rather than on those in the private sector). The solution most likely to be used to reduce inequity is the one that a person perceives as having the least cost.

The theory subsequently was attacked for lack of precision. Robert Pritchard (1969), a former student of John Campbell and Marvin Dunnette, argued that the modes of inequity resolution are the weakest part of the theory. Methods for reducing inequity are so numerous, he said, that individual differences undoubtedly exist regarding preferences among methods. Campbell, Dunnette, Lawler, and Weick (1970) concluded that:

> Predictions from equity theory are made very difficult by the complexity making up the input-output package and the multitude of ways in which inequity can be

---

[24]In 1958, Newell, Shaw, and Simon presented their theory of human problem solving that emphasized an information processing model. Shortly thereafter, the study of motivation in the workplace went cognitive; the employee was now immersed in thought. Years later Cappelli and Scherer (1991) blamed the "cognitive revolution" for limiting appreciation of the importance of context on organizational behavior.

resolved. However, the theory presents a clear warning to organizations that they must learn a great deal more about the nature of the input-output comparisons and the way they develop and change. (p. 382)

Because of these criticisms and because another theory—expectancy theory—was viewed by influential psychologists, particularly Lawler (1970),[25] as having greater predictive and explanatory power regarding performance in paid work settings than equity theory, the attention of I/O psychologists shifted to this theory.[26]

Expectancy Theory

Victor Vroom, a Canadian from Montreal, earned his undergraduate and master's degree from McGill, and his Ph.D. from the University of Michigan where he studied under N. R. F. Maier.[27] Rather than focus on factors in a job that energize and sustain behavior, Vroom (1964, p. 6) used "the term motivation to refer to processes governing choices made by persons or lower organisms among alternative forms of voluntary

---

[25]Lawler was a catalyst in the fields of HRM, I/O, and OB from the moment he came out of graduate school, especially in the domains of motivation and satisfaction in the workplace. Two primary themes of his work are the importance of participation in decision making and the importance of money. The criterion he uses in judging his work and the work of others is whether it has "high impact." Among the ways I gained credibility as a newly minted Ph.D. with the Weyerhaeuser Company's senior management team was to show Lawler's work to them. Lawler is currently the founder and director of the Center for Effective Organizations at the University of Southern California, where he and his colleagues do leading edge work in HRM.

[26]Adams's (1968) response was that: "The contrast between equity theory and expectancy theory implies that performance in work situations must be accounted for by either one or the other. Multiple motivation states may determine behavior, though one state may be dominant in an individual and in a group of individuals at a particular point in time. Under particular conditions the motivation to achieve equity may dominate, under others maximizing gain (expectancy) may be salient and under some conditions the two may be pitted each against the other. . . . I doubt that anyone seriously questions the fact that desire to manage outcomes is a powerful determinant of behavior, and there is now ample evidence that desire to achieve justice has considerable influence on behavior. The question of importance is not whether equity or expectancy theory accounts for such behavior as work productivity or quality, but under what conditions equity motives and gain maximizing motives account for certain proportions of observed performance variance" (p. 316). In a subsequent review of the literature, Mowday (1991) concluded that there is general support for the theory's predictions, particularly regarding piece-rate and hourly over-payment. People who believe they are overpaid perform higher than those who perceive that they are equitably paid.

[27]Vroom originally wanted to become a jazz musician. As an entering undergraduate student, he took the Strong Vocational Interest Test. It showed his love of music. He had been playing the clarinet and the saxophone for 5 years. His second highest score on the Strong Interest Test was psychology. The counselor who administered the Strong successfully convinced him of the wisdom of pursuing a career in the latter area. Nevertheless music has remained an important part of his life (Vroom, 2005).

activity." Influenced by the research of Tolman,[28] an experimental psychologist, as well as Lewin, a social psychologist, Vroom developed a cognitive theory based on a person's expectancies, valences, choices, and instrumentalities. Central to the theory are two propositions (Vroom, 1964).

> *Proposition 1.* The valence of an outcome is a monotonically increasing function of the algebraic sum of the products of the valences for all other outcomes and his conceptions of its instrumentality for the attainment of these other outcomes.

> *Proposition 2.* The force on a person to perform an act is a monotonically increasing function of the algebraic sum of the products of the valences of all outcomes and the strength of his experiences that the act will be followed by the attainment of these outcomes. (pp. 17–19)

That is, (1) the effort that people exert is a function of their expectation or subjective probability estimate that certain outcomes will occur as a result of their performance; and (2) the valence for them of those outcomes. The greater the valence of any outcome, the more likely the person is to choose to exert effort to take action. The valence of an outcome is, in turn, a function of its instrumentality for obtaining other outcomes and the valence of those other outcomes. Hence this theory is alternatively known as VIE theory (i.e., valence, instrumentality, expectancy).

Similar to equity theory, this theory states that people base their actions on their perceptions and beliefs. Unlike equity theory, which focuses solely on the outcomes of one's perceptions of fairness relative to a comparison other, expectancy theory was developed to explain virtually all work-related behavior ranging from occupational choice to performance on the job. Thus, expectancy theory was the first cognitive broad range theory of motivation developed by an I/O psychologist. The theory focuses on choice, effort, and persistence. In Vroom's words, the theory is "very similar to, almost taken from Kurt Lewin's field theory. The terms 'valence' and 'force' have exactly the same properties as in Lewin's writings. The concept of expectancy is a recasting of the term 'psychological distance,' which Lewin never well defined but had to do

---

[28]Tolman, an experimental psychologist at the University of California–Berkeley, was influenced by the Gestalt psychologists' research on goal directed action and the related positive and negative valences of objects, as well as the differences between drive like involuntary action vs. intentional acts. "Behavior as behavior, that is, as molar, is purposive and cognitive. These purposes and cognitions are of its immediate warp and woof" (Tolman, 1932, p. 6).

with the number of regions in the life space that had to be crossed in order to get to a goal. It also has some similarity to the notion that people choose in such a way as to maximize expected utility, although the terms 'utility' and 'valence of outcome' have different properties—utility implying a much greater degree of stability not subject to arousal. It's also very similar to Jack Atkinson's conceptions of aroused motivation being a function of motive, incentive and expectation, and to a similar formulation by Tolman" (Vroom, 2003, personal communication).

In short, expectancy theory operationalizes motivation in terms of four components. The first is effort. The second is the intrinsic valence in the outcome of high performance emanating from effort, the degree to which effective performance is desired for its own sake. Third, there is instrumentality—one's perceived causal connection between one's performance and the rewards one expects to receive as a result of this performance. Finally, there is the valence to the employee of the rewards (Vroom, 2003, personal communication).

Steers and Mowday, former students of Porter, along with Shapiro have described how Porter and Lawler (1968) expanded expectancy theory to take into account the employee's ability as well as role clarity in linking a person's effort to job performance (Steers, Mowday, & Shapiro, 2004).[29] Specifically, Porter and Lawler added a feedback loop to Vroom's theory to emphasize learning on the part of an employee regarding past relationships.[30]

In the previous decade, the belief that job satisfaction affects job performance had been shattered by Brayfield and Crockett. On the basis of expectancy theory, Lawler and his former mentor, Porter (Lawler & Porter, 1967), argued that it is nevertheless important to measure the satisfaction level that exists in organizations because it influences both employee attendance and turnover.[31] They then proposed the radical

---

[29]Lyman Porter (University of California, Berkeley, University of California, Irvine) mentored many doctoral students who subsequently made significant contributions to organizational psychology and behavior. In addition, to Edward Lawler, Rick Mowday and Richard Steers, these people include David Krackhart, Eugene Stone, and John Van Maanen.

[30]Although Vroom continued to publish extensively subsequent to his 1964 book on expectancy theory, none of it dealt with or even mentions valence, expectancy, or instrumentality. "For me the task was done" (Vroom, 2005, p. 252).

[31]Lawler's first doctoral student was Martin Evans. Based on his knowledge of expectancy theory, Evans developed the theory of path-goal leadership for his doctoral dissertation. Upon accepting a faculty position at the University of Toronto, Evans collaborated with Robert House, who was also at the University of Toronto, to refine the theory. Interestingly, the two did not publish together.

notion that rather than being a cause of performance, satisfaction is caused by it. They concluded that organizations should find ways of maximizing the relationship between performance and satisfaction rather than satisfaction itself.

Platt (1964) argued that a theory that cannot be mortally endangered cannot be alive. That expectancy theory was very much alive is evident by the voluminous research conducted to test it. In less than a decade there were two comprehensive reviews of this literature published in the prestigious *Psychological Bulletin* (Heneman & Schwab, 1972; Mitchell & Biglan, 1971). But by the mid-1970s, Miner and Dachler (1973, p. 381) concluded that "a closer examination of the literature reveals a number of inconsistent findings" and that it "is remarkably weak and contradictory in other respects" (p. 382). Locke (1975, p. 458) noted that "there are no consistent findings regarding which components are the best predictors of performance." Moreover, the results were suspect, he said, in that the theory predicts self-ratings of effort, attitude, and performance better than supervisory evaluations. Furthermore, Locke argued that the theory was incorrect in assuming (a) that people choose to maximize outcomes, or (b) that they usually perform complex calculations in making choices that will enable them to maximize outcomes. Finally, Frank Schmidt (1973) pointed out that the formulas involved in the theory assume a ratio scale when there is no known way of measuring valences on this scale. In an enumerative review of 31 studies testing the theory, House, Shapiro, and Wahba (1974) reached similar conclusions in their critique of the theory. A meta-analysis by Van Eerde and Thierry (1996) indicated that there is at best support for the individual components of Vroom's theory. The authors pointed out, however, that the vast majority of studies based on expectancy theory examined performance between groups of individuals. This was arguably inappropriate. Expectancy theory first and foremost provides a "within individuals" framework for predicting and explaining the choices a person makes. Yet very few experiments were conducted in this manner.

Years later, Vroom (2003, personal communication) himself stated: "The notion that people consider all possible outcomes in expectancy theory is implausible. Furthermore, the thought that they multiply these terms and add them up is really inconsistent with knowledge of information processing and cognitive psychology. They clearly don't do that, and I knew they didn't do that. But, I didn't have a theory of arousal—about what goals or expectations would be aroused in any given moment. That's the chief limitation of expectancy theory. It has naïve assumptions about arousal. I think the same thing was true of Kurt Lewin when he talked about valences being reflections of the tension systems that are aroused. So, that criticism of expectancy theory is a general one, and I completely agree with it." Vroom (2005) also acknowledged that eliminating the mathematical formulations might have helped to convey his belief that expectancy theory should be used for its heuristic value in providing a language for formulating questions about the role of beliefs and motives in work performance.

Behavior Modification

Following Vroom's heuristic theory based in part on research in experimental psychology, I/O psychologists ignored the concerns voiced two decades earlier by Ryan and Smith and began to examine the applicability of behaviorism to the workplace. The champion of environmental determinism in this time-period continued to be an experimental psychologist at Harvard University, B. F. Skinner.

In Skinner's (1974) advocacy of environmental determinism, behavior is said to be a function of reinforcers.

> Remove the gratuitous physiologizing, and the point is made that motives and purposes are in people while contingences of reinforcement are in the environment, but motives and purposes are at best the effect of reinforcements. The change wrought by reinforcements is often spoken of as the "acquisition of purpose or intention," and we are said to "give a person a purpose," by reinforcing him in a given way. These are convenient expressions, but the basic fact is that when a person is "aware of his purpose" he is feeling or observing introspectively a condition produced by reinforcement. (p. 58)

The frequency of a response, Skinner argued, can be changed by changing the schedule on which a reinforcer is presented. Systematic change, which alters the frequency of a response, is called operant conditioning (responses operating on the environment) or behavior modification as the emphasis is on observable behavior. Thus operant researchers, as had the founders of behaviorism, Thorndike (1911) and Watson (1925) continued to dismiss internal determinants, namely cognitions, as explanatory fictions.[32] Cognitions were said to be merely

---

[32]Ironically, Skinner himself was admitting to an explanatory determinant of behavior which resides inside the organism, namely, the organism's implanted history of reinforcement. As Bandura (2005a) noted, this history is an inferred inner cause rather than one that is directly observable.

epiphenomena of conditioned responses. Behavior, Skinner argued, is a function of its consequences. People learn contingent relationships between what they do and the concomitant result; it is these contingencies that determine their subsequent behavior, not cognition and certainly not the need hierarchy that Maslow espoused.

In an influential essay, Nord (1969) argued the similarities between McGregor's basic arguments and Skinner's emphasis on the environment in shaping a person's behavior. John Campbell (1971) endorsed Nord's viewpoint: "The operant conditioning model, in truth, has a great deal of structured similarity to the motivational theories of McGregor, Maslow and Herzberg. It simply gets to the heart of the matter more quickly" (p. 571). John Campbell argued further that it is behavior that is at issue rather than underlying causes or internal mediators.

Well-trained in experimental methods, I/O psychologists in this time period increasingly turned to both laboratory and field experiments in order to provide rigorous tests of phenomena that had been identified in correlational and case studies in the field. For example, Yukl, Wexley, and Seymore (1972), in a laboratory experiment, obtained results that were contrary to what might be predicted by instrumentality beliefs as posited by expectancy theory. Their results were consistent with Skinner's (e.g., Ferster & Skinner, 1957) research with rats and pigeons. Performance was higher when people were paid on a variable ratio schedule of reinforcement rather than on a continuous one.

Although rodents are highly prized in laboratory settings, the opposite is true in forest products companies. A mountain beaver is essentially a large rat with a hamster-like tail. Because it is largely a creature of habit, traps can be set effectively without bait to kill them. The necessity for doing so stems from the fact that they devour newly planted seedlings. A Weyerhaeuser Company VP became so frustrated with these rodents as well as with the employees whose job it was to trap them that he angrily exclaimed that he could step on more rodents than those employees could catch. Moreover, both the union executive committee and company managers were annoyed by the employees constantly filing nonsensical grievances because of job dissatisfaction due largely to boredom. The employees complained that the seats in the bus that took them to the woods were uncomfortable. They complained about the wind and the rain that resulted in them choosing to stay in the bus rather than persisting in trapping the rodents. They complained about their long hours. My solution—bring Las Vegas to the woods.

The trappers working side by side were randomly assigned to one of two groups. In group A, the trappers were paid on a continuous schedule of reinforcement. Each trapper received a $1.00 bonus over and above his hourly rate for each rodent he trapped. At the end of four weeks, the trappers were switched to a variable ratio four (VR-4) schedule in which they received $4.00 contingent upon trapping a rodent and correctly guessing the color of one of four marbles prior to drawing it from a bag held by the supervisor. Thus, each trapped rodent became the equivalent of a poker chip that a trapper could use to see how lucky he was in correctly predicting the color of a marble. In group B, the order of the schedules was reversed. Not only did employee productivity soar, but the grievances stopped. Excitement at the prospect of winning money replaced boredom in the workplace. Consistent with findings from animals studied in the laboratory, trappers who were experienced had higher productivity on the VR-4 than on the continuous schedule, while their inexperienced counterparts had higher productivity on the continuous schedule. Both the inexperienced and the experienced employees preferred the VR-4 schedule for monetary payments (Latham & Dossett, 1978).

Employee excitement with the reinforcement schedules that were used for distributing the monetary bonuses continued for years. Not a single grievance was ever filed. In examining employee reactions to the two schedules, Lise Saari and I found that the VR-4 schedule contributed to feelings of task accomplishment, recognition, and meaningfulness of the work (Saari & Latham, 1982). In addition, the trappers began to set goals regarding the number of rodents they would catch. A journal reviewer insisted that this fact be omitted from the article. There is no denying the efficacy of operant techniques. There is denial on the part of behaviorists of cognitive variables as root causes of a person's behavior.

In less than a decade following Nord's essay, Luthans and Kreitner (1975) published a book on ways to use behavior modification methodology in organizational settings. John Campbell's former mentor, Marvin Dunnette, (1976) referred to this methodology as one of seven milestones in I/O psychology because it makes explicit the operations that must be followed to increase the probability that an intervention will bring about a relatively permanent change in behavior. The methodology makes explicit the types of data that should be collected and the operations that should be followed in collecting these data. A *Handbook of Organizational Behavior Management* was published (Frederiksen, 1982). The *Journal of Organizational Behavior Management* was born. This journal publishes articles to the present day on the application of operant principles to issues in organizational settings.

Feeney (1973), a vice president at Emery Air Freight, popularized the notion that knowledge of results or feedback is explainable within a behavioristic framework. Scholars such as Komaki (1981) agreed with him. She showed that when performance during a baseline period is compared with performance after the introduction of feedback, often in the form of praise or recognition, performance invariably increases dramatically.

With few exceptions (e.g., Komaki, 1998, 2003), the interest of I/O psychologists in behaviorism quickly waned in the final quarter of the 20th century. Experimental psychologists such as Dulaney (1968) showed that even the simplest forms of learning may not occur unless people are conscious of what is required of them. Kaufman, Baron, and Kopp (1966) found that cognitive influences can weaken, distort, or nullify the effect of different reinforcement schedules. They showed that when people are rewarded on the same schedule, those who are told that they are being reinforced once every minute (a fixed interval schedule) produce a very low response rate (mean = 6); those who are led to believe that they are being reinforced on a variable ratio schedule maintain an exceedingly high response rate (mean = 259); while those who are correctly informed that their behavior will be rewarded, on average, every minute (a variable interval schedule), display an intermediate response rate. In short, identical environmental consequences can have different behavioral effects depending upon what the person is led to believe (cognition).

Many I/O psychologists were troubled by the philosophy of behaviorism, especially determinism and epiphenomenalism. Mitchell (1975) acknowledged that although the principles of behaviorism allow for the prediction of behavior, they do not permit an adequate explanation of why the behavior occurs.[33] Moreover, the exclusion of cognitive variables because they are not directly observable, he stated, is foolhardy. Drawing on the arguments of Nagle (1961), Mitchell pointed out that other sciences, including physics and astronomy, refer to unobservables as causal variables.

> These unobservables can be indirectly measured through their effects on other variables and eventually on observables. Through what is called a "logic of theoretical networks" (Cronbach & Meehl, 1955), we can ascribe meaning to these constructs and through a process of empirical confirmation provide support for this meaning. Thus . . . a logical positivists position is both an unnecessary

---

[33]Brief and Dukerich (1991) have stressed the point that sheer predictive power in itself is inadequate for explanation. Understanding the how, that is, the process, is the goal of scientific theory.

limitation on scientific inquiry and a poor representation of current thought in the philosophy of science (Kaplan, 1964). (Mitchell, 1975, p. 65)

In addition, Locke (1977, 1978) pointed out how behavior modification researchers in I/O psychology implicitly include cognitive processes. In disagreement with Komaki (1981), he (Locke, 1980) argued that the effect of feedback on performance cannot be interpreted as supporting behaviorism, because feedback is mediated by goal setting. As he and I subsequently noted, feedback is information (Locke & Latham, 1990a). Only when there is a standard for evaluating the feedback can it be appraised. A goal provides a standard by which the person can judge whether the feedback conveys "good," "neutral," or "bad" performance. In short, to explain the effect of feedback on behavior, one must know the goal or standard that was used by an individual to evaluate it.

Neither Locke nor I deny that people are influenced by environmental factors (Locke & Latham, 2004). But the causal effect is not deterministic. Rather, the effects of the environment depend on what people attend to and what conclusions they draw from the experiences they have and the situations they encounter. Much of Ben Schneider's work, to be discussed later, has looked at the issue of the effect of the environment on one's behavior in the reverse direction. His primary thesis is that an environment is formed by the people behaving in it.

Goal-Setting Theory

Edwin Locke was educated at Harvard University, the bastion of behaviorism in that time period. He subsequently did his Ph.D. at Cornell under the supervision of T. A. (Art) Ryan[34] and Patricia Cain Smith.[35] There he became an ardent critic of behaviorism.

---

[34]Art Ryan, recalled Pat Smith (2003, personal communication), was a brilliant researcher who was admired greatly by his doctoral students. Yet he was not a stellar teacher of undergraduates. Fearing that Art's low undergraduate teaching evaluations would be hurtful, a doctoral student broke into the room at Cornell where the evaluations were stored so that he could alter them for Art's benefit. Neither the administration nor Art ever learned of the incident. The perpetrator was not Ed Locke.

[35]In 1969 Patricia Cain Smith and two of her former doctoral students, Lorne Kendall and Charles Hulin, published what was to become among the most widely used scales to this day for measuring job satisfaction, the Job Descriptive Index or JDI (Smith, Kendall, & Hulin, 1969). Patricia Cain Smith earned her undergraduate degree from Nebraska under the supervision of J.P. Guilford, and her Ph.D. under the supervision of T.A. (Art) Ryan at Cornell. She is the grand dame of I/O psychology, not only because she is arguably the first woman to achieve prominence internationally

(Continued)

Ryan (Ryan, 1947, 1970; Ryan & Smith, 1954) argued that behavior is regulated by intentions. Needs, beliefs/attitudes, he said, affect behavior through intentions. Thus, once they are formed, intentions are the immediate antecedents for predicting and explaining behavior. Neither equity nor expectancy theory explicitly address intentions.

Locke's (1964) doctoral dissertation was based on a series of laboratory experiments to test Ryan's hypothesis regarding the effect of intentions. The culmination of these experiments (Locke, 1968) led to three propositions that would subsequently lead to the development of goal setting theory in 1990: (1) Specific high goals lead to higher performance than no goals or even an abstract goal such as "do your best"; (2) given goal commitment, the higher the goal the higher the performance, and (3) variables such as monetary incentives, participation in decision making, feedback, or knowledge of results affect performance only to the extent that they lead to the setting of and commitment to specific high goals. In short, goals have the effect of directing attention and action (*choice*), mobilizing energy expenditure or *effort*, prolonging effort over time (*persistence*), and motivating the individual to develop relevant strategies (*cognition*) for goal attainment (Locke, Shaw, Saari, & Latham, 1981). Given goal commitment, job performance improves because the goal provides a regulatory mechanism that allows the employee to observe, monitor, subjectively evaluate, and adjust job behavior in order to attain the goal.[36] Goal setting taps a fundamental attribute of human

---

(Continued)

as an I/O scholar, but because of the number of people who also achieved prominence under her mentorship, either as the chair or a member of their dissertation committee (e.g., John Bernardin, Charles Hulin, Lorne Kendall, Frank Landy, Ed Locke, Harry Triandis, Sheldon Zedeck). Lorne Kendall was among the kindest, brightest people I have had the privilege of calling my friend. As a Department Chair in Psychology, he could break the news of a non-tenure decision in such a way that the person thanked him before leaving his office. Sitting in my living room one night he closed his eyes and said that some people have difficulty thinking in three dimensions yet he had no difficulty thinking in five. He easily convinced me to join him at Simon Fraser University in Vancouver (Burnaby). After signing the requisite acceptance papers, we talked excitedly by phone. Three hours or so later, his wife, Mary telephoned me. While walking across the ice on March 27, 1977 following a curling game, she stopped as she observed Lorne bend over to, she initially believed, tie his shoes. Lorne never got up. He died that moment at the age of 43. He had once casually told me at a CPA convention in 1976 that he'd been born with a faulty heart valve and would likely die without a moment's notice. Sadly, he was correct. I no longer had a reason to accept Simon Fraser's job offer. I had lost a good friend.

[36]Originally, Locke and I used the term goal acceptance because the goals were assigned in our laboratory and field experiments. Later when our research interests, and those of colleagues expanded to include participatively set and self-set goals, we used the broader term, goal commitment.

behavior, namely, goal directedness (Lee, Locke, & Latham, 1989). In their reviews of the literature, both Austin and Vancouver (1996) as well as Mitchell and Daniels (2003) concluded that the one overriding common theme among almost all psychological approaches to motivation is goals.

As noted by Pervin (1989), the concept of goal as a motivational construct has a number of advantages over a sole focus on needs or external reinforcers. By emphasizing the cognitive representation or image of a goal, the employee is freed from the immediacy of a current stimulus. The employee is oriented toward the future as far as cognitive capacity permits.

The results regarding goal difficulty seemingly contradict those of Atkinson (1958), a social psychologist who had been a student of McClelland. Atkinson's theory of need for achievement states that task difficulty, measured as probability of task success, is related to performance in a curvilinear, inverse function. The highest level of effort is expended on tasks that are moderately difficult. Atkinson, however, did not measure personal preference goals or goal difficulty. His findings have not been replicated when task performance goals were measured.

McClelland (1961), a social psychologist, argued that people have a need to achieve success and avoid failure. He argued further that only the Thematic Apperception Test (TAT), a projective test should be used to assess this need because only this test assesses this need at the subconscious motive level. Among the few studies that used the TAT in work settings, null or negative results were obtained with regard to goal choice or performance (e.g., Roberson-Bennett, 1983; Howard & Bray, 1988). Matsui, Okada, and Kakuyama (1982), who did not use the TAT, found that achievement motivation has no effect on performance independently of goals that are set. Gary Yukl and I found that the goals people set predict their performance and level of satisfaction better than do personality measures of achievement (Yukl & Latham, 1978). However, R. Kanfer and Heggestad (1997) developed a 48-item scale that assesses a person's general motivation. Using this scale, they found that people who have high achievement and low anxiety traits excel in self-regulation. But, Bandura (1997) argued that empirical evidence shows that goal setting is a better predictor of ongoing level of performance than are measures of need for achievement. This lends causal priority to goal setting. Moreover, goal-setting theory, he stated, explains rapid shifts in motivational level through changes in mediating self-processes, whereas quick changes in a person's behavior pose explanatory difficulties for a dispositional motive determinant such as need for achievement. Nevertheless, Schneider (2004, personal communication) observed that McClelland's work,

> ... it is true, has not been adopted by I/O, but the work has been very useful in the training of people to be more achievement oriented, especially in India. I know I am terribly biased towards nAch, but if you read Roger Brown's (*Social Psychology*, 1965) description of the work you come away feeling that it was very worthwhile, astonishingly creative, and widely overlooked—likely because it rests on projective techniques.

A close reading of the book, however, suggests that McClelland's intervention included goal setting.

With regard to job satisfaction, Locke (1970), similar to Lawler and Porter (1967) viewed satisfaction as resulting from performance. However, he argued that it is the result of goal-directed behavior and value attainment as a result of reaching one's goal(s). Goal specificity delineates the conditional requirements for positive self-evaluation. An abstract goal such as "do your best" is at best a placebo. It provides little or no basis for regulating one's efforts, let alone for evaluating how one is doing. Its vagueness is too compatible with a wide variety of performance attainments.

In reviewing Locke's laboratory experiments, Hinrichs (1970, p. 525) questioned whether similar results "will carry through in the complex behaviors required in organizations." Similarly, in their review of expectancy theory, Heneman and Schwab (1972) stated,

> A noteworthy aspect of research on expectancy theory is the emphasis on investigating employees in their natural work environments, thus providing a high degree of external validity. In the case of motivation . . . this is in direct contrast to research on . . . goal setting theory (Locke, 1968) which has usually entailed student subjects working on laboratory tasks in experimental settings. The cost of external validity has been of course, a general inability to make causal inferences. (p. 8)

This was about to change with my work at the American Pulpwood Association (Latham & Kinne, 1974; Ronan, Latham, & Kinne, 1973), followed by my research conducted at the Weyerhaeuser Company (e.g. Latham & Yukl, 1975). Locke and I met in New Orleans in 1974 at the annual meeting of the American Psychological Association where we began a career-long collaboration on goal-setting theory (e.g., Latham & Locke, 1975, 1991; Locke & Latham, 1990a, 2002, 2005).

Concluding Comments

Disputes among researchers often lead to a change in theoretical insights. An article by Salancik and Pfeffer (1977) not only summarized the theories developed in this time period, it called into question need-satisfaction theories of motivation, specifically, Maslow's, Herzberg's, Hackman, and Oldham's, and even Vroom's expectancy theory.[37] The assumptions underlying these theories, they said, is that needs are universal, stable dimensions of people. Motivation is presumed to be the result of correspondence between a person's needs and the realities in the environment, namely, characteristics of one's job. To the extent the correspondence is high, people become satisfied and more motivated to perform their job because characteristics of their jobs are compatible with their needs. Liking one's job is assumed to be a component of arousal, leading to a behavioral reaction involving approach to rather than avoidance of one's job. Thus Oldham (1976), they pointed out, defined motivation in terms of satisfaction with one's work. Similarly, Hackman and Lawler (1971) defined motivation with the satisfaction of higher order needs with regard to an employee's reactions to characteristics of the job. Thus job design was viewed as a strategy to improve employee motivation. This is because people take action on the job to satisfy their needs. Needs are the origin of action.

Among Salancik and Pfeffer's criticisms of these statements were the following:

1. Drawing on attribution theory, they stated that people are able to see their environment more than they are able to see themselves behaving in the environment. Thus they select information from the environment which explains their behavior only because of its relative saliency. When a person behaves in an environment where there are few if any salient cues that are consistent with the behavior, a person is likely to use a personal construct such as "my attitude" to explain the behavior.

2. Need satisfaction models do not allow for the possibility that instead of reacting to an environment (e.g., job characteristics), people can take steps to change it or seek another one. Further, people can "construct meaning" in ways that make their job both satisfying and motivating for them.

---

[37]Lawler (1969) drew upon Vroom's expectancy theory in his study of job characteristics: A person will exert effort to the extent that effort leads to performance, and performance leads to valued outcomes. Outcomes Lawler said, are valued to the extent that they satisfy one's needs.

3. Needs are not completely biological; they are at least in part socially conditioned, that is, learned. They are modifiable through operant techniques.

4. Needs are poorly defined as evidenced by the ongoing debates as to the meaning of self-actualization. Poorly defined terms make it difficult to do research that can refute their applicability.

5. The characterization of job is a process. Who is to characterize it? Is the answer an employee, a supervisor, a researcher, or a naïve observer? Moreover, the way in which a person characterizes a job can be manipulated. Thus it does not appear that a job has absolute fixed characteristics. Therefore job characteristics are arbitrarily defined as a function of an observer.

6. Consistency effects occur on an attitude survey as a result of a person's awareness of his or her responses to one or more questions. The answers become salient information for respondents, which in turn constrain subsequent responses to items on the survey questionnaire. An employee's responses to: "To what extent would you like to have autonomy in your work?" "How much challenge does your job provide?" influence the person's response to, "How satisfied are you with your job?" In short, a previous response to an item on a questionnaire constrains a person's answer to a subsequent question.

7. A person's attitude is derived from whatever information is available when asked about the attitude. Through priming, it is possible to present a standard set of questions to people and then manipulate the results.

In short, they argued that job characteristics are socially constructed realities. Consistency and priming effects can explain the beneficial results of job environment studies rather than the alleged satisfaction of a person's needs. Finally, Salancik and Pfeffer questioned the focus of need satisfaction theories on an employee's attitudes, which they labeled an epiphenomenon, rather than on an employee's behavior.

Following Salancik and Pfeffer's critique, on top of those critiques described previously, few studies on Maslow's need hierarchy, Herzberg's job enrichment theory, Hackman and Oldham's job characteristics theory, or Vroom's expectancy theory were subsequently conducted in the 20th century.

With the concomitant decline of behaviorism in I/O psychology, a new theory was about to dominate the literature on motivation for the remainder of the 20th century, namely goal setting.

 **4** 1975–2000

The Employee Is Immersed in Thought

Introduction

By the final quarter of the 20th century, dust bowl empiricism—the emphasis on collecting data under the adage "if it works, use it"—was dead. In their *Annual Review of Psychology* chapter on attitudes and motivation, Miner and Dachler (1973) were able to restrict their focus to theory and theory-oriented research. While one theory of motivation that had appeared in the previous quarter continued to thrive in terms of theoretical and practical significance, interest in other theories waned as two others took their place.

In his "Annual Review of Psychology" chapter, Mitchell (1979, p. 252) reported that Maslow's theory, Alderfer's ERG model, and Herzberg's theory of job enrichment "have simply been absent from current research."[1] The same was true of equity theory. "While most people believe that a sense of justice is important in affecting work motivation, we still do not know much about how it is defined or its actual impact on performance" (Mitchell, 1979, p. 259). The answers would not be forthcoming until nearly a decade later when Greenberg, Folger, and their colleagues would publish their research on organizational justice.

Schneider (1985) observed that Roberts and Glick's (1981) highly critical review of Hackman and Oldham's job-characteristics theory resulted

---

[1]A cynic might argue that researchers abandoned one theory for another because of fad, fashion, or folderol (Dunnette, 1962). History, however, suggests that identification of methodological weaknesses of the predictive or explanatory power of a theory by respected scholars led to the development of and subsequent attention to a new theory. As Philips (1987) noted, "any position can be supported by positive reasons . . . but what really counts is how well the position can stand up to vigorous assault" (pp. vii-ix). Pinder (1998) argued that a theory should be parsimonious; if one theory can legitimately subsume another, it should do so.

in essentially no new work on it being published subsequent to 1983. As noted earlier, lack of reliability in measurement, lack of discriminant validity with other attitudinal measures of jobs, and halo error among perceived job characteristics were among the problems they cited.

After reviewing the literature, Ambrose and Kulik (1999) concluded that there have been little or no advances in expectancy theory research in the past decade. Moreover, goals have been shown to mediate the effect of expectancy theory constructs on performance (Klein, 1991). Thus Ambrose and Kulik concluded that there are few theoretical or applied reasons for additional research on the application of this theory in organizational behavior.[2]

Goal-Setting Theory

At the beginning of the fourth quarter of the 20th century there were a sufficient number of empirical studies on goal setting to warrant two literature reviews (Latham & Yukl, 1975; Steers & Porter, 1974). By the mid-1980s: "One topic that replaced expectancy theory for researchers was goal-setting theory, a work motivation theory unconcerned with individual differences in needs, desires, or instrumentality perceptions" (Schneider, 1985, p. 577). Miner (1984), in his review of organizational behavior theories, concluded that goal setting was one of only four theories that was both valid and practical. Pinder (1984, p. 169) stated that: "Goal setting theory has demonstrated more scientific validity to date than any other theory or approach to work motivation presented in this book." Boone and Bowen (1987) listed my paper with Locke on goal setting (Latham & Locke, 1979) as among the significant writings in management and organizational behavior. How did all of this occur so quickly?

In the same time period as Heneman and Schwab's (1972) favorable review of expectancy theory, the American Pulpwood Association wanted to identify the variables that differentiate the effective from the

---

[2]A highly arguable point is the merit of developing a theory deductively as Vroom did versus doing so inductively as was done with goal setting theory. See Locke and Latham (1990a, 2002, 2005) as to why we believe that an enduring theory is likely to be based on induction. Goal setting is an inductive theory that emerged from answers to five questions. (1) Does goal setting work? Do goals affect action? (2) Do the findings generalize to different populations of employees, different tasks, different settings, different countries? (3) What about lateral integration? How are goals related to participation in decision making, feedback, satisfaction, self-efficacy? (4) What about vertical integration? How are goals related to individual differences, personality, and values? (5) Are there boundary conditions or moderator variables?

ineffective logger in the rural southern United States. Ronan, Latham, and Kinne (1973) conducted a survey that through happenstance included items on goal setting. A factor analysis revealed that items measuring goal setting and items regarding the presence of a supportive supervisor loaded on the same factor as items that measured cords per employee hour and a low injury rate. Goal setting alone, that is, in the absence of a supportive supervisor, loaded on a second factor that included measures of voluntary turnover. The third factor was defined by measures of high supervisory supportiveness and equipment mechanization, but no goal setting. These behaviors correlated neither positively nor negatively with any performance criterion. The recommendations for practice formulated on the basis of that survey were greeted with skepticism by the industry sponsors (e.g., Georgia Kraft, International Paper Company, Owens, Illinois) of the American Pulpwood Association as they were aware that correlation does not imply causation. Moreover, the sponsors, many of whom were mechanical engineers, read with disbelief that mechanization, in which they were investing thousands of dollars, had no relationship with loggers' productivity. The loggers, many of whom had less than a middle school education, often ran the equipment with tires flat, sometimes without even checking to see if the equipment needed oil.

A serendipitous purview of the *Psychological Abstracts* led to my discovery of Locke's laboratory experiments. After reviewing the results of the logging survey in light of Locke's findings in the laboratory, a follow-up study was done to remove the skepticism of the value of goal setting on the part of the American Pulpwood Association's sponsor companies. Logging crews were matched on size, productivity, terrain, and level of mechanization. Each crew had a supervisor who was on the work site. The crews were randomly assigned to one of two conditions, namely a condition where the crews were assigned a specific high goal as to number of trees to cut down (cords) or a condition where they were urged to do their best to cut as many trees as possible. All the crews were paid on a piece-rate basis. Thus, the more trees they cut, the more money they made regardless of whether they were in the goal-setting or the do-your-best condition. Within a week, the productivity of the crews in the goal-setting condition as well as their job attendance was significantly higher than that of the crews in the "do best" condition (Latham & Kinne, 1974).

Why did this change in these two dependent variables occur so soon? Interviews revealed that people who were assigned goals immediately started bragging to one another as well as to family members as to their effectiveness as loggers. Goal setting had instilled in them a sense of purpose, challenge, and meaning into what had been perceived previously by them as a tedious and physically exhausting task. In short, goal pursuit and attainment led to enhanced task interest, pride in performance, and a heightened sense of personal effectiveness as well as an increase in pay. The problem with urging people to do their best, even when they are paid on a piece rate basis, is that they do not in fact do so. This exhortation is too vague, it is too abstract. There is no meaningful referent for evaluation of one's performance. Consequently, it is defined idiosyncratically. It allows for a wide range of performance levels that are acceptable to different people. Setting a specific high goal, in contrast, makes explicit for people what needs to be attained.

Thus, science had informed practice; goal setting did indeed increase employee productivity. On a variation of Parkinson's Law, a subsequent study revealed that when the wood supply is high and quotas are thus put in place to restrict the number of days that a company purchases wood from these independent loggers, the crews, who are paid on a piece-rate basis, harvest as much wood or more in those restricted days as they do in a normal work week (Latham & Locke, 1975). The quota, to the dismay of the forest products companies who had too great a wood inventory, became a challenging goal for the loggers that in turn led to a dramatic increase in their effort.

The Weyerhaeuser Company wanted to know whether the application of something so seemingly simple and straightforward as goal setting could be modified in ways to further improve productivity and lower costs. The majority of Weyerhaeuser loggers on the West Coast are unionized company operations rather than independent crews. These employees are paid by the hour rather than on a piece-rate basis. Would goal setting be effective with hourly workers? A time series design (Campbell & Stanley, 1972) showed that within nine months of goal setting, logging costs decreased by a quarter of a million dollars (Latham & Baldes, 1975). Goal attainment enabled these people to experience a sense of accomplishment. The truck drivers were now strategizing ways to increase the load of logs they were carrying without exceeding legal weight limits.

Umstot, Bell, and Mitchell (1976) noted that enriching jobs usually includes ways of increasing performance feedback. Feedback often leads people to set specific high goals. Using a job simulation, they found that job enrichment increases satisfaction, but it is goal setting that leads to significant increases in performance.

By the close of the 20th century, research had shown that setting specific difficult goals increases performance on over 100 different tasks, involving more than 40,000 participants in at least eight countries (Locke & Latham, 1990a, 2002). In short, goal setting was shown to be among the most valid and practical theories of employee motivation in organizational psychology (C. Lee & Earley, 1992).

Action theory, developed by German psychologists (e.g., Frese & Zapf, 1994) also emphasizes the importance of goal setting. The theory was specifically developed for application in organizational settings with the assumption that work requires actions. The theory states that "activeness" exists in every action to "appropriate" the environment to attain one or more goals. Self-regulation is posited to be dynamic and hierarchical in moving from conscious to unconscious or automatic regulation in redundant environments. "Work should be personally enhancing, thus one should use all aspects of the action sequence such as goal setting, information search, planning and feedback" (Frese, 2005, personal communication). In addition, the theory states that negative information is important; hence Frese's research interests, to be discussed later, include the positive benefits for people from making errors.

Goal Limitations

There are drawbacks to virtually all choices. This includes one's choice in setting a goal. Focusing on ways to attain goal A may preclude focusing on ways to attain goal B. For example, the downsides of trying too hard for quantity may lead to neglect of quality (Bavelas & Lee, 1978) and vice versa. In addition, those who are highly committed to attaining their goal may be less likely to help others to attain their goal (Wright, George, Farnsworth, & McMahan, 1993). When there are two or more goals, in the absence of prioritization, goal conflict may result. When this occurs, performance on both goals usually suffers (Locke, Smith, Erez, Chah, & Shaffer, 1994). People can, however, pursue more than one goal effectively when the goals are prioritized or causally interrelated (Edminster & Locke, 1987).

There have been five major disputes regarding goal-setting theory, one involving the role of feedback, the second regarding the importance of participative decision making in setting a goal, the third involving predictions based on expectancy theory, the fourth involving predictions on the basis of control theory, and the fifth on the relative effectiveness of urging people to do their best vs. setting a specific high goal.

The issue of whether feedback in itself affects behavior was resolved in a series of experiments which showed that it is completely mediated by the setting of specific goals; feedback, however, is a moderator of the effect of goals on performance (Locke & Latham, 1990a).[3] The importance of the method by which a goal is set is discussed subsequently in the section on controversies in the 20th century.

With regard to the third dispute, goal-setting theory states that there is a positive linear relationship between the difficulty level of a goal and the level of a person's performance. Since harder goals are more difficult to reach than easier goals, one's expectancy of success, across goal levels, will show a negative linear relationship to performance. Expectancy theory, in contrast to goal setting, asserts that there is a positive linear relationship between a person's expectancy of success and subsequent performance. In contrast to goal setting and expectancy theories, Atkinson's achievement theory states that a person's subjective probability estimate of success and subsequent performance is curvilinear, with the highest level of performance at moderate rather than low or high levels of expectancy. In short, the three theories make very different predictions.

The goal theory-expectancy theory conflict can be resolved in two ways: The first is to take into account within versus between group correlations. In goal-setting experiments, different groups are assigned different goals and they then rate their expectations of reaching them. Thus, each participant in the study rates his or her expectancy of attaining only one performance level, namely that which corresponds with the goal that was assigned. Because different groups of participants are assigned different goals, their expectancies pertain to the different performance levels. Therefore, rating the expectancy of goal attainment means different things in the different goal conditions. Thus people

---

[3]Conceptually, a mediator is an explanatory variable. It identifies and hence explains why there is a causal relationship between an independent and a dependent variable, as well as the relationship between a predictor and a criterion. Why is setting a goal so effective in increasing a person's performance? The mediators (explanation) include choice, effort, persistence, and cognition in terms of a strategy to attain it. For practitioners, identifying mediators is invaluable because this information can be used to modify an intervention or for adapting its principles to another area. Mediators answer the question as to why an intervention worked. Feedback affects performance, for example, only if it leads to the setting of and commitment to a specific high goal. Without goal setting, the feedback "goes in one ear and out the other." It is information that is not acted upon. Feedback, however, is a moderator of goal setting. It enhances the effectiveness of the goal regarding subsequent performance. Without feedback, a boundary condition, one has little or no idea as to one's progress toward goal attainment, let alone whether a different strategy is required to attain the goal. The importance of feedback as a moderator of goal setting was shown empirically by Miriam Erez (1977) while she was on a sabbatical at the University of Maryland where she worked with Ed Locke. Her finding was subsequently replicated by Bandura and Cervone (1983).

with high goals have higher performance yet lower expectancies than those with low goals and a low level of performance. But, the within-group correlation between a person's expectancy of goal attainment and subsequent performance tends to be positive (Garland, 1984; Mento, Cartledge, & Locke, 1980). This is because the within-group expectancy ratings are made regarding the same level of goal difficulty.

A second solution to the conflicting prediction of goal versus expectancy theory is to assess expectancy in terms of one's self-efficacy, that is, one's assessment of all factors that could affect one's performance (e.g., knowledge, ability, available resources) rather than the probability that one's sheer effort alone will lead to performing effectively. Self-efficacy typically is not assessed in terms of attaining a single goal or performance level, but to a range of performance levels. When self-efficacy is measured, goals and self-efficacy relate positively with performance regardless of whether goals are assigned or self-set. If goals are self-set, those with high self-efficacy set high goals. The between-group relation of both goal level and self-efficacy to performance is positive, as are the within-group relationships.

Regarding the concept of valence in expectancy theory, it is critical to note that a goal is simultaneously a target to strive to attain and a standard by which to evaluate the effectiveness of one's performance. Thus people with a high goal must perform at a higher level to become more satisfied than do those with an easy goal. Moreover, in the workplace, high performance typically leads to better outcomes (e.g., recognition, money, job advancement). In short, high goals not only require people to accomplish more in order for them to become satisfied, high goals also lead to more beneficial outcomes than easier ones.

With regard to Atkinson's findings, none of his studies included measures of self-efficacy or the setting of a specific high goal. Moreover, his findings of a curvilinear relationship between one's probability of success and subsequent performance is not a robust or replicable phenomenon.

Control theory, derived from cybernetic engineering by two social psychologists, Carver and Scheier (1981), also emphasizes goal setting.[4]

---

[4]Control theory was introduced to the work motivation literature by Robert Lord and a master's student, Michael Campion at the University of Akron (Campion & Lord, 1982). They criticized typical goal setting experiments for their focus on a static single goal. Control theory, they said, is capable of predicting and explaining multiple competing goals that are hierarchically arranged. Among Campion's later accomplishments were his election to the presidency of the Society of Industrial and Organizational Psychology and his appointment as editor of Personnel Psychology. Campion's dissertation supervisor was Paul Thayer, who was the Department Head of the Psychology Department at North Carolina State University.

As did Ryan (1970), Carver and Scheier stressed that, "when people pay attention to what they are doing, they usually do what they intend to do, relatively accurately and thoroughly." The theory asserts that the source of motivation is a negative feedback loop, metaphorically similar to a thermostat, that eliminates goal-performance discrepancies. Perceived discrepancy between performance and the reference standard, a goal, automatically triggers action on the part of a person to reduce the incongruence.

In disagreement with this position, both Bandura (1989) and Locke and Latham (1990a, 2002) argued that goal setting is also a discrepancy-creating process. Motivation requires feed-forward control in addition to feedback. After people attain their goal, those with high self-efficacy often set an even higher goal. The subsequent setting of a high goal creates rather than reduces motivation discrepancies to be mastered. "Self-motivation thus involves a dual cyclic process of disequilibratory discrepancy production followed by equilibratory reduction" (Bandura, 1989, p. 38). A regulatory process in which matching a standard begets inertness, argued Bandura, does not characterize self-motivation. Such a feedback control system would produce circular action that would lead nowhere. Moreover, people can increase their level of motivation by setting goals before any feedback is provided regarding a discrepancy between one's performance and the goal that has been set (Bandura & Cervone, 1986).

Bandura and Locke (2003) attacked the philosophy underlying control theory:

> The ontological foundations of control theory in its different versions have never been clearly articulated. This is no easy task given that this theory of cybernetic regulation is a discordant hybrid of agentic functions grafted on a mechanical feedback control system devoid of consciousness or any self-reflective capabilities. To further complicate matters, agentic functions have crept even into the allegedly automatic feedback system, although somewhat dissonantly, as when the cybernetic system is humanized by being equipped with complex information-processing components, endowed with a consciousness, and even granted a free will (Lord & Levy, 1994); furnished with scripts, causal attribution judgments, and calculation of utilities for alternative options (Klein, 1989); and affixed with affective self-evaluative motivators and self-efficacy beliefs from social cognitive theory (Vancouver et al., 2001). Carver and Scheier (1981) endowed the superordinate feedback loop with innumerable human attributes—self-consciousness, different types of selves, outcome expectations, attributional judgments, self-esteem, egotism, and the like. Where amid these sundry embellishments is control theory, and what unique perspective does it provide? (p. 97)

Cervone et al. (in press) argued that theoretical order is the hallmark of analyses that are recognized as advances in science. They critiqued control theory on the following grounds:

> Suppose a concert violinist self-regulates by comparing her ongoing performance to an ideal, but that the feature she desires to regulate, and thus the comparisons, involve a) the sound being produced, versus b) her motor movements while playing, versus c) her visual appearance before the audience. An embodied-cognition model such as the perceptual symbols systems approach of Barsalou and colleagues (Barsalou, Simmons, Barbey, & Wilson, 2003) would suggest that different mental structures, involving different modalities (auditory, motoric, visual), subserve the comparison functions in the different cases. There would, then, be no such thing—no single internal mental structure—that is "a comparator."
>
> Our point here is not that the positing of a comparator is "wrong." It merely is the following: The notion that a self-regulatory function (in this case, comparison) is carried out by a single corresponding structure (a comparator) is a strong claim. It requires careful explication and defense. (By analogy, imagine the defense required if someone posited that the function of remembering is carried out by "a rememberer.") Yet, in practice, the theoretical claim receives hardly any attention at all. In their definitive statement of control theory, Carver and Scheier (1998) devote little space to the question of how a structure central to their theory, the comparator, actually works: "How it [comparison] takes place is less important than that it takes place" (p. 11). But if one does not know how comparison takes place, there would appear to be no grounds for positing the existing of "a comparator" as opposed to positing that multiple distinct mental structures contribute to the function of comparison in different contexts. (Cervone et al., in press)

A fifth controversy occurred as a result of the findings by Ruth Kanfer and her husband, Phillip Ackerman.[5] They found that in the absence of knowledge or ability, setting a specific high goal can have a deleterious effect on a person's performance (Kanfer & Ackerman, 1989).

Both Bandura (1989) and Locke and I (Locke & Latham, 1990a) are in agreement with Kanfer and Ackerman that goal intentions in themselves do not automatically activate self-reactive influences of motivation. Knowledge or ability is a prerequisite. Given this prerequisite, certain properties of goals affect how strongly people will engage in given endeavors. These properties include not only specificity and difficulty level of the goal, but whether the goal is for the attainment of a performance

---

[5]Kanfer and Ackerman's study received the best paper award from the OB Division of the Academy of Management. I was one of the judges having been a recipient of this award the previous year (Latham, Erez, & Locke, 1988).

outcome that is valued, or the discovery of ideas or strategies to attain an outcome that is important to the individual, as well as how far into the future the goal is projected. Goal specificity and difficulty level were the focus of research in the 1960s–1980s. In the 1990s, attention shifted to the latter two issues. This is because goal attainment on tasks that are complex for people requires that problems associated with getting started and persisting until the goal is reached are effectively solved.

In studies of motivation, the relationship between the independent and dependent variables are typically studied with regard to choice, effort, and persistence. The effects of ability as well as environmental constraints are typically held constant across conditions (Campbell & Pritchard, 1976). In a simulation of air traffic control where the acquisition of ability had yet to occur, Kanfer and Ackerman (1989) found that urging people to do their best resulted in higher performance than the setting of a specific high performance goal. This is because a specific high performance goal imposes greater attentional demands on people when they are in a learning mode than is the case with a "do best" goal. As noted earlier, effective performance on tasks that are complex for people requires not only effort, but the discovery of appropriate task strategies.

Mone and Shalley (1995) replicated Kanfer and Ackerman's findings regarding the positive effect of urging people to do their best on a task that is complex for them. In addition, contrary to expectations, multiple performance trials over a three day period did not lead to the acquisition of appropriate task knowledge when a specific high performance goal was set. In fact, setting a specific high performance goal detracted from the effectiveness of the search for an effective strategy. In focusing on goal attainment, people appeared to be spending more time thinking about how to perform well rather than actually performing well. Worse, the dysfunctional effects of a specific high goal increased over the three-day period while the performance of those with "do best" goals became increasingly better.

The mediating variable that explained this finding is strategy. Individuals who had a specific difficult goal to attain consistently switched strategies relative to their counterparts who had been asked to do their best. This finding, Mone and Shalley reported, highlights the difference between mindlessly changing strategies versus searching systematically for effective ones. A goal to do one's best led to the discovery of strategies that were effective rather than a mad scramble to try different ways of attaining a specific goal. Thus, the setting of a specific high performance goal actually interfered with the processing of information and learning due to people constantly jumping from one strategy to another, strategies that were neither useful nor necessary.

Working independently of Mone and Shalley and with no knowledge of their findings, Dawn Winters and I reviewed Kanfer and Ackerman's study. We could find no methodological flaws in the way they had conducted their experiment. Thus, we hypothesized that their finding might be due to the type of goal that was set (Winters & Latham, 1996). To test this hypothesis, we first replicated Kanfer and Ackerman's findings.[6] Using a complex task involving the scheduling of college courses, we, too, found that urging people to do their best led to higher performance than setting a specific high performance goal. However, we also found that when a specific high learning goal is set in terms of discovering a specific number of ways to implement the scheduling task, it led to the highest performance. This is because a learning goal draws attention from the end result. It requires people to focus instead on understanding the task that is required of them, and developing a plan for performing it correctly. High performance is not always the result of sheer effort or persistence. It is also the result of cognitive understanding of the task, as well as the strategy or plan necessary for completing it (Frese & Zapf, 1994). When behavioral routines have yet to be developed, a specific high learning goal focuses attention on systematic problem solving and ultimately high performance (Seijts & Latham, 2005).[7] Hence, relative to a performance goal, a specific high learning goal increases the probability that a correct process or procedure will be discovered, mastered, and implemented. In such instances, commitment to a learning goal is likely to be higher than for a performance goal as a result of goal intensity, namely the amount of thought or effort that goes into formulating a plan of action required of the former relative to the latter. Consistent with goal-setting theory, a specific high learning goal leads to higher performance than urging people to do their best

---

[6]When highly competent researchers obtain contradictory findings, the explanation can often be found in differences in methodology regarding the procedure, the operational definition of variables, or the statistical analysis that was used. It increases your credibility with a scientific audience to replicate the other person's findings before showing how your alteration in procedure, statistical analysis, or operational definition leads to a different conclusion.

[7]Wood, Mento, and Locke (1987) had reported that the effect size of goals is smaller on complex than on simple tasks. This implies that some people are lacking the requisite skill or knowledge to perform effectively. Goal effects, they said, are often delayed on complex tasks, because learning is required. Hence, Dawn Winters and my hypothesis was that specific high learning goals should be set rather than performance outcome goals.

because it provides a standard by which they can monitor, evaluate, and, if necessary, modify their performance.

A variation of a learning goal is one that is qualitative. On the basis of their findings from two laboratory experiments, Staw and Boettger (1990) concluded that assigning a specific performance outcome goal can be damaging to an organization when a leader lacks the requisite knowledge to do so appropriately. In such cases, they recommended formulating the goal in vague terms, such as to do your best. Doing so, they said, would likely free knowledgeable subordinates to question and subsequently revise the task more so than they would if the goal were highly specific, yet the wrong one. Locke agreed with their conclusion.

On the basis of a subsequent set of laboratory experiments, however, Locke and Kirkpatrick (1990) found that an even more effective method is to make task revision an explicit qualitative goal, that is, specifically instruct people to challenge the assumptions underlying a given assignment, and to revise it where it is appropriate to do so. People told to do so had higher performance than those who were merely urged to do their best.

Social Cognitive Theory

Still another theory that emphasizes the importance of goal setting on motivation is Bandura's social cognitive theory. Albert Bandura, a social psychologist, was born and raised in Alberta, earned his undergraduate degree in psychology at the University of British Columbia and received his Ph.D. under the supervision of Kenneth Spence, the highly respected behaviorist at the University of Iowa.

In his "Annual Review of Psychology" chapter, John Campbell (1971) cited Bandura's (1969) authoritative book on behavior modification as an excellent source for extrapolating behavior modification principles to the work place. Shortly thereafter, Bandura repudiated behaviorism, because it embodies, he said, an erroneously "mechanistic" view of behavior. Reinforcing events change behavior through the intervening influence of thought (Bandura, 1974).[8] Similarly, Mischel (1973,

---

[8]In his autobiography, Bandura (2005) stated: "The behavioristic theorizing was discordant with the evident social reality that much of what we learn is through the power of social modeling. I found it difficult to imagine a culture in which its language, mores, familial customs and practices, occupational competencies, and educational, religious, and political practices were gradually shaped in each new member by rewarding and punishing consequences of their trial and error performance."

pp. 273–274) suggested that people regulate their behavior through goal setting and self-produced consequences to goal attainment: "Even in the absence of external constraints and social monitors, persons set performance goals for themselves and react with self-criticism or self-satisfaction to their behavior depending on how well it matches their expectations and criteria."

1977 was a watershed year for psychology with the publication of Bandura's theory in the *Psychological Review* (Bandura, 1977a) and described more fully in a book (Bandura, 1977b).[9] Originally called social learning, Bandura relabeled it social cognitive theory (Bandura, 1986) to avoid confusion with similarly named theories.[10] In brief, social cognitive theory states that behavior is a continuous reciprocal interaction among cognitive, behavioral, and environmental variables. Explicit in this view is the argument that behavior is both determined by and affects environmental consequences, which in turn affect the person's conscious intentions or goals, and vice versa (Bandura, 2001a). Thus, social cognitive theory provides a theoretical framework that encompasses the primary variables in both the cognitive and the behaviorist camps.[11]

Whereas behavioristic doctrine states that learning can occur only through performing responses and experiencing their effects, social

---

[9]In 1977 my office was located in Fred Fiedler's laboratory at the University of Washington. It was there that I received a preprint of the *Psychological Review* paper from Bandura. It was our first correspondence. Intrigued by the title, as well as the emphasis on goal setting, I immediately read it, then mailed a copy to Locke at the University of Maryland. Bandura, Locke, and I have been citing one another's work to the present day. As President of the Canadian Psychological Association (1999–2000), I appointed Bandura as the Honourary President. Bandura also served as President of APA in 1974.

[10]Social learning theory was used by Rotter (1966) to describe a person's beliefs regarding locus of control. Self-efficacy and locus of control are not only different phenomena, they are derived from different conceptual schemes. Whereas a person's self-efficacy concerns beliefs about one's capability to produce certain performances, locus of control refers to a person's belief as to whether a given outcome that is attained is dependent on one's actions (internal locus) or is due to fate, chance, or luck (external locus). The correlation between these two variables, self-efficacy, and locus of control is very low (Bandura, 1997). Locus of control is a dispositional trait whereas self-efficacy is a state.

[11]In Vroom's words (2003, personal communication), "Expectancy theory and Lewin's field theories were ahistorical with regard to causation; they didn't specify how the field of forces would come about or how it would be modified by learning. Bandura's is essentially a social learning theory, dealing with the modification and learning of expectancies through vicarious (among other) sources. It expands the nature of the issues, and the nature of the field."

cognitive theory enlarges this view by emphasizing vicarious, symbolic, and self-regulating processes in acquiring and maintaining behavior. The theory states that people can learn on a vicarious basis by observing the behavior of others and its consequences for them. Through the use of symbols, people are able to foresee probable consequences, set goals, and act accordingly. Consequently, as a result of self-regulatory processes, people learn to function as agents in their own self-motivation, through rewards for progress toward goal attainment.

The impact of this theory on I/O psychologists was immediate (e.g., Latham & Saari, 1979a) for at least two reasons.[12] Psychology, from the outset, had been concerned with the study of individual differences (Hull, 1928; Munsterberg, 1913). In contrast to this position, the behaviorists advocated a "black box" approach to psychology. The sole focus on observable stimuli, responses, and consequences of responses removed the necessity of peering inside an organism (the "black box"); consciousness, as noted earlier, was rejected and individual differences were dismissed as merely differences among organisms in their histories of reinforcement and thus were not of any particular scientific interest. Social cognitive theory, however, identified two individual-difference variables that play a critical mediating role among the stimulus, the response, the consequence, and the subsequent behavior (Bandura, 1982; Bandura & Adams, 1977; Bandura, Adams, & Beyer, 1977) These two cognitive variables are outcome expectancies (one's belief that the given outcome will occur if one engages in the behavior) and self-efficacy (one's belief that one can execute a given behavior in a given setting). "In regulating their behavior by outcome expectations, people adopt courses of action that are likely to produce positive outcomes and generally discard those that bring unrewarding or punishing outcomes" (Bandura, 2001b, p. 7).[13] "The likelihood that people will act on the outcomes they expect prospective performances to produce depends on their beliefs about whether or not they can produce those performances. A strong sense of coping efficacy reduces vulnerability to stress and depression in taxing situations and strengthens resiliency to adversity"

---

[12]Further evidence of the receptivity of I/O Psychology to Bandura's theory is that Melvin Sorcher was the first recipient of SIOP's award for Distinguished Contributions to Psychology as a Profession for his application of behavioral modeling principles in industry.

[13]Note the similarity of this aspect of the theory with Vroom's. A primary difference is that Bandura's outcome expectancy concept is free of the complex mathematical calculations for which Vroom's theory was criticized.

(Bandura, 2001b, p. 10). Low self-efficacy can thus nullify the motivating potential of positive outcome expectancies.[14] In short, more important than ability in affecting performance is one's belief regarding one's ability to perform a given task. Given the same low level of performance, people with high self-efficacy exert effort and persist until they have mastered the task, whereas those with low self-efficacy view their poor performance as a reason to abandon their goal. This belief system is the foundation of human agency, argued Bandura (1997). Unless people believe they can attain their goal through their actions, they are unlikely to persevere when confronted by difficulties. Thus, self-efficacy is a cognitive judgment that has motivational consequences.[15]

In contrast with Vroom's expectancy theory, goal setting is another core concept in social cognitive theory.[16] Had it been part of expectancy theory, one can infer from Bandura's research that specific goals would have been an outcome of the VIE process. This is because goals, argued Bandura, give direction to pursuits. They invest activities with meaning and purpose. The common factors conducive to enduring motivation, he stated, are setting goals in accordance with one's perceived capabilities (self-efficacy) and having informative feedback of progress toward

---

[14]In instances where one's performance solely affects the outcome, efficacy beliefs account for most of the variance in outcome expectancies. That is, when differences in self-efficacy among people are controlled statistically, outcome expectancies for performance make little or no independent contribution to the prediction of behavior. "Lack of independent predictiveness does not mean that outcome expectancies are unimportant to human behavior" (Bandura, 1997, p. 24). They are particularly important when outcomes are not controlled solely by one's performance. Similarly Locke, Motowidlo, and Bobko (1986) found that expectancies, as defined by Vroom, do not work solely through goals, but instead have an independent effect on performance.

[15]Self-efficacy has two dimensions, namely magnitude and strength. Magnitude refers to the number or levels of performance (e.g., 1, 3, 5 journal publications this year) that the person believes he or she can attain, while strength refers to the person's confidence in attaining a given level of performance (e.g., 1, 3, or 5 journal publications). To obtain an overall measure of self-efficacy, z scores from the magnitude and strength scores are added together. Lee and Bobko (1994) however, stated that these two dimensions can be combined using a single measure of self-efficacy, namely by summing the confidence rating for each level that the person states is attainable.

Note too that self-efficacy and self-esteem are not interchangeable concepts. Self-esteem is a trait, and hence is trans-situational. How much I like myself in Seattle is pretty much the same as how I like myself in Toronto. Self-efficacy is a cognitive judgment of how well I can perform a specific task. I can have high self-esteem and low self-efficacy regarding repairing the engine in my car; conversely I can have low self-esteem and high self-efficacy that I can give a lecture on motivation.

[16]At the 1978 meeting of the Western Psychological Association, upon meeting Bandura for the first time, I asked him to explain the primary difference between Vroom's theory and his own (Bandura, 1977a, b). Much to my surprise, Bandura at that point in time was not aware of expectancy theory.

goal attainment (Erez, 1977). Because self-judgment of one's capability is a major determinant of the goal one sets, the two are obviously positively correlated. The higher one's perceived self-efficacy, the higher the goal one sets, and the stronger one's commitment to it.

Wood and Bandura (1989) as well as Gist and Mitchell (1992) explained in detail the applicability of the theory to organizational settings. Meta-analyses of empirical research in work-related settings have shown the strong link between self-efficacy and a person's performance (Sadri & Robertson, 1993; Stajkovic & Luthans, 1998). Countless studies have shown that perceived self-efficacy contributes independently to subsequent performance after controlling for prior performance and indices of ability (Bandura, 1997). A strong belief in one's performance efficacy is essential to mobilize and sustain the effort necessary to succeed. After people attain their goals, people with high self-efficacy set even higher goals. These higher goals create new motivating discrepancies to be mastered (Bandura & Locke, 2003). As Locke (1965, p. 84) had shown years earlier, "getting closer to a 'standard' is both a source of satisfaction and an impetus to continued effort."[17]

In summary, in addition to the inclusion of goal setting, social cognitive theory differs from Vroom's expectancy theory in a number of ways. Expectancy theory states that motivation is governed by the expectation that effort will lead to performance which in turn will result in outcomes that are on a continuum of unvalued to valued.[18] Social cognitive theory argues that people exclude entire classes of options rapidly on the basis of their perceived efficacy. There is an important difference, Bandura and Locke (2003) argued, between belief in the utility of effort and belief that one can mobilize oneself to sustain effort in the face of perceived impediments and setbacks.

> Effort is but one of many factors that govern the level of quality of performance. People judge their capacity for challenging activities more in terms of their perceptions of the knowledge, skills, and strategies they have at their command than solely on how much they will exert themselves. Performances that call for ingenuity, resourcefulness and adaptability depend more on adroit use of skills and specialized knowledge than on dint of effort. . . . Hence, the aspect of self-efficacy

---

[17]Goal attainment, however, on tasks where there is no corresponding increase in the employee's growth or competence does not increase satisfaction (Latham & Yukl, 1976).

[18]A benefit of using self-efficacy rather than expectancy measures in goal-setting research is that self-efficacy is measured in terms of confidence in reaching each performance level across a range of performance levels, as opposed to any one performance level; thus the referent is always held constant (Locke, Motowidlo, & Bobko, 1986).

that is most germane to how much is accomplished is people's perceived perseverant capabilities—that is, their belief that they can exert themselves sufficiently to attain designated levels of productivity. (Bandura, 1989, p. 24)

Expectancy theory's emphasis on effort, Bandura said, limits its applicability to routine activities.

Goal-setting theory and social cognitive theory are similar in that both emphasize the importance of conscious goals for predicting, explaining, and regulating performance as well as the importance of feedback as a moderator of the goal-performance relationship. They provide the framework for self-management (Latham & Locke, 1991). The effect of self-management on self-efficacy and job attendance of unionized employees was shown by Frayne and Latham (1987).[19]

The two theories differ primarily in their relative emphasis on the variables that constitute them. The emphasis in goal-setting theory is on the core properties of an effective goal, namely specificity and difficulty level, as well as the mediators, namely direction, effort, persistence, and strategy, and the moderators, namely, ability, commitment, feedback, and situational constraints. Moreover, goal-setting research, relative to research on social cognitive theory, has focused on goal content (performance vs. learning) as well as on the method of setting goals (assigned, self, or participatively set). Goal-setting theory is not limited to but focuses primarily on motivation in work settings, including athletics (Locke & Latham, 1985). In contrast to goal-setting theory, social cognitive theory and the research that underlies it emphasizes the importance of self-efficacy as well as outcome expectancy, two different motivational systems that enhance goal commitment and persistence in the face of environmental difficulties. Social cognitive theory, unlike goal setting, specifies the ways that self-efficacy can be enhanced. There are no points of disagreement between the two theories in the assumptions that

---

[19]Frayne's doctoral dissertation, summarized in that paper, was the first and only dissertation to this date to win the award for best dissertation of the year from both the Academy of Management and the Society for Industrial and Organizational Psychology. What makes this remarkable is that she intentionally confounded variables such as goal setting, feedback, rewards, and punishers to create a "treatment package." I believe it is time to develop and apply treatment packages, where we already know the effects of the individual components of the package. I would like to see more studies on the effects of applying combinations of variables for the resolution of major issues confronting organizational decision makers. Robert Pritchard's work with ProMes as well as Michael Frese's on personal initiative are good examples of the benefits of doing so. Their work is discussed later in this book. To believe that one independent variable, holding all other variables constant, is going to resolve a complex problem in an organization is naïve.

underlie them. In fact, the concept of self-efficacy has been integrated with goal setting theory (Locke & Latham, 2002). People with high self-efficacy set higher goals, they are more committed to assigned goals, find and use better task strategies to attain the goals, and respond more positively to negative feedback than do those with low self-efficacy. Conversely, goals assigned by a leader can also affect self-efficacy in that they are an expression of confidence in an employee.[20]

Self-Regulation

Self-regulation involves processes that through modulation of thought, affect, and behavior enable people to guide their goal directed activities over time (Karoly, 1993). Among the first experiments on self-regulation that took place in the workplace were those conducted by Colette Frayne and I (Frayne & Latham, 1987; Latham & Frayne, 1989). Drawing on goal-setting and social cognitive theories, we adapted the methodology developed by a clinical psychologist, F. Kanfer (1980).[21] In brief, the methodology teaches people to assess problems, to monitor ways in which the environment facilitates or hinders goal attainment, and to identify and administer reinforcers for working toward, and punishers for failing to work toward, goal attainment. In essence, training in self-regulation teaches people skills in self observation, to compare their behavior with the goals that they set, and to administer reinforcers and punishers to bring about and sustain goal commitment.

Because of the diversity of clinical problems in which F. Kanfer had used this self-management technique effectively, and because of the strong theoretical rationale on which the training is based, we investigated its effectiveness with regard to increasing the job attendance of state government unionized maintenance workers. Interviews revealed that many of these people judged themselves as inefficacious in coping with environmental demands that they perceived as preventing them from coming to work. For example, some found it extremely difficult to take an hour off in the middle of the work day to accompany a child to a medical doctor's office.

---

[20]There is also evidence suggesting that goals and self-efficacy mediate the effect of visionary leadership on performance (Kirkpatrick & Locke, 1996).

[21]Fred Kanfer's daughter is Ruth Kanfer. After obtaining a Ph.D. in clinical psychology, she did a postdoctoral study in I/O psychology at the University of Illinois where her father was employed.

The self-management program itself consisted of eight weekly 1-hour group sessions followed by eight 30-minute one-on-one sessions. Each training group consisted of 10 people. The one-on-one sessions were conducted to tailor the training in self-management to the specific concerns of each individual, and to discuss issues that the person might have been reluctant to introduce in a group setting.

The first week an orientation session was conducted to explain the principles of self-mangement. The second week the reasons given by the trainees for using sick leave were listed and classified into nine categories, namely, legitimate illness, medical appointments, job stress, job boredom, difficulties with coworkers, alcohol and drug related issues, family problems, transportation difficulties, and employee rights (i.e., "sick leave belongs to me"). Of these nine categories, family problems, incompatibility with supervisor or coworkers, and transportation problems were listed most frequently.[22]

The trainees were taught to develop a description of the problem behaviors (e.g., difficulty with supervisor), to identify conditions that elicited and maintained the problem behaviors, and to identify specific coping strategies. This constituted the session on self-assessment. In this session, as in all sessions, the employees were assured that their comments would not be shared with anyone outside the training group.

The third week focused on goal setting. The distal goal was to increase one's attendance within a specific time frame (e.g., 1 month/3 months). The proximal goals were the specific behaviors that the respective individual had to engage in to attain the distal goal.

The fourth week focused on the importance of self-monitoring one's behavior. Specifically, the trainees were taught (a) to record their own

---

[22]Multiple measures of the construct of interest are advantageous because (a) most constructs cannot be measured without error, (b) it is difficult for a single indicator to adequately capture the breadth of a construct's domain, and (c) it is necessary to unconfound the method of measurement from the construct of interest (MacKenzie, Podsakoff, & Jarvis, 2005). In short, using multiple measures minimizes the probability of making a Type II error, that is, concluding erroneously that an intervention was ineffective when in fact it worked. Had Frayne and I only used typical measures of absenteeism rather than job attendance, we would have made this error, and an important discovery would have been lost. Because of the multiple classifications of an employee's absence used by most employers, and because of intentional as well as unintentional errors managers make in classifying an employee's absence from the workplace, measures of absenteeism are notoriously unreliable (Latham & Pursell, 1975). Thus we framed our intervention on ways to increase employee attendance as opposed to ways to decrease employee absenteeism. But, we measured both variables. The test-retest reliability of job attendance was .90; the test-retest reliability of the traditional measures of absenteeism was, in a word, terrible.

attendance, (b) the reason for missing a day of work, and (c) the steps that were followed to subsequently get to work. This was done through the use of charts and diaries. Emphasis was placed on the importance of daily feedback for motivational purposes as well as accuracy in recording their data.

In the fifth week the trainees identified rewards and punishers to self-administer as a result of achieving or failing to achieve the proximal goals. The training emphasized that the reward must be powerful and easily self-administered (e.g., self-praise, purchasing a gift). The punisher was to be a disliked activity, that was easily self-administered (e.g., cleaning the attic). Each individual developed specific response-reward contingencies.

The sixth week was essentially a review of the previous six sessions. This was accomplished by asking the trainees to write a behavioral contract with themselves. Thus, each trainee specified in writing the goal(s) to be achieved, the time frame for achieving the goal(s), the consequences for attaining or failing to attain the goal(s), and the behaviors necessary for attaining the goal(s).

The seventh week emphasized maintenance. Discussion focused on issues that might result in a relapse in absenteeism, planning for such situations should they occur, and developing coping strategies for dealing with these situations.

The theoretical rationale for combining variables into one treatment package has been articulated by Azrin. The assumption underlying self-management, he said, is that the intervention should "include as many component procedures as seem necessary to obtain ideally, a total treatment success" (Azrin, 1977, p. 144). Empirical support for combining goal setting, feedback, and self-monitoring into a treatment package can be found in both the organizational behavior and clinical psychology literature. For example, a laboratory experiment by Erez (1977) showed that goal setting in the absence of feedback has a minimal effect on behavior. A subsequent field experiment (Latham, Mitchell, & Dossett, 1978) found that feedback in the absence of goal setting has no effect on behavior. John Campbell (1982) concluded that little would be gained from further attempts to tease apart the relative effects of goal setting and feedback.[23]

---

[23] Years later, Rousseau and Fried (2001, p. 4) would remind us that "a set of factors, when considered together, can sometimes yield a more interpretable theoretically interesting pattern than any of the factors would show in isolation." I strongly agree.

A learning measure consisting of situational questions that contained a dilemma regarding obstacles to overcome in getting to work revealed no significant differences between the training and the control group prior to the study. Subsequent to acquiring skills in self-regulation, the difference in test scores between the training and the control group was highly significant as was the correlation between learning test scores and job attendance. To determine whether people retained their knowledge of self-regulation, the situational test was re-administered 6 and again 9 months subsequent to the training. The employees had not been told how well they had scored. Yet there was no significant loss of information across time. The same pattern of results was revealed regarding job attendance. Those who used self-regulation had significantly higher attendance than did those in the control group. Their self-efficacy for coming to work was significantly higher than their peers who had been randomly assigned to the control group. Self-efficacy assessed at the end of the training program predicted subsequent job attendance 9 months later. At the end of this 9-month interval, the employees in the control group were taught these self-regulation techniques. Within 3 months their job attendance increased to that of the employees in the original training group.

Job Characteristics Revisited

Hackman and Oldham's (1976) theory was resurrected during this time period when researchers discovered that it provided a mediational framework, particularly with regard to the effects of job autonomy as well as skill variety on an employee's job performance and satisfaction (Fried & Farris, 1987).[24] In addition, Campion and Thayer (1985), in a survey of 121 jobs in five plants, found that jobs that score high in enrichment have employees who are more satisfied, have higher job performance, and less absenteeism. The level of the job was a moderator variable. Similarly, a study in Germany showed that growth facilitating tasks increase one's personal initiative (Frese, Kring, Soose, & Zempel, 1996). Consequently, the importance of job characteristics was incorporated into the High Performance Cycle, a framework that Locke and

---

[24]Citation Classics reported that their three main publications (Hackman & Oldham, 1975, 1976, 1980) on this theory and the resulting measurement instruments are today among the most frequently cited studies in organizational behavior.

I developed (Locke & Latham, 1990 a, b) at the end of the 20th century for predicting, explaining, and influencing a person's work motivation.

A Comprehensive Framework:
The High-Performance Cycle

The high-performance cycle, shown in Figure 4.1, explains how to increase a person's performance. In addition to person variables, the high-performance cycle takes into account job characteristics. It is an inductive theory based on the accumulated findings of empirical research. In brief, the high performance cycle states that specific difficult goals, plus high self-efficacy for attaining them, are the impetus for an employee's high-performance. Goals and self-efficacy affect the direction of one's behavior and the effort exerted, as well as one's persistence to attain a goal. In addition, goals and self-efficacy motivate the discovery of strategies for effectively doing so. The effect of goals on a person's performance is moderated by ability, growth-facilitating characteristics of jobs, situational constraints, the feedback provided in relation to the goal, and a person's commitment to the goal.

High performance on tasks that are perceived as meaningful, growth facilitating, and sources of high external and internal rewards lead to high job satisfaction. The consequence is a willingness to stay with the organization and accept future challenges, hence the high-performance cycle.

The theoretical significance of the high-performance cycle is that it provides a comprehensive sequence of causal relationships that is consistent with research findings based on a number of different theories. The practical significance of the high-performance cycle is that it provides a model or framework for creating both a high performing and a highly satisfied workforce.

A decade later, we (Latham, Locke, & Fassina, 2002) reviewed the literature from 1990 through the spring of 2000 to determine the extent to which the high-performance cycle has been supported. An electronic search was conducted through PsycInfo and Proquest using key words from the high performance cycle. Approximately 107 studies relevant to the high performance cycle were located. Studies, not reviewed earlier in this book, are described next.

Demands Influence Performance

Goals. As stressed earlier, a goal is the object or aim of an action. A study of chronic musculoskeletal patients discovered that one's goal to

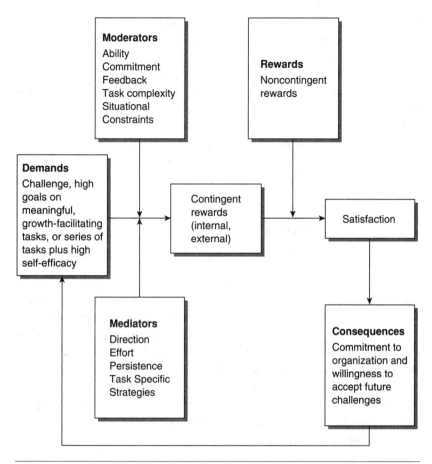

Figure 4.1   The High-Performance Cycle

Source: Locke & Latham (1990).

return to work is the single best predictor of a return to work (Tan et al., 1997). The positive effect of specific high goals on a person's behavior has also been obtained in the field of neurorehabilitation involving five studies of brain-damaged patients (Gauggel, 1999). No clinical or neuropsychological variable (e.g., time since onset of illness) was found to have a moderating influence. Assigned goals led to better performance than self-set goals. This is because the self-set goals were not as difficult as those that had been assigned. Self-set goals have also been found to be less challenging than goals that are assigned to people in the normal population (Hinsz, 1991, 1995).

Similarly, Von Bergen, Soper, and Rosenthal (1996) obtained a positive relationship between goal difficulty and performance. They also reported that people with low self-esteem perform worse when the goal is moderately difficult while those high in self-esteem perform best. Tang and Reynolds (1993) obtained the same finding. Those with low self-esteem had lower goals and lower performance than those with high self-esteem. Self-esteem was likely a proxy variable in that study for self-efficacy.[25]

From the standpoint of practice, there is a concern that very high goals could lead to a decrease in motivation and performance. This concern has not received empirical support (Bar-Eli, Levy-Kolker, Tenenbaum, & Weinberg, 1993; Jones & Cale, 1997). Rather, it is the person's perception, given the goal that is set, of how well he or she will perform on the subsequent trial or task that determines performance level (Weinberg, Fowler, Jackson, Bagnall, & Bruya, 1991). Hence the importance of one's self-efficacy.

Self-Efficacy. Performance is affected not only by one's goals, but by how confident one is of attaining them. As noted earlier, Bandura's (1997) research has shown that it is not so much our actual ability that holds us back or propels us forward as it is our self-efficacy. The higher one's self-efficacy in performing well on a task, the less difficult the goal is perceived to be (Lee & Bobko, 1992).

As noted earlier, self-efficacy influences the personal goals that one sets (Carson & Carson, 1993). The strong positive relationship of self-efficacy to personal goals and their relationship to performance have also been documented by Earley and Lituchy (1991) as well as Zimmerman, Bandura, and Martinez-Pons (1992). Lerner and Locke (1995) too found that self-efficacy affects an individual's personal goals.

In their review of the literature, Berry and West (1993) concluded that the consequences of high self-efficacy include the setting of high personal goals, the selection of challenging tasks, and high performance. Conversely, Hinsz and Matz (1997) showed that people with low self-efficacy regarding a task have low personal goals and subsequently perform poorly. Brown and Latham (2006) found that self-efficacy

---

[25]High goals also lead to high performance for groups. A meta-analysis revealed that the mean performance level of groups with specific high goals is almost one standard deviation higher than the performance of groups for which no goals are set (O'Leary-Kelly, Martocchio, & Frink, 1994). Klein and Mulvey (1995) and Mulvey and Klein (1998) showed that the difficulty level of a self-set group goal correlates positively with the group's performance. Crown and Rosse (1995) found that group goals for individual members who were committed to the group increased the group's performance on an interdependent task relative to any other condition.

correlates positively with goal level, goal commitment, and the team-playing behavior of MBA students in their respective study groups. Seijts, Latham, and Whyte (2000) found that the collective efficacy of a group affects performance, and in turn, a group's performance affects a group's efficacy. Seijts and Latham (2000a) found that a group's efficacy in making money, the group's goal commitment, and outcome expectancies that cooperation with others will lead to goal attainment correlates positively with a group's performance. Silver and Bufanio (1996) showed that collective efficacy affects the group goal difficulty performance relationship.

Button, Mathieu, and Aikin (1996) found no support for the hypothesis that over time assigned goals become less influential than self-efficacy on one's personal goals. Rather, they found that the effect of self-efficacy remains relatively constant and that normative information, that is, feedback that can lead to goal setting, becomes more influential as time progresses.

In summary, self- and collective efficacy are positively associated with the difficulty level of the goals that are set, goal commitment, and subsequent performance. An intriguing discovery by Tabernero and Wood (1999) revealed that people who have high self-efficacy have an incremental view of their ability. Consequently, they adjust their level of performance to negative feedback more effectively than do people who have low self-efficacy, and who are more likely to believe that their ability is fixed and hence unlikely to improve.

Growth Facilitating Tasks. Roberson, Korsgaard, and Diddams (1990) found that personal goals and task attributes have independent effects on satisfaction; the former effect may be the result of goal success. Tasks that are perceived as enriched facilitate high performance (Ambrose & Kulik, 1999; Campion, 1996), probably through their effects on goals and/or organizational satisfaction and commitment. Meta-analyses conducted by Mathieu and Zajac (1990) show that jobs that are perceived as enriched, not only produce high satisfaction, they induce high organization commitment.[26]

Kirkpatrick (1992), using a proofreading task, manipulated autonomy and responsibility in order to determine their effect on performance. Increases in responsibility led to increases in the difficulty level

---

[26]Meta-analysis permits the combination of data from conceptually related studies to reach generalizations based on statistical criteria. This procedure combines the data from separate studies by expressing each study's effect size in standard-deviation units.

as well as commitment to self-set goals. These goals, in turn, increased an individual's performance. Autonomy only affected a person's feelings of responsibility. These results suggest that enriching jobs through increases in responsibility increases an employee's performance through the process of goal setting.

In agreement with the findings obtained by Umstodt, Bell, and Mitchell (1976), Cordery (1996, 1997) argued that job enrichment in itself does not improve job performance. He found that the antecedents of effective job design/redesign outcomes are supervisory practices regarding (a) goal structure, the extent to which a supervisor ensures that an employee has specific attainable goals; (b) method structure, the extent to which an employee is able to exert control over work activity; (c) boundary protection, the extent to which an employee is provided the knowledge, skills, and resources to perform effectively; and (d) goal feedback, the extent to which a supervisor ensures that the individual is given timely information on progress toward goal attainment. These supervisory practices affect employee perceptions of their job.

In summary, enriched or challenging jobs appear to increase job satisfaction directly and independently of goal setting. Goal attainment, however, also affects job satisfaction. The effect of job enrichment on employee performance is indirect, namely through its effects on goals, feedback, satisfaction, and organizational commitment.

Individual Differences. The assertion that specific high goals lead to high performance is based on findings from over 400 empirical studies conducted prior to 1990 when the high-performance cycle was originally published. Thus there was minimal interest in or need for replicating this finding in the 1990s. And, because, as noted earlier, goal setting is a strong variable that masks individual differences (Adler, 1986; Adler & Weiss, 1988), personality variables were not included in the high-performance cycle when it was initially published.[27]

---

[27]Among the giants in industrial psychology in the 20th century were Ed Ghiselli, John Campbell, and Robert Guion. All three downplayed the importance of personality for predicting, understanding, or influencing behavior in the workplace. For example, Guion and Gottier (1965) asserted that there is no evidence that personality measures are related to work behavior. Ghiselli (1966) argued for a focus on past behavior rather than personality traits in the prediction of future behavior. Wernimont and Campbell (1968) emphasized the difficulty of determining what behaviors occur as a result of a specific trait. In addition Mischel (1968), a social psychologist, published a highly influential book where he argued forcefully that behavior is explained more by situational differences (recall Herzberg's work and Nord's interpretation of Skinner's research) than by differences in personality among individuals.

Toward the end of the 20th century individual differences became a subject of interest for those who studied work motivation. For example, Phillips and Gully (1997) identified, in addition to ability, a person's belief regarding locus of control (Do I control events or do events control me?) as having a positive relationship with self-efficacy and an indirect relationship with self-set goals. Lambert, Moore, and Dixon (1999) showed that self-set goals were more effective for gymnasts who have an internal rather than an external locus of control.

In summary, the relation of goals and personality traits when used to predict performance was still not fully understood nor extensively researched. However, there was emerging evidence of both mediation and moderation (interaction) effects. This topic was in obvious need of additional study. By the dawn of the 21st century it would come to dominate the motivation literature (see Part II).

Mediators

As noted earlier, and shown in Figure 4.1, four mediators explain how or why goals increase a person's job performance. The first three are primarily motivational, namely, direction, effort, and persistence. The fourth mediator, task specific strategies, is primarily cognitive. Each of these is discussed below.

Direction. Bagozzi and Warshaw (1990) proposed a theory of goal pursuit based on behavioral intentions. Attention or direction is a result of one's choice to attain a specific goal. Empirical support for this assertion was obtained by Hinsz and Ployhart (1998).

Kernan and Lord (1990), as well as R. Kanfer and her colleagues (Kanfer, Ackerman, Murtha, Dugdale, & Nelson, 1994), drew upon the cognitive resource allocation model to explain the relationship between goals and performance in multiple goal environments. Direction occurs through a prioritization process that is affected by situational cues, the personal importance of one goal relative to another, and feedback. Tubbs, and Ekeberg (1991) found that performance is highest when an individual is adept at shifting attention between levels in a multi-task hierarchy.

Effort and Persistence. In a study involving software engineers, Rasch and Tosi (1992) showed that goal difficulty affects the level of effort expended which in turn affects an individual's performance. With regard to persistence, Multon, Brown, and Lent (1991) found that some of the variance was accounted for by a person's self-efficacy.

That mediators do not always operate in isolation is shown in a study by Theodorakis, Laparidis, Kioumourtzoglou, and Goudas (1998). Effort, persistence, and task strategies jointly increased the performance of athletes on an endurance task relative to those with no goals. With regard to groups, Weldon and her colleagues (Weingart & Weldon, 1991; Weldon, Jehn, & Pradhan, 1991) found that effort, persistence, goal commitment, performance monitoring, and the identification of strategies to attain a group's goal mediate the effect of the goal-performance relationship.

Gellatly and Meyer (1992) found that attention, effort, and persistence are associated with arousal of the sympathetic nervous system, specifically changes in heart rate. Heart rate appears to mediate the goal difficulty-performance relationship. Duncan (1995) found that action is represented by a hierarchy of goals and subgoals activated in the prefrontal cortex of a person's brain.

Task-Specific Strategies. On a task that is complex for people, strategies have a stronger effect on performance than performance goals (Chesney & Locke, 1991).[28] This is because having the requisite knowledge is critical for performing such tasks effectively. Hence, as noted earlier, a specific difficult learning goal should be set rather than an outcome goal. A learning goal increases the likelihood of discovering the strategy necessary to perform the task.

Moderators

Moderator or boundary variables can enhance or attenuate the effect of demands, shown in Figure 4.1, on the employee's performance. These moderators include: a person's ability, task complexity, situational constraints, feedback, and goal commitment.

Ability and Task Complexity. Because goal-setting theory was conceived and developed primarily with regard to motivation, ability was taken as a given in most studies conducted prior to 1990. The tasks used

---

[28]Note that task complexity and a task that is complex for a person, although often highly correlated, are not interchangeable terms. Fixing a leaky faucet does not score high on task complexity; nevertheless, it is unbelievably complex for me. When we have a problem with a faucet, my wife always sends me to the basement, not for tools, but to get out of her way. By just looking at the faucet I can cause a geyser. Although obtaining funding for a research proposal scores high in task complexity, it is relatively straightforward and easy for me. And I don't require my wife's assistance.

were usually ones that the person already had the requisite knowledge and skill to perform well. This was done to minimize confounding of learning or ability with a person's motivation.[29] A problem confronting practitioners is that tasks in most organizational settings are inherently confounded in that both ability and motivation are required to excel on the job. This can be true for even easy tasks where there are multiple paths to accomplishment (Audia et al., 1996).

Locke and I (Locke & Latham, 1990a) included ability as a moderator in our theory of goal setting because lack of ability limits a person's capacity to pursue a specific high goal. Thus, there is a curvilinear relationship between goal difficulty and an individual's performance; that is, performance levels off once the limit of ability has been reached (Locke, Frederick, Lee, & Bobko, 1984). Furthermore, there is evidence that goal setting has stronger effects for high than for low ability people (Locke, 1982b).

Mathieu and Button (1992) found that previous performance, which is evidence of a person's ability, influences the setting of subsequent self-goals. Boyce and Wayda (1994) found that on tasks where the requisite skills to perform it have yet to be acquired, assigned goals lead to even higher performance than self-set goals. As both Kiesler (1971) and Salancik (1977) had noted years ago, the act of goal assignment, especially when the goal is high, increases self-efficacy in that it signals the belief by one's supervisor that one has the ability to attain it. This notion was subsequently supported empirically by Dov Eden. His work regarding Pygmalion effects is discussed later in this book.

As noted earlier, Kanfer and Ackerman (1989) had shown that setting specific high performance goals sometimes can be detrimental if individuals do not have the skill or knowledge required to attain them. In those instances, a specific high learning rather than an outcome goal should be set (Winters & Latham, 1996). A person's attention needs to be focused on discovering and mastering the processes and procedures for performing well, rather than on the attainment of a specific level of performance. This is because the attentional demands that can be placed on people are limited. Focusing on ways to attain a specific high outcome goal prior to knowledge acquisition places additional demands on people, so much so, that they are unable to devote the

---

[29]To further minimize the effects of ability contaminating experiments on motivation, people are randomly assigned to conditions, and performance on a pre-measure is often used as the covariate in an analysis of covariance.

necessary cognitive resources for task mastery. In addition, the assignment of a specific challenging performance outcome goal, prior to knowledge acquisition, usually makes people so anxious to perform at a high level that they scramble to discover the task-relevant strategies in an unsystematic way. Consequently, they fail to learn in a timely fashion the most efficient ways to accelerate their effectiveness. The solution is to set learning rather than performance goals, or to set proximal goals in addition to a distal goal.

Newman (1998) found that assigned learning goals in terms of identifying problem solving strategies necessitated fewer requests for assistance than was the case where students had performance outcome goals regarding their academic grades. VandeWalle and Cummings (1997) found that a primary benefit of learning goals is that they tend to induce appropriate feedback-seeking behavior.

In summary, these studies show that learning goals are effective on tasks that are complex for people because they focus their attention on identifying problem-solving strategies, they induce appropriate feedback-seeking behavior, and they increase self-efficacy regarding the attainment of the distal learning goal.

Seijts and Latham (2001) examined the effect of setting proximal goals in conjunction with either a distal learning or a distal performance outcome goal on a task that required learning in order to perform it correctly. As was found by Kanfer and Ackerman (1989), the people in the do-best condition performed significantly better than those with a distal performance goal. But, as was the case in the Winters and Latham (1996) study, performance was even higher when people were assigned a specific difficult learning goal. One reason is that a distal learning goal led to higher goal commitment than did the assignment of a distal outcome goal. A second reason is that self-efficacy increased across trials in the distal learning goal condition whereas in the distal performance goal condition it decreased. People with high self-efficacy were more likely than those with low self-efficacy to discover task relevant strategies. A mediator analysis showed that strategies had both a direct effect on self-efficacy as well as an indirect effect on performance.

The additional benefit of setting proximal goals with a distal learning goal is that they led to the formulation of the largest number of strategies. That proximal goals did not have a direct effect on performance may have been the result of the task that was used, namely one of high certainty rather than uncertainty.

In short, as Maier had pointed out years earlier, an individual's performance is a function of ability (e.g., strategy) and motivation (e.g., persistence). Important discoveries in this area in the 1990s include the documentation of when to set a specific high learning rather than a performance outcome goal. When people lack the knowledge or skill to perform a new task, a specific difficult learning goal should be set rather than an outcome goal; a specific difficult outcome goal should be set only when people already have the requisite knowledge or skill. Proximal goals, in addition to a distal goal, are often more effective than only a distal goal in generating high performance on tasks that are complex for people, especially if the task is characterized by uncertainty.

Situational Constraints and Uncertainty. Related to the moderating influence of an individual's ability on the motivational effects of goal setting, as well as tasks that are complex for an individual, are situational constraints. In the study referred to above, Lane and Karageorghis (1997) found that learning goals were more effective than outcome goals in getting people to discover ways of overcoming obstacles caused by co-workers.

Most recently, Brown, Jones, and Leigh (2005) examined the effect of role overload in an industrial selling context. They found that role overload is a boundary condition of both self-efficacy and goal level on an employee's performance. When role overload is not an issue, they found what countless other studies have shown, self-efficacy and goal level are positively related to performance. But when role overload is high, neither is related to a person's performance. In short, when people perceive that their resources are inadequate for them to do their job, in this instance lack of sales and administrative support, the normally positive effects of goal setting and self-efficacy are negated.

Uncertainty can attenuate the relationship between demands and performance when what the person knows to be true at one point in time is no longer true at later points in time due to the situation being in a state of flux. Using an assessment center simulation where high school students were paid on a piece-rate basis to make toys, as was the case in the Kanfer and Ackerman study, Latham and Seijts (1999) found that urging people to do their best led to higher performance than setting a difficult, distal outcome goal. However, setting a proximal in addition to a distal goal led to the greatest monetary earnings in an ever-changing market place. This is because proximal goals, through self-efficacy and performance feedback, focus a person's attention on task-appropriate strategies in coping effectively with uncertainty.

Based on my observations of individuals in a consortium of telephone companies in Canada, I hypothesized that a social dilemma can be a situational constraint for the normally positive effects of goal setting. Employees were torn between doing what was best for themselves versus the industry as a whole. In addition, the size of the group appeared to moderate the social dilemma. To test these hypotheses, a job simulation was used. In a money-making task, Seijts and I (Seijts & Latham, 2000a) obtained no main effect for goal setting. However, we found that high personal goals that are compatible with the group's goal enhances group performance; in contrast, a personal goal which is incompatible with the group's goal has a detrimental effect. Individuals in seven-person groups were less cooperative, had lower collective efficacy, a lower commitment to the goal, and lower group performance than those in three-person groups.

Feedback. Cellar, Degrendel, Sidle, and Lavine (1996) found that feedback in relation to a quantity goal leads to higher performance than goal setting alone. A meta-analysis (Neubert, 1998) confirmed this finding. Specific behavioral feedback in relation to goal setting has also been found to increase transfer of training effectiveness (Shoenfeld, 1996).

Vance and Colella (1990) found that negative feedback in relation to one's goal not only decreases goal commitment, it leads to a lowering of personal goals on subsequent trials. However, as noted earlier, Tabernero and Wood (1999) found that identifying substandard performance relative to goal attainment is highly effective in increasing the performance of those who have an incremental or dynamic belief about their ability; consistent with the finding of Vance and Colella, this increase did not occur for individuals who believed that their ability was a fixed entity. Undoubtedly, these various beliefs have potent effects on self-efficacy.

The assertion by control theorists that action stops when feedback indicates that the goal has been attained was shown to be incorrect by Phillips, Hollenbeck, and Ilgen (1996). Contrary to control theory, people actively created goal-performance discrepancies by setting a higher goal upon goal attainment. Seeking and striving are inherent in goal setting.

In summary, empirical evidence continues to show that feedback allows people to track progress in relation to their goal. In addition, feedback provides information regarding one's degree of enactive mastery. This in turn affects self-efficacy.

Goal Commitment. When commitment is lacking, goals have little or no effect on behavior (Wofford, Goodwin, & Premack, 1992).[30] Fortunately, commitment is usually easy to obtain in both laboratory and field settings when the goal is perceived as legitimate by the participants. This is especially true when there are strong ties between leader-members (Klein & Kim, 1998).

A meta-analysis showed that goal commitment moderates the relationship between goal difficulty and performance (Klein, Wesson, Hollenbeck, & Alge, 1999). The correlation between goal difficulty and performance is higher among individuals with high rather than low goal commitment. However, this analysis, as well as the study by Seijts and I (Seijts & Latham, 2001), also revealed that goal commitment can have a main effect on performance when all participants are trying to attain reasonably difficult goals.

Allsheid and Cellar (1996) found that commitment has a direct effect on performance. Similarly, in a field experiment involving supervisors, Morin and Latham (2000) found that goal commitment correlated positively with both self-efficacy and a supervisor's performance.

Another meta-analysis revealed that goal commitment accounted for only 3% of the variance in the goal-performance relationship (Donovan & Radosevich, 1998). This is undoubtedly due to restriction of range, because as noted, most people readily accept assigned goals. A second reason for this finding is very likely the different operationalizations of goal commitment (DeShon & Landis, 1997; Seijts & Latham, 2000b). For example, Tubbs and his colleagues (Tubbs, 1993, 1994; Tubbs & Dahl, 1992; Tubbs & Ekeberg, 1991) operationalized goal commitment as the absolute discrepancy between assigned and self-set goals. They found that such a measure consistently moderated the relationship between assigned goals and performance. To the extent, however, that ability influences the choice of one's goals and one's subsequent performance, the observed relationship between the discrepancy measure and performance is partly spurious. When ability is partialled out, Wright and his colleagues (1994), in a re-analysis of Tubb's data, showed that the correlation between the discrepancy measure and performance was reduced significantly.

Seijts, Meertens, and Kok (1997) found that within very difficult goal conditions, people who perceive the task as meaningful have higher

---

[30]Klein et al. (1999), using meta-analysis and confirmatory factor analysis, found that goal commitment is unidimensional, and that 5 of the original 9 self-report measures on Hollenbeck et al.'s (1989) self-report attitudinal scale appear to be a robust psychometrically sound measure of goal commitment.

performance than those who view it as unimportant to them. Presumably, meaningfulness is a proxy variable for goal commitment.

In summary, goal commitment is a function of the expectancy that the goal can be attained and the importance the individual attaches to its attainment (Locke & Latham, 1990a; Tubbs & Dahl, 1991; Wofford et al., 1992). Advances have been made regarding an understanding of goal commitment, specifically in documenting its interaction with goal difficulty, identifying the best items for measuring it, and showing the effect of anchoring on it (Seijts & Latham, 2000b). Goal commitment can affect performance directly when goal difficulty is held constant and is at a high level.

Performance Leads to Rewards That Affect Satisfaction

The belief that high performance should lead to high rewards is all but axiomatic in western society.[31] In a series of laboratory experiments, Mento, Locke, and Klein (1992) found that high goals are perceived as instrumental in gaining many positive outcomes including a sense of pride in accomplishment, an increase in perceived competency, as well as career and life success. Consistent with the predictions of both expectancy and social cognitive theories, a series of meta-analyses by Eby et al. (1999) found that perceived competency, which implies success, increases job satisfaction.

Anshel, Weinberg, and Jackson (1992) found that high goals lead to increases in intrinsic motivation. But, easy ones decrease it when rewards are not contingent on performance. Kernan and Lord (1991) found a positive relationship between goal-performance discrepancy and satisfaction; the higher a person's performance in relation to the goal the better. They concluded that it is the amount of the discrepancy rather than the person's absolute performance that influences satisfaction. This is because, as noted earlier, a goal is a standard for judging one's performance.

With regard to extrinsic rewards, Farh, Griffeth, and Balkin (1991) found that satisfaction is high when people are allowed choice. High ability people chose piece-rate pay; those low in ability chose fixed pay. Their subsequent goals and performance were consistent with their selection. (Of course, satisfaction is also high when people actually get rewards that they value.)

The goal-performance relationship is influenced by external rewards only when people believe that the rewards are attainable (Bandura,

---

[31]The effect of societal culture on a person's performance is addressed in Part II of this book.

1997; Lee, Locke, & Phan, 1997). High dissatisfaction occurs when rewards are perceived as unfair, as too impersonal, or as punishment. The latter can occur when high performers are consistently assigned more work than low performers (Doherty, 1998).

Further support for this aspect of the high performance cycle can be found in a field study by Summers and Hendrix (1991) of restaurant managers. They reported a positive relationship between employee perceptions of pay reward fairness and pay satisfaction; pay satisfaction is a component of overall job satisfaction.

Satisfaction Leads to Organization Commitment

Commitment, defined by Meyer and Herscovitch (2001), is a force that binds a person to a course of action that is relevant to a particular target. Hence, commitment is a powerful source of motivation, and it can lead to persistence in a course of action, even in the face of opposing forces (Meyer, Becker, & Vandenberghe, 2004). In contrast to the concept of motivation, which can have short-term implications for behavior, the binding nature of commitment has relatively long-term implications for an employee. Hence, commitment to the organization is a key variable in the high-performance cycle, because it can affect a person's willingness to remain in the organization and to continue to set and commit to high organizationally relevant goals (Meyer & Herscovitch, 2001). A meta-analysis by Cooper-Hakim and Viswesvaran (2005) revealed 185 samples where organizational commitment correlated positively with job performance.

An earlier meta-analysis found that job satisfaction and organizational commitment, though related are distinct concepts (Tett & Meyer, 1993). Satisfaction is viewed in the high-performance cycle as enhancing commitment.[32] Another meta-analysis found that the satisfaction-commitment relationship is higher in the private than in the public

---

[32]Among the leading researchers on organizational commitment is John Meyer who is at the University of Western Ontario. He believes that:

> ... satisfaction can come before affective and probably normative commitment, and could be involved in their development. I think that I would be more likely to develop an affective commitment if I was happy with my work, co-workers, supervision, etc. I might develop a normative commitment if I felt that the treatment I received was extraordinary and required reciprocation. Continuance commitment usually correlates near zero with job satisfaction so causal priority might not be an issue. However, those with a high continuance commitment might stay with a job in spite of the fact that it is not satisfying (which could

(Continued)

sector, and higher for professional than for clerical workers (Cohen & Lowenberg, 1990). In total, Cooper-Hakim and Viswesvaran (2005) found that job satisfaction was correlated in 879 samples with organizational commitment.

Mathieu and Zajac (1990), using meta-analysis, found that job satisfaction yielded significant correlations with organization commitment. This supported their earlier finding that job satisfaction has a direct influence on level of organizational commitment (Mathieu & Hamel, 1989).

Unlike the external validity of goal setting across countries (Locke & Latham, 1990a), culture may be a moderator variable of the above findings. No correlation was found between satisfaction with one's job and organizational commitment among people in the United Emirates (Alnajjar, 1996). However, a study of dairy workers in Ireland and New Zealand found that satisfaction with intrinsic and extrinsic rewards was a significant predictor of affective commitment to the organization (O'Driscoll & Randall, 1999). The necessity for future research to take a cross-cultural look at organizational commitment was stressed by Cooper-Hakim & Viswesvaran (2005).

After reviewing this literature, we (Latham et al., 2002) concluded that the high-performance cycle has withstood the test of time. Although the model would benefit from studies that use more elaborate statistical analyses, the extant empirical studies conducted during the 1990s suggest that such tests would yield significant results. Specific high goals do indeed lead to high performance. High performance on enriched tasks often leads to high rewards which in turn promote satisfaction which subsequently encourages commitment to the organization.

A limitation of the high-performance cycle is the relative emphasis on cognition and the environment or job context. Affect in the high-performance cycle is limited primarily to feelings of job satisfaction and

---

(Continued)

contribute to a negative correlation). Moreover, we recently found some evidence that satisfying conditions can be perceived as a "cost" of leaving (which could contribute to a positive correlation—see Powell & Meyer, *Journal of Vocational Behavior*, 2004). To complicate the matter even further, I think that commitment can also lead to satisfaction. For example, affectively committed employees who put in extra effort and perform at a very high level are likely to experience higher levels of task/performance satisfaction. Again, this raises the issue of what one means by job satisfaction. (J. Meyer, 2004, personal communication)

In support of Meyer's comments, Farkas and Tetrick (1989) found that job satisfaction and affective commitment have reciprocal effects.

organizational commitment. The effect on motivation of one's feelings with regard to trust in organizational decision makers, particularly with regard to feelings of fairness or justice in the workplace, is not included in this framework.

Principles of Organizational Justice

Toward the end of the 20th century, O'Reilly (1991, p. 432) found that: "The bulk of organizational behavior continues to focus on two dominant theories: goal setting and equity." The issue of equity, specifically organizational justice, was now being addressed by Jerald Greenberg, who had received his Ph.D. under the supervision of Gerald Leventhal at Wayne State University and Robert Folger who had received his Ph.D. under the direction of Adams (Greenberg & Folger, 1983). Organizational justice principles fill the void noted earlier by Mitchell (1979) in that they provide a new framework that specifically addresses fairness and trust in the workplace. Organizational justice answers the question in the title of Leventhal's (1980) article, "What Should Be Done With Equity Theory?" Greenberg's and Folger's work supplanted Adam's equity theory as a central role in promoting organizational well being.

Few things kill an individual's motivation faster than the feeling that someone else is getting a better deal. Organizational justice principles state that in addition to being fair, the people who make decisions must be perceived as fair (Greenberg, 1990a, 1993). Thus, this body of work is arguably as much about leadership as it is about employee motivation. Distributive justice focuses on: "What was distributed to whom?" "Who got what?"[33] Procedural justice is concerned with such questions as: "Are there procedures, processes, or systems in place for determining what was distributed to whom?" If not, feelings of injustice among the workforce are likely to skyrocket. If yes, are they representative of the thinking of the majority of us, or only of a select few? If they are representative, are they applied consistently or are exceptions the norm? If they are representative, and they are applied consistently, are they ethical?

Justice principles were adapted by Greenberg and Folger (1983) from the socio-legal literature on conflict resolution. These principles, and

---

[33]Recall that Adams's equity theory, which influenced Folger as well as Greenberg and Greenberg's mentor Leventhal, focuses on the motivational effects of distributive justice.

the empirical data that support them, further state that the more employees feel that the procedures are fair, the more they evaluate positively their boss and trust management, and the less inclined they are to leave their jobs (Lind & Tyler, 1988).[34]

Two key factors that affect feelings of procedural justice are a priori criteria for making decisions, and "voice." To the extent that the a priori criteria are applied consistently, suppress bias, are based on accurate information, are correctable if the information is later discovered to be inaccurate, are representative of the interest of all parties, and are ethical, people are likely to accept and understand the basis for an organizational decision even when they do not necessarily agree with it. This includes an organization's strategic plan (Kim & Mauborgne, 1993), appraisal system (Folger & Cropanzano, 1998), and drug screening policy (Konovsky & Cropanzano, 1993). Voice advances the concept of participation in decision making in that people must see that their viewpoint was taken into account before the final decision was made. To the extent that people feel that their voice is heard, they are likely to support decisions that are not congruent with their earlier viewpoint.

Two complementary explanations for these findings are as follows: First, adherence to procedural justice principals is seen by most employees as beneficial for them. It is therefore in their self-interest to support the procedure. Second, most people value procedures that promote group cohesiveness rather than creating an in-group versus an out-group (Greenberg, 2000).

Consistent with the concept of procedural justice, Bies and Moag (1986) advanced the idea that feelings of fairness are also affected by the interactions among people, particularly with the leader. Hence the term, interactional justice.[35] Two underlying premises of interactional justice are that once a decision is made by a leader, (1) the logic or rationale must be given and (2) the person who gives it must be seen as sincere (Greenberg, Bies, & Eskew, 1991). Logic and sincerity foster understanding, trust, respect, and acceptance, not necessarily agreement.

---

[34]Years earlier, McGregor (1960) had argued that fairness and trust are central issues in creating a positive "managerial climate."

[35]In this time period there was considerable debate on whether interactional justice is a unique construct apart from procedural justice, and if so, whether it is unidimensional in nature (Greenberg, 1993).

Logic involves informational justification, that is, providing people with the information that they need to understand the rationale underlying the procedures that are or will be affecting them. Sincerity involves social sensitivity, including treating people with dignity and respect.

When interactional justice is perceived to be high, people are likely to accept what they feel are undesirable outcomes. For example, employees who smoked expressed greater willingness to support the introduction of a company's smoking ban when the rationale was thoroughly explained, and when it was done so in a socially sensitive manner. Failure to do this by other leaders in the organization resulted in smokers rejecting the ban (Greenberg, 1994). Similarly, where the explanation for a temporary cut in pay was provided without a rationale, and it was given in a distant uncaring manner, employee theft was twice as high as in areas of the company where employees viewed that they had been given the logic for the pay cut with care and sensitivity (Greenberg, 1990b). In yet another organization, the better the logic people received for them being laid-off from work, and the more dignity and respect they received in the process of being let go, the less likely they were to take legal action for wrongful dismissal (Lind, Greenberg, Scott, & Welchans, 2000).

When distributive justice is either low or difficult for a person to evaluate, particularly with regard to social comparisons, procedural justice issues have a greater effect on feelings of fairness than do distributive issues. Moreover, procedural issues increase in importance when the trustworthiness of authority figures are difficult to discern (Van den Bos, Wilke, & Lind, 1998). Brockner and Wisenfeld (1996) found that adherence to procedural justice principals reduces the psychological distance between the authority figures who are distributing outcomes and the recipients of those outcomes. When the outcomes that are distributed are perceived as favorable by an individual, the importance of procedural justice principals to the person decreases.

The practical benefit from following these principles was demonstrated by Nina Cole and me (Cole & Latham, 1997). Supervisors in Canada were taught to follow procedural justice principles in taking disciplinary action. Human resource managers and labor lawyers, "blind" to both the hypotheses and the experimental conditions, observed these supervisors in role plays with actual unionized employees. Those who followed the principles were judged to be more fair than those randomly assigned to the control group. In two subsequent field experiments, Dan Skarlicki and I (Skarlicki & Latham, 1996, 1997) found that the organizational citizenship behavior of union members in Canada increased significantly when the union leaders adhered to principles of procedural justice.[36] Greenberg (1999) trained managers in principles of procedural justice in a retail store where they had been described by their employees as being disruptive, uncaring, insensitive, unconcerned with their welfare, and routinely ignoring them in the decision-making process. Compared to employees in a second store where the managers received training on an unrelated topic, and a third store which served as a control group, the employees, whose managers received training in procedural justice principles showed significant increases in job satisfaction and commitment as well as decreases in both turnover intentions and theft. The widespread applicability of principles of organizational justice to the workplace explains the attention it has received from scientist-practitioners.

Concluding Comments

In this final quarter of the 20th century, the cognitive revolution in the study of organizational behavior became firmly established. Behaviorism, which enjoyed a long reign in the other domains of psychology, was now dead. So was dust bowl empiricism. With the methodological discovery of ways to study mediators and moderators, cognitive variables were shown to predict, explain, and influence an employee's choice, effort, and persistence in organizational settings. Affect, in addition to cognition, captured the attention of many behavioral scientists in this final quarter. Feelings of trust and fairness in the workplace were now being studied within the framework of organizational justice principles. Soon this focus would encompass the study of the employee's mood and emotions.

---

[36]An in-depth history of organizational justice theory is provided by Byrne and Cropanzano (2001).

⬛ 5   20th-Century Controversies

E mpirical research and theory development did not take place in the 20th century without spirited debates about their scope, underlying assumptions, and the methods used to test them. As noted earlier, the Hawthorne experiments as well as Maslow's and Herzberg's theories were well publicized and well accepted by practitioners and the public, yet pummeled by scientists for methodological weaknesses. The scientific community in HRM, I/O, and OB abandoned behavior modification even more quickly than they had embraced it because of the philosophy, behaviorism, on which the methodology is based. In addition, four controversies dominated research and theory throughout the 20th century, namely, the importance of money as a motivator, the distinction between intrinsic and extrinsic motivators, the causal relationship between job satisfaction and job performance or the converse, and the importance of participation in decision making as a motivational technique.

Money

The job choice literature shows that pay is among the most important factors that people take into account in seeking and accepting a job offer (Barber & Bretz, 2000). But to what extent does it influence effort and persistence? In the first quarter of the 20th century, engineers concluded that money is the primary incentive for engaging in efficient and effective behavior (Taylor, 1911). In the second quarter, Viteles (1932), on the basis of countless attitude surveys showed that money is only one of many motives of the worker. The prime element "is the wish to enjoy the feeling of worth-recognition and respect on the part of others" (p. 582). This conclusion was buttressed by interpretation of the Hawthorne studies (Mayo, 1933). In the third quarter, Herzberg (1966) concluded that money can have an adverse effect on job dissatisfaction, but no effect on job satisfaction. Both equity (Adams, 1965) and expectancy theories (Lawler, 1971) explained how money affects job performance as well as job satisfaction.

Edward Lawler, as I noted earlier, has had a career-long interest in the influence of money on an employee's behavior.[1] Drawing upon both need-hierarchy and expectancy theories, Lawler (1971) presented a model that contends that pay is important to the extent that it is perceived to be instrumental in satisfying a person's needs, and to the extent that these needs are important to the person. He cited empirical evidence that this is particularly true when pay is seen by employees as instrumental for satisfying their needs for autonomy and security, and less likely for satisfying their needs for affiliation and self-actualization.

In addition, Lawler provided evidence that pay motivates employees when it is closely tied to their perceptions of their performance. Hence, he argued for employee participation in decisions regarding job evaluation because (1) the resulting decision is improved by the information contributed by job incumbents, and (2) because the job incumbents are more likely to accept decisions if they are involved in making them. A zero relationship between job satisfaction and performance or a negative one, he said, is indicative of a poorly functioning reward system. In such cases, employee motivation is usually low because rewards are not closely tied to an individual's performance. In a situation where rewards are tied to performance, a positive relationship between satisfaction and performance usually exists. In a setting where good performers are paid the same as poor performers, a negative relationship typically exists between job satisfaction and performance. In short, Lawler argued that satisfaction can be both a cause and a consequence of performance. Initially, satisfaction in a behavioral sequence is usually a dependent variable; later as performance leads, or does not lead, to monetary rewards it influences a person's motivation and performance. In short, the relationship between job satisfaction and job performance reflects a continuous ongoing process where at one point in time one

---

[1]While I was in college, I had a summer job working on the docks in Alexandria, Virginia. When ships came in and had to be unloaded, there was a great deal of work to do, and people worked a great deal of overtime. When no ships were being unloaded, there was considerable "slack." I was intrigued by how fast the work pace was when overtime was likely to be required and how slow it was at other times. A little investigation by me revealed most employees tried to manage their overtime pay. When work was slow, they worked slowly in order to be sure they got a full day's work. When there was a heavy work load, they worked hard so they wouldn't have to work "too much" overtime. They wanted to earn overtime, but didn't want to work more than 50 to 55 hours, so they would work hard to get things done. My conclusion was that pay affects behavior, but in complex ways, and that I wanted to learn more about its impact! (Lawler, 2005, personal communication)

factor is causing another, and where at a later point in time it is being caused by it. Thus, for Lawler, the issues around pay directly affect the controversy discussed in a subsequent section regarding the relationship between an employee's job satisfaction and job performance.

Edward Deci (1975), a social psychologist, claimed on the basis of his laboratory experiments, that money can kill a person's intrinsic motivation. The latter was defined as continuing to perform a task in the absence of an externally administered reward. He proposed that extrinsic rewards, especially if excessive, that are given for performing well on tasks that are intrinsically valued are perceived as "controlling" by an individual. Deci's theory of self-determination states that when this perception occurs, motivation as well as satisfaction decreases. He argued that people have the need to feel that their actions are chosen freely. Receiving a monetary reward for doing what one would have done anyway, because of its intrinsic appeal, causes one to make an attributional shift regarding the cause of one's behavior from self to others.[2]

Locke and I (Locke & Latham, 1984, 1990a) argued that money has no effect on behavior unless it leads to the setting of and commitment to specific high goals. Bandura (1989) stated that a focus on monetary incentives neglects the affective self-evaluative rewards of goal attainment. Forethought regarding outcomes influences a person's effort and performance. For example, the prevalent forethought of employees expressed in attitude surveys in the 1930s was fear of job loss. Forethought regarding this outcome explains the restriction of output and hostile attitudes of people toward management, described by Viteles, that occurred despite the widespread use of monetary incentives.

The high-performance cycle (Latham, Locke, & Fassina, 2002; Locke & Latham, 1990a) states that performance contingent rewards increase a person's performance only if they increase satisfaction with the job, commitment to the organization, and the acceptance of future challenges. A meta-analysis of studies designed to test Deci's conclusion

---

[2]Deci was influenced by the philosopher Jean-Jacques Rousseau who argued that the freedom to pursue momentary whims and freedom from social control fosters human creativity. Harry Harlow, an experimental psychologist, and a past president of the American Psychological Association, instigated research in this area with his discovery that monkeys repeatedly solve puzzles presented to them without being rewarded with food for doing so. Thus intrinsic motivation is said to be taking place when an activity is engaged in for its own sake; extrinsic motivated behavior is said to be occurring when it is followed by a reward (e.g., money, verbal praise). Interestingly, Maslow too was affected by Harlow's work in this area when he was pursing his doctoral studies at the University of Wisconsin where Harlow was a faculty member.

shows that extrinsic rewards are not inherently de-motivating for people (Eisenberger & Cameron, 1996).[3] This study is described in the next section.

Intrinsic vs. Extrinsic Motivation

This controversy parallels the controversy over the effects of money on performance. Empirical research conducted by the University of Michigan's Survey Research Center (1948, p. 10) led to the conclusion that: "The use of external sanctions, of pressuring for production, may work to some degree, but not to the extent that more internalized motives do." No one subsequently promulgated this belief more than Deci. Similar to his claim regarding the negative effect of money on behavior, Deci (1975) stated that people judge their motivation on the basis of the circumstances in which they behave. If they perform activities for external rewards, such as money, they infer a lack of personal interest whereas if they perform without external inducement, they judge themselves to be in control and hence intrinsically motivated. Deci then came to the provocative conclusion that extrinsic incentives reduce intrinsic motivation because they create the impression for people that their behavior is externally precipitated. This in turn weakens their feelings of competence and self-determination. This inference was drawn by comparing the amount of time a person spends on a task after the experiment had allegedly ended ("free time") and no reward was being given versus the amount of time spent on the task prior to the administration of the reward.

Bandura (1977b) argued that the deficiencies of this reasoning are at least fourfold. First, intrinsic motivation is an elusive concept. It is usually defined as performance of activities for no apparent external reward. Identifying the existence of intrinsic motivation on the basis of persistence of behavior in the absence of noticeable extrinsic incentives is no easy task. It is all but impossible, he said, to find situations that completely lack external inducements (e.g., situational, physical, and social

---

[3]Deci's typical dependent variable was time spent on a laboratory task after money to persist was terminated. He did not examine the external validity of his findings in the workplace. Schneider (2004, personal communication) commented that Deci might be tapping affect for the task. Goals were not set in Deci's studies. Goal attainment, we know, typically leads to positive affect. Money tied to goal setting, when done properly, can lead to dramatic increases in productivity (Latham & Wexley, 1994; Locke, 2005; Locke, Feren, McCaleb, Shaw, & Denny, 1980).

structures, the materials they contain, expectations of others). The activation of behavior is the result of a continuous interaction between personal and situational sources of influence. Second, Bandura pointed out that the methodology used in the experiments that led to Deci's conclusion is flawed. The abrupt withdrawal of a monetary reward is not a neutral event. Not rewarding behavior after it has been rewarded consistently functions as a punisher that reduces performance. Moreover, satiation and tedium affect one's level of activity. When incentives are used to get people to repeatedly perform the same behavior, they eventually tire of it. Finally, Bandura attacked Deci's logic. Decreases in performance often reflect reactions to how incentives are presented rather than to the incentives themselves. Incentives can be used coercively (e.g., "you will not get any money until you do x"), as an expression of appreciation (e.g., "this is in recognition of your doing y"), or to convey evaluative reactions (e.g., "this is what this performance is worth to us"). In short, the same incentive can have differential effects on an individual's behavior depending on the message conveyed. As Bandura noted, it is unlikely that concert pianists lose interest in the keyboard just because they are offered high recital fees.

Locke and I (Locke & Latham, 1990a) have also criticized Deci's conceptualization of intrinsic motivation as well as the inferences he has drawn regarding the negative effects of monetary rewards. First, we noted that in studies where behavior is the dependent variable, Deci typically fails to measure the mediating variables he has asserted to be responsible for its effects, namely feelings of competence and self-determination. Second, Deci has not distinguished between liking an activity for its own sake and liking it because it makes one feel competent. Third, intrinsic motivation, defined by Deci as time spent on a task during a free period is not very relevant to the workplace. Work life tends to almost always include assigned deadlines, imposed standards, and pay. Finally, it seems unlikely that the need for self-determination and competence can be wellsprings of human motivation, and at the same time be so fragile that their effects are negated by the most common of life's exigencies.

Eisenberger and Cameron (1996) attacked Deci's theory for failing to specify the mechanism which explains why dissatisfaction associated with a perceived decline in self-determination lessens a person's intrinsic intentions in performing a task, as opposed to anger at the individual who is no longer providing the anticipated reward. Based on a meta-analysis by Cameron and Pierce (1994) of studies conducted between 1971 and 1991, plus their own review of subsequent research, they reached the following conclusions which are dramatically different from Deci's:

1. If a person is rewarded for completing a task, or attaining a goal for quality, and if that reward is abruptly stopped, the person still spends as much time on the activity as was spent prior to the reward being introduced in the experiment (i.e., baseline performance).

2. When the reward is verbal praise, people spend more time on a task, despite the cessation of the praise, than they did prior to the introduction of praise in the experiments.

3. Moreover, people reported that they like the task more after receiving praise or money.

4. Reward for high creativity in one task enhances creativity in an entirely different task.

5. The only reliable effect of a reward having a detrimental effect on a person's performance during "free-time" occurred when an anticipated reward was presented on a single occasion without regard to quality of performance or task completion.

Nevertheless, beginning with Dyer and Parker (1975), the conclusion that the distinction between intrinsic and extrinsic motivation is meaningful continues to be debated (Cameron & Pierce, 1994; Ford, 1992). For example, my co-author on the 2005 chapter in the *Annual Review of Psychology* on motivation, Craig Pinder, disagrees with me on the relevance of Deci's work:

> The central tenets of the Deci and Ryan tradition are about competence and self-determination. The issue of competence (regardless of what it is called) figures into so many other theories (VIE, goal setting, self cognitive, etc.), that it is clearly significant. What Deci and Ryan add is the self-determination angle, which I think is a major Western value underlying our norms for freedom and self-determination at both the individual and national levels. Self-determination is a critical thread in the fabric of our society. It counters determinism in favor of free will.
>
> In addition, I have no doubt about the value of the concept of intrinsic motivation, both in our field as well as in related fields (e.g., education, health, mental health, developmental psychology, and others). I think that many people are hung up on the old battles centered on Deci's early work (which I always thought wasn't that bad for pioneering work) and have not paid sufficient attention to the newer work that has evolved far beyond the 1972 and 1976 experiments. (Pinder, 2005, personal communication)[4]

Performance and Satisfaction

In the first quarter, Thorndike (1917) found that speed and quality of work remained the same despite a decrease in work satisfaction. By the second quarter, the measurement of attitudes toward work was believed to be the pathway to discovering the motives of the worker. The attitude most frequently measured was job satisfaction (Pinder, 1998). Viteles (1932) equated work motivation with employee performance and morale. Thus a primary variable of interest to HRM, I/O, and OB researchers was employee morale or satisfaction. The highly productive employee is one who has positive attitudes toward the job.

In the third quarter, Brayfield and Crockett (1955) challenged that belief by showing that there was little or no relationship between these two variables. A decade later Vroom (1964) showed that the median correlation between a person's satisfaction and performance was only 0.14. Near the end of the decade, Lawler and Porter (1967) argued on the basis of expectancy theory that it is performance that leads to satisfaction rather than the reverse. People enjoy that which they do well.

---

[4]Choosing the "right" colleagues in our field to co-author a paper invariably leads to a motivating experience; choosing the wrong person can be de-motivating for everyone concerned. I have used one or more of the following principles to good advantage: (1) I choose someone who can complement my skill set. (2) I choose an individual whose opinion I hold in high regard, but who has a slightly different point of view. Differences in viewpoints can contribute substantially to both the over-all quality of a study and the subsequent write-up of it. The issue of mutual respect is important because differences in opinion can lead to friction. Locke and I as well as Yukl and I have argued vehemently over the choice of an appropriate word—a single word. (3) I choose a person who I find enjoyable, a person with whom I find it easy to laugh. Science is unarguably a serious endeavor; that in no way implies that it cannot be fun. For example, Craig Pinder and I laughed repeatedly during our two visits with one another to integrate and polish our respective contributions to the 2005 *Annual Review of Psychology* chapter on motivation. Laughter, along with respect, seems to induce an environment where my co-authors and I are comfortable giving and receiving constructively critical comments. (4) I get agreement prior to doing the study or writing a paper on the order of authorship. I get consensus as to who will do what as a result of the order of authorship (e.g., I will write the introduction and method section, you do the results, let's write the discussion together; you do the first draft and I will polish a final one and run it by you). A rule of thumb that I find useful is that you should be first author if the original idea is yours, and you have asked me to join you in testing your idea.

In many instances I choose my research assistants to collaborate with me on a paper. How can I do otherwise when we faculty emphasize the importance of them making presentations at scholarly societies and publishing in top tier journals prior to receiving the Ph.D.? Generally I discourage them from attempting to do so alone, or to attempt to do so with a fellow doctoral student. There is an art to getting research published that most graduate students have yet to master. There is an art to responding to a journal reviewer who is less than competent, especially in delivering a well-placed punch to the nose that in turn makes a journal editor smile, as well as accept the paper for publication.

In the final quarter of the century, Bandura (1989) argued on the basis of social cognitive theory that when people master valued levels of performance, they experience a sense of satisfaction. Locke and I (Locke & Latham, 1990a), on the basis of goal-setting theory, stated that satisfaction is the result of the attainment of valued goals. This is because, as noted earlier, a goal is not only a specific standard of proficiency to be attained within a given time frame, it is a standard by which to evaluate the adequacy of one's performance. Similarly, Bandura (1997), as well as his former doctoral student Cervone, along with co-authors Jiwani and Wood (1991), found that self-satisfaction from the attainment of valued goals often leads people to set even higher goals for themselves rather than lapse into a state of contentment. The result is enhanced rather than diminished performance. Self-satisfaction that is conditional on one's future level of performance, however, is even more predictive of performance motivation than is satisfaction with one's past performance (Bandura & Cervone, 1983).

A meta-analysis by Judge et al. (2001) revealed a mean average corrected correlation of .30 between performance and job satisfaction. They did not attempt to validate causal direction. They found, however, that the relationship is stronger than that reported in previous reviews when the criterion is overall performance, rather than a measure of an individual's productivity, with the former including organizational citizenship behavior. The moderator is job complexity; the correlation is stronger in enriched than in simplified jobs. Goal attainment that is not accompanied by an increase in perceived growth/competence can contribute to dissatisfaction (Latham & Yukl, 1976; Parker, 2003). This explains the findings of both Brayfield and Crockett as well as Vroom. Unenriched simplified jobs dominated the literature that they had reviewed. Organ (1977, 1990) found that job satisfaction does lead to organizational citizenship behaviors (e.g., helping co-workers, helping customers, doing the "little" things for the organization).

Schneider (1985) argued the proposed causal relationship between satisfaction and performance is, in actuality, a hypothesis at the group or organizational level of analysis. That is, when morale is high the productivity of the organization is also high. Indeed, Ostroff (1992) found that satisfaction aggregated to the organizational (school) level of analysis correlated significantly with a school's performance.[5] The

---

[5]Recall the distinction noted by Guion and Stagner in the 1950s between satisfaction and morale. It is likely that Argyris and McGregor, who focused on organizational effectiveness, would agree with Ostroff's finding.

organizational effectiveness measures reflected the cumulative responses and interactions among employees. In short, individual level attitudes and behaviors become shared and produce an emergent collective structure of attitudes, norms, and behaviors that affect organizational outcomes.

My viewpoint on this issue, from the standpoint of a practitioner, is as follows: If the primary concern of an organization is to find ways to increase an employee's satisfaction with the job, one obviously has to start somewhere. For me, the beginning point is usually job performance. Find ways to increase the person's performance, and then set specific high goals. The benefits for doing so are described above by Bandura, Locke, and me. Self-satisfaction accrues from the attainment of valued goals. This leads to reciprocal determinism where, as Lawler (1971) has stated, a person's performance is a causal variable at one point in time and a dependent variable affected by job satisfaction at a later point in time. This is shown graphically in Figure 4.1 depicting the high-performance cycle.

A literature search that Locke and I did (Locke & Latham, 1990a) revealed that the relationship between successful performance and subsequent task performance is an extremely reliable one. The mean weighted correlation is .51. A person's success was typically defined in the literature as either the number of successes or as the degree of discrepancy between the goal and performance. The literature review also indicated that when people perform well, they not only feel satisfied, they generalize their positive affect to the task.

A limitation or boundary condition to my approach of focusing initially on performance is that a person's performance may already be high, and/or the goal or goals that have been set may not be valued by the person. The high-performance cycle is an excellent diagnostic tool for me in these situations. It provides a checklist for ascertaining where the problem lies. For example, among the questions I ask are: (1) What goal or goals does the person value? (2) Does the person have high or low self-efficacy to attain them? (3) Are the tasks "growth facilitating"? (4) Is lack of ability a problem for attaining valued goals? (5) Is the person receiving timely performance feedback? (6) Are there situational constraints? (7) Are the strategies necessary for performing effectively known? (8) Does the person see that rewards are contingent upon performing well? (9) Is the person satisfied as a result of receiving these rewards? (10) Consequently, is the person willing to accept new challenges, new goals?

Participative Decision Making

As noted earlier, the war with repressive Fascist regimes in Europe led to the Lewin, Lippitt, and White (1939) studies on autocratic, democratic, and laissez-faire studies of leadership styles and motivation. Participation was considered to be an inherent attribute of democracy and thus an antidote to fascism. Coch and French (1948), former students of Lewin, maintained that participation in decision making overcomes resistance to change in the workplace. Sashkin (1984) went so far as to argue that employee participation in the decision-making process is a moral imperative. Nevertheless, more than 30 years ago, Campbell, Dunnette, Lawler, and Weick (1970, p. 422) stated: "Surely the same prescription cannot be made for all subordinates, all managers, all tasks, and all conditions." Vroom's (1959, 1960) research suggested that the answer is no. His correlational studies involving employees in a package delivery firm showed that people who scored low on measures of authoritarianism and high on need for independence tended to be highly productive under participatory leaders. But, the opposite correlations were obtained for employees who scored high on a measure of authoritarianism and low on need for independence. High productivity on the part of those employees correlated positively with a highly directive style of supervision.

The thrill, the excitement of programmatic research is akin to being a detective or an investigative reporter in searching for the correct answer. The finding from practice (Ronan, Latham, & Kinne, 1973) of the necessity for a supportive supervisor when goals are assigned corroborated two of three propositions of Likert's (1967) systems 4 theory of leadership, namely, the principles of supportive relationships and goal setting.[6] The third, participation in decision making was not investigated in that study. In response to a question from Weyerhaeuser Company's senior management as to whether the positive benefits of goal setting could be improved upon, participative decision making in goal setting was included to assess its effect on the company's logging crews. Science informed practice. Productivity was highest in the crews that were randomly assigned to the participative goal condition (Latham & Yukl,

---

[6]Likert's (1967) research showed that a leader's style could be classified as exploitive authoritative (systems 1), benevolent authoritative (systems 2), consultative (systems 3), or participative group decision making (systems 4).

1975). Noted only parenthetically in our journal article was the fact that goal difficulty was significantly higher in the participative than in the assigned goal condition. However, a subsequent study with the company's word processors revealed that lines typed per hour were the same regardless of whether the goal was assigned or set participatively. Again, it was noted parenthetically in the journal article that there was no significant difference in goal difficulty between goal conditions (Latham & Yukl, 1976). Practice was about to inform science.

An advantage of practice, especially when the practitioner is a colleague of the people who are the beneficiaries of an intervention, is the ability to make first-hand observations of behavior in a natural environment. I saw that the word processing supervisors in the assigned goal condition lowered the goal when an employee had difficulty attaining it, and raised the goal when no such difficulty was experienced. Through enactive mastery, the supervisors in all likelihood were increasing the employee's self-efficacy regarding productivity. Enactive mastery and self-efficacy were two concepts which were unknown at the time.[7] The difficulty level of the goal in the participative condition remained constant throughout the 10-week study period.

In a symposium at the American Psychological Association, Porter (1976) suggested that the positive effect of goal setting on performance might be limited to relatively low level jobs. The following year allowed a test of this assumption. Weyerhaeuser's senior management team decided to lay off a significant number of engineers/scientists in R&D. To prevent this occurrence, the R&D senior vice president persuaded the president of the company that within a year, scientists/engineers would be motivated to attain a level of excellence that would eliminate the desire of management to seek cutbacks in R&D as a way of reducing costs.

Step 1 required a job analysis to define excellence. The result was the development of behavioral observation scales or BOS (Latham & Mitchell, 1976; Latham & Wexley, 1977, 1994). Step 2 involved a 3 (assigned goal, participative goal, do best) × 3 (praise, public recognition, and monetary bonus) factorial design plus an additional 10th cell. The 10th condition was a control group consisting of people in R&D who were unaware that they were involved in this project. All the people

---

[7]Bandura's theory was not published until the subsequent year.

in the other 9 conditions were not only aware that they were participating in this project, they were aware of who was in each cell.

The results of this six-month field experiment showed that the scientists and engineers in the "do your best" condition performed no better than those in the 10th cell, namely, the control group. This occurred despite the fact that they received feedback and either praise, public recognition or a monetary bonus, and despite the fact that they knew that the participants in 6 of the 9 cells were setting specific high goals to attain for their performance appraisal (Latham, Mitchell, & Dossett, 1978). This finding is consistent with goal-setting theory which states that these variables have no effect on performance unless they lead to the setting of and commitment to a specific high goal. Participative goals led to the highest performance, yet goal commitment was the same across all 6 goal-setting conditions. Goal difficulty, however, was higher in the participative than in the assigned condition. That is, the participatively set goals were significantly higher than those that were assigned by a supervisor unilaterally. Practice informed science. It appeared that it was not the method by which the goal was set that influences performance, but rather the difficulty level of the goal. The benefit of goals that were set participatively was not an increase in goal commitment but rather an increase in goal difficulty. Goal-setting theory states that the higher the goal, the higher the performance. Science had informed practice.

Weyerhaeuser's word processing supervisors requested assistance in the selection of employees and the appraisal of their operators. The results of one study showed that there were no significant differences between the assigned and participative goal conditions on the operators' performance or goal commitment. The second study showed that performance and goal commitment was higher in the assigned than in the participative goal condition (Dossett, Latham, & Mitchell, 1979). As a result of these contradictory findings, it was time to go into the laboratory.[8]

---

[8]A controversy that took place in the latter half of the 20th century was whether field experiments are inherently better than laboratory experiments. There was seemingly blind condemnation of the applicability of laboratory findings to problems in the workplace (Brief & Schneider, 1986). A firestorm occurred when a laboratory experiment by Lise Saari and me was accepted by the reviewers, one of whom was Ed Locke, and rejected by an Associate Editor of the *Journal of Applied Psychology*, Frank Landy. In the annual journal editorial board meeting held at SIOP, the editor, Bob Guion supported Frank's decision which Ed had vocally attacked. As a member of the

(Continued)

Numerous theories in organization psychology (e.g., Argyris, 1964; Likert, 1967) emphasize the importance of participation in decision making for ensuring employee commitment. Goal-setting theory, however, does not specify which method for setting a goal is preferable. It simply states that given goal commitment, the higher the goal the higher the performance. Consequently, students were randomly assigned to one of three groups. All participants in all three groups were informed that the Weyerhaeuser Company was in need of ideas to increase log exports to Asia. The goal for number of ideas agreed to by a participant in the participative condition was given to a participant in the assigned goal condition. The participants who were in the third condition were urged to do their best to generate as many ideas as possible because the economy in the American Northwest at that time depended in large part on the profitability of companies such as Weyerhaeuser.

The results of the study informed both science and practice. With goal difficulty held constant, goal commitment and performance were the same regardless of whether the goal was assigned or set participatively. Both goal-setting conditions led to significantly higher performance than urging people to do their best (Latham & Saari, 1979b). These results were replicated in a second study (Latham & Marshall, 1982) involving brainstorming as part of a job analysis in a Canadian government agency regarding effective supervisory behaviors. With goal difficulty held constant, there was no significant difference among the two goal-setting conditions regarding goal commitment or actual performance. Both methods of goal setting led to a greater number of ideas than urging employees to do their best. This was true regardless of the employee's age, education, position level, years as a supervisor, or length of time employed in the government.

Performance appraisals are conducted once a year within approximately the same time period at Weyerhaeuser. In this next study, students were informed that the company needed people to check the arithmetic on

(Continued)

editorial board, I listened quietly. Not being able to change the editorial decision, Ed organized a symposium for the 1984 Academy of Management. This was followed by an edited book (Locke, 1986) which provided "an empirical sword to slay the dragon of negativism about laboratory research . . . , the message is clear: the data do not support the belief that lab studies produce different results than field studies. Perhaps college students really are people. After all, probably the vast majority of them work, or have worked at a job. Why their disguise fools many observers into thinking otherwise is not clear" (J. Campbell, 1986, p. 276). Note that Locke's actions were consistent with Michael Frese's work on personal initiative to be discussed later. Frese contends that negative emotion often leads to constructive behavior in making a change for the better.

each appraisal instrument (BOS) as the accuracy of the total score was obviously of extreme importance to an employee. The experimental design that had been used in the two preceding studies was used in the present experiment with the exception that a fourth condition was included. In this fourth condition, there was an assigned goal that was set significantly higher than the participatively set goal.

As was the case in the preceding studies, the performance of those with participatively set and yoked assigned goals resulted in the same high level of performance. Both goal-setting conditions led to significantly higher performance than the do best condition. But, the highest performance was in that fourth condition where the assigned goal was higher than in the two yoked goal conditions (Latham, Steele, & Saari, 1982). Science (Latham & Saari, 1979b; Latham, Steele, & Saari, 1982) was indeed informing practice which in turn (Latham & Marshall, 1982) was informing science. Participation in decision making is not a variable of importance for motivation; the variable of importance is the difficulty level of the goal.

By this time proponents of participation were beginning to take notice of these contradictory findings to mainstream theories in organizational behavior. Tolchinsky and King (1980) criticized the above goal setting studies for confounding goal setting and participative decision making.[9] Consequently, a 3×2 factorial design was used to compare participatorily set goals, yoked assigned goals, and "do your best" vs. participative decision making and individual decision making in the assembling of toys. This task is one that is often used in assessment centers (Bray & Grant, 1966) for selecting and developing managers. A main effect was obtained for goal setting only. Performance was the same regardless of whether decision making was done participatively (Latham & Steele, 1983).

The controversy regarding the effect of assigned versus participatively set goals seemed to be settled. Participation is a motivational benefit only if it leads to the setting of a higher goal than one that is assigned. Later that same year, however, the first of a series of four studies by Miriam Erez and her colleagues appeared in the literature (Earley &

---

[9]Confounding means that two independent variables, in this instance goal setting and participation, are manipulated together within the same experimental condition. If the dependent variable changes, we are unable to discern whether the change is due to goal setting, to participation in setting the goal, both (that is additive effects) or due to the combination of the two independent variables (an interaction effect).

Kanfer, 1985; Erez, 1986; Erez, Earley, & Hulin, 1985; Erez & Kanfer, 1983). The results of these studies can be summarized in one sentence: Latham is wrong. This type of conclusion can be rather disconcerting regardless of where one fits on the scientist-practitioner continuum.

Fortunately for me, there were at least 10 studies that had replicated my findings (Chacko, Stone, & Brief, 1979; Chang & Lorenzi, 1983; Dossett, Cella, Greenberg, & Adrian, 1983; Ivancevich, 1976, 1977; Leifer & McGannon, 1986; Shalley, Oldham, & Porac, 1987; Vanderslice, Rice, & Julian, 1987; Wexley & Baldwin, 1986). The 10th study eliminated the rival hypothesis that the results reflected experimenter bias on my part: "Results from the study concerning assigned vs. participative goal setting were contrary to our initial expectations as well as preference for more participative approaches . . . " (Kernan & Lord, 1988, p. 84).

When highly competent researchers obtain contradictory findings, chances are that both research camps may be correct (Campbell & Stanley, 1972). The explanation may be in a boundary condition or moderator variable. The discovery of such a variable in this case is as important to practice as it is to science.

Locke is a close friend of both Erez and me. Consequently, Locke was chosen by us to be the mediator. The result was a study that won an award from the Academy of Management (Latham, Erez, & Locke, 1988) as it was the first published paper in HRM, I/O, and OB based on the collaboration of two antagonists who worked with a neutral party to resolve their differences (see also Campbell, 1992; Erez, 1992; Latham, 1992; Locke, 1992).[10]

The first step involved Locke conducting an interview of Erez and me over dinner on hypothesized reasons for our contradictory findings:

1. Task importance: In my laboratory experiments/simulations, the task was always stressed to the participants as important to Weyerhaeuser. The importance of the task was not stressed by Erez to the participants in her studies.

2. Group discussion: Erez's participative condition almost always involved groups discussing and then setting the goal. With the exception of logging crews, the participative conditions in the studies I conducted involved dyads.

3. Self-set goals: Erez had people set their own goal. She then "forced" them to abandon the goal in favor of one that was assigned or set participatively. This process might have irritated the participants in the assigned goal condition.

---

[10]This study has been cited by the Nobel Prize winner, psychologist Daniel Kahneman (2003), as an ideal way of resolving contradictory scientific findings.

4. Self-efficacy: I always stressed the likelihood the goal can be attained and the positive effects that one can expect as a result of goal setting (e.g., "previous work has shown that goal setting increases . . ."). This was not done by Erez.

5. Value differences: Erez suggested that Israelis may be more collectivistic than North Americans. However, this did not explain the results she obtained in her research conducted while on sabbatical at the University of Illinois.

The second step involved empirical research. Two of the four studies that were conducted (Latham, Erez, & Locke, 1988) failed to find support for any of the five hypotheses. Locke "interrogated" Erez's former research assistant, Christopher Earley. As a result of Earley's comments, the third and fourth experiment yielded the answer to the puzzle (see Cummings & Earley, 1992). To everyone's surprise, the explanation was not a result of differences in the way in which the goals were set participatively in the Erez versus my studies. The explanation was the difference in the way the goals were assigned. Erez, Locke, and I found that when the assigned goal is given with a logic or rationale, it is as effective as one that is set participatively. When the goal is assigned tersely (e.g., "Do this . . .") or when participants are told that they don't have to try to attain it, as was done in the Erez studies, an assigned goal is indeed inferior to one that is set participatively.

As a doctoral student, I became a strong admirer of Rensis Likert's work with regard to participation in decision making. Thus I believed that Erez was correct in her assertion that participation in decision making in goal setting is preferable to a goal that is assigned. But, as was the case with Kernan and Lord (1988), my data for the most part never supported my belief. There was, however, an exception to this statement.

On a Sunday morning in 1977 I received a telephone call from Rensis Likert.[11] He suggested that the reason why no differences were found between goal-setting conditions in my experiments is that the supervisor/experimenter behaved in a supportive manner regardless of

---

[11]Rensis Likert telephoned to invite me for breakfast along with his wife Jane at the forthcoming Academy of Management meeting. Truly honored, I readily accepted. During that breakfast, he said that if he were to revise his theory he would do so by emphasizing the importance of supportive relationships, followed by goal setting and participation in decision making in that order, rather than the reverse.

At the end of World War II, Ren was among the founders of the Institute for Social Research at the University of Michigan. There he did groundbreaking work in showing the interrelationship among leadership, motivation, and organization design on employee performance. He used attitude surveys as an effective feedback tool for setting goals and involving people in the decision-making process on ways to improve an organization's effectiveness.

whether the goal was assigned or set participatively. Consequently, my research assistant, Lise Saari, and I conducted a laboratory experiment (Latham & Saari, 1979c) that supported the findings from the factor analysis of the survey of pulpwood producers (Ronan, Latham, & Kinne, 1973). We found that supportive behavior resulted in higher goals being set than nonsupportive behavior. In further support of Likert's systems 4 theory, we found that participatively set goals led to better performance than assigned goals even when goal difficulty was held constant, and even though there was no significant difference between conditions in goal commitment. But, because this laboratory experiment was the only one of four experiments (Latham & Marshall, 1982; Latham & Saari, 1979c; Latham & Steele, 1983; Latham, Steele, & Saari, 1982) that obtained this finding, I had forgotten it. Worse, I had forgotten the final conclusion of that experiment, namely, that participation can increase understanding of what is required to perform the task. The people in the participative condition asked far more questions than did those in the assigned goal condition.

Serendipity struck. I periodically re-read Campbell, Dunnette, Lawler, and Weick (1970), my "academic bible." In re-reading it, it occurred to me that Erez might be right for the wrong reason. The benefit of participation might be primarily cognitive rather than motivational. In the literally hundreds of goal-setting studies conducted in the past 50 years, the vast majority of tasks required primarily choice, effort, or persistence to perform them. This is because goal setting is viewed primarily as a motivational technique (Locke & Latham, 1984); hence the task researchers selected was almost always one that did not necessitate the acquisition of knowledge or skill.

Quality circles at Weyerhaeuser are used to generate ways for employees "to work smarter rather than harder." Inherent in quality circles is goal setting regarding the generation of concrete ways for continuous improvement. Both the literature (science) and practice (quality circles) led to a hypothesis, namely, that the benefit of participative decision making is primarily cognitive. Consequently, Winters, Locke, and I (Latham, Winters, & Locke, 1994) randomly assigned individuals to an assigned or a participative goal condition in which people worked in a group (participation condition) or alone. No main effect was obtained for goal setting as the two conditions were yoked. But, there was a main effect for decision making with performance significantly higher in the participative than in the individual decision-making condition on a task that was highly complex, a task requiring the scheduling of course offerings for a university. This main effect of participative decision making on performance, however, was completely mediated by self-efficacy and task strategy. The people who participated in decision making were able to make higher quality decisions than those who worked alone. This increase in knowledge enabled better task strategies as well as higher self-efficacy.

A meta-analysis by Wagner (1994) corroborated the findings of the above experiments. The effect of participative decision making alone on a person's performance has statistical yet lacks practical significance. Locke, Alavi, and Wagner (1997), in their review of the literature, corroborated Wagner's conclusion. The primary benefit of participation in decision making is cognitive rather than motivational. It is effective when it stimulates information exchange among knowledgeable people, and increases their confidence that they can do so productively.

The practical significance of the discovery of these two mediators, self-efficacy and task strategy, should not be lost on anyone who has attended a university faculty meeting. The participation of the faculty is seldom an issue. Virtually everyone talks in these meetings; virtually no one listens. Since little is heard, even less subsequently gets done. It is only to the extent that participation in decision making increases self-efficacy and the discovery of the appropriate task strategy(s) that much is accomplished.

The above finding may run counter to the prevailing ideology of some behavioral scientists. The issue of participation in decision making, however, should be viewed as a pragmatic rather than a moral one. Contrary to the assertion that letting people have a say or choice generates feelings of control or commitment, and thereby better performance, it would appear that assigning a goal accompanied by a rationale is in itself an indirect means of increasing a person's self-efficacy. This is especially true when the goal is high, because it implies the person is capable of attaining it (Salancik, 1977). Choice in itself, choice in the absence of self-efficacy will not lead to high performance.

Seismic Events: Summary and Overview of the 20th Century

From a Scientist's Viewpoint

The seismic events that influenced research on and theories of employee motivation in the 20th century are at least tenfold (Latham & Budworth, 2006). The first two occurred as a result of research in experimental psychology and the methodology of engineers rather than the discoveries of HRM, I/O, and OB researchers. Thorndike's law of effect, in the words of Vroom (1964), is among the most substantiated findings of experimental psychology and is at the same time among the most useful findings for applied psychology concerned with influencing human behavior. Time and motion studies by engineers resulted in the routinization and simplification of tasks. Monetary incentives were tied to task completion, and performance increased significantly. The implicit theory in the first quarter of that century was that money is the primary, if not the sole, motive of the worker.

I/O psychology's contribution to knowledge of motivation in the workplace occurred in the second quarter. "Restriction of output" by workers had become widespread despite the fact that bonuses were paid contingent upon performance. Attitudes toward management were hostile as people during the Great Depression feared losing their jobs. The third seismic event was Rensis Likert's publication of findings from his doctoral dissertation regarding the measurement of attitudes. His methodology demonstrates the ease with which employee attitudes can be surveyed. On the basis of countless employee surveys, Viteles was able to argue forcefully that money is only one of many motives that influence an individual's choice, effort, and persistence to perform well. His argument was supported by a fourth seismic event, the Hawthorne studies. These studies were interpreted as supporting the conclusion that low employee morale and negative attitudes toward one's job were the result of routinizing work through time and motion studies. In addition, they suggested the interrelationships among motivation, satisfaction, and performance as well as the myriad ways that they can be increased.

Research in the second quarter of the 20th century was largely atheoretical. The implicit theory was that the pathway to discovery of the worker's motivation was through the identification of attitudes toward work; the satisfied worker is a productive worker. Attitude surveys coupled with the Hawthorne studies led to the controversial conclusion that job satisfaction is the primary cause of job performance.

The end of the second quarter and the beginning of the third witnessed the formal development and use of theory to guide research on employee motivation. The fifth seismic event that influenced understanding of motivation was Maslow's need hierarchy theory. Not only was it the bedrock for (a) McGregor's Theory Y, it was the basis for the (b) first series of empirical studies on employee motivation by an I/O psychologist based on theory, namely the early research by Porter, and, in addition, (c) it spawned subsequent theory, Alderfer's ERG. Finally, (d) it focused the attention of researchers such as Herzberg on the job itself as an enabler or frustrator of the attainment of a person's higher order growth needs.

Maslow believed that the source of motivation was within the individual, namely, needs. Needs give rise to goal directed behavior that satisfy a need. Once gratification is achieved, the need does not disappear as a factor in behavior, it simply accounts for less of the force working on the person, as the satisfaction of other needs become salient. Failure to satisfy a need increases the importance of satisfying a lower need. Although a critic of Maslow's emphasis on a hierarchy of needs, Locke (1991) has argued that needs are indeed the basic set of factors underlying human behavior.

Nord et al. (1988) observed that a theory often reflects the sociopolitical environment in which it is formulated. Because workers for the most part were uneducated in the first quarter of the 20th century, the focus of engineers was on work simplification. A largely illiterate workforce was no longer the case subsequent to World War II. Upon returning home, former soldiers, particularly those in Canada, the United Kingdom, and the United States enrolled in universities in record numbers.

Following World War II, Herzberg, influenced by Maslow, believed that people have two basic sets of needs, and that characteristics of the job affect the attainment of these needs. The first set of needs are those concerned with survival; the second are the employee's growth needs. Thus, the sixth seismic event was the conclusion that rather than simplifying jobs, jobs should be enriched. To form job attitudes that motivate employees, Herzberg argued that motivators must be built into jobs that facilitate the attainment of their growth needs. This latter conclusion is a seismic event because it shifted the attention of HRM, I/O, and OB researchers to the importance of job design. It is a practical theory (Brief & Dukerich, 1997) in that it stimulated practitioners to view the world of work and to take courses of action in ways they might not have done otherwise.

The development of theory in the latter half of the 20th century was an ongoing progressive process. In the third quarter the emphasis shifted away from needs that people may or may not be aware of that influence their choice, effort, and persistence. Emphasis instead was on cognitive/perceptual theories. The seventh seismic event was Vroom's expectancy theory that viewed the employee as an information processor. Vroom argued that it is not only the presence or absence of characteristics of the job that are important to motivation in the workplace, it is the employee's perception of those characteristics that cause him or her to form beliefs and attitudes about choices to be made. Choice is determined by the person taking into account anticipated valences, expectations, and instrumentalities. These cognitive variables, argued Vroom, instigate and direct an employee's behavior. People attempt to maximize their overall best interest on the basis of their evaluation of this information.

Ryan, Locke's dissertation advisor, argued that needs, beliefs, and values determine behavior through an intervening variable, conscious intentions; and that people strive to act intentionally. Ryan's work was the precursor to the eighth seismic event in advancing knowledge of employee motivation, namely goal-setting theory. Whereas intention is a representation of a planned action, a goal is the object or aim of such an act, the target of one's intentional act. It is the standard by which one evaluates one's performance.

Similar to expectancy theory, goal setting is a cognitive theory. Unlike expectancy theory, it is more easily operationalized, measured and tested. Mitchell and Daniels (2003) stated that at the close of the 20th century Locke and Latham's (1990a) goal-setting theory "is quite easily the single most dominant theory in the field, with over a thousand articles and reviews published on the topic in a little over 30 years."

Although vehemently disagreeing on the philosophy of science, there are relative points of agreement between the behaviorists and the cognivitists. Both camps agree that a reward is a valued outcome, that these outcomes should be tied to desired behavior, as well as the effect of context on behavior. Job characteristics are important in that they influence perceptions regarding expectancy and instrumentality; they are antecedent stimuli for behavior as well as factors that affect the consequences of the behavior. The points of view between the two camps are also arguably complementary. Expectancies influence choice. Consequences or outcomes influence the probability that the behavior will reoccur. These similarities led to the ninth seismic event, Bandura's social cognitive theory. The theory postulates reciprocal determinism among a person's cognitions, behavior, and the environment. "External events may create the reason for doing something, but except in simple reflexive acts, they are not the originators of affect and action. External stimuli give rise to course of action through personal agency" (Bandura, 1986, p. 12).

Social cognitive theory too emphasizes the importance of goal setting. Whereas Vroom had argued the importance of expectancy, namely one's subjective probability that effort will lead to performance, Bandura, working without knowledge of Vroom's theory, formulated the concept of self-efficacy, a similar yet broader concept that has generative properties. Self-efficacy can stimulate the behavior in question. To the extent that proximal subgoals promote and authenticate self-efficacy, they increase motivation through enhancement of perceived personal causation. In agreement with expectancy theory, this theory states that the person's perceptions and thought processes mediate the impact of the job environment (Wood & Bandura, 1989). In agreement with Porter and Lawler's contention that high performance leads to high job satisfaction, the theory states that people develop an enduring interest in those activities where they feel self-efficacious. When people master valued levels of performance, they experience a sense of satisfaction.

Ford (1992) argued that at least three sets of variables are necessary for a complete theory of motivation, namely, goals, emotions, and agency. The tenth seismic event of the 20th century that advanced understanding of motivation focused on the second of these three variables, namely feelings of trust and fairness. Greenberg and Folger's principles of organizational justice focus on a person's perceptions and attitudes, specifically evaluations of those perceptions. Similar to Adam's equity theory, their research shows that perceptions of inequitable treatment generate motivational forces that instigate behavior to reduce these feelings. The distribution of outcomes as well as the procedures for determining what is distributed to whom determines perceptions of fairness and feelings of trust.

In closing this historical review of the 20th century, at least one question remains: What is work motivation? A comprehensive definition that reflects the history of research and theory on this subject is Pinder's (1998, p. 71): Motivation is "a set of energetic forces that originate both within as well as beyond an individual's being, to initiate work related behavior, and to determine its form, direction, intensity, and duration." This definition takes into account psychological processes in the direction, energization, and regulation of behavior. The definition is consistent with James, Freud, and Vroom in that it accommodates the arguments that behavior is determined by motive states that are not in awareness as well as those that are conscious. It acknowledges that features of the environment such as job characteristics trigger motivational forces.

The concept of force, Pinder stated, is central to this definition. Energetic forces suggest the multiplicity of both needs and external factors. The definition suggests that motivation will manifest itself through effort. The notion of improvement also emphasizes the importance of internal as well as external origins. Thus Pinder's definition takes into account the importance of the environment in arousing as well as shaping behavior without downplaying the importance of the employee's needs, values, attitudes or the belief that effort will lead to a desired outcome(s). Importantly, the direction of the motivated forces is also inherent in this definition. To predict and understand work motivation, one must know the specific goal toward which motivated energy is directed. Motivated arousal occurs to the extent that the goal is difficult. Duration or persistence occurs to the extent that the goal is perceived to be attainable (self-efficacy).

From a Practitioner's Viewpoint

A fundamental value of science is to criticize what is known for the purpose of advancing knowledge. The 1970s–1980s witnessed criticism that was tantamount to a civil war in the field of motivation as theorists and researchers engaged in an on-going attack of one another's work. As noted previously, Wahba and Bridwell (1976) critiqued Maslow's theory. They found no evidence of five universal needs let alone a hierarchy. Their critique as well as Salancik and Pfeffer's (1977) were so thorough that no further research was conducted on this theory for several decades. Both Vroom (1967) and Locke (1975) showed that Herzberg's notion of a two-factor theory of satisfaction versus dissatisfaction is a methodological artifact of the critical incident technique. Roberts and Glick (1981) attacked Hackman and Oldham's job characteristics theory for its lack of discriminant validity with other attitudinal measures, as well as halo error among perceived characteristics of jobs. Heneman and Schwab (1972) critiqued both expectancy and goal-setting theories, the latter for its lack of external validity in that time period. Hinrichs (1970) too questioned whether Locke's laboratory findings would generalize to organizational settings. Pritchard (1969) attacked equity theory for lack of precision regarding how people identify their inputs, outputs and comparison others, while Lawler (1971) argued that expectancy theory provided a more useful framework for explaining phenomena studied by equity researchers. Schmidt (1973) stated that the mathematical formulas of expectancy theory assume a ratio scale when there is no known way for assessing valences on this scale. Locke (1975) argued that Vroom was incorrect to assert that people are always rational decision makers and that he was also wrong to believe that they make complex calculations when they are making choices. Leventhal (1980) opinioned: "What shall we do with equity theory?" And despite the usefulness of Skinner's methodology for predicting and influencing behavior, the vast majority of HRM, I/O, and OB researchers rejected the philosophy on which it is based, behaviorism.

Three bright spots emerged in this era. First, voluminous field experiments showed the generalizability of goal-setting findings from the laboratory to work settings (e.g., Latham & Lee, 1986; Latham, Mitchell, & Dossett, 1978). Second, Bandura (1977a) presented social learning theory, later renamed by him as social cognitive theory (Bandura, 1986). The third was Robert Folger and Jerald Greenberg's (Greenberg & Folger, 1983) answer to the question asked by Greenberg's mentor, Leventhal, as to what should be done with equity theory, namely, develop principles of organizational justice.

Neither scientists nor practitioners expect a "perfect" experiment or study, nor do they expect a theory to be accurate in every way. I am pleased when a piece of research or a theoretical framework forces me to confront possibilities that would not have occurred to me otherwise. In this context, I was then and I am prepared today to take action on the basis of the research and theories presented thus far. I am reluctant to discard old clothes; I am even more steadfast in hanging onto old theories. This is why I am not overly critical of them. My nature is to focus on what can be useful in field settings rather than on what should be discarded. I don't expect every reader to agree with my opinions in this regard. Rather, I expect that the following opinions will be a basis for debate:

1. For me, attitude surveys continue to be an excellent way of assessing the current thinking and affect of employees and using the results to problem-solve with them ways to improve systems, processes and procedures that affect the attainment of employee and employer goals. Normative-based surveys are helpful for gauging whether specific attitudes in an organization are typical of those in the wider workforce. However, I also find surveys that are tailor made for the organization, based on interviews with a random sample of employees or with focus groups, very useful. They can become the basis for very productive dialogues.

2. I am not prepared to argue that all psychological needs identified by behavioral scientists in the West are universal. I agree that there is no consensus on definitions of needs such as self-actualization. Nevertheless, I take needs into account in my practice. As the area doctoral coordinator here in the business school, I immediately want to know if a student lacks adequate living expenses, has yet to find a satisfactory place to live, and is experiencing trouble in making friends with fellow graduate students. Maslow's theory provides a checklist for me to problem-solve with a student when I find that the person is not doing well in the first term of the graduate program.

3. In working with client organizations on a "start-up" or on a redesign of the workplace, it would be outrageous, in my opinion, not to draw upon Herzberg and Hackman and Oldham's work. In addition, I recommend giving people a realistic job preview (Wanous, 1973). If a person dislikes task variety, autonomy, recognition, opportunities to increase his or her skills, and feedback, the person can reject the job offer. I have yet to meet someone who did so.

4. That cognition mediates the effectiveness of operant techniques has in no way lessened their effectiveness for me in applying them in the field.

5. Expectancy theory is invaluable for me in casual conversations with individuals as well as people in focus groups.

(a) I want to know whether people believe that if they "knock themselves out" (effort), they will perform effectively.
(b) Further, I want to know the outcomes they expect for performing effectively. I know intelligent teenagers who feel they will be rejected by peers for doing well in school. I know employees who believe their goals will be raised to impossible levels if they attain the current ones.
(c) Hence, I want to know the value a person attaches to one or more outcomes of performing well. All of the above helps me and the client predict what people are likely to choose to do on the job.

6. Equity theory is similarly valuable to me. This theory showed me the importance of identifying "comparison others." Are our doctoral students in HRM-OB comparing themselves to their counterparts in marketing? Psychology Department? Other HRM, OB, and I/O departments in the United States? Who? I ask similar questions of salaried and hourly workers in the organizations where I am a consultant.

7. Set specific high goals. If I am in the role of a coach with executives, I prod them to consider the value of self-set high goals. I do

likewise when teaching self-management skills to people lower in the organization. When assigned goals are necessary because of an organization policy, I ensure that they are accompanied by a logic or rationale. I explain the value of participatively set goals to organizational leaders in terms of the likelihood that the person or persons will set an even higher goal than one that is assigned. Moreover, participation among knowledgeable people stimulates information exchange which can lead to better task strategies as well as high self-efficacy regarding their implementation. I stress the importance of setting sub-goals if the environment is characterized by high uncertainty. I advocate learning goals when people lack the knowledge or ability to attain specific high-performance outcome goals.

8. I draw upon expectancy and equity theory in applying goal setting principles. (a) Set specific high goals that are perceived to be difficult yet attainable. (b) Ensure that their attainment is tied to outcomes that are valued, and (c) appraised as equitable by employees.

9. Drawing on social cognitive theory, I focus on ways of increasing an individual's self-efficacy for attaining a difficult goal. As a coach I probe to see whether people see the relationship between what they do and the outcomes that they can expect.

10. In doing all of the above, organizational justice principles are on my mind. For example:

(a) What will be distributed to whom? Who will get the promotion? Salary increase? New office? New hire?
(b) Are there agreed-upon procedures, processes or systems for determining who gets what?
(c) Will people understand the logic underlying a decision?
(d) Will the person who will communicate a decision be viewed by the listeners as "sincere"?
(e) Do people believe that their viewpoints were taken into account before a decision has been finalized?

I could not practice effectively in organizations without the benefit of the scientific theories and research underlying these 10 steps.

Part II

The 21st Century

EXAMINING THE PRESENT: 2000–2005

6 Needs

The Starting Point of Motivation

Introduction

With the closing of the 20th century, HRM, I/O, and OB scholars had done what William James (1892) suggested at the end of the previous millennium. They had taken conscious motivation seriously. Consciousness, Bandura (2000) stated, is the very substance of mental life. A functional consciousness, he said, involves intentional accessing, and deliberative use of semantic and programmatic information to manage life events. The human mind is not only reactive, it is creative, and proactive.

At the dawn of this new millennium, it would appear that cognitive theories of motivation will likely be integrated with personality as well as affective processes. This is evident in the review by Brief and Weiss (2002) on moods and emotions. A review by Eccles and Wigfield (2002) underscores the conclusion by Seijts and B. Latham (2003) to continue to integrate social and I/O psychology theories as the former already provides frameworks for examining affective processes more fully.

Miner (2003) concluded that motivation continues to hold a significant position in the eyes of scholars in the present century. "If one wishes to create a highly valid theory, which is also constructed with the purpose of enhanced usefulness in practice in mind, it would be best to look to motivation theories . . . for an appropriate model" (Miner, p. 29).

Predicting, explaining, and influencing employee motivation in the 21st century can now be done by taking into account seven variables.[1] (1) *Needs* for physical and psychological well being and (2) personal *traits*, as the latter historically have been viewed as needs or drivers.

---

[1]This taxonomy was adapted and modified by Latham and Pinder (2005) from one that was originally put forth by Locke and his former doctoral student, Henne (Locke & Henne, 1986).

An individual difference variable rooted in needs is (3) *values*, which one considers good or beneficial and acts to gain or keep. Because (4) *context* affects the extent to which needs are met and values are fulfilled, (a) societal *culture*, (b) *job design* characteristics, and (c) *person-context fit* must be examined. Needs and values affect (5) *cognition*, particularly goals, the situationally specific form of values, the specific object or aim of an action. Cognition plays an integral role in each of these concepts. Although (6) *affect* or emotion does not depend on cognition (Bandura, 1997), the two are usually reciprocally related (Lord & Kanfer, 2002). Affect is the form in which one experiences automatized value appraisals, or subconscious beliefs. Emotion-focused coping encompasses both cognitive and behavioral strategies (Kanfer & Kantrowitz, 2002). Affect is also influenced by culture as well as by organizational norms (Lord & Harvey, 2002). (7) Finally, as emphasized in the high performance cycle discussed earlier, an employee's motivation is affected by rewards or incentives. However, they affect effort and persistence only to the extent that they satisfy one or more values of an employee.

Need Hierarchy Theory

Needs are physiological as well as psychological. They affect a person's survival and well being. Hence, needs are the starting point of motivation (Locke, 2000). The form in which one experiences needs is through pleasure and pain. Need satisfaction is pleasurable. Need frustration is not only uncomfortable, it can be life-threatening. Consequently, there is a resurgence of interest on needs by behavioral scientists, including a resurgence of interest in Maslow's (1943) hierarchical need theory.

Toward the end of the 20th century, Wicker, Brown, Wiehe, and Reed (1993) had argued that Maslow's theory is better at predicting a relationship between a person's intentions and behavior than with the person's ratings of "importance" and subsequent behavior. Greater deficiency in a need, they said, increases one's intentions to act on the need even if one does not give it a high importance rating. Borrowing from one of their examples, I rated writing this book as much more important to me than keeping cool, but there was a point of discomfort on my part during the summer where I stopped writing in order to turn up the air conditioner.

Wicker et al. found that between-goal correlations and partial correlations across four data sets support Maslow's theory when intentions to act are rated rather than measures of importance. Moreover, intentions to act appear to be stronger with lower than higher needs because of greater negative salience.

Ronen (2001), using multidimensional scaling and smallest space analysis rather than factor analysis of data collected in 15 countries, found support for the taxonomic element of Maslow's theory. Kluger and Tikochinsky (2001) advocated ongoing efforts to find ways to operationalize the theory validly before concluding that Maslow's hierarchy argument is incorrect. Locke (2000), however, believes that it is unlikely that strong evidence will ever be found for a "built-in" need hierarchy for employees in the workplace. Different people are capable of prioritizing their needs in different ways, based on their chosen values. It is not the case, he said, that physical needs are always more important to a person than psychological needs. People who have very low self-esteem may commit suicide.[2]

VanDijk and Kluger (2004) argued that needs, such as those listed in Maslow's taxonomy, reflect strategic adaptation challenges. Hence a person's needs dictate the way motivation processes operate. Threats to safety, regardless of individual differences among people regarding their traits or personality, almost always take precedence over them finding ways of increasing or promoting their effectiveness in the workplace. It is only the latter that is affected by individual differences.

Van-Dijk and Kluger (2004) argued that needs explain the contradictory findings of control theory studies versus those virtually always obtained in studies of goal setting and social cognitive theories. When a need is salient, people become highly aware of whether it is met. When their goal for security is attained, one's motivation to act to further attain this need is reduced. That is, a higher or more difficult goal to attain regarding one's personal security typically is not set. This finding is consistent with the prediction of control theory. On the other hand, when the need to increase one's skills and worth to self, employer, or society becomes salient (e.g., self-actualization), the attainment of one's

---

[2]Schneider (2004, personal communication) argued that it is important to point out that Maslow's theory was a developmental theory of personality not a theory of inter-individual differences—the way it has been studied. The only way to study Maslow's theory and the hierarchy proposition is to study people over a life—or at a minimum until they are 21 or more. If we only study adults, we should find differences in where people are more or less locked on the need hierarchy and make predictions based on where they are. So, people with high security needs buy more insurance, have smaller mortgages, and invest less in the stock market—and want to be paid a salary rather than paid based on an incentive system, and so forth.

goal typically leads to the setting of an even higher goal. This finding is consistent with the position of both goal setting and social cognitive theories (Bandura & Locke, 2003).

Haslam, Powell, and Turner (2000) presented a process-based analysis of need structure and need salience derived from the social identity approach to organizational behavior. To understand motivation, they argued that one must understand aspirations for the self that exist in a hierarchy. When personal identity is salient, needs to self-actualize and to enhance self-esteem through personal advancement and growth become dominant. When social identity is salient for an individual, the need to enhance group based self-esteem through a sense of relatedness, respect, peer recognition, and attainment of group goals dominate. The authors stated that McGregor's (1960) Theory Y assumptions apply when the supervisor and employee share the same identity; Theory X assumptions apply when they do not do so. People are motivated to attain those goals that are compatible with their self-identity. Needs associated with a specific group membership are internalized; they serve as a guide for behavior in a specific working context. Haslam et al.'s analysis of survey data of Australian employees were interpreted as supporting social identity theory.

Ajila (1997) and Kamalanabhan, Uman, and Vasnathi (1999) argued that there is now widespread acceptance of the practical significance of Maslow's theory. Physiological needs are considered in decisions regarding space, lighting, and overall working conditions; safety in terms of work practices; love in regard to forming cohesive work teams; esteem through responsibility and recognition; and self-actualization in terms of providing opportunities for creative challenging jobs or tasks. This is particularly true in developing countries. Employees in four manufacturing companies in Nigeria rated lower needs (i.e., physiological, security) as the most important to satisfy followed by the higher order growth needs, once these lower-order goals were obtained (Ajila, 1997). Among bank employees in India, officers attached greater importance to the growth needs than did clerks whose need for job security was an ongoing concern for them (Rao & Kulkarni, 1998).

Socioanalytic Theory

A different taxonomy of needs has been proposed by Robert and Joyce Hogan. Their taxonomy is the basis for socioanalytic theory. This theory

(Hogan & Warremfeltz, 2003) states that people have innate biological needs for (a) acceptance and approval; (b) status, power, and control of resources; and (c) predictability and order. These needs translate into behaviors for getting along with others, getting ahead in terms of status, and making sense of the world. Hogan (2004) argued that the agenda for personality theory is to explain individual differences among people in their ability to get along and get ahead; the agenda for personality assessment, he argued, is to predict individual differences in people's potential for doing so.

Socioanalytic theory is a segue to the subsequent discussion of personality. The theory states that personality should be defined from the perspectives of both the person and the observer. Personality from the person's view is his/her identity. It is defined in terms of the strategies one uses to satisfy the needs for acceptance and status. Personality from an observer's point of view is a person's reputation. It is defined in terms of trait evaluations. Hence reputation reflects the observer's view of the characteristic ways the person behaves. Reputation describes a person's behavior; identity explains it (J. Hogan, & Holland, 2003)

Concluding Thoughts

Although need-based theories explain why a person must act, they do not explain why specific actions are chosen in specific situations to obtain specific outcomes. Moreover, they do not easily account for individual differences. Hence, along with needs there is a resurgence of interest in individual differences particularly with regard to the relationship between the person and the environment.

7 Personality Traits

Distal Predictors of Motivation

Introduction

Traits have long been considered needs or drivers, the satisfaction of which leads to pleasure, and the lack of fulfillment to displeasure (Allport, 1951). Nevertheless, Mitchell (1979) had found that personality variables control little or no variation in behavior in the workplace. The few empirical results that were statistically significant lacked practical significance. The inability to specify the mechanisms linking particular personality traits to job performance led most researchers in the 20th century to downplay the importance of an employee's personality in the workplace (Hough & Schneider, 1996).[1] Subsequent findings in the present century from meta-analyses, however, have shown the importance of personality variables for predicting and explaining performance (e.g., Barrick, Mount, & Judge, 2001). Failure to express one's traits can lead to anxiety (Cote & Moskowitz, 1998). Mitchell and Daniels (2003) reported that research on personality is now the fastest growing area in the motivation literature. Why has this "suddenly" occurred?

Until the end of the 20th century, there was no agreed-upon personalogical frameworks from which to study the dispositional basis of motivation (Erez & Judge, 2001; Hogan, 2004). Many researchers were

---

[1]This was not the case in vocational psychology. John Holland (1973) advanced the proposal that vocational choice is affected by personality type, there are six personality types, and a model environment for each type. Vocational adjustment occurs, he said, to the extent that people pursue a career in an environment that matches their personality type. Today this is among the most widely recognized and well-replicated findings in the history of vocational psychology (Rounds, 1995), and Holland's theory is overwhelmingly popular among users—clients as well as vocational guidance counselors (Dawis, 1996).

clinical psychologists who focused on psychopathology (e.g., Rogers). Others were humanists (e.g., Murray) who were interested in an individual's uniqueness. Still others were psychometricians (e.g., Cattell) who examined the factor analytic structure of personality.

Hogan (2004) credited two discoveries for garnering the attention of HRM, I/O, and O/B scholars in individual difference variables. The first was the finding that measures of a person's integrity not only predict job performance, they do so with no adverse impact regarding women and minorities. The second is the development of the Five Factor Model or FFM (Wiggins, 1996), which assesses extroversion, conscientiousness, neuroticism, openness to experience, and agreeableness. Research that has a theoretical basis for linking a personality construct and a job performance outcome has significantly higher predictive validities than those obtained in exploratory studies (Tett, Jackson, Rothstein, & Reddon, 1994). A meta-analysis of the relationship between the FFM and three theories of employee motivation, namely goal setting, expectancy, and social cognitive, revealed that the "Big Five" traits have an average multiple correlation of .49 with motivational criteria in the workplace.

Thus, the argument for studying traits in the present century is, as articulated by Hogan (2004), threefold. First, traits are real. Second, an individual's personality can be described in terms of traits. Third, an employee's action is explainable in terms of traits. Empirical studies support Hogan's contention.[2] For example, Moskowitz & Cote (1995) had recently shown that a person's dominance score on a personality test correlates positively with dominant behavior and negatively with submissive behavior. Moreover, they found that when people behave in ways that are counter to their personality traits, they experience negative affect. Therefore, all things being equal, people behave consistently with predictions from their personality traits (Glomb & Welsh, 2005).

A fourth interrelated reason for the current emphasis on personality is the demand by organizational leaders for ways to identify people who are adaptive, flexible, versatile, and tolerant of uncertainty. The world of work in the 21st century is characterized by ever-changing dynamic environments.[3]

---

[2]Personality measures, however, are distal predictors of behavior. Hence, intermediate variables should be considered in terms of mediating and moderating effects. Personality measures are best viewed as antecedents. They assess a person's predisposition to behave in certain ways.

[3]Jack Welch, the former CEO of General Electric Company, during his visit to our business school in September 2005, stated that a key to a leader's success is the selection of team players with high energy and passion, who can energize others and who have an edge to them yet are people sensitive. "HRM is King," he said.

In a review of predictor domains, Schmitt, Cortina, Ingerick, and Weichmann (2003) concluded that personality is a primary predictor of elements of motivation. This is because, as Spangler, House, and Palrechar (2004, p. 252) noted, "traits are stable consistencies in expressive or stylistic behavior that affect the expression of motives." Motives energize and focus behavior in the presence of environmental or situational factors. Specifically, the extant research shows that traits predict and/or influence job search, choice of job, as well as job performance and satisfaction. In addition to the FFM, these traits include self-regulatory and self-monitoring strategies, core self-evaluations, goal orientation, as well as three traits that affect the perception of one's self and the environment. These three traits, autonomy, control, and impersonal orientation constitute the basis of Deci's self-determination theory.

Five Factor Model (FFM)

Gray (1994) argued that two separate neural pathways explain reactions to perceived positive and negative events. Extroverts are differentially sensitive to cues of reward; people who score high on neuroticism are sensitive to punishment cues. Barrick et al. (1998) found that teams whose members score high on extroversion score high on supervisory assessments of team performance. The mediator was cohesiveness. Furnham, Forde, and Ferrai (1999) found that extroverts are attracted to enriched jobs. Those who score high on neuroticism are attracted to jobs that excel on hygiene variables.

Mount and Barrick (1995) showed that conscientiousness is particularly important in jobs that allow autonomy. Peterson, Owens, and Martorana (2000) reported that the scores of chief executive officers on conscientiousness as well as agreeableness correlate with flexibility in decision making on the part of the senior management team as well as with the firm's performance. Witt and Ferris (2003) found that the relationship between conscientiousness and job performance that requires interpersonal effectiveness is moderated by social skill. Among workers low in social skill, the relationship between conscientiousness and performance was either not significant or negative.[4]

---

[4]Hogan and Shelton (1998) argued on the basis of socio-analytic theory that social skill, a learned ability, is necessary for one's motivation to lead to success. High needs for achievement or power are likely frustrated, they said, among people low in social skill.

Barrick, Stewart, and Piotrowski (2002) showed that motivational constructs can be measured by first identifying basic goals that regulate a person's behavior across work settings, and then determining the traits that impact them. Drawing upon Hogan's socioanalytic theory, and the FFM, they found that "status striving" and "accomplishment striving" mediate relationships between conscientiousness and extroversion with supervisory evaluations of sales performance.

Witt, Burke, Barrick, and Mount (2002) found that personality traits interact with one another to determine behavior. The results from seven independent samples of employees showed that the relationship between conscientiousness and job performance was higher for people high rather than low on agreeableness. Barrick, Parks, and Mount (2005) similarly found that characteristics of the person, as opposed to the situation, restrict the extent to which an individual behaves in accordance with one or more personality traits. Employees high in emotional stability, extroversion, or openness to experience who were low on self-monitoring achieved the highest levels of interpersonal performance.

Despite the usefulness of the FFM, a number of concerns have yet to be resolved. First, as Perrewé and Spector (2002) pointed out, the five dimensions of the FFM are not independent constructs. If neuroticism is reverse-scored and renamed "emotional stability," all five factors are positively correlated. Second, the FFM is not a comprehensive assessment of personality. For example, it does not assess one's belief in internal versus external locus of control. Third, the wisdom of shrinking all personal characteristics to only five global traits is questionable. Hogan (2004) concluded that seeking the structure of personality by factor analysis is little more than a psychometric method in search of a theory. Finally, there is considerable doubt that the FFM is applicable in the less-developed world (Triandis & Suh, 2002).

Leaetta Hough (2005, personal communication), the president of SIOP, 2005–2006, believes that

> the FFM provides a useful set of terms for researching and discussing personality variables. Indeed, at the dawn of this century, it is not in vogue to criticize the FFM. However, considerable evidence exists that additional personality variables are important for describing and understanding intra- and interpersonal behavior as well as for predicting work behavior. For example, although variables such as core self-evaluations and integrity can be considered compound variables made up of combinations of FFM variables, not all of the variance in these compound variables is explained by the FFM and its facets, and some of these variables may be emergent rather than simply multi-faceted. Nor are important characteristics such as emotionality, social competence, ego strength, and narcissism, often

considered part of personality, well represented in the FFM. Similarly, some personality disorders are not well presented in the FFM. The FFM is an important model but it is unwise to embrace it solely and without reservation.[5]

Self-Regulatory/Self-Monitoring Personality

Ruth Kanfer, trained originally as a clinical psychologist, and her colleague Heggestad (1997) proposed a developmental theory that distinguishes between distal influences on action, in the form of relatively stable motivational traits, and proximal influences that are associated with individual differences in self-regulatory or motivational skills.[6] They argued that motivation control and emotion control are two types of

---

[5]Georgia Tech, when I was a student there, emphasized the importance of studying individual differences. Since I had tried to no avail in the 1970s to find a mediator on moderator effects of personality on goal setting, and since I was persuaded by my colleague Terry Mitchell's *Annual Review of Psychology* chapter that it was useless to persist, I am somewhat awestruck by the highly respected people in our field who did not give up. Hence my question of Leaetta Hough as to why she stuck with this topic. "For as long as I can remember, I've been fascinated and delighted by the richness of individual differences. When I began conducting job analysis in the 1970s to identify individual differences critical to job performance, job incumbents often told me "attitude" was the most important determinant. They described "attitude" by referring to temperament or personality characteristics. At the same time, I was learning about the Five-Factor Model of personality in the graduate classes in the Psychology Department at the University of Minnesota, but my enthusiasm for what I was learning was tempered by the zeitgeist of the time-personality variables were not useful for predicting work-relevant criteria. Fortunately, my mentors, Marv Dunnette and Auke Tellegen, were steeped in the Minnesota tradition of differential psychology and dust-bowl empiricism, and they appreciated my interest in seeking alternatives to the Big Five. Soon my work gave me the opportunity to test different models. I was assigned responsibility for the personality component of the predictor domain for Project A, the personnel selection project of the 1980s. Using construct-oriented thinking and a different structure of personality variables than the Five-Factor Model, we demonstrated through meta-analysis and our own empirical evidence that what job incumbents had earlier told me was correct—personality is indeed an important determinant of job performance" (Hough, 2005, personal communication).

[6]Recall that Lyman Porter was trained as an experimental psychologist, and Ed Locke, who was trained as an I/O psychologist later received training in clinical psychology. The interrelatedness among the fields of psychology is further demonstrated by Ruth's career. "My transition from clinical to I/O psychology followed a natural progression. In clinical training at Arizona State University, I focused on psychological attributes and intra-individual dynamics, largely irrespective of context. I studied the foundations and methods for psychological and intellectual assessment, personality and psychopathology, social influence processes, and treatment evaluation methodologies. As such, I was fortunate to take course work in both experimental and differential approaches to human behavior. As a post-doctoral quantitative fellow at the University of Illinois, I focused on intra-individual dynamics in the context of work, studied the application of

(Continued)

motivational skills or self-regulatory strategies that people use to control their cognition, affect, and behavior during the process of goal attainment. Motivational skills refer to individual differences in sustaining effort and persistence through goal setting. Emotion control skill pertains to self-regulatory strategies to manage anxiety and worry. In Kanfer's words:

> My work focuses on individual differences in personality traits and tendencies that relate directly to achievement motivation and goal striving tendencies; namely, the various trait tendencies that affect an individual's investment of intellectual and energetic resources and the execution of this investment. My approach has been to focus on the development of meaningful trait complexes comprised of old and new traits that share substantial variance. I use both correlational and experimental methods to identify these complexes and to test their differential and incremental predictive validities over component traits for learning and performance. This trait complex approach has proved useful for identifying communalities among seemingly disparate constructs in motivation theorizing, as well as for understanding the role of different motive classes on work behavior over time and across settings. (Kanfer, 2005, personal communication)

Heggestad and Kanfer (1999) developed a multiple trait-motivational inventory. The scale has convergent and discriminant validity with regard to measures of motivation versus intellectual abilities (Kanfer & Ackerman,

---

(Continued)

assessment methods for personnel selection, training methods and evaluation, and social, interpersonal, and organizational determinants of job performance and satisfaction. I also learned new methodologies for investigating person-situation interactions and their impact on the individual over time. I/O psychology attracted my interest during my last year of clinical training because the workplace seemed to provide an excellent context for studying adult behavior from an interactionist perspective that unfolds overtime. My advisor, Tony Zeiss, and my father, Fred Kanfer, encouraged me to pursue my training and interest in I/O psychology after I completed my clinical internship and Ph.D. My work on motivation and self-regulation during clinical training further provided me with the foundations for understanding achievement in the workplace. Since both clinical and I/O psychology require strong foundations in both experimental and differential psychology, and because both fields are concerned with the scientific study of behavior in the context of practical concerns, my transition from clinical to I/O psychology felt quite natural. At Illinois I was fortunate to have the opportunity to work with a number of faculty and talented graduate students, including Allen Lind, Fritz Drasgow, Phil Ackerman, Chris Earley, Maureen Ambrose, John Sawyer, Laurie Weingart, Mavee Park, Mary Rosnowski, and David Harrison. But my primary mentor for I/O psychology at Illinois was Chuck Hulin. His breadth of knowledge, clear thinking about the nomological network of relations among key constructs in I/O psychology, and steadfast demand for innovative and programmatic research inspired me. He asked thorough questions that caused me to think broadly yet ever more precisely about motivation and emotion in the context of work (Kanfer, 2005, personal communication).

2000). In a study of job search by unemployed individuals, Wanberg, Kanfer and Rotundo (1999) found that motivation control was the only nondemographic factor that predicted sustained job search. Specifically, the self-regulatory skills of goal setting, planning and cognitive rehearsal were more important than an individual's self-efficacy for success, or financial hardship, in sustaining overall search intensity over time.

A meta-analysis by Kanfer, Wanberg, and Kantrowitz (2001) examined the relation of personality measures with respect to self-regulation regarding job search. The results showed that self regulation is more strongly related to positive than to negative affective variables.

A meta-analysis of a self-monitoring personality by Day, Schleicher, Unckless, and Hiller (2002) revealed a robust positive relationship with job performance, as well as a relatively strong positive relationship with advancement into leadership positions. This is because self-monitors are motivated to meet the expectations of others, which in turn enhances their likeability. Likeability is a key to job progression (Hogan, 2004). In an enumerative review, Day and Schleicher (in press) concluded that self-monitors outperform those who are low on needs to get along and get ahead. The evidence is relatively mixed on the need to make sense of the environment.

Self-monitoring is not represented well in the FFM (Day et al., 2002). In fact, it may be as much if not more so a skill rather than a trait as it correlates highly with the ability to manage one's image.

Core Self-Evaluations

Judge, Locke, and Durham (1997) developed a theory of traits that they labeled core self-evaluations with regard to one's appraisal of people, events, and things in relation to self.[7] In short, these are "bottom line" conclusions that people hold about themselves. Core evaluations are manifested in four highly correlated traits, namely, self-esteem (self-perceptions of one's worth, value and importance), locus of control (personal degree of influence over life events), neuroticism/emotional stability (tendency to be secure and well adjusted), and generalized self-efficacy (overall

---

[7]The original idea for an assessment of one's core evaluations in work settings was Locke's. He developed the idea after reading the clinical psychology literature. Judge linked the concept to the trait literature. Subsequently, Judge, Locke, and Locke's wife, Cathy Durham, collaborated on their initial paper. Judge, whose mentor was Charles, "Chuck" Hulin, a cohort of Locke's in graduate school, is among the most prolific scholars in our field in this time period.

confidence in one's ability to deal with a variety of situations in one's life). Judge et al. argued that these core evaluations influence a person's appraisal of job characteristics/environments which, in turn, influence a person's job satisfaction and behavior. Thus, core self-evaluations, they said, have a greater effect on a person's behavior because they have more connections to other traits, beliefs and evaluations than peripheral traits

A meta-analysis showed that this aggregation of four traits is a strong dispositional predictor of an employee's job satisfaction (Judge & Bono, 2001). Erez and Judge (2001) found that a person's core self-evaluations predict motivation and performance, whereas the individual traits did so inconsistently. They also found that motivation, that is, persistence and desire to perform well, mediated about half the relationship between core self-evaluations and performance. Hence they concluded that core self-evaluations are indeed assessing motivation, and that this explains its prediction of job performance.

Wanberg, Glomb, Song, and Sorenson (2005) found that this aggregate of traits affects persistence with regard to job search despite experiencing rejections along the way. These results, they said, suggest the power of thinking positively. The authors also suggested that assessing a person's core self-evaluations should prove useful for predicting and understanding the difficulty level of goals people set.

Judge (2005, personal communication) stated that:

> One thing that we have consistently shown, unlike researchers of other approaches to the assessment of personality, is that core self-evaluations are value adding beyond the FFM rather than an alternative measure to it. This is because core self-evaluations are just that—evaluative whereas the FFM assesses traits that are descriptive, more peripheral, and less central or basic to one's self-concept.

Johnson, Mosen, and Levy (2006) offered a number of suggestions for improving the use of this construct. First, a meta-analysis has shown that self-esteem and generalized self-efficacy are so highly intercorrelated ($r = .86$) as to be redundant (Judge, Erez, Bono, & Thoresen, 2003). They are measuring the same phenomenon. The measure of general self-efficacy in core evaluations should be replaced with a measure of extroversion. The basis for this second recommendation is that there is ample evidence from research with animals and human beings of two basic independent motivation systems, one is approval and the other is avoidance (e.g., Higgins, 2000).[8] Emotional stability or neuroticism,

---

[8]An approach or promotion focus is a personality disposition to strive to attain positive outcomes whereas people with a prevention or avoidance disposition strive to avoid negative ones.

one of the four core evaluations, assesses an aversive or avoidance motivation system (i.e., a heightened sensitivity to punishing events; anxious-
calmness emotions; fight or flight response). A complementary measure
of an approach motivation system should likewise be included in core
evaluations (i.e., appetitive motivation is typically activated in a setting
where perceptions of anticipated rewards are salient). If emotional stability is in the model, they argued that a measure of extroversion should
be included too.

Goal Orientation

Farr and his colleagues (Farr, Hofman, & Ringenbach, 1993) were
among the first to draw the attention of HRM, I/O, and OB scholars to
Dweck's work in educational psychology on goal orientation, a trait that
is not the same as goal setting, which is a state. On the basis of her
studies of children, Dweck (1986) argued that:

> The study of motivation deals with the causes of goal-oriented activity. Adaptive
> motivational patterns are those that promote the establishment, maintenance, and
> attainment of personally challenging and personally valued achievement goals.
> Maladaptive patterns, then, are associated with a failure to establish reasonable,
> valued goals, to maintain effective striving toward those goals or, ultimately, to
> attain valued goals that are potentially within one's reach. (p. 1040)

In contrast to the FFM which embeds five broad motivational traits in
a framework or taxonomy of personality, Dweck's (1999) goal-orientation
theory embeds motivational traits in a narrow structure of goal striving
that emphasizes the ways that a person's behavior is affected by approach
and avoidance tendencies. Specifically, she argued that people's conception of their ability influences the goals they pursue. Incrementalists
have a learning goal orientation; they focus on the acquisition of knowledge and the perfecting of competence. Hence, they approach tasks
that are challenging for them. Errors are viewed by them as allowing
opportunities to learn from mistakes. Entitists, on the other hand, view
their ability as fixed. They have a performance goal orientation,
whereby they avoid tasks that do not allow them to easily demonstrate
their proficiency.

Don VandeWalle, who did his Ph.D. under the supervision of
Larry Cummings at the University of Minnesota, is among the leading
researchers in organizational behavior who has shown the application
of one's goal orientation to behaviors in work settings. He developed
and validated scales to assess goal orientation (VandeWalle, 1997). In

doing so, he found that there are two dimensions to a performance goal orientation: (1) People with a proving goal orientation focus on finding ways to demonstrate their competence as well as making a favorable impression on others. Hence, they tend to choose tasks where they can excel. (2) Those with an avoid goal orientation focus on finding ways to avoid tasks where they may be shown to be incompetent as well as avoiding making a negative impression on others. A high avoiding goal orientation can be emotionally draining (VandeWalle, Cron, & Slocum, 2001).

Those with a learning goal orientation focus on mastery (learning) of complex tasks while those with a performance goal orientation choose tasks in which they believe they can excel. Moreover, a learning goal orientation is positively correlated with openness to new experiences and optimism (VandeWalle, 1996), internal locus of control (Button et al., 1996), desire for hard work (VandeWalle, 1997) and effort (VandeWalle, Brown, Cron, & Slocum, 1999). In addition, VandeWalle et al. (1999) found that a learning goal orientation correlates positively with sales performance, but it is mediated by self-regulation (goal setting, effort, planning). A performance goal-orientation disposition, on the other hand, correlates negatively with self-efficacy, which is a cognitive state (Phillips & Gully, 1997). They concluded that: "There is considerable evidence of goal orientation existing as a stable individual difference" (p. 250).

Brett and VandeWalle (1999) reported that goal orientation does not have a direct relationship with performance, but that it is mediated by the content of the goals (performance vs. learning goal) that individuals select. Those with a learning goal-orientation disposition select a learning goal, and those with a performance goal orientation select a goal that they believe is attainable. This longitudinal study showed that goal orientation influences initial emotional reactions and subsequent self-regulation in the face of negative feedback.

Self-Determination Theory

Deci's ongoing concern for a distinction between intrinsic and extrinsic motivation and their differential effect on motivation as a result of feeling controlled led to the development of self-determination theory (Deci & Ryan, 1990; Ryan & Deci, 2000). In brief, this theory states that giving people the freedom to make personal choices leads to personal empowerment, a higher sense of autonomy, and a higher level of interest in a task. This, in turn, results in people spending more time

Locke (2004) conducted a 6-year follow-up study of entrepreneurs. They found that two traits, tenacity and passion, have indirect rather than direct effects through specific, non-trait mechanisms—namely, vision, goal setting, and self-efficacy. Yet it is possible that some trait effects, such as need for achievement, are direct and thus are not mediated. Research is needed on if, when, and why this occurs.

Bandura (2001b), as noted above, continues to have little or no use for the study of personality variables. The personal determinants of motivation and subsequent performance, he said, are cognitive. They include people's knowledge structures, their skills, self-beliefs of efficacy to manage given activities and environmental demands, and self-regulatory capabilities that operate through goals and outcome expectancies rooted in a value structure. Since these variables typically indicate or explain the predictive relationship between one or more characteristics of a person's personality and performance, why not focus solely on them? Ruth Kanfer, a strong supporter of Bandura's work, answered my question:

Bandura has made many very important contributions to understanding motivation processes independent of personality. The next step is to understand the relations of these process variables to stable individual differences in preferences and action tendencies (personality) that arise from the joint influence of biology, experience, and cultural affordances and constraints. The ultimate value of studying personality versus process variables is determined by the nature and strength of the linkages between personality and proximal process constructs, as well as the purpose of the investigation. In an applied perspective, proximal variables, such as goals or self-efficacy beliefs, represent the critical levers for achieving behavior change. Their malleability, however depends upon personality and the environment. Distal personality traits add predictive power for understanding performance across time and classes of situations that entail motivational processing. (Kanfr, 1980; 2005, personal communication)

8 Values

Trans-Situational Goals

Introduction

As is the case with personality characteristics of an employee, values too are an individual difference variable. They are rooted in needs and hence provide the principle basis for a person's goals. Indeed, values can be viewed as trans-situational goals, varying in importance (Schwartz & Sagie, 2000). Because they are relatively enduring, values serve as guiding principles in the life of a person (Prince-Gibson & Schwartz, 1998). Values are similar to needs in their capacity to arouse, direct, and sustain behavior. Whereas needs are inborn, values are acquired through cognition and experience. Thus values are a step closer to action than needs because values are what a person takes action on to acquire or keep. Moreover, values influence behavior because they are normative standards used to judge and choose among alternative behaviors.[1] Although values can be subconscious, they are usually more easily verbalized than needs.

Values are inherent in most work motivation theories (Locke & Henne, 1986). These theories focus on the influence of one or several particular values such as perceptions of fairness on action or on the effects of values in general (expectancy theory). Goals are similar in meaning to values except that they are more specific. They hold the

---

[1]Milton Rokeach, a social psychologist, is considered to be the "trail-blazer" in this research domain. His work has been a basis for Jennifer Chatman's subsequent research on person-organization fit in terms of congruent values. Both individuals agree that because values transcend situations, they are able to guide a person's actions beyond immediate goals to more ultimate goals (Chatman, 1991; Rokeach, 1973).

same means–end relationship to values as values do to needs. Goals are the mechanism by which values lead to action.

Verplanken and Holland (2002) explored *how* values affect choices. Outcomes with the potential to activate a person's central values instigate the acquisition of information and motivate choice decisions in accordance with pursuing the values in question. That is, activation and information collection mediate the relationship between values and the choices one makes.

In a longitudinal study, Malka and Chatman (2003) examined the extent to which values act as moderators of one's "subjective well-being" and job satisfaction. They hypothesized that money should affect a person's subjective well-being to the extent that money is relevant to one's values. They found that business school graduates who have an external work orientation reported higher job satisfaction and subjective well-being than those who reported an orientation toward the intrinsic aspects of work. No data were collected on performance.

Srivastava, Locke, and Bartol (2001) developed a scale for assessing the different motives people have for making money. A motive is the reason underlying an individual's choice of a goal. They isolated 10 factors ranging from wanting money for the purposes of enhancing family security, to gaining a sense of justice, to enjoying greater freedom. There were also negative motives. Some people, for example, use money as a way of feeling superior to others and as a way of gaining power. If self-doubt, however, is the root cause of their value for money, the pursuit of money will not assuage it because lack of money is not the cause. The motive to accumulate money comes from the person's insecurities (Locke, McClear, & Knight, 1996; Richins & Dawson, 1992). Srivastava et al. found that positive motives were neutral with respect to their relationship with measures of a person's subjective well-being, that is, a self-evaluation of one's overall life. There was a negative relationship between the importance that people attach to money and their subjective well-being when the motive for wealth is to overcome their self-doubts. In summary, wealthier people are not necessarily happier than their poorer counterparts. The motive underlying the value for money is the determining factor.

Context

Personality variables, viewed as irrelevant subject matter for work motivation throughout much of the 20th century, have been profitably rehabilitated. What is lacking, argued Johns (2006), is comparable progress in understanding the different ways that context affects an employee's behavior. Context, as noted earlier, affects the extent to which an employee's needs are met and values are fulfilled. As Johns noted, context can have a direct effect, or can interact with personality variables, to affect a person's behavior in the workplace; hence it can have both subtle and powerful effects on research results.[2] As a result of globalization, however, values are now being studied within the context of a person's societal culture, in addition to job and person-environment fit.

Societal Culture

Values were defined by Geert Hofstede (2001) as a broad tendency to prefer certain states of affairs over others. Hofstede founded and managed the Personnel Research Department of IBM, Europe.[3] The effect of society on an employee's values was shown in a landmark study he conducted in the previous century. In analyzing responses to 32 value questions from more than 116,000 IBM employees in 50 countries, Hofstede (1980, 1984) discovered that each country could be described in terms of four broad values—power distance, individualism, masculinity, and uncertainty avoidance. Power distance defines the extent to which the less powerful person in a given society accepts and considers inequality in power as normal. An individualist culture emphasizes

---

[2]Rousseau and Fried (2001) have also emphasized the importance of context in linking observations to a set of relevant facts and events in one's research. A fascinating study of data from the Center for Creative Leadership on 12,000 managers in 142 organizations underscores Johns' point that the environment can have a direct effect on one's personality. Schneider, Smith, Taylor, and Fleenor (1998) found that there is a main effect for organizations on personality. That is, you can predict the personality of managers in an organization once you know the organization where they work. Similarly, there is a main effect for industry on personality.

[3]Hofstede worked with David Sirota who was manager of Personnel Research for the IBM World Trade Corporation, of which IBM Europe is a subsidiary. He conducted his work in the small town of Blariaum, a short distance from Amsterdam, where IBM had a Management Development Center in a charming, large old castle. Hofstede also did global surveys with Allen Kraut who replaced Sirota in 1970. In 1972, Hofstede went on a two-year sabbatical leave to IMEDE, now called IMD in Lausanne, Switzerland, where he did much of the analysis and writing that he published in his book *Culture's Consequence*. Although he did not return to IBM, he received the company's support to complete what would become "landmark" work. John Hinrichs replaced Hofstede in Europe after Hofstede left for IMEDE. Today, Lise Saari is the director, IBM Global Workforce Research that includes Asia Pacific, Europe/Middle East/Africa, and the Americas (Allen Kraut, 2004, personal communication).

enlightened self-interest, whereas a collectivist (Hofstede uses this term in the anthropological rather than the political sense) society places value on the enhancement of the group's interests. Masculine cultures value such personality traits as assertiveness, ambitiousness, and competitiveness, especially in regard to material success; whereas a feminine culture values quality of life, interpersonal relationships, and value for the weak. Uncertainty avoidance is a cultural characteristic that defines the extent to which people are made nervous by situations that they perceive to be unstructured, unclear, or unpredictable. Strict codes of behavior and a belief in absolute truths typify this society. Cultures with a weak uncertainty avoidance are said to be relatively unemotional, accepting of personal risk, and tolerant.

Brett (2000) reported that normative behavior of people with low status in a high power distance culture is to minimize challenges to high status members. In high power distance cultures, conflicts within one's class are usually resolved by a superior.

Brockner et al. (2001) found that societal culture moderates perceptions of organizational justice. In four independent studies, people responded less favorably to low levels of voice in low power distance countries (the United States and Germany) than their counterparts in high power distance countries (People's Republic of China, Mexico, and Hong Kong).

Miriam Erez (2000) and her colleague Christopher Earley (Earley, 2002; Erez & Earley, 1993) developed a "model of cultural self-representation" to guide employee behavior and managerial practices in cross-cultural settings.[4] They argued that people strive to fulfill values for self-enhancement, efficacy, and self-consistency. Their model is based on individualism vs. collectivism and high vs. low power distance. Three principles are advanced to assist human resource managers design and implement motivation and reward systems: (1) identify the cultural characteristics of a country regarding collectivism/individualism and power distance; (2) understand yourself and the cultural values you

---

[4]Christopher Earley and Miriam Erez have maintained a lifelong working relationship. Chris obtained his Ph.D. in psychology at the University of Illinois where he was Miriam's research assistant while she was there on sabbatical. Miriam subsequently served as the dean of the Faculty of Industrial Engineering and Management at the Technion University in Israel. Chris is currently the dean of the Business School at the University of Singapore. In 2005, Miriam Erez was awarded one of the highest honors an academic can receive from her country, the Israel Prize for Management Science for her contribution toward integrating psychology and management.

represent; and (3) understand the meaning of various managerial practices (such as differential vs. flat salary reward distribution and top-down vs. two-way communication styles) in each country. Projecting values onto people from other cultures that differ on the above key dimensions can create dysfunctional consequences in terms of employee motivation, interpersonal communication, and overall performance.

Dirks and McLean Parks (2003) gave an example of the tragic effect of failing to take into account cultural differences:

> In high context cultures, meaning relies heavily on "reading between the lines," or understanding what is said through the context of the situation. In contrast, in low-context cultures, meaning is explicitly delineated—what you say is what you mean. Even with the 20-20 vision of hindsight, one wonders what role communication style may have played in the September 11, 2001, terrorist attack on the World Trade Center in New York City. In the 3 years before the terrorist attack, the United States and Taliban leaders met to discuss bringing the terrorist Osama bin Laden to justice. According to former CIA station chief Milton Bearden (Ottaway & Stephens, 2001), "We never heard what they were trying to say. . . . We had no common language. Ours was, 'Give up bin Laden.' They were saying, 'Do something to help us give him up'" (p. AO1). When the Taliban publicly stated that they no longer knew where bin Laden was, the low-context United States interpreted it as an effort to evade responsibility for turning him over. However, a more high-context interpretation of the statements suggests that the Taliban more than once set up bin Laden for capture by the United States. Bearden noted (Ottaway & Stephens, 2001), "Every time the Afghans said, 'He's lost again' they are saying something. They are saying, 'He's no longer under our protection'. . . . They thought they were signaling us subtly, and we don't do signals" (p. AO1). High-context cultures communicate using signals, yet low-context cultures apparently don't "do" signals, potentially with disastrous results. (pp. 292–296)

An axiom of North American psychology is that one should create a strong tie between one's performance and the rewards one receives. However, doing so in many developing countries may conflict with societal values that emphasize collectivism rather than individualism. Thus, global adherence to this axiom may have a deleterious effect on an international organization's performance. For example, individualistic cultures value competition, achievement, and personal goals. Employees want pay plans that reward their performance. But collectivistic cultures value cooperation, interdependence, and group goals. Employees want pay plans that foster harmony within their group (James, 1993; Leung, 1997).

Leung (2001) argued that: (a) people in collectivistic cultures have higher levels of unconditional benevolence and positive social identity which, in turn, lead to higher levels of in-group involvement than is the case for people who value individualism; (b) productivity and performance levels are more homogenous (not necessarily higher or lower) in collectivistic cultures than in individualistic cultures; (c) motivational strategies by superiors have more effect on subordinates in cultures with high levels of power distance than in cultures low in power distance; and (d) negative reactions from supervisors in high power distance cultures generate more negative reactions among workers than is the case in low power distance cultures.

Bagozzi, Verbeke, and Gavino (2003) observed that national cultures vary in the ways in which the self, others, and the relationships between the self and others are construed. In the West, self is viewed as a relatively independent, autonomous entity. In the East, self is viewed as a social, interdependent entity where one's thoughts and feelings are formed in reference to those of significant others. There is an emphasis in the East on fitting into the shared network of social relationships. These findings are supportive of those reported by Hofstede.

In an attempt to tie together needs and values, Steers and Sanchez-Runde (2002) stated that one's national culture influences three key sets of distal sources of motivation: (1) people's self-concept including personal beliefs, needs, and values; (2) norms about work ethic and the nature of "achievement," tolerance for ambiguity, locus of control, etc.; and (3) "environmental factors" such as education and socialization experiences, economic prosperity and political or legal systems. Based on this conceptual model, it would appear that these distal factors influence self-efficacy beliefs and work motivation levels and goals as well as the nature of incentives and disincentives to perform well.

In an enumerative review of the literature, Aguinis and Henle (2003) reported that employees in individualistic cultures are more motivated when they are working alone than when they are part of a team; in contrast, those who work in collectivistic societies perform better in teams. Social loafing on the part of an individual is a more common occurrence in the West than it is in the East. Interestingly, the performance of employees in both Eastern and Western cultures is lowered when they are required to work with "out-group" members. But the magnitude of this effect is moderated by societal culture. Those in a collectivistic culture are more opposed to working with out-group members than are employees in cultures that are individualistic.

In support of the findings referred to above by Brockner et al. (2001), the authors also concluded that societal culture moderates the effects of employee participation in the decision-making process. Cultures characterized by high power distance as well as individualism are more likely to favor decisions made by individual managers or employees; collectivistic as well as low power cultures are more likely to benefit from an intervention that introduces participation in decision making to the workplace.

Departing from Hofstede's early research, Earley (2002) proposed a three-level construct which he labeled "cultural intelligence," in which a person's self-efficacy vis-à-vis social discourse in cross-cultural settings plays a key role in the effectiveness of such interactions. Consistent with Bandura's (2000) research, high self-efficacy resulted in an individual initiating cross-cultural interactions, persisting in the face of early failures, and engaging in problem solving as a way of mastering the necessary skills.

Sue-Chan and Ong (2002) investigated the effect of goal assignment on goal commitment, self-efficacy, and performance of people from 10 different countries. Self-efficacy mediated the effect of goal assignment on performance for those low in value for power distance.

Scholz, Dona, Sud, and Schwarzer (2002) found that not all motivation-related values vary across cultures.[5] A study of more than 19,000 participants from 25 countries showed a high degree of consistency in the psychometric properties of a scale assessing general self-efficacy—an arguably important concept in the mechanisms related to goal setting and self regulation. The distinction between general and specific self-efficacy is discussed later.

Bagozzi et al. (2003) reported, in a comparative study of salespeople in the Philippines versus the Netherlands, that shame, as defined by intense feelings that one has not met the expectations of salient others, was experienced emotionally similarly across the two cultures. However, an examination of employee performance revealed strong context effects. Dutch employees hid from customers in whose presence they felt ashamed, and hence their performance decreased; the Filipino salespeople approached such customers so as to repair the damage to the relationship.

---

[5]Based on their research findings, Schwartz and Sagie (2000) argued that two sets of values generalize across cultures. Specifically, they found two bipolar dimensions: First, openness to change vs. conservation; second, self-transcendence vs. self-enhancement.

The basis for many of these differences in values among societies, argued Nisbett (2003), can be traced back 2,500 years to ancient Greece and China. The Greeks encouraged personal agency which included valuing the individual, a sense of debate, and a curiosity for the larger world. The Chinese espoused collective agency which valued the in-group, harmony, and a lack of worldly wonderment. Today, Westerners believe that individuals are separate units and therefore enter into social contracts with one another that guarantee certain rights and freedoms. Asians, on the other hand, view societies not as aggregates of self-contained individuals but rather as natural wholes of interacting elements. Consequently, they place less value on the rights of the individual.

Nisbett's research shows that today people in the East (e.g., Chinese, Japanese, and Koreans) and West (e.g., North Americans) see, think about, and mentally organize the world in fundamentally different ways. A series of social psychology experiments revealed that Asians are more attentive to content while Americans are more prone to extract objects from their environment. Asians are more likely to anticipate changes in the directions of trends in contrast to North Americans. North Americans, Nisbett found, are prone to thinking linearly; they believe that trends will continue. Asians are likely to seek compromises to conflicts; North Americans are likely to polarize alternatives and adopt an argumentative approach. North Americans often fail to recognize the role of situational constraints on a speaker's behavior relative to their Korean counterparts. When given two seemingly contradictory propositions, North Americans tend to polarize their beliefs whereas Chinese tend to accept equally both propositions.

Trompenaars and Hampden-Turner (1998) differentiated societal cultures in terms of universalism-particularism. Cultures that embrace universalism rely on rules for assessing what is right versus wrong or appropriate vs. inappropriate, and rely on the courts to enforce these norms. Cultures that score high on particularism take into account the context in determining right versus wrong. For example, was the rule broken by the person intentionally? In particularist cultures, understanding the reasons the person took action is essential for assessing whether a "wrong" has taken place. Therefore, universalists often perceive particularists as untrustworthy because of the "exceptions" that are made. They view concepts and definitions used by particularists as arbitrary or capricious. Conversely, particularists appraise universalists as untrustworthy for being so "cut and dry."

In summary, starting with Hofstede's landmark research with IBM in the last century, significant progress has been made in the present century in understanding cross-cultural differences in work motivation. Mediating mechanisms explain why motivational strategies vary in effectiveness in different countries. As Hofstede warned 20 years ago, transposing job design characteristics that are effective motivators in one culture (e.g., North America) to other cultures (e.g., Asia) must be done with caution. If there is a mismatch between the values of society and the values of an intervention, such as job or organization redesign, the intervention is doomed to fail.[6]

Job Characteristics

As Chatman (1989) noted toward the end of the 20th century, the implicit hypothesis underlying the study of individual differences is that a person's behavior is optimally predicted by measuring traits, values, and motives. This is because these variables are relatively stable and hence are reflected in a person's behavior.

In contrast to this position, situationists in the 20th century (e.g., Herzberg; Hackman, and Oldham) believed that context (e.g., job characteristics) is a primary determinant of an employee's behavior,[7] hence their focus on job and organization design. Among the leading situationists in the present century are two Australian researchers, Cordery and Parker.

Cordery (1997), an I/O psychologist at the University of Western Australia, argued the necessity of differentiating the importance of three dimensions of job autonomy, namely (1) method control as defined by the amount of discretion one has over the way in which work is performed, (2) timing control in terms of the influence one has over scheduling of work, and (3) allowing supervisory discretion in setting performance goals. He found four interrelated dimensions that affect job autonomy, namely the extent to which the supervisor (1) provides

---

[6]Years earlier, Faucheux, Amado, and Laurent (1982) made a similar point. The assumptions of Theory Y were found to be contradictory to the social reality of Latin America as well as the Catholic ethic in Latin Europe; and, in many areas of France and Italy the human relations movement was considered naïve. Locke (2003) suggested a research agenda to increase understanding of the universality or lack thereof regarding motivational interventions. If intervention A does not work in culture B, is it because people in culture B refused to use it? Is it because people refused to use it initially but eventually used it effectively? Did the intervention fail because it was poorly implemented? Will the intervention be effective if it is adapted/modified so as to be congruent with the values of the society in which it will be implemented?

[7]The person-situation debate in the HRM, I/O, and OB literature parallels the ongoing nature vs. nurture/heredity vs. environment debate in experimental psychology.

clear attainable goals, (2) exerts control over work activities, (3) ensures that the requisite resources are available, and (4) gives timely accurate feedback on progress toward goal attainment. The first three influence employee perceptions of autonomy.[8]

An analysis of survey data from Australian employees led Wright and Cordery (1999) to conclude that affective well-being declines with traditional job designs, particularly where there is production uncertainty, but increases under "high control" job designs. Production uncertainty, is an important contextual variable that, similar to supervisory practice, has the potential to improve the prediction and explanatory capability of job design theories. Where the work is routine and predictable, attempts to increase decision control (autonomy) within an operator's job begs the question, they said, of "control over what?" Where the opposite is true, they found that job design can be effective in increasing motivation in the workplace.

Building on her research with Wall (Parker & Wall, 1998), which shows that work-related stress can result in emotional exhaustion and psychosomatic illness, Parker (2003) conducted another study that showed that unenriched, simplified jobs stemming from lean processes can affect an employee's level of job depression.[9] The mediator was job characteristics. Job characteristics also partially mediated organizational commitment. To the extent that lean processes can be introduced in such a way as to allow job autonomy, skill use, and participation in decision making, the employee's well being and motivation increases. Failure to do so, she argued, is not likely to be conducive to an employee's self-efficacy. These findings, from a UK-based company, are consistent with those obtained earlier by Theorell and Karasek (1996). They found that lack of job autonomy can increase the risk of cardiovascular disease. It would appear that Herzberg was correct in his

---

[8]Note that job autonomy is viewed here as a state, that is, a characteristic of the job rather than a growth need or individual difference variable.

[9]"What goes around comes around." Lean processes, originating in Toyota, Japan, is similar to Frederick Taylor's work discussed at the beginning of this book. The objective is to improve efficiency, quality, and responsiveness to customers by removing wasted time and motions. A primary distinction between lean processes and Taylor's approach is that the work standards are determined by the employees rather than by industrial engineers.

Parker, a faculty member of the Australian Graduate School of Management, did her dissertation under a renowned researcher, Toby Wall. In an earlier study (Wall & Jackson, 1995), she found that job autonomy can facilitate the time necessary for learning and development which in turn increases job performance.

hypothesis that the job can affect a person's mental health; it can affect one's long-term physical health as well.[10]

Parker's hypothesis regarding the possible mediating effect of self-efficacy regarding job characteristics is supported by Bandura's (2001a) social cognitive theory. When people believe themselves to be ineffacious, they are likely to exert little or no effort even in environments that provide opportunities for their growth. Conversely, when people view their environment as controllable regarding job characteristics that are important to them, they are motivated to fully exercise their perceived efficacy which, in turn, enhances their likelihood of success.

Houkes et al. (2001) obtained findings similar to Cordery and Parker. In their studies of a Dutch bank and school, they used a Dutch translation of the Job Diagnostic Survey (Hackman & Oldham, 1980). The data revealed a positive relationship between work content, specifically skill variety, and work motivation as defined by the desire to perform well, and between erosion of work content and emotional exhaustion in both organizational settings. The latter variable was also predicted by lack of social support.

The Multimethod Job Design Questionnaire (MJDQ) can be used for assessing the characteristics of a job. Originally developed by Campion and Thayer (1985) and refined by Edwards, Scully, and Brtek (1999), the MJDQ is valid, comprehensive, and applicable across contexts. Eighteen of the items assess motivation, 8 tap mechanistic properties of jobs, 10 focus on biological variables, and the remaining 12 measure perceptual-motor requirements of jobs.[11]

Edwards, Scully, and Brtek (2000) found that mechanistically oriented job designs that focus on such things as work simplification and specialization are associated with efficiency-related outcomes. Motivationally oriented job designs are associated with satisfaction related outcomes. Paradoxically, these two designs typically produce outcomes that have strong negative relationships to one another.

Using the MJDQ within a pharmaceutical company, Morgeson and Campion (2002) outlined a process to minimize the tradeoff between employee efficiency and satisfaction: First, define task clusters that form a natural work process. Second, quantify the task clusters in terms of

---

[10]That lack of autonomy in a Western country can lead to heart disease suggests a study for someone to conduct in the East where employees may be higher on external than internal control. Would designing jobs characterized by high autonomy lead to adverse health effects?

[11]Their analyses indicate that the MJDQ is best represented by a first order model with 10 factors, each of which represents a distinct aspect of work.

their motivational (e.g., autonomy) and mechanistic (e.g., specialization) properties. Third, combine task clusters to form a job core.

Aguinis and Henle (2003), in their enumerative review of the literature, found support for Herzberg's fundamental premise, namely, that two motivators appear to be universally applicable: the desire by employees for both growth and control of their environment. Jobs that facilitate growth are desired by employees in China, Russia, the United States (Silverthorne, 1992), Bulgaria, Hungary, the Netherlands (Roe, Zinovieva, Dienes, & Ten Horn, 2000), Australia, Canada, and Singapore (Popp et al., 1986). The importance of being able to exert control over one's environment was expressed by employees in foreign subsidiaries of companies in Belgium, Columbia, Germany, Italy, Japan, Mexico, Spain, and Venezuela (Alpander & Carter, 1991).

In summary: (a) the importance of an employee's job environment, particularly, the importance of designing jobs that allow autonomy for such outcomes as learning, performance, organizational citizenship behavior, and satisfaction has been shown by a multitude of empirical studies. Unenriched routine jobs can result in job depression. (b) A questionnaire with excellent psychometric properties now exists to assess job characteristics. (c) Morgeson and Campion (2003) have shown that there are three major components of jobs, namely, complexity, the social environment, and physical demands. The latter two have been relatively ignored by HRM, I/O, and OB researchers. As a result of research on how best to design jobs, more than 90% of Fortune 1000 companies have incorporated task autonomy (Lawler, Mohrman, & Ledford, 1995) because, as noted by Hackman and Oldham (1980), autonomy can lead to the critical psychological state of experiencing responsibility for work outcomes that, in turn, leads to an increase in an employee's satisfaction with the job.

Langfred and Moye (2004) developed a model that highlights for practitioners possible moderators regarding job autonomy. When there is low task interdependence and high task variability, an organization should select people who have a strong need for autonomy. In settings where an employee lacks the requisite knowledge to make informed decisions, task autonomy can have a deleterious effect on performance due to the increase in cognitive load on the person. When task technology requires high levels of task interdependence in which an employee's work is tightly coupled, introducing task autonomy can decrease performance. However, when task variability is high, task autonomy usually is highly beneficial to an employee's performance. But when the task comes with highly formalized rules and procedures, granting a person job autonomy can be an oxymoron. In short, before designing jobs with autonomy, organizational decision makers need to take into account: (a) how motivated the workforce is by job autonomy, (b) their task-specific knowledge, (c) the complexity and interdependency of the different tasks performed by different people, (d) task variability, and (e) the extent to which the rules and procedures for performing the task are formalized. Autonomy should not be granted to employees who do not value it, who lack the knowledge or ability to perform interdependent tasks that are complex for them, as well as tasks that are low in variability and are enshrined in codified rules and procedures. These findings point to the necessity of taking into account context, namely "person-environment fit."

Person-Environment Fit

Leonard Ferguson (1962) credited Walter Dill Scott and his consulting firm, the Scott Company, for being the first to recognize the importance of person-environment fit.

> Working (1919-1923) directly with its clients, forty of which were large industrial organizations and later, through Scott and Clothier's book, *Personnel Management: Principles, Practices and Point of View* (A.W. Shaw Company, 1925) the Scott Company developed . . . the 'worker-in-his-work unit.' . . . In contrast with notions held by Hugo Munsterberg . . . the Scott Company held that there were no square pegs (i.e., men) to be found for square holes (i.e., jobs). Rather that both 'men and jobs' [were] plastic [both] yielding here and giving there to outside pressure. Therefore, recognizing the fact that a job and a person will interact, each influencing, changing, and modifying the other, industry's task became, said the Scott Company, not "the connecting of a man with a job but 'the creation of worker-in-his-work unit.'" (pp. 15–16)

Research on person-environment fit 40 years later had as its impetus the attack by Mischel (1968), a highly respected social psychologist, on the study of personality. Paying no attention to Scott, Mischel argued that it is the situation rather than the person that causes behavior. This sparked a strong response from a social psychologist at York University, Norman Endler (Endler & Magnusson, 1976; Magnusson & Endler, 1977). The essence of the retort is that it is the person in interaction with the situation rather than the person or situation alone that is critical in predicting, understanding, and influencing a person's behavior.

An employee's environment, namely the job and the employing organization, affects and is affected by a person's needs, personality, and values. Research emphasis in the present century is primarily on a person's needs, personality, and values rather than on the environment. This may be a reaction by HRM, I/O, and OB researchers to the emphasis in the previous century on the environment to the near exclusion of personality variables. Ambrose and Kulik (1999) reported that between 1970 and 1990, more than 200 studies were conducted on characteristics of jobs that are determinants of attitudinal and behavioral outcomes.[12] However, to believe that motivation is solely a function of the person or solely a function of the job is as naïve as believing that area is primarily a function of length rather than width.

Motivation is both an internal psychological process and a transactional one. That is, motivation is the result of the reciprocal interactions between people and their work environments and the fit between these interactions and the broader societal context (Franko, Bennett, & Kanfer, 2002). Thus, to fully understand, predict, and influence employee behavior, one must, as Scott stated nearly a century ago, take into account both the person and the environment. Researchers who embrace this approach, as noted earlier, are referred to as interactionists.

Employees typically differentiate between two varieties of person-environment fit: (1) "needs-supplies" where an employee's needs, desires, or preferences are met by the work environment; and (2) job demands-abilities where a person's abilities are commensurate with what the job requires (Cable & DeRue, 2002; Dawis & Lofquist, 1984; French, Caplan, & Harrison, 1982). The person-environment interface can be further differentiated in terms of a complementary and a supplementary fit (Cable & Edwards, 2004; Muchinsky & Monahan, 1987). A complementary fit exists to the extent that a person's psychological need such as job autonomy (needs-supplies fit) is fulfilled (Kristof, 1996) and an individual's skills meet environmental needs (demands-ability fit) (Muchinsky & Monahan, 1987). A supplementary fit occurs when the employee and the employee's environment are similar.

---

[12]Recall that highly influential psychologists such as Terry Mitchell (1979) had concluded that there was little to be gained from studying individual difference variables with regard to motivation. Similarly, Locke, Shaw, Saari, and Latham (1980) reported that the only consistent finding regarding the effect of individual difference variables on goal setting was inconsistency.

Recalling that the Hawthorne studies focused in part on the adjustment and maladjustment of an employee to the work setting, Barsade, Brief, and Spataro (2004) commented that the findings suggested the importance of person-context fit.

A supplementary fit exists when an employee and an organization attach similar importance to the same values, that is, the importance a person and an organization place on a particular attribute. Thus, what distinguishes needs from values with regard to person-environment fit is the conceptual division along which needs and values vary, that is, an employee's desired amount for one or more psychological needs versus the importance of one or more values to an employee.

Complementary needs-supplies fit is obviously important because it leads to the fulfillment of a person's needs. People display positive attitudes to the extent that their needs are fulfilled. Supplementary fit satisfies a fundamental need for consensual validation of a person's perspectives (Kristof-Brown, Zimmerman, & Johnson, 2005; Van Vianen, 2000). Demands-abilities fit has a smaller relationship on an employee's attitudes because the fit is based on meeting environmental rather than a person's needs.

A study that took place in four water-treatment agencies involved employees ranging from laborers to executives. In that study, Cable and Edwards (2004) found that psychological need fulfillment and value congruence were equally predictive of a person's work attitude. Yet each predicted unique variance in the dependent variables. What this study tells us is that value congruence is working through mechanisms of similarity-attraction and value validation rather than a need fulfillment mechanism.

Shaw and Gupta (2004) defined supplies-value fit as the congruence between the desired level of a certain task characteristic (values) and the level of that characteristic available in the job (supplies).[13] Values are the conscious desires held by the person, whereas supplies refer to the amount, frequency, or qualities of a job characteristic that a person values. The process underlying the supplies-value model are cognitive comparisons that employees make regarding the congruence between the job characteristics that they value as opposed to those they experience. Shaw and Gupta conducted three studies which showed that psychological as well as physiological strain occurs when there is a misfit. Excess values create emotional distress and arousal by eliciting too much cognitive rumination regarding the discrepancy, and then

---

[13]Note that here values refer to the desired amount, which is how needs are characterized earlier. Unfortunately, P-E researchers use the terms *need* and *values* inconsistently, such that each term sometimes refers to desired amount and other times refers to importance (Edwards, 2005, personal communication).

activating defense mechanisms that dampen an employee's mood. Conversely, over-supply also creates emotional distress and cognitive rumination; it increases strain through depletion. In short, a person-environment misfit affects strain when supplies exceed a person's values due to the fact that the job is more complex (e.g., variety, autonomy, work level, skill requirements) than the individual prefers, or when supplies fall short of an individual's values because the job is simpler than the individual prefers.

Shaw and Gupta found that job performance is a contingency factor that either heightens or lessens the effects of a supplies-value misfit on an employee. This is because job performance can heighten or lessen the attention a person pays to a misfit. Performing poorly increases the number and direction of supplies-values comparisons that an individual makes and in addition increases the intensity of the person's deliberation. Performing effectively, however, reduces the penchant for introspection, lowers the perceived importance of a misfit, and curtails external cues that trigger cognitive rumination of a discrepancy.

Parker's research, described in the previous section, is arguably taking into account both the person and the environment.[14] She and her colleagues hypothesized that the design of work (e.g., permitting autonomy or job control) and one's personality contribute to both a person's mental health and job performance. In a longitudinal study of customer service center employees in the United Kingdom, these researchers found that the beneficial effects of designing jobs that allow people autonomy is enhanced for those employees who score high on psychological acceptance. The latter refers to a willingness to experience all psychological events, including thoughts, feelings, and sensations, without attempting to change, avoid, or otherwise control them. By accepting these internal events, people are able to effectively use their energies, formerly allocated to resignation, avoidance, or control, to act in ways that are congruent with their values and goals. This is because acceptance involves the transfer of

---

[14]I use the word arguably because the person and environment were not assessed on commensurate dimensions. For instance, to study needs-supplies fit concerning autonomy, a measure of the amount of autonomy in the environment should be paired with a measure of the amount of the autonomy desired by the person (e.g., Edwards & Rothbard, 1999). In contrast, Parker operationalized the person in terms of psychological acceptance. Although this concept is conceptually relevant to environmental autonomy, it does not refer to autonomy itself. Studies of this type are not equipped to test P-E fit, because it cannot be determined whether the environment exceeds or falls short of the person when the two are assessed on different metrics (e.g., it does not make sense to say that a score of 3 on an environmental autonomy scale matches a score of 3 on psychological acceptance because the scales do not refer to a common content dimension).

scarce attentional resources from controlling internal events to making and enacting behavioral choices on the basis of what will lead to valued goals rather than on the basis of what thoughts or emotions the person may be experiencing in the workplace. In short, these data show that psychological acceptance is a moderator of the relationship between job autonomy and measures of an employee's mental health and productivity.

Person-context fit, not surprisingly, affects the ability of personality measures to predict a person's job performance as well as satisfaction. The ability to do so increases when characteristics of the job are taken into account (Gustafson & Mumford, 1995). Tett, Jackson, Rothstein, and Reddon (1999) reported that this is also true for occupational context. For example, people who score high on extroversion are generally high performers. However, occupational context can negate this personality-performance relationship. Specifically, extroversion was shown to be contraindicated for accountants, for whom professional accountability and limited job autonomy are a requisite.

To what extent can a poor fit in one area (e.g., team/environment) compensate for a good fit in the other (e.g., person/team)? In a highly innovative experiment, using a computer simulation originally developed for the U.S. Department of Defense, Hollenbeck et al. (2002) answered this question by examining fit in terms of (a) the person's intelligence and personality with (b) the structure of the team, departmental vs. divisional, and (c) the uncertainty of the environment. Departmental teams emphasize narrow specialized roles and high interdependence among team members. Divisional teams emphasize relatively broad independent roles.

In a predictable stable environment, department teams usually perform better than divisionally structured teams. This is because department teams are efficient in that redundancy across people is minimized, and high levels of functional expertise are developed. Divisional teams, on the other hand, perform well in an unstable environment because they promote flexibility; they are able to react quickly to local, idiosyncratic opportunities as well as threats.

In the present study, the task confronting the teams was highly complex. The results showed that a good person-team fit exists when the person is intelligent and the team is structured divisionally, and, when the team must perform in an uncertain unstable environment. However, the benefit of a good person-team fit was negated when the team-environment fit was poor. When the environment became predictable, this team structure became inefficient. No amount of intelligence on the part of team members could compensate for a misalignment between team structure and the environment.

Emotional stability on the part of people in the misaligned team-environment fit partially offset the negative effects of a divisional structure in a predictable environment. Nevertheless, all things being equal, it was still optimal for team performance for the teams to be structured functionally when interacting within a predictable environment.

In the functional department teams that performed in a predictable environment, the hypothesis that a person's agreeableness is important was not supported. Hollenbeck et al. concluded that this is because this is a "strong" environment that masks individual differences.

In the 1960s, a University of Toronto professor, Marshall McLuhan, coined the term, a *global village*. This village is now a reality. In the ever-changing nature of work, virtual teams have become commonplace within the past decade. These teams consist of individuals who interact on interdependent tasks, yet they are geographically and sometimes even organizationally dispersed, and hence they must rely primarily, if not solely, on information and communication technologies for the coordination and communication necessary for them to perform team tasks. Maruping and Agarwal (2004) are among those researchers who are beginning to examine fit in terms of task and technology to ensure performance effectiveness of these virtual teams. This research is based on media synchronicity theory (Dennis & Valacich, 1999) which is essentially a framework for making informed choices of available communication media. The theory attempts to match the requirements of the communication task to the capabilities of the medium. The theory proposes that a team's tasks consist of two critical communication processes: the exchange and subsequent deliberation of the meaning of the communication, and convergence regarding the development of the shared meaning of the information.

Empirical research based on this theory is in the embryonic stage. The early evidence suggests that the nature of the task is indeed an important factor in choosing an appropriate communication medium. In addition, the developmental stage of a virtual team must be taken into consideration. Newly formed virtual teams typically need richer media that facilitate socialization and trust among members (e.g., tele-conferencing). Established teams may be able to perform optimally using less rich media (e.g., audio conferencing). In short, the theory states that choice of media is governed by the nature of the task and the developmental stage of the team.

Among the leading interactionists with regard to the fit between the person and the organization, as opposed to person-job fit is Benjamin Schneider, professor emeritus at the University of Maryland.[15] He and his colleagues developed the attraction, selection, attrition (ASA) model. ASA states that people gravitate to organizations and jobs that are congruent with their values.[16] For example, Cable and Parsons (2001) found that value congruence between the person and the organization at time of hire predicts subject's perceptions of fit two years later. The more job offers available to an employee, the greater the likelihood of an appropriate fit. To the extent that value congruence was low, turnover occurred. In short, people are attracted to and tend to remain with employers whose values are similar to their own. They often leave (attrition) when this is not the case. With regard to selection, Ryan, Sacco, McFarland, and Kriska (2000) found that people voluntarily drop out of the selection process when they perceive a misfit. This supports an earlier finding that organizational and occupational factors determine the types of people who join and remain in an organization (Schaubroeck, Ganster, & Jones, 1998).

ASA also stresses the dysfunctional consequences of interpersonal homogeneity (e.g., the dangers of limited perspectives for decision making, groupthink, etc.) as well as the putative benefits such as high levels of

---

[15]He is famous, in part, for his dictum: The people make the place. This is because "people come to organizations already presocialized as a result of the attraction, selection, attrition (ASA) process, and the organization refines them; organizations do not make silk purses out of sow's ears. Organizations that claim large impact for their socialization practices (e.g., police and fire departments, medical schools) attract particular kinds of people who already empathize with the norms and values of these organizations" (Schneider, 2004, personal communication). He has been interested in person-environment interaction since the earliest days of his doctoral studies with Jack Bartlett.

> Somehow I knew it was wrong to study either individual differences or the situation and think you had all the answers. My dissertation topic was a field study of the interaction of ability and situation in the prediction of performance. Later, I had an ONR Contract to further study this issue and ran a small conference on ability-situation interaction. In reviewing the literature I discovered that the only time such interactions were found were in laboratory studies and that truly piqued my curiosity so I began messing around with ways to conceptualize the fact that true interactions only happen in extreme conditions. In about 1979 I ran across a 1973 paper by Kenneth Bowers in *Psychological Review* on interactional psychology, and he gave me the answer: lab studies randomly assign people to situations, but that is not the way the real world works. (Schneider, 2004, personal communication)

[16]In support of Schneider's ASA model, George Hollenbeck, a former staff psychologist with Merrill Lynch and a fellow member of the Summit Group, sent him a cartoon from the *New Yorker* where the cat boss (with many cat workers in the background) states to the dog employee: "Let's face it. You and this organization have never been a good fit."

interpersonal harmony and job satisfaction (Schneider et al., 2001). To date however, there is little or no ASA research regarding an employee's job performance. This is because the ASA model is critical of the current and historical emphasis on the individual as the focal point for analysis. The ASA model focuses instead on organizational effectiveness and predicts an organization's demise over time when person-environment fit is high. The irony here, as Kristof-Brown (2005, personal communication), a former student of Schneider, commented is: "The dysfunctional consequences are all for the organization. There are very few people who believe that fit creates negative consequences for the individual. This is the great complication of the levels of analysis in fit. What is good for the person is not necessarily good for the organization."

The ASA has been critiqued by Simmering et al. (2003) for failing to take into account the possibility that people who experience a misfit may change themselves, or their environment, rather than simply leaving the organization. In a longitudinal study, they found that people who score high on conscientiousness proactively engage in developmental activities when their needs for autonomy are not being met.

In addition to Schneider, Jennifer Chatman at the University of California, Berkeley, is a long-time advocate of examining person-organization fit. Her research takes into account the importance of context regarding an organization's values (e.g., O'Reilly, Chatman, & Caldwell, 1991). Person-organization fit exists to the extent that there is congruence between the values of the organization and the values of the employee. Determining "fit" enhances the ability to predict the extent to which an employee's values will change as a function of being employed in a given organization and the extent to which the employee will adhere to the employing organization's values. Her research shows that person-organization fit is positively related to an employee's engagement in organizational citizenship behavior. This finding was replicated by Lauver and Kristof-Brown (2001) in their study of office personnel and drivers in a national trucking company. However, if there is a poor fit because the person's values are not aligned with values that are held strongly by the employing organization, the person's values are likely to change, given that the individual is open to being influenced. If the latter is not the case, the employee is likely to seek employment elsewhere. On the other hand, if the person has high self-efficacy, and/or if the person enters the organization with a large cohort whose values, too, are discrepant with those held by the organization, it is the organization's values that are likely to change over time rather than those held by the employee(s). Chatman's model of person-organization fit is shown in Figure 8.1.

In short, people are constantly both producers and products of their social systems. "Goodness-of-fit" models simultaneously consider the compatibility between individuals and the environment in which they work. The basic assumption underlying these models is that the relationship between person variables (such as needs or values) and both individual and organizational outcomes is contingent upon various features of the environment (e.g., characteristics of the job, the team, and the organization).

A limitation of person-environment fit research is that interactions between the person and characteristics of the job or organization are usually treated as stable rather than as dynamic states.[17] Moreover, there are no agreed-upon ways of assessing dynamic interactions (Borman, Klimoski, & Ilgen, 2003). Hulin and Judge (2003) lamented that on balance the conceptual advantages of goodness-of-fit models have yet to yield the significant gains that might be expected in understanding an employee's performance. This may have been due to treating the environment as somehow independent of the employee, even though the employee affects the environment (cf. Bandura, 2001a). Clarity regarding person-environment fit has been very much needed on the extent to which a person's performance, as opposed to satisfaction, is increased. This clarity has been provided by Kristof-Brown et al. (2005).[18]

These authors conducted a meta-analysis of the person-environment fit in terms of person-job, person-group, person-organization, and person-supervisor. Among their findings are that:

---

[17]"Classic presentations of P-E fit theory (e.g., French et al., 1974, 1982) emphasize that people can respond to P-E misfit by modifying the person, the environment or both (French and colleagues describe these responses in terms of coping and defense). Thus, although some discussions of P-E fit do not address the dynamic aspects, such oversights do not characterize P-E fit theory itself, and the dynamic aspects of P-E fit have been discussed for quite some time" (Edwards, 2005, personal communication).

[18]Amy Kristof-Brown's long-term interest in P-E fit began during an impression management study she did as a graduate student with her professor, Cindy Stevens. They found that applicants who indicate that they are "a good fit" are judged highly favorably in a selection interview (Stevens & Kristof-Brown, 1995). Subsequently, she took a doctoral seminar with Ben Schneider where she wrote a paper on P-E fit. "He is the one who encouraged me to take it to *Personnel Psychology* where I got a great set of reviewers who took the paper to a whole other level" (Kristof-Brown, 2005, personal communication). As I stated in my 13 critical incidents, at the outset of this book, mentors can have an enduring influence on a person's career.

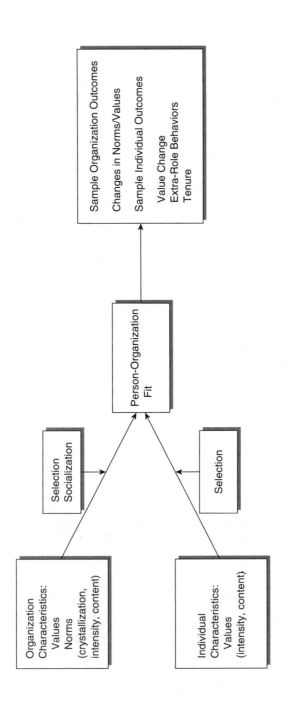

Figure 8.1   A Model of Person-Organization Fit

Source: Reprinted with permission from Chapman, J. A. (1989). Improving International Organizational Research: A Model of Person-Organization Fit. *Academy of Management Review, 4,* 333–349.

1. Person-environment fit is a multidimensional concept. The four definitions of fit, listed above, are only moderately related to one another. People can discern these four different aspects of their environment when assessing their fit.

2. Person-organization fit has a weak correlation with overall job performance, but a moderate correlation with organizational citizenship behavior, a moderate negative correlation with intention to quit and a low correlation with actual turnover. The primary benefit of person-organization fit is its positive relationship with an employee's organizational commitment and job satisfaction.

3. Person-job fit has a modest correlation with overall performance. Needs-supplies fit is a stronger predictor than demands-abilities. Person-job fit has a strong relationship with an individual's job satisfaction and organizational commitment.

4. Person-group fit has a low correlation with an employee's overall performance and organizational citizenship behavior.

5. Person-supervisor fit has a strong relationship with a person's job satisfaction but not organization commitment.

6. In comparing the different types of fit, (a) organizational commitment was most strongly related to person-organization fit followed closely by person-job fit. It was weakly related to person-group fit. (b) Satisfaction with co-workers was highest for person-group fit, followed by person-organization and person-job fit. (c) Not surprisingly, satisfaction with one's supervisor was highest for person-supervisor fit.

7. With regard to performance, the correlations were at best modest for person-job (.20), person-group (.19), and person-supervisor fit (.18).

In science, it is seldom the case that anyone has the last word. In this instance, Jeff Edwards (2005, personal communication) pointed out that:

Several of the studies reviewed (e.g., Cable & Parsons, 2001; O'Reilly et al., 1991) operationalized fit using profile similarity indices, which have numerous methodological shortcomings (Cronbach, 1958; Edwards, 1993). These problems do not merely weaken effects, nor should they be addressed by warning researchers to interpret results "with caution." Rather, these problems often invite conclusions that are flat wrong. Moreover, profile similarity indices shield P-E fit theory from falsification, because the construction of these indices assumes the similarity between the person and environment drives outcomes without testing that assumption. Thus, studies that have used profile similarity indices (or difference scores) are inconclusive. Note that this inconclusiveness applies to most of the studies reviewed by Kristof-Brown et al. (2005), and aggregating these studies with meta-analysis does not rectify the problems with the studies themselves.

Locke and I (Locke & Latham, 2004) noted that person-environment studies generally focus on the effect of "strong" or constrained situations where employees feel less free to act as they want or "really are" as compared to when they are in "weak" situations. What has yet to be studied is strong vs. weak personalities. As Schneider's ASA model emphasizes, people are not simply dropped into situations. Research is now needed on ways they choose, create, and change the characteristics of their job and their team, as well as their organization, and the role, if any, of personality traits in doing so.[19]

Concluding Comments

As was the case in the 20th century, the number of HRM, I/O, and OB researchers in the 21st century who are studying physiological and psychological needs per se is relatively small. However, the picture changes when the definition of needs is broadened to include personality traits. As of the end of the 20th and the beginning of the 21st centuries, this field of study is receiving a great deal of attention with regard to motivation in the workplace. The effect of the environment alone as a main effect on motivation is studied by a relatively small number of researchers today relative to yesterday. Instead, context—particularly job characteristics—is being taken into account as a moderator of the predictability of traits regarding an employee's performance.

As is the case with personality traits, the importance given to employee values by HRM, I/O, and OB researchers is relatively recent. Influenced by Hofstede's work in the 1980s, scientists and practitioners are now sensitive to the dangers of a North American bias in the behavioral science literature. The effect of societal differences on employee behavior is increasingly receiving attention by researchers.[20] And again, similar to the study of traits, researchers are taking into account the importance of context. Specifically, they are looking at reciprocal or

---

[19]As noted earlier, Bandura remains highly skeptical of finding any significant role played by traits. His research shows that three cognitive variables, namely goals, self-efficacy, and outcome expectancies, are the important determinants of motivation. The meta-analysis results by Kristof-Brown et al. (2005, p. 318) "strongly call into question the use of personality similarity as an indicator of P-O fit."

[20]Given Hofstede's data are from one organization, IBM, and given the current era of globalization in which most organizations now function, the importance of replication studies cannot be overstated.

interaction effects of characteristics of the job, the structure of the group or team, and the congruence or fit between the values of the organization and the values held by the person on his or her motivation in the workplace.

9 Cognition

Goals, Feedback, and Self-Regulation

Introduction

As noted earlier, behaviorism was the dominant paradigm in psychology for the first 60 years of the 20th century. In the 1970s, there was a cognitive revolution that has prevailed to the present day.[1]

Motivation arguably has developmental primacy over cognition in that needs are present at birth. Needs are even present before one's first perceptual experience. Needs confront us with the requirement of taking action to ensure our survival. But when it comes to choice of action beyond a reflexive response, cognition usually has primacy over motivation. A need cannot be met without the knowledge required to understand what can be done to satisfy it.

Pritchard et al. (in press) defined motivation as the process that determines how energy is used to satisfy needs. Motivation is a cognitive resource allocation process where a person makes choices as to the time and energy that are to be allocated to an array of motives or tasks. Thus motivation includes the direction, intensity, and persistence of this allocation process. Similar to Vroom's expectancy theory, Pritchard and his colleagues view motivation as a future-oriented concept in that people, they said, anticipate the amount of need satisfaction that will occur when specific outcomes are received. The perceived relationship between applying energy to actions, and this resulting need satisfaction, influences how much of the energy pool is devoted to that action. Empirical studies are now needed to test the predictive, explanatory, and operative power of Pritchard's theory.

---

[1]With few exceptions (e.g., Komaki et al., 2000) little attention is given any more to the philosophy of behaviorism as an approach to motivation in the workplace.

Cognition is inherent in motivation in that the sensations of pleasure and pain are informational. Based on needs, values, and the situational context, people set goals and strategize ways to attain them. They develop assumptions of themselves and their identity. This, too, affects their choice of goals and strategies. In short, while cognition and motivation can be partly isolated for research purposes, they are rarely separate in everyday life. Thus we now examine the research from the late 1990s to the present on goal-setting theory, feedback and self-regulation. Social cognitive theory, the Pygmalion effect, and action theory with regard to their relevance for the workplace are examined in Chapter 10.

Goal-Setting Theory

Empirical research on goal-setting theory in the present century continues unabated. As noted earlier, Mitchell and Daniels (2003, p. 231) concluded that it is the single most dominant theory in the field.[2] Goals are the situationally specific form of one's values (Locke, 2000). To predict what an employee will do in a given situation requires knowledge of how values are translated by the person into specific goals. Thus goals are the immediate precursor of action. They affect action in three ways. First, goals affect the facts people choose to act on. They regulate the direction of action by focusing attention and behavior on value-goal-relevant behavior at the expense of non-goal-relevant action. Second, values and goals affect the intensity of one's actions and the concomitant emotions dependent upon the importance of the goal to the person. The more difficult a valued goal, the more intense the effort to attain it. Third, valued goals affect persistence.

After reviewing the goal-setting literature in the 20th century, Locke (2000; Locke & Latham, 2005) concluded that all goal effects are mediated by knowledge and ability to perform the requisite task. Goal setting without adequate knowledge is useless. A goal may affect choice, effort, and persistence, but the employee will not be able to attain the goal unless that individual knows how to do so. The converse is also true. Knowledge in the absence of goals is also useless to the extent that the person has no desire to take action, to make use of that knowledge.

In this section, the current literature on conscious and subconscious goals are reviewed as is the moderating or boundary effect of context;

---

[2]In an earlier version of their paper, they used the metaphor of an 800-pound gorilla to describe the ubiquitous presence of goal-setting theory and research in the HRM, I/O, and OB literature.

feedback too is reviewed as it is an important moderator of goal setting. Finally, the self-regulation literature is reviewed as goal setting and feedback are two critical variables in the self-regulation of behavior.

Conscious Goals

Goal commitment is most important and relevant when the goal is difficult (Klein et al., 1999). Current measures of goal commitment now exist that have high reliability and validity (Klein et al., 2001; Seijts & Latham, 2000a).

Brown and Latham (2001) found that unionized telecommunication employees have high performance and high job satisfaction with their performance appraisal process when specific high goals are set. Moreover, self-efficacy in this study correlated positively with subsequent performance.

Despite the voluminous literature that now exists on both goal setting and goal orientation, goal setting and goal orientation researchers rarely, if ever, take into account one another's findings. My colleagues and I (Seijts, G. Latham, Tasa, and B. Latham, 2004) offered four reasons why this is so.[3] First, the focus of most goal orientation studies is how ability is viewed by a participant, whereas that of goal-setting studies is almost always motivation. Second, the tasks used in goal orientation studies are usually complex for people as the emphasis is on the acquisition or avoidance of knowledge and skill. The tasks typically used in goal-setting studies are straightforward for people as the emphasis is on motivation, on ways to increase their effort and persistence. Ability is treated as a given. Third, inconsistent findings are the rule when personality variables have been investigated as possible moderators of goal setting effects on performance. As Adler and Weiss (1988) had noted, a specific challenging performance goal creates a strong situation that attenuates the effect of personality on a person's behavior.[4] Hence the fourth reason. Goal orientation researchers rarely, if ever, include the setting of a specific high goal in their experiments. Goal orientation is usually treated as a trait.

---

[3]Brandon Latham is my son. He was a research assistant for Gerard Seijts, who had been my research assistant a decade earlier. Like Watson, a century earlier, Brandon left psychology for a career in advertising. Unlike Watson, he did so in the absence of controversy. Watson left Johns Hopkins University at the peak of his career after becoming romantically involved with a graduate student.

[4]Recall Mischel's (1977) distinction between strong vs. weak situations.

Using a business simulation of the U.S. cellular phone industry, Seijts et al. (2004) conducted an experiment to determine whether a specific difficult learning goal versus a learning goal orientation is likely to increase market share, and whether goal orientation is a moderator of the goal performance relationship. In support of our hypotheses, we found that setting a specific high learning goal leads to higher performance than either a specific high performance goal or a vague goal "to do your best." Self-efficacy and information search, which were reciprocally related, mediated the effect of specific high learning goals. Both a prove and an avoid goal orientation correlated negatively with performance in the "do your best condition," while a learning goal orientation correlated positively with performance in the do best condition, as well as in the condition where a specific high learning goal was set.[5] This latter finding suggests that the effect of learning goals on performance is further enhanced for people with a learning-goal orientation. The greater influence of goal setting than goal orientation as a determinant of performance tempers the practical significance of developing selection tests for assessing goal orientation. The usefulness of such tests would appear to be limited to jobs that people do alone, or almost alone, and that offer little or no training. Through training, people can be taught to set specific, high goals (e.g., Latham & Kinne, 1974); they can be taught, moreover, when to set specific, high learning goals versus specific, high performance goals. Because a goal is a situational variable that in general masks the effect of goal orientation as a dispositional variable, an emphasis on training programs rather than selection tests is likely to prove beneficial to organizations in this regard.

Using an Internet search task and a proofreading task, Kaplan, Erez, and Van-Dijk (2004) obtained similar findings regarding the effect of goal setting on another presumed trait. Specifically, they found that a person's "prevention/promotion focus" affects performance only when a specific difficult goal is not set. A specific high goal directs people toward goal attainment, regardless of their regulatory focus.

Meyer, Becker, and Vandenberghe (2004) presented the case for introducing a new concept to the goal-setting literature, namely goal regulation. Goal regulation, they said, is a mindset regarding the reasons for

---

[5]As noted earlier, VandeWalle did a factor analysis that showed that a person's performance goal orientation has two dimensions. A prove orientation is a predisposition to choose tasks that will enable the person to perform effectively in the eyes of others; an avoid orientation is a predisposition to avoid tasks where the person is likely to be seen as incompetent or ineffective.

and the purpose of a person's course of action that is either being contemplated, or is in progress. Differences in mindsets, the authors said, parallel Meyer and Allen's (1991) three-component model of organizational commitment, namely, affective (personal involvement, value congruence), normative (perceived obligation to remain, receipt of benefits that activate a need to reciprocate), and continuance (perceived costs of leaving the organization). Understanding goal regulation mindsets, Meyer et al. asserted, is becoming increasingly important. Changes in the workplace, they said, make it increasingly difficult for managers to specify, monitor, and regulate desired behavior on the part of employees. As an employee's discretion over what to do and when to do it increases, the nature of that person's commitment becomes increasingly important.

Goal regulation draws upon both Deci's and Higgins' research discussed earlier in that it is hypothesized to have two components, locus of causality and perceived purpose. These two components can change in response to variations in the environment. Meyer et al. offer the example of an employee who initiates a course of action to comply with a supervisor's request (extrinsic), and who has a strong desire not to fail (prevention focus). This person may come to appreciate the intended outcome (intrinsic) and see it as an ideal to be attained (promotion focus). Conversely, the person might see the futility of pursuing a goal yet continue to do so because of concern for the anticipated outcomes of failure to do otherwise (extrinsic; prevention focus).

Employees who have a strong affective commitment to the organization, team, or supervisor are likely to share the "target's" values and to experience assigned goals as autonomously regulated, and hence as ideals to be attained (a promotion focus). Those with a strong normative commitment are likely to view goal acceptance as an obligation. Meyer et al. described employees who are committed to a target primarily because of necessity, as having continuance commitment. These employees are likely to perceive the goal as externally regulated. Thus, they will pursue the goal to avoid the loss of desired outcomes (a prevention focus). Hence, Meyer et al. described goal commitment as a multidimensional concept because it is the result of different mindsets. Employees can pursue a goal because they want to, because they think they should, because they must, or some combination of the three.

The extent to which these notions actually affect employee behavior in significant ways remains to be tested. One intriguing hypothesis offered by these authors is that the benefit of affective relative to continuance commitment is most likely realized when it is difficult to specify all of the required behaviors, or to anticipate all of the potential obstacles to goal attainment. Affective commitment is believed to be an antecedent of discretionary as opposed to proscribed behaviors.

Contextual Conditions

The importance of context on goal setting is now being studied regarding the goals of the individual versus those of the group, the complexity of the task, environmental change and uncertainty, deadlines for multiple goals, and environmental inducement for corruption. For example, Seijts and I (Seijts & Latham, 2000b) examined the applicability of goal-setting principles when one's personal goals are incompatible with those of the group. As noted earlier, we found that a social dilemma is a boundary condition for the usual positive effect of goal setting. A self-enhancing personal goal has a detrimental effect on a group's performance. People in seven-person groups are more competitive than those in three-person groups. Only when the individual's goal is compatible with the group's goal is the group's performance enhanced. This finding is similar to Chatman's work, discussed previously, on the importance of value congruence between the person and the employing organization.

Our findings highlight what is sometimes a drawback of goal setting. When two or more people believe that their goals are competitively rather than cooperatively related, they are likely to be tempted to pursue their self-interest single-mindedly. Knowing that their partner(s) may subsequently feel exploited, there is evidence that they may even engage in subtle forms of deception to cover-up their opportunistic behavior (Wathne & Heide, 2000). For example, conflict can occur when one party perceives that another party is interfering with or preventing goal attainment. A meta-analysis by Zetik and Stuhlmacher (2002) revealed that negotiators, who by definition have conflicting goals, nevertheless consistently achieve higher profits when they have a specific goal than those who do not set goals. Consistent with goal-setting theory, the higher the goal the higher the outcome. No effect was found for participation in setting the goal.

The pursuit of self interest, however, does not have to preclude collaboration. It is the way that goals are perceived that determines how people subsequently behave (Deutsch, 1973; Tjosvold, Leung, & Johnson, 2000). The prevalence of opportunism and exploitation depends on the extent to which partners believe their goals are interdependent.

Goals may be seen as cooperatively, competitively, or independently related. Cooperation is likely to occur if two or more people view the attainment of their respective goals as positively correlated, that is, as others reach their goals, a person also attains his or her goal. Competition is likely to occur if two or more people view the attainment of their respective goals as negatively related; people believe that the attainment of another person's goal decreases the probability of them attaining their goals. Goals are viewed as independent if the attainment of one person's goal is viewed as having a little or no bearing on whether another person's goal is attained.

When goals are viewed as competitive between or among parties, people are likely to withhold information and ideas. They may even obstruct the goal progress of another (Stanne, Johnson, & Johnson, 1999). When one views the goals of others as independent, one often withdraws from interaction with them and becomes indifferent to their interests. My own experience is that this characterizes many large law firms as well as business schools and departments of psychology. How my colleagues in finance perform has minimum direct bearing on me as a faculty member, and hence I have minimum interaction with them.

I have argued that a solution to these problems with goal setting is to set a superordinate goal or vision (Latham, 2004). Wong, Tjosvold, and Zi-Ya (2005) obtained empirical support for this assertion. A shared vision unites employees; it gives them a common cause to rally around which, in turn, reduces opportunistic behavior and replaces it with cooperative interdependence. Hence a superordinate goal is an antecedent for cooperative goal setting.

Working with companies and their suppliers in China, Wong et al. found that the relationship between a high level of a shared vision among employees and low levels of opportunism was partially mediated by cooperative goal setting. Once partners see their interests as positively and mutually beneficial, they are less likely to exploit the other. A shared vision strengthened cooperative goal setting by drawing the boundary lines of "in-group" around the two organizations and their suppliers, thereby reducing the out-group feelings that frequently occur in alliances. A shared vision with cooperative goals gives people reasons to believe that they will not be exploited; rather, their partners will work with them openly for mutual benefit. "Indeed, partners who are committed to pursuing their self-interests and recognize that these interests are cooperatively related may engage in minimal opportunism and, more generally, may be prepared to make their partnerships highly effective" (Wong et al., 2005, p. 789).

How a person's appraisal of stress as a challenge vs. a threat interacts with high goals on performance on a complex task has been investigated by Drach-Zahavy and Erez (2002). With goal difficulty held constant, people who perceived the situation as a threat had significantly lower performance than those who appraised the situation as a challenge. Consistent with the findings of Winters and Latham (1996), people who were given a learning goal regarding the discovery of appropriate strategies had higher performance than those who were assigned either a specific performance or a general do best goal, particularly under the threat condition.

Drach-Zahavy and Erez's finding regarding perceptions of stress suggest that the way a goal is presented and framed in terms of striving to attain positive versus avoiding negative outcomes moderates the effectiveness of goal setting. This is exactly what Roney, Griggs, and Shanks (2003) found. A negatively framed goal ("Try not to miss answering more than 3 of these 15 anagrams") led to worse performance than either a positively framed goal ("Try to answer 12 out of these 15 anagrams") or a do-your-best goal.

Errors inevitably occur in the pursuit of one's goals. However, these errors can be framed positively: "The more errors you make, the more you learn." Frese's research shows that the combination of providing people with (a) ample opportunities to make errors and (b) explicit encouragement to learn from their errors improves their performance. A moderator is task complexity; tasks for which the person already possesses the requisite knowledge and skill do not result in many errors. [6]

It is likely that learning goals facilitate or enhance metacognition, namely control over one's cognitions (Ford, Smith, Weissbein, Gully, & Salas, 1998, p 220). [7] This involves planning, monitoring, and evaluating progress toward goal attainment. Skill in metacognition is particularly necessary in environments with little or no external structure or guidance (Schmidt & Ford, 2003). Learning goals appear to prompt people to generate solutions to an impasse, implement them, and monitor their effectiveness.

---

[6] Frese's research on error management has been limited mostly to computer training; the external validity of his findings has yet to be tested. I am confident that his findings are generalizable to a multitude of other tasks. This area is ripe for theses and dissertations.

[7] Metacognitive training involves teaching people strategic questioning while studying problems. Sample questions include: Am I getting closer to my goal? What worked? What did not work? (See Schmidt & Ford, 2003.)

Keith and Frese (2005) found that error-management training induced both emotion control and metacognitive activity during training, and these processes enhanced performance on tasks that required finding new solutions. Error-management training and learning goals go hand in hand in that both involve discovery type activities. Yet, to date, the two methods have not been examined within the same experimental design. [8]

Ironically, there can be a downside to one's success. Audia, Locke, and Smith (2000) found that past success increases strategic decision makers' satisfaction. But their satisfaction led them to continue to use their previously successful strategies. Higher satisfaction was associated with higher self-efficacy as well as higher performance goals. This, in turn, increased dysfunctional persistence subsequent to a radical change in the environment. Hence, another impediment to the usual positive benefits of goal setting is environmental uncertainty as the information required to set specific high goals may become unavailable or obsolete due to rapid ongoing environmental changes.

Bandura (1997) noted that a distal goal is sometimes too far removed in time to provide effective incentives and guides for present action. Seijts and I (Latham & Seijts, 1999), as discussed earlier, paid high school students on a piece-rate basis to make toys, and the dollar amounts paid for the toys changed continuously without warning. We replicated the findings of Kanfer and Ackerman (1989). Setting a specific high distal outcome goal resulted in profits that were significantly worse than urging the students to do their best. But when proximal outcome goals were set in addition to the distal outcome goal, self-efficacy as well as profits were significantly higher than in the other two conditions. This is because in highly dynamic situations, it is important to actively search for feedback and react quickly to it (Frese & Zapf, 1994). In addition, Dorner (1991) has found that performance errors on a dynamic task are often due to deficient decomposition of a goal into proximal goals. Proximal goals can increase what Frese and Zapf (1994) labeled error management. Errors provide information to employees as to whether their picture of reality is congruent with goal attainment. There is an increase in informative feedback when proximal or subgoals are set relative to setting a distal goal only.

---

[8]Keith and Frese looked at goal orientation as a trait rather than setting a specific high learning goal which is a state. They found that "error training is powerful enough to wipe out the effects of a personality variable" (p. 353). Hence, they rejected their hypothesis that people with a high learning goal orientation should benefit more from error training than people with a performance goal orientation.

In addition to being informative, the setting of proximal goals can also be motivational relative to a distal goal that is set for performance attainments far into the future. Moreover, the attainment of proximal goals can increase commitment, through a person's enactive mastery, to attain a distal goal (Bandura, 1986; Bandura & Schunk, 1981).

In a follow-up study, Seijts and Latham (2001) examined the effect of setting proximal goals in conjunction with either a distal learning or a distal outcome goal on a task that required learning in order to perform it correctly, namely, the scheduling of university classes. As was found in the previous studies, participants who were instructed to do their best significantly outperformed those who had been assigned a specific difficult outcome goal. But, once again, the results revealed that performance was significantly higher when people were assigned a specific difficult learning goal than when urged to do their best. This is because a distal learning goal resulted in higher goal commitment than setting a distal outcome goal. This appears to have been due to the fact that self-efficacy increased across trials in the distal learning goal condition, and decreased across trials in the distal outcome goal condition. There was a significant correlation between self-efficacy and performance on the second and third trials. Support was found for Winters and Latham's (1996) assertion that individuals with high self-efficacy are more likely than those with low self-efficacy to discover and implement task-relevant strategies. Mediation analyses showed that strategies had both a direct effect on self-efficacy and an indirect effect on performance. Proximal goals had no direct effect on performance. They did so indirectly by increasing the number of strategies people discovered. A primary difference between this study and the previous one is that the scheduling task was stable across time, whereas the toy-making task was dynamic and hence highly unpredictable. Proximal goals appear to be critical on the latter type of tasks.

Durham, Knight, and Locke (1997) also found that on tasks that are complex for people, there are often goal-strategy interactions, with goal effects strongest when effective strategies are used. Similarly, strategies moderate the positive effect of difficult goals on work that is highly complex for people (Knight, Durham, & Locke, 2000). However, a job analysis can obviate the necessity of a learning goal when the solutions to a task are already known by subject matter specialists. This is because the behaviors necessary for attaining high performance are made explicit for people (Brown & Latham, 2002). Hence, a job analysis enables the setting of a specific high behavioral goal. A learning rather than a behavioral goal is appropriate only when solutions to performing a task effectively have yet to be discovered.

A relatively neglected but important context regarding goal setting is the motivational processes that occur when people work toward the attainment of multiple goals that have deadlines. Mitchell, Lee, Lee, and Harmon (2004) speculated on how these goals influence the pacing of resource allocation (time, effort) to a particular task, as well as the spacing of resources. The major components of this process are the deadlines, the plan, goal attainment/discrepancy appraisals, context such as the number of different tasks to be completed, and the decisions regarding spacing and pacing of resources. Drawing on attribution theory (Weiner & Graham, 1999), they elaborated on the ways people interpret performance discrepancies, their emotional reactions, and subsequent decisions to either continue to try to attain or abandon a goal, or switch to another activity.

Pacing and spacing decisions, they argued, mediate the relationship between goals and performance. Six attributes of goals that influence pacing and spacing decisions are the (1) importance, (2) difficulty level, and (3) specificity of the goals for the person; (4) the temporal range (distal vs. proximal) as well as the (5) urgency of the goals; and (6) the accountability of the person for attaining them. With regard to importance, employees take into account the outcomes that they expect for goal attainment. The higher the importance of these expected outcomes for the person, the higher the goal commitment and the allocation of resources to attain it. The more difficult the goal, the more resources that are allocated to attaining it. A distal goal that includes proximal goals is more motivating than a distal goal alone (Seijts & Latham, 2002). Accountability occurs through the setting of a specific deadline and being held responsible for meeting the deadline (Frinke & Klimoski, 1998).

The bridge between deadline goals and the actions to attain them are the plans people make regarding resource allocations and time frames. Once the goal is pursued, people make judgments as to whether they will meet the deadline. A goal performance discrepancy, Mitchell et al. said, prompts attentional processes that enable a person to thoughtfully assess the causes of the discrepancy.

Drawing on three theories, Mitchell et al. proposed that a goal will likely be pursued even if the person's performance is falling far short of it if (a) the goal is important (goal-setting theory), (b) if the person has high self-efficacy (social cognitive theory), and (c) if the person attributes (attribution theory) the cause to lack of effort and/or temporary bad luck. Emotional reactions such as guilt or moderate anxiety lead to an increase in resource allocation while anger or depression result in the person abandoning the goal.

Mitchell et al. also drew upon attribution theory to predict and explain behavior when the goal performance discrepancy is positive. Contrary to the control theorists, they argued that if people attribute their high performance to effort and skill, they will speed up so that they can quickly attain the goal and then switch to another one. If the attribution is that their initial judgment of goal difficulty was faulty, they are likely to slow down. The former occurs because finishing early due to one's efforts is the basis for not only positive emotion, it is also the basis for an increase in self-efficacy ("I can do this; I can get this done"). Note that the concept of outcome expectancy is also a key predictive and explanatory variable. If the expected outcome of attaining a goal early is that additional difficult goals will be assigned, people are likely to pace themselves to ensure that deadlines are at best met rather than beaten. Attaining a goal early, because it proved to be easier than expected often generates little if any positive emotion. Thus the person is likely to slow down so as to finish on time.

Switching to other tasks, Mitchell et al. stated, occurs once the goal is attained. Switching also occurs when one becomes bored or fatigued while working toward the goal when there are one or more disruptive events or when switching goals is part of the person's plan to do so. The latter specifies the time that will be allocated to one or more tasks. Empirical research is now needed to test Mitchell et al.'s assertions.

Fried and Slowik (2004) argued for incorporating time as a contextual variable into goal-setting theory, particularly regarding challenging vs. relatively easy goals when multiple goals are being pursued. Because there is a limit to the ability of a person to pursue multiple challenging goals that heavily tax cognitive resources, the most effective solution, they argued, is to use clock-time reallocation. An employee can reschedule one or more activities or mix tasks in a particular clock-time period such that some goals are simpler to attain than others. Again, empirical research is needed to test these hypotheses.

Mainemelis (2001) argued that frequently exposing employees to challenging goals provides the momentum necessary for them to generate new ideas and also prevents degradation of their skills. However, Fried and Slowik hypothesized that challenging goals over an extended time period, without sufficient time periods between them, is likely to lead to a deterioration in both the person's ability and motivation to perform effectively. The longer the time period, they stated, the greater the likelihood that a high goal for the original task will remain motivational.

In a knowledge-based firm that strives for innovation, specific high learning rather than performance goals should be set regarding creativity. A performance goal deadline for creativity can be detrimental to performance (Amabile et al., 2002; Winters & Latham, 1996). Again, outcome expectancies are important for predicting, understanding, and influencing an employee's performance. If the anticipated outcome is that organizational decision makers will view goal failures as transitory and part of the learning process, high learning goals will likely be repeatedly set. If failure is judged severely, less difficult or vague abstract goals are likely to become the norm in the workplace.

Kehr (2004) proposed a model for integrating implicit and explicit motives. The framework is designed to enable answers to such questions as to why some people attain their goals relatively easily, whereas others, equally skilled, fail to attain them. Why do some people dislike goals that they themselves set voluntarily? Inherent in the framework is the premise that implicit and explicit motives are dual systems, and that the two systems can be in conflict. Implicit or latent motives are associative networks in that they connect contextual cues with affective reactions as well as with a person's behavior. They are related to unconscious as well as basic and organismic needs. Hence, they are usually subconsciously aroused and lead to affective preferences and implicit behavior impulses that are relatively independent of social demands in later life. Explicit motives, on the other hand, are consciously accessible. They are strongly influenced by social and normative pressure. They, in turn, influence cognitive choices including one's intentions and goals. Consistent with social cognitive theory, perceived rather than actual ability is included in the model as the focus is on motivationally relevant antecedents of behavior.

Kehr hypothesized that goal attainment does not necessarily lead to an increase in a person's satisfaction. Discrepancies between implicit and explicit motives cause intrapersonal conflict because of conflicting behavioral tendencies that can result in impaired well being. Volational regulation is required for conflict resolution in favor of cognitive preferences and to suppress unwanted implicit impulses.

With regard to the alleged corruption effect of extrinsic rewards such as money on intrinsic motivation, Kehr argued that extrinsic rewards only do so to the extent that they activate new goal representations ("I want an increase in salary of X%") and deactivate the original aroused implicit motive ("I can no longer enjoy this job unless I get this salary increase"). Where this does not occur, extrinsic rewards, he hypothesized, can enhance intrinsic motivation.

Kehr's propositions have yet to be tested. Among his recommendations is to determine whether affective ("I really like this task") and cognitive preferences ("I consider this task important and I really want to do it") can serve as proxy variables for one another. Research is needed on the relative weights and different interactive effects for implicit motives, explicit motives, and perceived abilities for different classes of behavior. Setting specific high goals may be contraindicated, according to this framework, if the goal is not supported by implicit motives, and the volitional resources of the employee are low.

As Locke and I (Locke & Latham, 1984) pointed out more than 20 years ago, there are potential downsides to any intervention; goal setting is no exception. For example, when goals are perceived as impossible, offering a monetary bonus for goal attainment can lower a person's motivation (Lee, Locke, & Phan, 1997). Locke (2001) argued that monetary incentives affect performance only when goal commitment and self-efficacy are high.

My personal experience working with high-level managers is that when monetary bonuses are tied to goal attainment, some managers will find ingenious ways to make moderately difficult goals appear to their superiors to be highly difficult goals. [9] Jensen (2001) reported that cheating to earn bonuses for goal attainment is now endemic in the workplace. For example, some managers ship unfinished products in order to reach sales goals, while some accountants "manage earnings," particularly in the fourth quarter, to meet stock analysts' expectations. Jensen's observations are supported by a laboratory experiment which

---

[9]Donald Peterson, a former CEO of Ford Motor Company is an alumnus of the University of Washington. The dean, Nancy Jacob, in introducing me to him, mentioned my work on goal setting. He immediately expressed his dissatisfaction with tying management by objectives to monetary incentives for the reason I gave above. At Ford, we hire very smart people, he said. They quickly learn how to make relatively easy goals look difficult so that they can secure their bonus. Jack Welch, in his visit to our business school, stated that the purpose of goal setting is to stretch one's imagination so as to foster the discovery of great ideas. Then the individual gets hammered for not attaining these stretch goals. The solution Welch said that he favors is to tie monetary bonuses to how well a leader's division performed relative to an a priori agreed-upon competitor such as Westinghouse.

showed that people who come close to but fail to attain their goal are more likely to overstate their performance than those who are not close to attaining their goal or those who are urged to do their best. This was true regardless of whether there was a monetary incentive for goal attainment (Schweitzer, Ordonez, & Douna, 2004). Fortunately, the college students, even though they were anonymous to the experimenters, did not take money they did not earn. Nevertheless, one-third of them overstated their performance. This study shows that management must be vigilant for unintended consequences of the goals that are set.

Locke (2004) described four methods for practitioners to consider when linking monetary incentives to goals. At this time there are, unfortunately, no published field or laboratory experiments comparing the relative effectiveness of these methods. Cheating can occur under any one of them. Hence, organizations need a strict and enforced code of ethics and a well-designed control system regardless of the method of choice.

The first method Locke suggested, is to assign people difficult goals and give them a substantive bonus only if they are attained. This removes all ambiguity as to what is required to earn the bonus. A disadvantage of this method is that high performance, which falls slightly short of the goal, is not rewarded. The outcome can be temptation for employees to exaggerate their results so as to create the impression that the goal has been attained.

A second method that overcomes this problem is to have multiple goal levels with a different bonus level contingent upon reaching a given goal level. A limitation of this method is that people may not strive to attain the highest goal. In my opinion, pride, recognition, and the desire to be, and to be seen as, highly effective mitigates this limitation. Coaching on ways to increase self-efficacy (e.g., "the top goal is in fact attainable") and outcome expectancies (e.g., "see the relationship between what you are doing and what you have to do to attain the top goal") will likely lead to commitment to the highest goal.

A third method is a variation of the second; namely, to implement a continuous linear bonus system (e.g., a 2% bonus for every 1% increase in sales). In this way, there is no loss for falling marginally short of the highest goal; an employee is paid exactly what has been accomplished; moreover, there is no upper limit on the bonus. In both this and the previous method, a person must attain a minimum goal that is acceptable to the organization before a monetary bonus is given.

A fourth method is one that I favor. Employees are given specific challenging goals, and the decision about offering a bonus is made after the fact so as to take into account the context in which the goal was pursued. Thus, an employee who does not attain a high goal but nevertheless persisted in the pursuit of it under very difficult conditions (e.g., a downturn in the economy) would be given a larger bonus than a person who exceeded what was initially believed to be a difficult goal but in reality turned out to be relatively easy due to factors beyond the person's control (e.g., a drop in fuel costs). This method requires the exercise of judgment on the part of subject matter experts (e.g., members of the senior management team who are aware of what the person did in a given environment). A panel of judges is necessary in order to minimize bias on the part of any one observer. A downside of this method is that it can lead to feelings of injustice on the part of an employee. The antidote for fostering feelings of justice is discussed in a subsequent section. Suffice it to say here that this method is used by J. P. Morgan Chase, professional consulting firms, and the University of Washington. In the latter case, the full and associate professors evaluate the performance of the assistant professors in their respective areas (e.g., HRM/OB), and the full professors evaluate the associate professors. The department chair makes an independent evaluation. These evaluations are then reviewed by all the department chairs in the business school as a group. The group meeting, which typically lasts two to three days, is chaired by the dean. This process makes it difficult for an individual's evaluation to be unfairly inflated or deflated. Regardless of the method chosen, transparency and logic must be a bedrock of the decision-making process.

Implementation Intentions and Subconscious Goals

A limitation of our theory of consciously set goals (Locke & Latham, 2002) is that it does not take into account that the subconscious is a storehouse of knowledge and values beyond that which is found in awareness at any given time. In an acknowledgment of this fact, we stated that unlike the conscious mind, the subconscious has an enormous storage capacity (Locke & Latham, 2002).[10] Basically, it stores what comes into focal or partial awareness. Subconscious storage is essential to learning. It frees the mind to focus on new facts and make

---

[10]As scientist/practitioners, we were concerned primarily with how effectively people perform in work settings. Because human action at work is largely consciously directed, we chose to focus on conscious goals. Details on what we did and why we did it in collaborating to develop the theory of goal setting are described elsewhere (Locke & Latham, 2005).

new integrations. The challenge for researchers is to identify and measure the subconscious or implicit knowledge that people bring to bear on a task over and above their extant knowledge. In taking up this challenge, it is noteworthy that most researchers in this century have distanced themselves theoretically and empirically from Freud's early work on the subconscious (Barsade, Brief, & Spataro, 2003).

Arguably, the most exciting research in this domain is occurring in social psychology. Gollwitzer (1999) and his colleagues (e.g., Brandstäetter, Lengfelder, & Gollwitzer, 2001) found that goal intentions that are accompanied by implementation intentions on tasks that are complex for people lead to a higher rate of goal attainment than goal intentions only.[11] An implementation intention is a mental link that is created between a specific future situation and the intended goal directed response. Thus it is subordinate to goal intention. Implementation intentions specify when, where, and how behavior is likely to lead to goal attainment. Thus, holding an implementation intention commits the person to goal-directed behavior once the appropriate situation is encountered. By forming implementation intentions, people switch from conscious effortful control of their goal-directed behavior to being automatically controlled by preselected contextual cues. Implementation intentions lead to heightened activation of these prespecified cues. Thus, once this situational context is encountered, it triggers the goal directed behavior specified by an implementation intention in the absence of conscious intent. This automaticity stems from one mental act of pairing a desired goal-directed behavior with a situation that is critical to the person. Hence, nonconscious goal pursuit occurs as a result of automatic association. If an employee tends to have the same goal whenever she is with a given person or group, the sight of that person or group is enough to trigger that goal. Once activated, motivation guides one's behavior toward goal attainment without the employee realizing it.

In a study of adults living in East Germany, Brandstätter, Heimbeck, Malzacher, and Frese (2003) found that adding goal intention and then implementation intention significantly increases the ability to predict whether a person will seek ways to further their education. However, implementation intentions only work when there is high commitment

---

[11]Gollwitzer found that this is not the case on tasks that are straightforward for people. Automatization through implementation intentions has a strong facilitating effect only when the initiation of action is difficult.

(Gollwitzer, 1999). When this is the case, implementation intentions affect behavior even after considerable time has elapsed between the formation of the intention and an encounter with the critical situation.

Bargh and Ferguson (2000) summarized research findings that suggest that automatic or nonconscious goals produce the same outcomes as conscious goal pursuit in information processing, memory storage, social behavior, and task performance as well as self-efficacy, self-evaluation, and a person's mood state. They differ from conscious goals in that they operate without awareness or the necessity for conscious guidance. The effect of priming on nonconscious goal-setting appears to be so powerful that it may some day raise ethical issues in the workplace. For example, Bargh et al. (2001) found that a primed goal resulted in people continuing to work on a task after being told to stop doing so. On the positive side, primed goals have also been found to reduce prejudice (Bargh, 1994).

Consistent with goal-setting theory, feedback is a moderator; it guides behavior toward the automatized goal (Bargh & Ferguson, 2000).[12] The environment can activate a person's goal within a given situation as part of the preconscious analysis of the situation. The habitual plan for carrying out the goal is activated automatically without conscious planning. To the extent that environmental features become associated with the goal, the importance of conscious choice is removed entirely.

Bargh and his colleagues primed goals by taking advantage of associations between the goal and semantically related words. Shah (2005) examined two other associations, namely, goals associated with those things that help bring about their attainment—that is, instrumental goal priming, and goal association with other individuals—interpersonal goal priming.

Because a particular goal is often pursued in particular settings while one is engaging in specific behaviors or activities, the goal may become associated with such settings. The instrumental or means-goal association is not dependent on the semantic relation of the means and goal but rather on their perceived functional relationship, that is, said Shah, the degree to which the means is seen as facilitating the attainment of one's goal. The stronger the association, the higher the likelihood that encountering the setting, or the means to attain it, will automatically

---

[12]Recall that the word moderator means in this instance that goal-setting effects on performance increase when feedback is present (Erez, 1977).

lead to the pursuit of that goal. In short, Shah has argued that surrounding a person with various means to attain a specific goal is likely to move that goal to the center of a person's attention, thus enhancing that individual's commitment to attaining it.

In addition to semantic and instrumental goal priming, a third source of goal priming is the people who are significant to an individual. Shah (2003a) found that when people are presented the name of a close significant other subliminally, that is, a person who would want them to do well on the task, the salience of the task goal increases, as does persistence and actual performance. Shah also found that priming a person's "significant other" decreases pursuit of the goal if a person's significant other does not support the goal or is strongly associated with the pursuit of a different or unrelated goal.

In still another study, Shah (2003b) found that a person's significant other affects how a goal is consciously perceived and expressed by the person who is pursuing it. A significant other "automatically" affects the perceived difficulty and importance of a goal and how the person feels emotionally about success and failure regarding goal attainment.

Interpersonal goal priming even affects subsequent social interactions. Fitzsimons and Shah (2005) subliminally presented words to prime a goal to achieve academically. People, randomly assigned to an experimental group, relative to their counterparts in the control group, reported feeling significantly closer to those they perceived could help them attain the goal. In addition, they indicated that they intended to spend less time with those people who they perceived as not facilitating their academic success.

The sine qua non of these experiments is the individual's report of being unaware: "Once activated, the (subconscious) goals operate to guide subsequent cognition and behaviors in the same way that consciously held goals do, all without the individual's awareness of the goal's guiding role" (Chartrand & Bargh, 2002, p. 15). A major problem in obtaining reliable data indicative of "unawareness" lies in the operational definition of this concept. The adequacy of a verbal or written report serving as an indicator of unawareness is dependent upon several stringent subcriteria, namely: (a) the adequacy of the person's interrogation in terms of the precision and clarity of the questions; (b) the person's motivation to respond truthfully; (c) controls for the probability of the questioning process itself inducing awareness; and

(d) an a priori categorization procedure for classifying responses as aware or unaware (Ericksen, 1960; Latham & Beach, 1974).[13] Double-blind experiments should be conducted by HRM, I/O, and OB researchers when they examine the external validity of these laboratory findings in organizational settings. An organizational setting may be sufficiently structured, relative to social or laboratory settings, that it masks the effect of automotive or subconscious goals.

No published study as yet has compared the effect on job performance of subconscious priming with explicit conscious goal setting. However, preliminary findings from two laboratory experiments conducted by Stajkovic, Locke, and Blair (in press) suggest that they do interact.

In their first experiment, they chose a task that has often been used in studies of conscious goal setting but not in priming studies. MBA students were given a word search puzzle in which they had to find and circle 7 achievement-related words (e.g., win, compete, succeed, strive, attain, achieve, master) in a 10 × 10 word matrix containing 13 words. Words could go in any direction. The people who were not primed circled seven non-achievement-related (neutral) words in a matrix that contained only neutral words. The dependent measure was the number of uses for a wire coat hanger (overlapping uses such as hang a coat, hang a shirt, did not count). Awareness questions, adapted from Bargh, were given in writing to the students when the experiment ended. People who either did not identify all the primed words or who showed awareness that the primed words were achievement-related were deleted from the analysis.

The people who were primed gave significantly more uses than the no-primed participants in the control group. This is the first experiment in I/O OB to show that subconscious priming can affect performance on a task that has been used frequently in laboratory experiments on conscious goal setting.

---

[13]Experimental studies purportedly demonstrating learning in unaware subjects date back to the 19th century (e.g., Pierce & Jastrow, 1885). But the reliability and validity of these data were attacked throughout much of the first half of the 20th century largely on the grounds that the data could be interpreted without reference to an aware-unaware continuum (Eriksen, 1960). Hence the conclusion that there was no evidence to justify the belief that learning or discrimination can occur without awareness. This conclusion was successfully challenged by Kenneth Spence (1966) through the effective use of a masking task in a classical conditioning experiment involving the blinking of a person's eye. Egeth (1967), after reviewing the literature on selective attention, found that directing attention away from a channel may effectively lower the messages received by it. Cats, observing a mouse, can withstand increasing magnitudes of electric shock to their feet when normally the slightest amount would result in them immediately escaping from the situation.

Stajkovic et al. then examined how priming effects on performance compare to the effects of conscious goals. Both subconscious (primed) and conscious goals were manipulated in this experiment. The interaction effect between conscious and primed goals was of primary interest to the researchers. If both conscious and primed goals are set, the total motivation force might be stronger. There had been no previous research on this issue.

The participants were undergraduate and graduate students. This experiment used a 2 (primed, no-primed) × 3 (easy, do your best, and difficult goals) factorial design. Priming involved a Scrambled Sentence Test. Participants were asked to construct a grammatically correct four-word sentence (e.g., *The eagle flew around*) from a set of five randomly positioned words (e.g., *flew, eagle, the, blue, around*). In the primed groups, 12/20 sentences (60%) included words related to achievement (e.g., *prevail, compete*) and in the no primed groups, all words in each of the 20 sentences were neutral. Conscious goals were set in three conditions (easy, do your best, difficult) in relation to a performance task (giving uses for common objects). The easy goal required 4 uses (expected success rate of 90%), and the difficult goal was to provide 12 uses (expected success rate of 10%).

As always, the participants were administered a post-experimental awareness questionnaire. Participants were excluded from the data if they did not complete the priming manipulation correctly, and/or if they indicated awareness of the priming (e.g., "Something to do with achievement, success, motivation").

There was a main effect for primed goals, as well as a main effect for conscious goals on the individual's performance. The two-way interaction between primed and conscious goals was also statistically significant. In the "no-primed-conscious goal" groups, the performance for an easy goal was virtually identical to that for the "do your best goal." In the difficult goal condition, performance increased 17.2% relative to the "do your best" goal. In primed-conscious goal groups the "do your best goal" increased performance 27.5% over the easy goal, and the difficult goal increased performance 44.3% over the easy goal, and 24% over the "do your best goal." In terms of the between-group means, the performance of the "no primed-easy goal" groups were virtually identical. However, "do your best" participants in the "primed condition" outperformed the "do your best" participants in the "no-primed" condition by 23.7%. The people with a difficult goal in the primed condition did better than the people who had a difficult goal in the "no-primed condition" by 29.2%.

After one day, there was a main effect for "priming" on performance as well as a main effect for goals on performance. The two-way interaction was also significant. In the "no-primed-conscious goal" groups, the performance means for easy and do your best goals were similar. Difficult goals increased performance by 20% relative to the people who only had "do your best" goals. In the "primed-conscious goal" groups, those with do your best goals increased their performance by 36.6% over those who had easy goals, and those with difficult goals had performance that was similar to those who had "do your best" goals. The performance of those in the "no-primed-easy goal" condition and "primed-easy goal" conditions was also similar. However, those people with "do your best" goals in the priming group outperformed those with difficult goals in the no primed group by 34.1%, and those with difficult goals in the priming group outperformed those with difficult goals in the no primed group by 17.3%. This is the first time that such interaction effects have been found. In addition, the performance difference between hard and easy goals was 47.71% greater than that between the primed and no-primed groups on Day 1, and 38.5% on Day 2. This indicates that conscious goal effects are stronger than unconscious effects.

These exciting findings with regard to the effect of unconscious goals on performance now need to be replicated on dependent variables that are relevant in organizational settings. It would appear that the fields of I/O and OB will soon come full circle from William James' exhortations at the opening of the 20th century to study consciousness to the increasingly growing focus at the beginning of the present century on the subconscious. Would Freud be pleased? Miner undoubtedly is happy.

A 20th-century voice in the wilderness of HRM, I/O, and OB advocating the importance of assessing the subconscious was John (Jack) B. Miner, a former editor of the *Academy of Management Journal*.[14] Trained as a clinical psychologist, he subsequently worked as a personnel specialist at the Atlantic Refining Company, now part of Arco. In 1960, he became an academic and remained so until his retirement in 1994. His research output

---

[14]Lyman Porter (2005, personal communication) stated: "As one who was involved in Academy leadership throughout a good part of the 1970s, I believe I can say, without fear of contradiction, that in his role as *AMJ* editor at that time, Jack Miner—through the standards he invoked for acceptance of articles—was extremely influential in helping to turn the journal from a so-so quality publication into one of the premier journals in the management discipline. In other words, he deserves considerable credit for a true scholarly contribution to the development of *AMJ* as we know it today."

includes the development of a projective test, namely, the Miner Sentence Completion Scale (MSCS). He developed this test because of his belief that a projective measure is superior to a self-report measure of personality. The latter, he said (Miner, 2005), taps conscious self-attributed motives, while a projective test unearths both conscious and unconscious implicit motives with heavy emphasis on the unconscious. He quoted approvingly the differentiation between these two types of measures that was promulgated by another clinician, G. Meyer (1996):

> Implicit motivations are viewed as being more unconscious and physiologically related, as developed earlier in life and not requiring language and verbal mediation to solidify, and being more strongly associated with long-term spontaneous behavioral trends. In contrast, self-attributed motives are understood as having different historical antecedents and as being better predictors of conscious choices and immediate, situationally defined behaviors. . . . Cross-method disagreement is thus not a question of test invalidity. Rather it is a phenomenon that can lead to a more refined identification of people and more accurate behavioral predictions. (p. 575)

Miner used his MSCS to assess phobic reactions of managers to their multiple role requirements (e.g., relations with authority, competing with peers, imposing wishes on subordinates). Their responses to his sentence completion stems indicate, he said, whether a manager possesses a particular motive pattern (e.g., favorable attitude toward supervisors, desire to compete, desire to exercise power). He provided them with psychoanalytic interpretations of their unconscious motives so as to enable them to cope with the anxiety associated by their roles as managers. The results, compared with those obtained in a control group, showed an increase in a person's managerial motivation (e.g., Miner, 1960).

Unfortunately, to correctly interpret a projective test requires as much art as it does science, if not more so. No one questions Miner's results; but very few people have attempted to use his projective scale or to replicate his findings due to concerns regarding the construct validity of the MSCS and the lack of reliability in scoring it.

Ann Howard, a past president of the Society of Industrial and Organizational Psychology, examined whether subconscious or conscious motives are more powerful in predicting long-term managerial success at AT&T. Specifically, Howard (2005) examined scores on McClelland's (1961) Thematic Apperception Test (TAT). Like the MSCS, this, too, is a projective measure. Specifically, the TAT assesses a person's need for achievement. Howard compared TAT responses with a conscious measure of goal setting. Both measures were taken between 1956 and 1960.

In addition to the TAT, the job incumbents took two other projective tests, the MSCS and the Rotter Incomplete Sentences Blank. The assessment of conscious goals were coded from interviews where people stated the highest management level they wanted to attain in their career (i.e., 1, entry level management, to 7, company president).

"In contrast, to the other measures, goals showed a very strong correlation with advancement (r = .54), even when the influence of cognitive ability was eliminated (r = .43)" (Howard, 2005, p. 8). For the people who left AT&T to become entrepreneurs, conscious goals were a strong predictor of their salary. The TAT motive patterns showed no significant linear relationship with the management level the person attained 25 years later. But a composite measure of the projective tests showed a small but significant relationship with an employee's advancement. Moreover, multiple regression analyses revealed that conscious goals plus the composite projective measures contributed independent variance to the prediction of an employee's promotion in AT&T. As of 2005, the door has been opened for the study of a person's unconscious goals in the workplace.

Feedback

As has been emphasized earlier in this book, feedback and goal setting are interrelated (Locke & Latham, 2002). The effect of feedback on performance is mediated by goal setting. That is, feedback leads to an improvement in performance only to the extent that it leads to the setting of specific high goals (e.g., Locke, Cartledge, & Koeppel, 1968). Feedback, however, is a moderator of goal setting. The increase in performance over time increases more in the presence rather than the absence of feedback regarding goal attainment. In short, goals and feedback consistently work better together than either one does alone (Locke & Latham, 2002, 2005).

Seeking feedback is important because it increases the likelihood of goal setting, which, in turn, increases quality and quantity of performance (Renn & Fedor, 2001). Ashford, Blatt, and VandeWalle (2003) stated that the processing of feedback involves monitoring the environment in an automatic preconscious fashion through visual, auditory, and relational cues. Significant changes in the environment, or in the preconscious monitored cues themselves, may cause a shift to the conscious seeking of feedback, and the conscious evaluation of the costs and benefits of doing so. Having sought feedback, and resolving uncertainty associated with the interruption, a person returns to the automatic processing of information.

Unsolicited feedback is often discarded (Roberson, Deitch, Brief, & Block, 2003). But, as the perceived value of feedback increases, people usually seek it actively and frequently (Tuckey, Brewer, & Williamson, 2002). There are at least three primary motives for why a person seeks feedback: (1) Instrumental to attain a goal and perform well, (2) ego-based to defend or enhance one's ego, and (3) image based to protect or enhance the impression others have of oneself (Ashford & Black, 1996). Only the first, instrumental feedback seeking on the part of the person, is likely to enhance future performance.

Ashford and Tsui (1991) reported that seeking negative feedback creates an image of one's effectiveness. This is because managers who do so are viewed as attentive to and caring of the opinion of others. Showing a preference for only positive feedback hurts the image of a manager in the eyes of others.

Consistent with the literature reviewed earlier, context, personality, and self-efficacy have been shown to moderate the positive effects of feedback. With regard to context, societal culture affects the type of feedback that is sought. In individualistic cultures where most people want to "stand out," feedback regarding one's successes is more frequently sought than feedback regarding failures. The opposite is true in collectivist societies where the emphasis for most people is to find ways of "fitting in" (Bailey, Chen, & Don, 1997). Taking into account individual differences in personality, Heine, Kitayama, Lehman, Takata, Ide, Leung, and Mtsumoto (2001) found that the above finding can be explained on the basis of different motives of self with regard to self-enhancement vs. self-improvement.

Individual differences in self-esteem, task vs. ego focus, promotion vs. prevention focus, and performance vs. a learning goal orientation have also been investigated in terms of their moderating effect on feedback. Williams, Miller, Steelman, and Levy (1999) found that a feedback source that is perceived as supportive increases feedback seeking. Nevertheless, people with low self-esteem often lack the desire to seek negative feedback for fear that it may corroborate their negative self-appraisal (Bernichon, Cook, & Brown, 2003).[15]

Kluger and DeNisi (1996) conducted a meta-analysis which shows that the effect of feedback on performance is variable. In fact, they found that 38% of feedback interventions had negative effects on a person's performance. However, feedback sign (positive vs. negative)

---

[15]There is also evidence that some people seek feedback that is consistent with their self-view. Thus some people with low self-esteem often seek negative feedback (Swann, 1990).

was not shown to be a moderator of the effect of feedback on an individual's performance. They proposed that task focused individuals who receive feedback are likely to allocate their cognitive resources to the task, whereas ego involved people allocate their cognitive resources to themselves. In the latter case, this decreases the potential for future task success following the feedback the person receives.

Context can be helpful in masking the effect of this personality variable, task vs. ego focused. Heimbeck, Frese, Sonnentag, and Keith (2003) found that error management instructions (e.g., "I have made an error. Great!") helps to keep the person's attention on the task and away from self. This is true for tasks where the feedback provides information on factors that are under the control of trainees so that their understanding of what is required of them increases (Debowski, Wood, & Bandura, 2001). This is because errors can enhance one's mental model of a task by leading to new insights and creative solutions. By minimizing opportunities to make errors, the initial benefit of specific feedback decreases. People fail to learn how to correct errors. They fail to learn how to be resilient, subsequent to ineffective performance, through systematic exploration. Goodman, Wood, and Hendrickx (2004) found that the more systematic a person is in the exploration process, the less confusing the information obtained, and the more beneficial the feedback for performance.

Recall that control theory (Carver, Sutton, and Scheier, 2000) states that failure motivates more than success, while goal-setting (Locke & Latham, 2002) and social cognitive theories (Bandura, 1997) state that positive feedback in relation to goal pursuit increases effort and goal difficulty levels. On the basis of personality differences among people, Van-Dijk and Kluger (2004) conducted a series of experiments that they argued resolve these contradictory predictions. They showed that people who either receive positive feedback under a promotion focus, or negative feedback under a prevention focus, have higher motivation (i.e., intention to exert effort) than people who receive feedback that is incongruent with their regulation focus.[16] As was the case with the trait, goal orientation (Seijts et al., 2004), regulatory focus was easily manipulated/induced by the researchers. Thus, it is questionable

---

[16]A prevention focus is activated by security needs where a promotion focus is triggered by growth and development needs. People who have a prevention focus tend to frame situations in terms of loss vs. no-loss, whereas those who have a promotion focus view situations as gain vs. no gain. Consequently, a prevention focus sensitizes people to the presence or absence of punishers, the use of avoidance strategies, and to emotions ranging from agitation to quiescence. In contrast, a promotion focus sensitizes people to the presence or absence of rewards, the use of approval strategies, and to emotions ranging from elation to dejection. Maslow would likely agree.

whether a person's regulatory focus should be considered only as an individual difference variable, let alone whether feedback sign should be tailored to different occupations as suggested by the authors (e.g., positive feedback for people in artistic and investigative jobs).[17] A limitation of this study is that performance was not measured.

Goal orientation, argued by some to be a personality variable, influences one's interpretation of the purpose with which feedback is given. Both Taberno and Wood (1999) as well as VandeWalle (1999) found that people who have a learning goal orientation disposition are more likely than those with a performance goal orientation to effectively process negative feedback on ways to improve performance. The extent to which a person perceived feedback seeking as valuable fully mediated the effect of a learning goal orientation on actual feedback seeking in VandeWalle's study. Individuals with a learning goal orientation are able to put negative feedback into perspective, and quickly rebound from any distress that it initially causes them.

Frese (2005) and his colleagues have shown that people can be easily taught, through instructions, to embrace negative feedback by framing errors as beneficial to the learning process, and to be resilient, subsequent to making an error, through systematic exploration. The issue of resiliency by increasing an individual's self-efficacy is discussed shortly. Future research should examine the additive effects of setting specific high learning goals in the context of error management training.

With regard to goal orientation, cross-situational consistency is needed to substantiate a claim for its dispositional influence on behavior; the longer the temporal separation between the measurement of personality and job performance, the stronger the dispositional inference (Staw, 2004). This has yet to be shown. Given ongoing questions on the psychometric properties and factor structure of goal orientation scales (e.g., Button, Mathieu, & Zajac, 1996; VandeWalle, 1997), given that a learning goal orientation correlates positively with effort, self-efficacy, and goal setting level (VandeWalle, Cron, & Slocum, 2001), given that a learning goal orientation is easily induced (Elliott & Harackiewicz, 1996), and given that goal setting masks its effects (Seijts et al., 2004), it would appear that it is time to stop examining the influence of dispositional goal orientation and continue to examine its effects as a state. As VandeWalle (2003) stated, when the situation

---

[17] Goal-setting theory (Locke & Latham, 2002) does not predict anything on the basis of feedback being positive vs. negative. The key issue is how people assess the feedback and what they do next. Negative feedback motivates those people who have high self-efficacy to set specific high goals.

provides strong cues, the dispositional goal preference is overridden. Goal orientation does not appear to be a stable individual difference trait across different situations. Thus, in regard to feedback, a learning goal orientation should be induced rather than passively accepted as a trait that is inherent in a person.

Dweck (1999) herself now believes that goal orientation is a domain-specific personality pattern. She stated that a person may have a perfor-mance goal orientation in one domain and a learning goal orientation in another. Given the fluctuating nature of this construct in the literature (see Grant & Dweck, 2003), it would appear prudent in the workplace to set specific high learning goals and foster a learning goal orientation on those tasks that are complex for an individual. Induced mental framing of a learning goal orientation should be conducive to increasing an employee's self-efficacy that the competency necessary for performance effectiveness can be acquired (Seijts et al., 2004; VandeWalle, Cron, & Slocum, 2001).[18]

In a study of salespeople, Brown, Ganesan, and Challagalla (2001) found that self-efficacy moderates the effectiveness of information seeking from supervisors and co-workers regarding role expectations and performance. People with high self-efficacy use feedback to increase their motivation, task focus, and effort as well as to decrease their anxiety and self-debilitating thoughts. Similarly, Heslin and Latham (2004) found that managers in Australia change their behavior in a positive direction in response to feed-back from subordinates when they have high self-efficacy to do so.

Nease, Mudgett, and Quinones (1999) found that self-efficacy tends to be influenced by numerous rather than single instances of feedback.

---

[18] Bandura's (2000, personal communication) observation is that:

Dweck's work on conceptions of intelligence is fine as far as it goes, but it is thin on theory, i.e., it fails to specify the mechanism through which construing ability as an entity or as an incremental skill affects performance attainments. In the experiment with Bob Wood, in which we manipulated conceptions of ability experimentally, we demonstrated that they exert their effects through perceived self-efficacy and goal setting.

Her experiment comparing learning and performance goals has several methodological flaws. She confounded her manipulation of high and low ability by telling all the children that they had high learning ability. Schunk has shown that belief in one's learning ability fos-ters achievement. Dweck casts her study in terms of perceived ability. But children's percep-tions of their ability were never measured. Given the confounded manipulation, the children's beliefs in their ability remain unknown. These methodological flaws dispute her conclusion that children with learning goals exhibit mastery behavior regardless of per-ceived ability.

Future studies should allow for a systematic analysis of quartiles to test possible configured relationships. Self-efficacy may have a low positive effect, or even a negative effect at very low and very high levels of performance and a high positive effect at moderate levels of performance (2nd and 3rd quartiles).

Self-Regulation

Self-regulation can be defined as a multi-component, multi-level, iterative, self-steering process that targets the person's cognition, affect, and behavior, as well as environmental factors that can facilitate or inhibit an individual's effort and persistence regarding goal attainment (Boekaerts, Maes, & Karoly, 2005). The various models of self-regulation are based on the common meta-theory that cognitive factors are significant contributions to one's own behavior (Bandura, 2005a). Goal setting and feedback seeking in relation to progress toward goal attainment are the core of self-regulation (Latham & Locke, 1991; Wood, 2005). This is because self-regulation involves setting, attaining, and maintaining one's goals.

Self-regulatory processes supporting goal implementation have been examined by Golliwitzer and Bayer (1999). They offered a time perspective on goal striving and self-regulatory processes as mediating the effects of intentions on behavior. The latter consists of four phases: predecisional (choosing among competing goals, based on expected value); preactional (forming implementation intentions in the service of the goal intention); actional (bringing goal directed actions to a successful end) and post actional phases (evaluation as to whether further action is necessary). Brandstäetter et al. (2003) inferred from field interviews that the portion of variance accounted for in action initiation increases by adding expected value and goal intention step by step.

Roe (1999) and Frese and Fay (2001) argued the importance of personal initiative, defined as self-starting proactive behavior that overcomes barriers to the attainment of self-set goals. Employees high on personal initiative are able to change the complexity of and control over their workplace even when they do not change jobs (Frese, Garst, & Fay, 2000). Personal initiative, measured within the framework of a situational interview (Latham & Sue-Chan, 1999) has adequate inter-rater reliability as well as construct validity (Fay & Frese, 2001). This work is discussed in greater detail in the subsequent section on action theory.

Godat and Brigham (1999) provided training in self-management to employees who chose the behaviors they themselves wanted to regulate (i.e., their general health). The training involved 8 weekly, 2-hour sessions ranging from acquiring self-monitoring skills to ways of shaping and rewarding one's behavior. The results showed a significant change in behaviors relative to those in the control group. Drawing on her earlier work with unionized employees (Frayne & Latham, 1986; Latham & Frayne, 1989), Frayne (Frayne & Geringer, 2000) trained insurance salespeople in the use of self-management techniques based on goal setting, self-monitoring, and self-administering rewards. The result was an increase in sales performance as a result of increases in self-efficacy and outcome expectancies.

Donovan and Williams (2003) examined goal revision processes of varsity-level college track and field athletes over an 8-week competitive season. Consistent with Bandura's (1997) argument of discrepancy production, the athletes set their distal goals for the season at a level of performance that was considerably higher than their best performance during the previous season. Their initial proximal goal for their first competitive meet, however, was slightly lower than their best previous performance. Proximal goals were used by them to work up to performance levels that were compatible with their distal ultimate goal. For both the competition and the end of season goals, athletes whose performance was below this goal tended to revise their goals downward in proportion to the magnitude of the discrepancy, while those who surpassed their goal revised it in an upward manner in proportion to the magnitude of the positive discrepancy.

Temporal factors also exert an influence on goal revision. Athletes were found to be more likely to revise their goals when there was a goal-performance discrepancy in the second half than they were in the first half of the season. The moderator was their beliefs regarding ability. Consistent with findings regarding goal orientation (Dweck, 1999) as well as learned helplessness (Seligman & Csikszentmihalyi, 2000), athletes who believed that their ability is fixed also believed that their performance would stay relatively the same over time, no matter how hard they tried. Faced with a large negative discrepancy, they lowered their end of season distal goal. This was not true for those who attributed the discrepancy to nonability factors.

Ilies and Judge (2005) also focused on the processes individuals use to regulate their goals across time. People typically lower their goal following feedback they perceive to be negative; they increase their goal when they feel that the feedback is positive. The mediator is affect. It influences a person's subsequent goals and performance through the emotions that are experienced.

Positive affectivity has an energetic arousal component (e.g., interest, enthusiasm) that increases optimism regarding the attainment of a subsequently assigned goal. Part of this is also likely to be mediated by an employee's self-efficacy. Ilies and Judge concluded that "social cognitive theory more adequately explains motivational self-regulation across time, compared with control theory. That is, the present results suggest that, in general, after meeting or exceeding their goals, individuals do not maintain their goal level and decrease effort in order to minimize the positive discrepancy between performance and goals, but rather set higher goals that motivate them to increase performance, as predicted by social-cognitive theory" (Ilies & Judge, 2005, p. 463).

With regard to implications for practice, Ilies and Judge first quoted Bandura (1997, p. 130): "Notable attainments bring temporary satisfaction, but people enlist new challenges as personal motivators for further attainment." Second, they concluded that negative feedback is only beneficial when the difference between a person's performance and goal is relatively small. Repeated or extreme negative feedback leads many people to give up. The results of this study suggest that a person's affect, especially positive affect, mediates the feedback subsequent goal relationship.

A self-management technique has been developed that involves computer-assisted implementation, including the internet (Bandura, 2004a). The computer mails personalized reports that include feedback on an individual's progress toward proximal goals. The feedback also provides guides on ways an individual can cope with troublesome situations. The program induces participants to set new proximal goals for them to attain when facing situations where they are experiencing difficulties. In short, this computerized implementation system is able to provide intensive individualized guidance in self-management to large numbers of people. Bandura reported that employees in the workplace were able to lower their cholesterol through this approach.

Vancouver and Day (2005) concluded from their review of the literature published between 1979 and 2004 that self-regulation interventions in organizational settings are indeed effective. The outcomes that have been examined in these studies range from an individual's job attendance to job performance, as well as self and team efficacy. Sonnentag (2002) reached a similar conclusion. She found that self-regulatory mechanisms, namely, goal setting, feedback, and self-efficacy play a crucial role in fostering a person's "well being" and performance.

Pritchard et al. (2002) have shown the effectiveness of these procedures when employees apply them to the organization as a whole. ProMes, as discussed earlier, emphasizes goal setting and feedback. It is a step-by-step process that identifies (a) organizational objectives, (b) a measurement system of the extent to which the objectives are met, and (c) a feedback system regarding performance. Productivity is defined as how well a system uses its resources to achieve its goals. ProMes has led to organizational level productivity improvements in European countries regardless of differences among cultures. Using single case, repeated measures designs, Pritchard et al. reported an average increase between baseline and post intervention productivity of 1.42 standard deviations across 55 implementations in seven countries. A limitation of this methodology, pointed out by the authors themselves, is that it is effective primarily in stable rather than dynamic environments. Research is now needed on organizational contexts and work arrangements that can act as facilitators or inhibitors of self-regulatory processes (Wood, 2005).

Because of the striking similarities among goal setting, social cognitive and action theories, I will forego a Concluding Comments until the end of the next chapter, where the latter two theories are discussed.

10 Social Cognitive Theory

Bandura's social cognitive theory also dominates the work motivation literature in the present century. This theory emphasizes dual control systems in the self-regulation of motivation, namely a proactive discrepancy production system that works in concert with a reactive discrepancy reduction system (Bandura, 2001a). As noted earlier, research on social cognitive theory shows empirically that the effect of environmental antecedents and consequences are mediated by cognitive variables. People are motivated by the foresight of goals, not just the hindsights of shortfalls. A specific high goal creates negative performance discrepancies to be mastered. People mobilize their effort and resources based on their anticipatory estimates of what is necessary for goal attainment. Therefore, at the outset, a goal can enhance performance before any feedback is provided.

Self-Efficacy

Upon goal attainment, people with high self-efficacy set an even higher goal as this creates new motivating discrepancies to be mastered. If the goal is not attained, self-efficacy and goal commitment predict whether people re-double their effort, react apathetically, or become despondent. Meta-analyses by Sadri and Robertson (1993) and Stajkovic and Luthans (1998) of wide-ranging methodological and analytic work-related laboratory and field studies provide overwhelming evidence that efficacy beliefs influence the level of motivation and performance. Colquitt, LePine, and Noe (2000) found that self-efficacy even affects the transfer of training independent of skill acquisition.

Nevertheless, social cognitive theory has been attacked by Vancouver and his colleagues (Vancouver, Thompson, & Williams, 2001). In a laboratory experiment, they found that as people near their goals, self-efficacy was negatively related to performance. Hence, they claimed that self-efficacy is not a cause of high performance. High self-efficacy, they said, creates complacency that undermines performance.[1] On the basis of nine meta-analyses conducted by other scholars across diverse spheres of functioning, using cross sectional as well as longitudinal designs, Bandura and Locke (2003) concluded that this contradictory finding was an artifact of the particular laboratory task that Vancouver used, namely a guessing game in which the same activity was performed repeatedly in the same session under invariant conditions. The participants had to guess the correct color and order of four colored squares randomly preset before each game. There was nothing learnable or transferable from one game to another. Consequently, no skill was being acquired, and no improvement in performance could occur across trials.

In commenting on the distinctions between the positions advocated by goal setting and social cognitive theory researchers vs. advocates of control theory, Kanfer (2005) argued that it is unlikely that sufficient evidence will emerge for falsification of the theoretical tenets of either camp. Instead, she advocated a search for important boundary conditions, and a focus on pressing practical questions that have arisen as a result of the changing nature of work in this new millennium. I would add the observation that in contexts where no learning is possible from one task to the next, the benefits one can expect from increases in self-efficacy are indeed attenuated. Thus, high self-efficacy with regard to playing a roulette wheel is likely to prove beneficial for the gambling casino rather than for the gambler.

Evidence that high self-efficacy does not always lead to desirable outcomes has been shown by my colleagues Glen Whyte and Alan Saks (Whyte, Saks, & Hook, 1997). They found that it can be the source of inappropriate task persistence. Dysfunctional persistence has been shown to be the result of high goals, self-efficacy, and satisfaction with one's past performance. The result was less rather than more seeking of information following a radical change in the environment (Audia, Locke, & Smith, 2000). The correction for the downside of seeking success, however, is not to diminish a person's self-efficacy. As Bandura (2000) noted, a resilient belief that one has of what it takes to succeed provides the necessary staying power in the

---

[1]The practical significance of this finding, observed Bandura and Locke (2003), would be for athletic coaches to send their team onto the playing field in a self-doubting frame of mind so that they will not play complacently. "We would lay heavy bets against a team coached according to Vancouver's control theory" (Bandura & Locke, 2003, p. 97).

face of repeated failures and setbacks, not to mention skeptical as well as critical social reactions that are inherently discouraging for people.[2] The correction for inappropriately high self-efficacy lies in developing ways of identifying ongoing practices that have exceeded the point of utility so that people do not misread their environment. Future research is required to find ways to preserve the functional value of resilient self-efficacy while at the same time instituting informative monitoring and social feedback systems that help people identify the practices that are no longer useful (Bandura & Locke, 2003). For example, setting proximal or sub-goals can provide information as to when to alter versus "stay the course" regarding the pursuit of a distal goal (Latham & Seijts, 1999).

As noted earlier in the discussion of personality, social cognitive theory rejects resorting to traits in order to explain human behavior. Perceived self-efficacy and outcome expectancies, are not contextless global dispositions that should be assessed by an omnibus test. Bandura conceptualizes self-efficacy as task specific. It is a state variable rather than a dispositional trait. "There is no all-purpose specific self-efficacy scale. It is a contradiction in terms. Specific scales are tailored to particular domains of functioning. An already developed specific scale is usable in other studies only if the activity domain is the same as the one on which the scale was developed" (Bandura, 2003, personal communication; Bandura, 2005a).

Nevertheless, Eden (2001) has validated a measure of general (GSE) rather than task-specific self-efficacy. GSE, he stated, represents one's belief about general self-competence across a variety of different situations. Eden and his colleagues (Chen, Gully, & Eden, 2001, 2004) found that GSE is distinct from self-esteem in predicting important outcomes in organizational settings. Moreover, Eden (2001) found that

---

[2]The importance of staying power has been described by White (1982) with regard to people who achieved eminence in spite of repeated rejection. James Joyce's *The Dubliners* was rejected by 22 publishers. Gertrude Stein submitted poems to editors for 20 years before one was finally accepted. The Impressionists had to arrange their own art exhibitions because their works were routinely rejected by the Paris Salon. Van Gogh sold only one painting during his lifetime. Frank Lloyd Wright's architectural works were widely criticized during much of his career. Fred Astaire was initially rejected for being only a balding, skinny actor who could dance a little. Decca records turned down a recording contract with the Beatles because groups of guitars were "on the way out." As Bandura observed, persistence in the face of massive unintermitting rejection defies explanation in terms of reinforcement or utility theories. It is a person's self-beliefs of efficacy that determine how much effort will be exerted in an endeavor, and how long the individual will persevere in the face of obstacles.

a person's belief in the efficacy of the resources available to perform the requisite work can be as motivating as task specific self-efficacy.[3]

Both Perrewé and Spector (2002) as well as McNatt and Judge (2004) believe that GSE is a stable dispositional trait that is likely to be highly resistant to change. Future research is needed to determine how GSE and task-specific self-efficacy relate to one another, especially in light of the finding from a factor analysis that these two concepts loaded highly on the same factor (Judge et al., 1998). It seems likely that in assessing task specific self-efficacy, a person takes into account available resources and one's ability to use them effectively.

Outcome Expectancies

In addition to an individual's goals and self-efficacy, outcome expectancies is a third cognitive variable in Bandura's theory. When self-efficacy is high, and positive outcome expectancies are low, behavior can become dysfunctional. To the extent that one understands the outcomes that people expect, one can understand why they do what they do. Change the outcomes that people expect, and one can change their behavior. As a way to determine a person's outcome expectations, I developed an empathy box, shown in Figure 10.1.

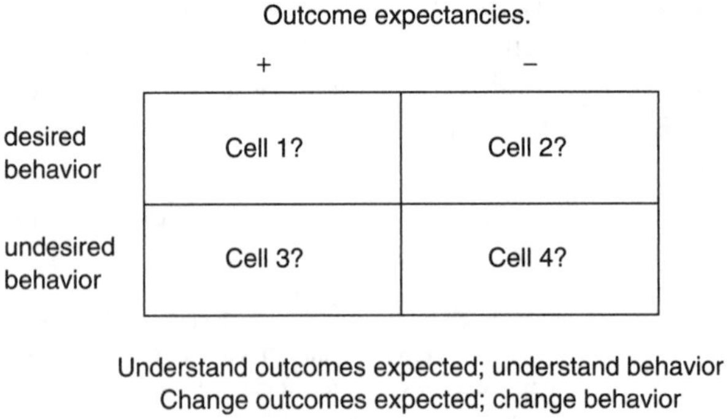

Outcome expectancies.

	+	−
desired behavior	Cell 1?	Cell 2?
undesired behavior	Cell 3?	Cell 4?

Understand outcomes expected; understand behavior
Change outcomes expected; change behavior

Figure 10.1   Empathy Box

[3]Bandura would likely be pleased if Eden's GSE was defined in terms of Guzzo et al.'s (1993) conception of potency. Whereas efficacy beliefs are task-specific in that they refer to beliefs about performance on specific tasks, potency refers to a generalized belief about one's general effectiveness across multiple tasks.

A problem confronting a forest products company was an inordinate amount of theft by employees. Theft was so bad that the unionized employees were even stealing from one another. Hence, the union as well as the company selected names from a hat for me to interview (Latham, 2001b). Random selection works in that among the individuals chosen for me to see were the very people who were stealing from their colleagues as well as from the company. Self-efficacy on the part of an employee on ways to be honest was not an issue. Thus, the randomly selected employees were asked the following questions, in accordance with cells 1–4 in the empathy box, regarding their outcome expectancies for honesty versus theft.

(1) What positive outcomes do you expect for being honest? That is, what are the upsides, how will you come out ahead if you are honest? The answers for the most part were "nothing."

In using the empathy box, so named because it is a tool for assessing the perspective of other people, one must often "bite one's tongue" or the outcome is likely to be a "socially desirable response" to the interviewer's question. Thus, a display of anger to the above answer is likely to minimize any value to further questioning an employee.

(2) What negative outcomes do you expect for being honest? In other words, what are the downsides? How might you get hurt for being honest? Representative answers to this question included ostracism by peers. Supervisors explained how they were castigated by the human resources manager for the number of grievances filed as a result of asking people to open their lunch boxes as they were leaving the plant gate at the end of a shift.

(3) What positive outcomes do you expect for stealing? No one said they were selling or even using the stolen goods. No one reported "getting even" with the company as an explanation for theft. Instead, people discussed their pride in their performance as thieves. They described the planning and organizing of a theft as well as the sense of camaraderie and team-playing that occurs throughout the planning process. They even asked me to become involved: "Doc, tell us what you want and we can get it out within 45 days; we are that good." The expected outcome for these people was the thrill and excitement of executing a seemingly impossible theft successfully.

(4) What negative outcomes do you expect from stealing? No one feared for their jobs since they were members of a strong militant union. Further, they were aware of the company's guarantee of an uninterrupted supply of logs to Japan. The company, they reasoned,

would not fire them for fear that such action might lead to a strike. The only downside for stealing, they said, was the anger of spouses because of the space the stolen material was taking in the garage, the basement, and attic.

Change the expected or anticipated outcomes, change behavior. Thus, the fifth question was: "What needs to shift or change to get people into cell 1?" The answers can often be found in the responses to the second and third questions. Consideration in this instance was given by management to profit sharing. This idea was discarded due to possible precedent setting for other unionized mills. Redesigning the jobs so that the excitement and challenge is in the work was discussed in detail. This idea, too, was discarded because of the monetary expense of a job redesign intervention for this mill—a mill that exists primarily as a thorn in the side of competitors. Instead, the expected outcomes of the thieves were changed by adopting a policy from the public library.

Effective on a given Friday, employees were told that they could now borrow from the company what they once stole.[4] Effective on the subsequent Friday, as is done by libraries, an amnesty day was declared. The company stated that the assumption would be made that the person who returned the company's property was not the person who removed it; rather, it would be assumed that the person was returning property on behalf of a friend; no questions would be asked.

The material was returned by the truckload. People did not want to miss the opportunity for increasing space in their garages, basements, and attics. The amnesty was so effective that it was extended an additional two days. No subsequent theft occurred, as the thrill of doing so was now gone. Nor did these employees subsequently demonstrate other counterproductive behaviors. There was no "symptom substitution." And no one borrowed the equipment. There was no longer any thrill or excitement in possessing it.

Moral Disengagement

I used the empathy box as a way to understand why employees were stealing from the company and fellow employees. What motivates leaders of organizations to behave unethically? We know from Bandura's work

---

[4]This caused apoplexy on the part of the company's lawyers—which in itself was a bit of a thrill. They prepared reams of paper for employees to sign which stated that the company was not liable for someone getting hurt off the job while using company equipment (e.g., a chainsaw).

that self-reactive influence enables people to regulate their own motivation and behavior rather than respond like weathervanes to whatever situational influences happen to impinge upon them. In this self-regulatory process, we also know that people set goals or standards, monitor and evaluate their performance relative to their goals and the constellation of contextual events operating at the time, and then react self-approvingly or self-critically.

To answer the above question, Bandura, Caprara, and Zsolnai (2000) drew upon social cognitive theory to explain transgressions made by leaders who break rules ostensibly in the interests of their company as well as their own. Specifically, they reviewed the moral disengagement strategies of (a) Union Carbide India Limited where a gas leak from a pesticide plant killed 2,500 people, injured 10,000 seriously, partially disabled 20,000, and adversely affected 180,000 others in one way or another; (b) Ford Motor Company senior managers' decision to sell the Pinto despite the warning by the company's engineers of serious design problems, and the resulting burn deaths of 500 people; (c) Nestle Company knowingly selling powdered infant formula to Third World countries that is harmful when mixed with water supplies of poor quality; and (d) the near explosion equivalent to a 1-megaton bomb at Three Mile Island.

Transgression conduct addresses the exercise of moral agency through two sets of sanctions—social and personal. Social sanctions are administered in the form of social ostracism and external punishers. Self-sanctions operate through self-condemnation of one's behavior in relation to one's moral standards.

At least six factors enable people to commit transgressions without experiencing self-sanctions: (1) Moral justification occurs by people portraying a detrimental act to others as advancing the attainment of a valued social or moral goal; (2) finding a euphemistic label to mask a reprehensible activity or even conferring a respectable status to it; (3) displacing personal responsibility for one's actions to the dictates of others, especially legitimate authority figures; (4) disregarding or distorting the consequences of one's actions; (5) dehumanizing the injured party of human qualities; and (6) attributing the cause of one's behavior to forcible provocation by the other person or persons.

Among the strategies that Bandura and his colleagues recommended to counteract moral disengagement is to (1) constantly monitor and publicize corporate practices that have detrimental human effects; (2) increase the transparency of the discourse by which the deliberation of corporate policies and practices are formulated; and (3) expose "sanitizing language" that masks inappropriate behavior.[5] Empirical research is now needed to determine the effectiveness of this proposed intervention.

Pygmalion Effect

In addition to enactive mastery and modeling, social cognitive theory states that a person's self-efficacy is affected by persuasion from a "significant other." People tend to behave in accordance with the expectations of those who are significant to them. Persuasion by those who are significant to us can be a powerful source of a behavior change (Bandura, 1997). To the extent that a leader is held in high regard, this person needs to be purposeful in what is said, lest the leader "gets what the leader says" (e.g., "you are awful at this" vs. "you have the ability to master this").

Long before the current studies by social psychologists on sub- or pre-conscious goals, let alone self-efficacy, Merton (1948, p. 195) brought to prominence the concept of the self-fulfilling prophecy (SFP). Specifically, a self-fulfilling prophecy "is in the beginning false, a false definition of the situation evoking a new behavior which makes the originally false conceptions come true." In short, a person's actions sometimes fulfill their own prophecies/expectations or the prophecies/ expectations of significant others. The Pygmalion effect is a special case of a self-fulfilling prophecy (Rosenthal, 2002). It refers to the effect of nonconscious mental processes that lead a person (e.g., teachers) to treat others (e.g., students) in accordance with his or her expectations. People tend to respond in accordance with the way they are being treated. This effect has been studied extensively by Eden and his colleagues with regard to Israeli military officers as well as managers with their respective subordinates.

The Galatea effect refers to the direct manipulation of a person's self-expectations (Eden & Sulimani, 2003).[6] Self-expectations are a mediator of the Pygmalion effect. As Bandura's (1997) research has shown, high

---

[5]Jack Welch (2005) during his visit to our business school, scoffed at creating a cover story for people who are fired for lack of integrity (e.g., the person left to spend more time with family). Welch believes in making an example of the person's termination to others throughout the company.

[6]Galatea is the statue that the mythical Pygmalion sculpted. The Galatea effect differs from the Pygmalion effect in that the former is a self-produced/induced expectation whereas the latter effect is produced among subordinates by inducing their supervisors to expect great things of them. The Golem effect refers to the negative impact of low expectations of a significant other on a person's performance (Eden, 2003).

self-expectations lead to high performance. Thus, Eden's studies on the Galatea effect have essentially been exercises in ways to increase self-efficacy through persuasion by a "significant other" (e.g., the leader).

In the typical SFP experiment, Eden, as an eminent behavioral scientist, effectively (mis)leads managers within 5 or so minutes into believing that some subordinates, namely those he randomly assigned to the experimental group, have high potential.[7] These managers then become unwitting prophets who fulfill their own subsequent expectations of these people. That is, a manager subsequently spends the time necessary with the designated high potentials to facilitate them achieving more than those people who were assigned by Eden to the control group (Eden, 1990).

The effectiveness of an SFP intervention on performance improvement has been corroborated by a meta-analysis of the accumulated results of experimental research in organizational settings (McNatt, 2000). The process works as follows: (1) High leader expectations result in (2) improved leadership of the person, (3) which, in turn, increases a person's self-efficacy, (4) resulting in greater motivation that includes (5) intensification of effort, which is manifested in (6) an increase in performance. With regard to steps one and two, nonconscious mental processes result in leaders treating subordinates in accordance with their expectations of them. The practical significance of this technique, however, is limited in that it is based on deception. As Eden and Sulimani (2002) acknowledged, few psychologists or organizational behavior consultants are likely to base their relations with clients on an intervention that deceives people no matter how worthwhile the performance outcomes.

The question remains as to whether raising supervisors' expectations of subordinates' capabilities without deception is as effective as a SFP intervention.[8] A systematic experiment to compare these two conditions

---

[7]Born in the United States, Barry Fine changed his name to Dov Eden in 1971 upon completing his Ph.D. at the University of Michigan under the supervision of Stan Seashore, and emigrating to Israel. There he served as a major in the Israel Defense Forces. He is a long-time faculty member of Tel-Aviv University.

[8]Schneider (2004, personal communication) believes that Theory X and Theory Y are both unconscious expectations of what motivates others and hence clearly fit the SFP model. "I actually think that any and all theories of leadership should contain this kind of explanation for the effects achieved. I also believe that the reason why leader personality gets reflected in subordinate behavior can be tied to the relationship between leader personality and the expectancies generated by leaders for subordinates. For example, conscientious leaders have expectancies of followers that they also will be conscientious! I firmly believe that founders' personalities get played out in organizations because of the implicit expectancies created for followers—Schein (1992) would agree with this, I am sure."

has yet to be conducted. On the basis of social cognitive theory, the answer would appear to be an emphatic yes. Eden and Sulimani (2002) focused on what they called means efficacy in addition to self-efficacy. The former term, they said, is the aggregate subjective judgment of the utility of the means (e.g., tools, equipment, resources) available for performing one's job. Specifically, in a one-day workshop they successfully taught instructors in the Israeli military ways to use these two concepts to motivate trainees to increase performance through verbal modeling and persuasion. There was no deception.[9]

McNatt and Judge (2004) conducted a 3-month field experiment on the Galatea effect on a person's job performance. No deception was used; instead, they drew upon Bandura's (1997) methodology for increasing an employee's self-efficacy, namely, verbal persuasion from managers. Specifically, the managers emphasized to newly hired auditors, who were randomly assigned to the experimental condition, of the competitive hiring process, the qualifications and skills that resulted in them being hired, the auditors' past successes stemming from effort and ability, as well as the ongoing support that they (the auditors) could expect from the managers. In the first month, 55% of the auditors who received this intervention performed above the median, compared with only 45% of the control group; but, this positive effect disappeared in the remaining two months. Thus, the positive effect of this intervention on performance was temporary. Nevertheless, based on McNatt and Judge's methodology, it would appear that further Galatea interventions to raise employee expectations of themselves should be conducted within the framework of Bandura's social cognitive theory rather than through the use of deception. Deception, in addition to being unethical, limits Pygmalion effects to settings where there has been minimal previous interaction between a "deceived" leader and subordinates (Eden, 2003). When the leader has had prior experience with and has acquired knowledge of an employee, the Pygmalion effect does not occur. Knowledge of an employee is not a moderator of the positive effect of training procedures for knowingly increasing an employee's self-efficacy. So, why resort to deception to increase a person's personal initiative when it is not necessary to do so?

---

[9]Consistent with Bandura, Locke (2003) stated that means efficacy is not a valid concept: Instrumentality is the proper term, he stated, for Eden to use. Moreover, both Bandura and Locke would agree that a self-efficacy measure takes into account the benefits of tools, equipment, and resources available to an individual.

Action Theory

The champion of this theory continues to be Michael Frese (2005). He is unarguably the most cited HRM, I/O, and OB German researcher in journals published in the West. As noted earlier, action theory states that most action is goal-oriented behavior. Anticipated results are visualized and hence motivate a person to attain them. A key proposition of action theory is that the better one can visualize and imagine goal attainment, the greater the motivating function of the goal.

A goal can be the result of a person's wish or can be derived from an organizational task. Opportunity for action, time to do something about it, the importance of the goal, and one or more means to attain it are important parameters that lead to goal attainment. The key factor that differentiates a goal from a mere wish is whether the person has developed at least a rudimentary plan for its attainment. People tend to abandon a goal that they find difficult in the absence of specific detailed plans. Goal commitment and persistence are likely to increase if people have developed detailed plans and are in the process of executing them. Goal attainment is unlikely to occur if one merely indulges in positive fantasies about attaining the goal or only worries about not attaining it (Oettingen & Mayer, 2002).

Action theory states that to excel at organizational tasks the person must translate or redefine them into internal goals. The effectiveness of this redefinition process depends in part on the person understanding and accepting the task.

Goals are organized into hierarchies. Distal goals have less regulatory power than proximal goals. Because of action styles, contradictions between proximal and distal goals often go unnoticed. This is because automatic heuristics regulate how people set their goals, plan, monitor, and process feedback. Actions are usually regulated at a conscious level only when barriers, opportunities for new goals, or environmental pressures appear. When high routinization is achieved, the person no longer has to think consciously regarding the actions they take. This explains why experts often find it difficult to teach novices.

Frese (2005) has used action theory as a framework for developing a training program to increase a person's personal initiative in the workplace. Personal initiative is defined as changing one's environment rather than only reacting to it, going beyond what a person has been told to do, and initiating improvements in work procedures. In short, personal initiative involves the pursuit of self-set goals. Self-set goals require people to think proactively, particularly with regard to ways to overcome obstacles to goal attainment.

The core of Frese's training program consists of goal development, collecting information for making a prognosis, planning and monitoring action, and seeking feedback. That is, after the goal is set, a person seeks the information necessary for goal attainment, and, in dynamic settings makes a prognosis regarding future environmental states. Plans are developed, executed, and monitored based on this information. During monitoring, feedback is used to adjust one's actions when necessary.[10]

Frese's training program has considerable practical use. Unemployed people with a high degree of personal initiative were able to find a job faster than those with low personal initiative (Frese et al., 1996). The personal initiative taken by owners of small businesses in Africa was shown to be related to their firm's subsequent success (Frese, 2000). The widespread use of training in personal initiative in medium size companies in Germany led to increases in company profitability (Baer & Frese, 2003).

These findings are consistent with those conducted within the frameworks of goal-setting and social cognitive theories. Action theory and Frese's research, as Frese readily explained (Frese, 2005), reflects the preference by German psychologists for all-encompassing theories that are often excessively complex. From the standpoint of a practitioner, however, Frese has put together a comprehensive treatment package that works. Frese's work on personal initiative, for example, encompasses personality factors, knowledge skills and abilities as antecedents, environmental supports, and goals. In addition to proactive planning, it contains a training module on innovation to persuade people to invest time and effort to generate creative techniques; and emotion regulation based on Ellis's (1999) work so that they do not become angry if things do not work out, and skills in self-management.

Action theory appears to borrow heavily from social cognitive theory. The similarities between them are striking. Four core features of the social cognitive theory are goals, forethought, self-reactiveness, and

---

[10]This methodology parallels Frayne's and my self-management studies described earlier (Frayne & Latham, 1986; Latham & Frayne, 1989).

Frese and Fay (2001) found that there may be a personal initiative personality. Responses to their personal initiative situational interview correlates positively with Bateman and Crant's (1993) proactive personality.

self-reflectiveness. People, Bandura (2004a; 2005a) argued, through forethought, set goals and anticipate likely outcomes of prospective actions to guide and motivate effort. The person monitors and regulates action relative to the goal that is set. Hence, self-regulation occurs. In addition to being an agent of action, people are self-examiners in that they reflect on their efficacy, the meaning of their pursuits, and whether adjustments in their actions are necessary. By exercising self-influence, Bandura concluded that people operate generatively and proactively, not just reactively. To the extent that parsimony is valued, this theoretical framework can explain Frese's impressive results.

Concluding Comments

The cognitive revolution that took place in the 1970s has been an enduring one. This is hardly surprising, given that the people consistently think. To believe that the psychology of the individual could be predicted, explained, and influenced solely by examining behavior and its consequences, in retrospect, appears ludicrous.

Two cognitive theories continue to dominate the HRM, I/O, and OB literature, namely, goal setting and social cognitive. A third, action theory, which is popular in Germany, overlaps strongly with these two theories. These three theories have provided effective frameworks for successfully training employees in self-regulation/self-management in the workplace.

Goal-setting theory explains the effect of goals and feedback on self-regulation. They prompt people to engage in self-reflective as well as self-evaluative thinking. Social cognitive theory explains the effect of self-system variables that exert their influence on a person's behavior in performance contexts where there is specific feedback on goal progress. Thus, self-management can be understood via complementary analyses of goal-system and self-system variables. Goal setting and goal commitment can be understood in terms of cognitive processes involving self-efficacy beliefs and outcome expectancies.

Both the *Academy of Management Journal* (Steers, 2001) and the *Journal of Applied Psychology* (Klein & Zedeck, 2004) were successful in soliciting theoretically driven articles with the goal of advancing and understanding organizational behavior. Many of these articles (e.g., Fried & Slowik, 2004; Kehr, 2004; Mainemilis, 2001; Meyer et al., 2004; Mitchell et al., 2004) provide a rich research agenda, particularly for empirical studies on goal setting.

Whereas the vast majority of studies emanating from the cognitive revolution have focused on consciousness, the new frontier, emanating from social psychology experiments, is the subconscious. HRM, I/O, and OB scholars have speculated on its importance with regard to goal setting, feedback, and self-regulation. Empirical studies in the workplace have yet to be conducted.

Given the need long expressed by managers and practitioners for passion in the workplace (e.g., Peters & Waterman, 1982), the domain that remained inexplicably unexplored by HRM, I/O, and OB researchers during the 20th century is emotion. As shown in the next chapter, this vacuum is currently being filled by meaningful research.

11 Affect/Emotion

The Employee Has Feelings Too

Introduction

In the 21st century, organizations are scrambling to compete effectively in a turbulent global marketplace. This is requiring three arguably new agendas:[1] (1) a new intellectual agenda for creating value in the marketplace; (2) a behavioral agenda for implementing newly discovered strategies; and (3) new emotions and passions for internalizing the new, while letting go of former strategies and behaviors that are no longer effective. The second and third agendas are the province of HRM, I/O psychology, and organization behavior. In the 20th century HRM, I/O, and OB theory and research were limited primarily to employee cognition and behavior. Emotions were ignored for the most part. This oversight is rapidly being corrected in the present century.

Mowday and Sutton (1993) were among the first to argue against an overemphasis on cognition in the study of motivation. This is because affect, which includes moods and emotions, influence goal level and commitment as well as the attainment of complex long-term goals in the face of obstacles (see Barrett & Bartunek, 2004; Lord & Kanfer, 2002). Indeed, failure to regulate one's emotions, coupled with failure in job performance, can ultimately undermine one's problem-focused coping efforts and intensify feelings of hopelessness (Kanfer & Kantrowitz, 2002). Thus, a theoretical framework of motivation that fails to take into account human emotion is incomplete (see Feldman, Barrett, & Bartunek, 2004).

---

[1]David Campbell (2005), a senior fellow at the Center for Creative Leadership, maintains that globalization of the economy is by no means new. In the early days of the 20th century, Singer Sewing Machines, International Harvester Reapers, and Woolworths "Dime" stores could be found throughout the world. I would add that England thrived in the 18th and 19th centuries as a result of the country's emphasis on a global economy.

Just as there was a cognitive revolution in the 1970s, Barsade, Brief, and Spataro (2003) observed that HRM, I/O, and OB are currently undergoing an "affective revolution." Affect is viewed by most researchers as a phenomenalogical state described in terms of emotions such as sad, happy, or enthusiastic (Thorensen et al., 2003). Whereas state affect refers to feelings in a given situation in a given point in time, trait affect is considered to be a stable personality dimension.

Studies on feelings of trust, fairness, exploitation, and revenge in the workplace continue to be studied within the framework of organizational justice. Hence, the empirical research on feelings of justice as well as emotions is also reviewed in this chapter. This chapter ends with a discussion of the psychological contract.

Emotions and Moods

Locke (2003) defined emotion as the form in which one experiences automatic, subconscious value appraisals. As such, emotions contain built-in tendencies or impulses to take action. Emotions can be long lasting when the situation is long lasting, when a person's subconscious continues to make appraisals of a given event, or when an individual is consciously brooding over an issue. Emotions can also endure when there is a chemical imbalance in the brain.[2] In their *Annual Review of Psychology* chapter, Brief and Weiss (2002) defined moods as "generalized feeling states not . . . identified with a particular stimulus and not sufficiently intense to interrupt ongoing thought processes" (p. 282). Whereas moods are generally characterized as positive or negative, emotions are usually labeled specifically (e.g., fear).

In the 20th century the study of affect was primarily limited to the study of job satisfaction since many people believed that job satisfaction leads to high job performance.[3] Fisher and Hannah (1931) viewed dissatisfaction in terms of vocational maladjustment due to "nonadjustive emotional tendencies." Mild employee maladjustments, they concluded,

---

[2]Note there is scarcely a subject or topic in workplace motivation that Locke has not influenced. In 1975, I invited Lawler to make a presentation to the Weyerhaeuser Company. Aware of my newly formed friendship with Locke, he made the jovial comment that Locke has thought deeply about 99% of the issues in our field and is right on about 90% of them. Thirty years later, I continue to agree with that observation.

[3]A historical perspective on the study of affect in the workplace has been written by Weiss and Brief (2001).

are manifested by the person's petty jealousies and lack of "cheerful cooperation." More severe maladjustments are evident by the employee making frequent job changes, reporting feelings of exhaustion, and even hearing voices at work. In short, job satisfaction was not attributed to characteristics of the workplace but rather to the emotional maladjustment of the employee. Viteles (1932, p. 589) concluded, on the basis of Fisher and Hannah's work, that "one half of the amount expended annually because of labor turnover is spent on the replacement of emotionally maladjusted workers." Thus, the focus of job satisfaction was on employee emotions. Fisher and Hannah went so far as to argue further that employees are usually unaware of the source of their emotional maladjustments and consequently misattribute it to characteristics of their job. Hence, they remain unhappy from one job setting to another. It was not until subsequent sundry interpretations of the Hawthorne studies that the pendulum of opinion swung fully to the polar opposite; job characteristics came to be viewed by behavioral scientists as a primary, if not the sole determinant of job satisfaction.[4] As this latter research paradigm developed, employee mood and emotion were soon forgotten (Weiss, in press). By the final quarter of the 20th century, both Organ and Near (1985) and Brief and Roberson (1989) observed that typical measures of job satisfaction are far more cognitively than affectively laden.

Interest in emotion was fully resurrected in 1996 when Weiss and Cropanzano presented their affective events theory (AET). This theory provides a framework for studying emotions in the workplace. It discusses both the causes and the consequences of affective experiences, particularly the effects of a person's moods and emotions on performance as well as satisfaction with the job. Among its key theoretical elements is the distinction made between affect and job satisfaction. AET states that the former is one's evaluative judgment of the job; it is the consequence of a person's affective experiences at work as well as the person's belief about the job. The person's affect and belief jointly influence overall job satisfaction in that this judgment is influenced by affective experiences as well as by beliefs about the job. An employee can

---

[4]Not everyone was sanguine regarding this pendulum swing. As discussed in Part I, Pfeffer and Salancik (1978) warned that motivation cannot be reliably predicted by job characteristics. Motivation, they said, is socially influenced and transient. Preliminary work by Jennifer George (2000), a former doctoral student of Art Brief, supports this position. She found that the mood of the leader influences the mood of the followers.

distinguish between pleasant and unpleasant experiences while working, and abstract beliefs about such things as pay and career opportunities. When one is called upon to evaluate one's job, both of these are
taken into account. The process by which this occurs, as well as the
influence of affective experiences on beliefs and vice versa, is not yet
well understood. What is known is that:

> (1) More recent affective experiences carry more weight in the judgment. (2)
> People don't seem to simply add up their affective experiences. They provide some
> sort of meaning structure to the experiences, and that is what influences a person's
> overall judgment. Think of going to a very sad movie. Throughout the movie you
> are in a negative affective state, yet your judgment at the end is positive. (3)
> Frequency of affective experiences is a better predictor of overall judgments than
> is intensity. Life satisfaction is higher with a history of small but frequent pleasant
> experiences than it is with a history of infrequent, but intense pleasant experi-
> ences. Presumably, job satisfaction works the same way. (Weiss, 2005, personal
> communication)

AET also emphasizes the causal role of environmental events in influencing a person's affect and job performance. An event usually has
emotional consequences that, in turn, influence a person's behavior.
This influence is relatively immediate. Since a person's mood states vary
across time, the relationship between affect and performance must be
studied as it unfolds over time.

On the basis of AET, Ilies and Judge (2005) argued that goal regulation explains in part the links among emotion, action tendencies, and
intentional behavior. Performance feedback is an affective event that
influences an employee's affective state and, through the goals a person
subsequently sets, behavior.

Forgas and George's (2001) affect infusion model (AIM) states that
attitudes regarding one's job are partially a function of the affect that
colors one's cognitive processes in forming evaluations. Thus, AIM is a
direct effects model in that it does not assume any mediating influence
between affect and social judgments (Thorensen et al., 2003).

A definitive book of original chapters by leading behavioral scientists
in the field on emotions in the workplace has been edited by Lord,
Klimoski, and Kanfer (2002). Consistent with AET, the thrust of the
chapters is that emotions mediate environmental events and the person's subsequent behavior. Strong negative emotions frequently have
strong associations with specific types of behavior (classical conditioning), and thus are likely to produce such behavior. Because emotions are
often urgent and passionate, the behavior often is manifested so quickly

that little if any cognitive processing occurs.[5] This is because an emotional reaction to a psychological or physical event can occur in a time span as short as 300 milliseconds (Klinger, 1996).

Murphy (2001) reviewed neurophysiological as well as behavioral evidence that shows that affect does not always require conscious input. The conscious and subconscious can operate independently, and they can influence each other. The emotional unconscious can be described as the conscious awareness of one's emotional state, but a lack of awareness of the source of that state (Kihlstrom, Mulvaney, Tobias, & Tobis, 2000). Thus, a person's emotion may be the result of implicit memories that reflect the effect of a previous event on an ongoing experience, regardless of whether the person is aware of or can recall the specific event.

In short, people do not always deliberate and plan before they act (Seo et al., 2004). Motivational processes are not always cognitively based, discrete choice processes. Nevertheless, there is usually a continual interplay between emotion and cognition; the causal arrow can go in either direction (Lord & Harvey, 2002).

Seo et al. (2004) defined core affective feelings as an ongoing stream of transient, patterned alterations in ongoing neurophysiological states and autonomic activity. Hence, affective feelings can exist in the subconscious as well as in awareness. Seo et al. argued that core affect is the central construct affecting both the processes and outcomes of work motivation via their influence on judgment processes, particularly with regard to goal setting.

Self-regulation, Seo et al. maintained, provides a conceptual linkage through which motivation and emotion can be integrated theoretically. They proposed that core affective feelings have two independent

---

[5]Metcalfe and Mischel (1999) used the words hot vs. cold to describe the motivational antecedents of behavior. Specifically, they differentiated between a hot emotional system and a cold cognitive system. Locke (2005, personal communication) takes issue with the above statement. He believes that motivational processes are indeed cognitively and value based in that they are subconsciously stored information and are affected by values. It may be more accurate, however, to assume that all workings of the mind are "cognitive" whether they are memories triggered by an emotion, deliberate actions based upon careful consideration, or well-learned procedures. It would be incorrect to assume that "cognitive" only refers to "conscious" deliberations that require most of the capacity of working memory. Implicit memory stores that contain automatic procedures still require some degree of attention. For example, once one has become skilled at driving a manual transmission car, it takes little attention to be successful, but the act of shifting gears still requires some attention—so, it can still be considered a cognitive process (e.g., attending to the visual and auditory context for selecting and successfully engaging the correct gear, accessing memory stores for proper kinesthetic procedures). Even the act of eliciting an emotion from a memory rather than an environmental situation requires "cognitive" input from a memory store.

dimensions, namely pleasantness at the level of subjective experience, and activation in terms of one's physiological energy. Core affective states are believed to be inherently motivational in that they have their own action tendency, or readiness, such as "moving toward, away from, or against." Thus, Seo et al. stated that people in a positive core affect behave generatively by exploring ways to obtain positive expected outcomes in contrast to those in a negative core affect who focus on ways to avoid negative expected outcomes. The activation of core affective experiences influences the intensity of a person's motivation (i.e., effort). To the extent that it is positive, people set, commit to, and persist until they attain high rather than easy goals.

There is growing interest among organizational scholars in emotion regulation. Heckhausen and Schultz (1999) proposed that individuals rely primarily on two processes to control their emotions. People take action to modify their environment (e.g., change jobs; seek tasks that they enjoy). When that is not possible, they take internally directed action. With regard to the latter, Pugh (2002) has discussed ways of exerting control over when to experience and express one's emotions. Response modulation is dependent upon the environment (e.g., cultural or organizational norms) as well as cognition. Initially a consciously controlled process, emotional regulation, through practice eventually becomes automatic. Power differentials in dyads (e.g., boss/subordinate) also influence emotion regulation. Powerful people have more freedom to express their emotions in the workplace relative to less powerful people. The latter are expected to keep their emotions in check.

Emotion appraisals usually involve cognitive value judgments of events that are interpreted as having motivational significance for the person (Lazarus, 1991).[6] This sets the stage for expressed emotion, emotional expressions, and emotion regulation. Consistent with the philosophy of reciprocal determinism underlying social cognitive theory, experienced emotions are posited to be inputs from physiological, cognitive, and behavioral systems (Kanfer & Kantrowitz, 2002). Emotion regulation is understanding and influencing "the process of initiating, maintaining, modulating, or managing the occurrence, intensity, or duration of internal feeling states and emotion-related physiological

---

[6]A strong supporter of Lazarus' research on emotion, Locke (2003) defined emotion appraisals in terms of a four-step process: First, the object or event is perceived. Second, there is a conceptual evaluation. The subconscious automatically classifies the perceived object or event based on one's stored knowledge. Third, there is a value appraisal in the form of subconscious, psychological evaluation. Fourth, there is an emotional experience that involves physiological reactions.

processes, often in the service of accomplishing one's goals" (Eisenberg, Fabes, Guthrie, & Reiser, 2000, p. 167).

Seo et al. (2004) have speculated that a person's core affect at the time of goal setting influences information processing regarding the situation, the options for action, and a person's expected outcomes. This is because momentary feelings often act as a judgment-simplifying heuristic. Thus, the more positive/pleasant a person's core affect at the moment a goal is set, the more likely the person is to commit to and exert effort to attain it. With regard to goal attainment, emotion regulation may be initiated to replace one emotion with a more productive one, such as reframing task threats into challenges and thereby increasing task motivation (Kanfer & Kantrowitz, 2002).[7] With practice, this may occur nonconsciously in response to detection of a discrepancy between one's goal and one's performance. Individual differences in personality traits (e.g., negative affectivity) likely influence the instantiation of emotion regulation through their influence on the monitoring of one's behavior. Seo et al. predicted that people who are experiencing positive core affect make judgments regarding their progress in attaining their goal less frequently, less thoroughly, and more favorably than those experiencing negative core affect. Hence the former individuals persist in their intended course of action longer than those in a negative affective state when there is a large discrepancy between their performance and their goal. Empirical research with external validity is now needed to test these hypotheses. To date, the majority of experiments on the effect of emotions on a person's performance have been restricted to simulations and laboratory settings (Barsade, Brief, & Spataro, 2003).

There is emerging evidence that goal setting not only has a positive effect on a person's performance, it has a positive effect on a person's overall sense of well-being.[8] A meta-analysis by Koestner, Lekes, Powers, and Chicoine (2002) of nine studies showed that goal attainment is

---

[7] Recall the study discussed earlier by Drach-Zahavy and Erez on a person's appraisal of stress as a challenge or a threat regarding high goals.

[8] Well-being is a loosely used umbrella term for affect. The criterion measures for assessing this concept typically include three or more measures of interest to the researcher. The focus on well-being suggests the ongoing evolution within the fields of HRM, I/O, and OB from an effectiveness/efficiency emphasis to one that is more balanced in terms of benefits to both the employee and employer. A problem with this research focus is the lack of consistency among researchers in operationally defining subjective well-being. This explains why different studies by highly competent researchers can yield contradictory findings (recall the study by Wright et al. vs. Smithey et al. on the relationship between HRM practices and an organization's effectiveness). Another problem is that research on this topic does not appear to be taking into account and hence benefiting from

(Continued)

associated with increases in a person's positive affect and decreases in negative affect. This is particularly likely when the goal is difficult.

In a study involving people in a broad range of managerial and professional jobs in Germany, Wiese and Freund (2005) found that only those adults who perceived their goals as difficult to attain reported a change in positive and negative affect, job satisfaction, and perceptions of occupational success over a 3-year period. Goal progress was a strong predictor of self-reports of occupational success. It was also related to positive affect when goal difficulty was perceived to be high, but not when the goal was viewed as having been relatively easy to attain. Moreover, there was no data suggesting that feelings of exhaustion were predominant among the people who had set high goals. The relationship between the attainment of one's work goals and affective well-being was especially strong when the goal was perceived by the person to be important. Among the most interesting findings from this study is that lack of goal attainment in one's personal life appears to be related to higher degrees of well-being when the person experiences goal progress on the job. Compensatory switching occurs so as to enable a person to concentrate emotion regulation in the work domain.

Keith and Frese (2005) found that metacognitive ability and emotion control are independent mediators of a person's performance. They then posed two questions that have yet to be answered: (1) Does metacognitive activity positively affect emotion control because people who engage in metacognitive activity forget to become upset over an error? (2) Or is emotion control a prerequisite for metacognitive activity because only if people can control their negative emotions can metacognitive activity take place? Future self-regulation research will likely provide a framework for integrating emotion and cognitions into a common model.

An issue that has yet to be thoroughly explored is when disengagement or abandonment of a goal is appropriate for enhancing worker-related well-being (e.g., increase in job satisfaction and reduction in

---

(Continued)

seminal studies in related fields such as vocational psychology. For example, Lofquist and Dawis's theory (Dawis & Lofquist, 1984) of work adjustment based on an interactive person-environment system is seldom cited. This theory views response capabilities and reward preferences as person characteristics, response requirements and reward systems as work environment descriptors, correspondence between person and work environment as the primary predictor, and satisfaction and satisfactoriness as the twin criteria of a person's adjustment. This is just one example of many for the necessity of a "boundaryless" psychology to be discussed in Chapter 12 of this book. Over-specialization is making us ignorant of relevant findings in related fields.

stress and emotional exhaustion). Disengagement from a goal that is truly unattainable is an adaptive strategy because it frees up resources that can be invested in attainable goals, and it reduces the experiences of accumulated failures.

A study involving nurses in a Dutch hospital found that high self-efficacy employees who abandoned goals that were within their control showed a decrease in work-related well-being a year later. Surprisingly, those who attained their goal despite their low self-efficacy for doing so also reported a decrease in work-related well-being. Pomaki and Maes (2005) concluded that the typically beneficial effect derived from goal attainment can be thwarted by self-defying attributions (e.g., I attained the goal through luck).

A key factor affecting pursuit versus abandonment of a goal may be actual or perceived controllability. In a review of the literature on stress and resilience, Hawkley et al. (2005) concluded that seeing a stressful situation as controllable, and coping actively in response to it, not only increases the likelihood that the stress will be resolved, it produces physiological benefits from diminished autonomic and neuro-endocrine activity. Of course, if the stressor is perceived as controllable when in fact it is not, the consequences can be maladaptive if the reduction in autonomic activation is inadequate to endure the uncontrollable stressor. The authors found that people who experience severe chronic stress are at significantly greater risk of developing disease (recall Herzberg's assumptions and Parker's empirical research). The metabolic requirement posed by psychological stressors takes its physiological toll on resilience. Included in the authors' examples of such stressors are pressing deadlines, unreasonable bosses, and perceived injustices. Is it time for HRM, I/O, and OB researchers to do collaborative research with neuro-psychologists?

Principles of Organizational Justice

Today there is an abundance of excellent laboratory and field research on organizational justice principles. The literature on conceptualizations of organizational justice mushroomed in the 1990s following the review by Greenberg (1987). Cropanzano and Greenberg (1997) reported that by the mid-90s, justice was the most popular topic of papers submitted to the Organizational Behavior Division of the Academy of Management. A search of 20 psychology and management journals on the Web of Science database revealed that from 1989–1992 there were only 15 publications where the terms justice or fairness were used;

from 1993–1996, there were 53; and from 1993–2000, the figure had grown to 100 (Colquitt & Greenberg, in press). Despite these facts, Greenberg (2004, personal communication) observed that there is as yet no unified theoretical approach to organizational justice. Rather, there are multiple conceptualizations of justice in the workplace. Hence Greenberg prefers the umbrella term "organizational justice" minus the word *theory* to describe this large rapidly growing body of work. A grand theory, he contends, remains to be developed that refines and consolidates current conceptualizations of justice.

Colquitt, Conlon, Wesson, Porter, and Ng (2001) conducted the first meta-analysis review of the justice literature. With regard to the dimensions of justice, their results showed that distributive and procedural justice are unique though highly intercorrelated constructs. The correlations between procedural and interactional justice also led them to conclude that these two dimensions should be treated separately. As Bobocel and Holmvall (2001) noted, procedural and interactional justice have (1) different causal effects on outcomes, (2) different antecedents, and (3) correlate with organizational outcomes to different degrees. Thus, justice appears to have three components: distributive, procedural, and interactional. Currently, there is debate as to whether there is a fourth. This argument is based on the merits of breaking interactional justice into two components: interpersonal and informational (Colquitt & Greenberg, 2003). Kernan and Hanges (2002), in a study of survivor reactions to a reorganization, found that not only was procedural justice strongly related to trust in management, interpersonal and informational justice added unique variance to the prediction.[9]

Masterson (2001) discovered a trickle-down effect between distributive and interactional justice. Teachers who felt they were compensated fairly for their effort felt more committed to their organization and consequently put more effort into their interactions with their students. This, in turn, led to high student evaluations of their instructors.

A study involving a random sample of city residents revealed that the three dimensions of justice, namely distributive, procedural, and interactional, are linked negatively to feelings of depression and emotional exhaustion (Tepper, 2000). These three dimensions also correlate negatively with work–family conflict. This is because organizational factors that do not match one's contributions can exacerbate tensions between

---

[9]Locke (2003) has argued strenuously against using the concept of interactional justice on the basis that it is overly broad in the number of behavioral categories that are subsumed under it.

one's work and family. Judge and Colquitt (2004) found that lack of procedural and interactional justice are the primary drivers of stress in the workplace; they recommended training programs for leaders on ways to act in a just manner (e.g., see Cole & Latham, 1997; Skarlicki & Latham, 2005).

Harlos and Pinder (2000) reported the results of a qualitative study of 33 individuals who reported having been unjustly treated in the workplace. Interactional injustice was defined as "perceived interpersonal mistreatment by a hierarchical superior or authority figure." Systemic injustice was defined as "perceptions of unfairness involving the larger organizational context within which work relationships are enacted." Emotions were shown to be antecedents and consequences of injustice experiences. Superiors' expressions of anger and their widespread lack of emotion were common causes of emotional responses by these employees. Fear, anger, hopelessness, sadness, excitement, and a decrease in emotionality among the employees were common consequences of perceived injustice. These same emotions, in addition to several others including rage, irritation, shame, embarrassment, guilt, dread, and cynicism appeared in the accounts of many wronged individuals. These findings are similar to those obtained in another study where unfair treatment had a visceral physiological effect on employees (Vermunt & Steensma, 2001). Subsequently, based in part on incidents in the Canadian military, Pinder and Harlos (2002) developed a conceptual model of the relationship between being victimized by injustice and employee silence. Two forms of silence—quiescence and acquiescence—were proposed, along with hypotheses regarding how wronged employees move into and between these two states.

Perceptions of lack of fairness occur when an outcome, procedure, or person is viewed unfavorably, when the person or organization is seen as having multiple options, and when the option exercised is perceived by others as violating their moral principles and beliefs (Folger & Cropanzano, 1998). Because people frequently have to acquiesce to the authority of others, questions of trust arise. When this occurs, people often rely on heuristics or cognitive shortcuts to guide their behavior (Lind, 2001). In short, *would, could,* and *should* judgments of the fairness of situations can occur either systematically or automatically (Cropanzano, Byrne, Bobocel, & Rupp, 2001).

Justice matters to people because it is in their best interest with regard to both material and interpersonal outcomes. It affirms their identity within groups that they value, and it is aligned with a fundamental respect for human worth (Ambrose, 2002). Hence, Cropanzano et al. (2001) concluded that justice matters to people to the extent it serves one of four interrelated psychological needs: i.e., control, belonging, self-esteem, and a meaningful existence. When people feel that they are unfairly treated, their commitment to the organization declines, their job performance drops, and they are unlikely to engage in organizational citizenship (Konovsky, 2000).

Colquitt et al. (2001) found that procedural justice has a mean meta-analytic correlation of .36 with performance. The dependent variables that have been shown to be influenced by employee feelings of fairness, however, are not limited to traditional measures of job performance, citizenship behavior, or job attitudes. Additional variables affected by feelings of fairness or the lack thereof include theft (Greenberg, 2002), exploitation as well as self-sacrificing decision allocations (Turillo, et al., 2002), retribution (Mclean Parks, 1997), workplace revenge (Trip, Bies, & Aquino, 2002), and sabotage (Ambrose, Seabright, & Schminke, 2002).

Employees who feel they have been treated unfairly typically become motivated to re-establish a sense of fairness. Interactional justice is arguably the most deeply personal type of injustice an employee may experience. Inness, Barling, and Turner (2005) found that this experience can lead to aggressive retaliation against one's superior if the person is perceived to be abusive or unfair. Their study showed that this retaliatory behavior is due largely to situational factors; it is not moderated by individual difference variables such as a person's self-esteem. If, however, an employee has a history of aggressive behavior, the behavior is exacerbated in the setting where the abuse is experienced.[10]

Skarlicki and his colleagues have focused on justice principles with regard to layoffs and retaliatory behavior in work settings (Skarlicki, Ellard, & Kelln, 1998; Folger & Skarlicki, 1998). In their most recent study (Barclay, Skarlicki, & Pugh, 2005), they examined the relationship between fairness, emotion, and retaliation among people who were laid off from work. Specifically, they looked at negative inward emotions, namely, shame and anger since these are often associated with events that hinder a person's goal attainment (Lazarus, 1991). These interrelated

---

[10]Kenneth B. Clark, the eminent psychologist whose research influenced the Supreme Court in *Brown v. Board of Education* (1954) to hold racial segregation in public education unconstitutional, stated that: "Injustice results in violence either in personal, small group, or larger contexts as shown in riots. You cannot have injustice without violence of some degree" (Jones & Pettigrew, 2005).

emotions are typically directed at self. The outward focused emotions that they studied were hostility and anger toward others who are perceived to be the cause of an injustice.

An outcome or event, in this instance a layoff from work, is typically the driving force behind a two-part appraisal process: (1) determining the relevance of an event to one's values and goals, and (2) identifying who or what is responsible for the event. Barclay et al. found that when confronted by an uncertain or unclear situation, employees focus on procedural and interactional justice information as a way to understand what has happened (i.e., a distributive outcome) to them. Perceived violations of procedures or treatment predicted anger. When employees attributed the cause of the layoff to external sources (e.g., their employer), they engaged in retaliatory acts. When procedural and interactional justice were perceived to be high, the greater the shame and guilt employees felt since they were unable to deflect blame to others. This latter finding points to the need for interventions to boost the self-esteem of people who no longer have jobs as well as their self-efficacy for finding re-employment. In short, when employees feel unfairly treated, they respond both affectively (e.g., low commitment) and behaviorally (e.g., decrease in helping behavior and an increase in retaliation).

The Psychological Contract

Procedural justice can also affect psychological contracts positively to the extent that they minimize uncertainty and ambiguity (Van den Bos & Lind, 2002). From the employer's perspective, "the experience of justice begets an obligation on the part of employees to reciprocate and thus fosters the development and maintenance of a social exchange relationship, with the expectation that such a relationship will lead to the exchange of valued benefits between the parties" (Blader & Tyler, 2005). Adherence to procedural justice principles is negatively associated with an employee's perceptions of a breach in the psychological contract (Flood et al., 2001; Tekleab, Tekeuchi, & Taylor, 2005).

Among the first scholars to coin the term "psychological contract" is Chris Argyris (1960). He defined a contract as unwritten expectations between an employee and the employing organization. The employee's expectations include a sense of dignity, worth, and an expectation that the organization will provide opportunities for the individual to learn and grow on the job. The employer's expectations include loyalty and commitment from the employee.

Nicholson and Johns (1985) argued that a psychological contract is the essence of an employee's linkage to an employer. This is because it results from a promise of reciprocity in exchange for some action. Violations of an exchange occur frequently when implied promises by a recruiter or one's "boss" disappear when one or both of them disappear from the organization without informing relevant others of these commitments. Interestingly, psychological contracts cause more negative reactions than is the case when one's expectations are violated.[11] Wilson (1999, p. 186) made the point poignantly: "Contractual agreement so thoroughly pervades human social behavior, virtually like the air we breathe, that it attracts no special notice—until it goes bad." Hence there is the necessity for renegotiation of the psychological contract as conditions change with either the employer or employee.

A violation of a psychological contract is typically an emotional and negatively affective experience for an employee. It develops from a cognitive process of interpreting a situation and formulating a belief that the organization has failed to fulfill or maintain its obligations (Morrison & Robinson, 1997; Robinson, 1996). The results include feelings of distrust, resentment, and indignation on the part of an employee that, in turn, can lead to a decrease in a person's organizational commitment and citizenship behavior, task performance, and an increase in an employee's intentions to leave the organization (Robinson & Morrison, 2000).

No one has expanded our understanding of psychological contracts more than Denise Rousseau, now at Carnegie Mellon University, and her former doctoral student, Sandra Robinson, now at the University of British Columbia. The genesis of Rousseau's work can be traced back to her father's work experiences:

> I am a blue collar kid, who listened to dad complain over dinner most every night about the company he worked for (Pacific Tel and Tel, before the ATT break up). It wasn't the physical work (climbing poles in 110 degree summers or stormy

---

[11]In the early 1990s, Glen Whyte, then an assistant professor, was recruited by Wharton largely through the efforts of Bob House. Panic stricken over losing a stellar researcher in decision making and negotiations, Roger Wolff, then our dean, and I put a package together that included a large office—an office unbeknown to us that had been promised by a previous dean to a senior professor when it became vacant. To this day, that individual dislikes me. He feels his unwritten contract with the earlier dean, who had left long ago for another university, had not been honored and hence his contract had been unfairly violated. The root of the problem is that the faculty member failed to see the necessity for renegotiation of the psychological contract when conditions changed with the employer, namely the new vs. the former dean. The good news is that Glen stayed at Toronto.

winters) or the long hours (overtime and call ups to return) that bothered him. It was the supervisors, their abusive treatment, inconsistent demands, and overall disregard for my dad and his coworkers, that made him miserable. When my dad had a chance to become a supervisor (as a senior worker) he was horrified, and I realized it was because dad couldn't imagine a supervisor who actually behaved appropriately to his employees. Of course, he declined.[12]

I knew there had to be a better way, but didn't see how to make it so until I took industrial psychology at Berkeley from Milton Blood.[13] The pieces fell into place. Young, naïve, and ever-optimistic (still the latter today) I thought that if I could capture what the interaction workers had with their company looked like from a worker point of view it would help managers behave more responsibly and respectfully to employees. Along the way, of course, I came to realize that a lot of managers are themselves treated by senior executives in just the same ways that workers experience.[14] My great disappointment has been that research, as yet, has so little impact, the reasons for the presidential speech I gave at the Academy of Management in 2005 regarding why we need evidence-based management.

Psychological contracts are fascinating to me because in this psychic space is where people LIVE in the day to day, managers, coworkers, too. But the real hook for me is "mutuality," when people actually share an understanding of what they owe the organization and each other. So much attention is given to violation, but most employment relations continue for some time and maintaining some level of fulfillment and performance.

We don't fully understand why or how—we must if we want to build organizations that bring out the best in people while serving the needs that can only be met by the complicated coordination that organizations can provide.

I believe that the heart of effective psychological contracts is not so much consistency, but redundancy, lots of supporting practices that provide resources and direction that sustain exchanges between people and companies over time.

In the States there is NO real voice for labor, so it is absolutely necessary that individual workers have voice in their own employment relations (mutuality cannot be coerced), and thus individual influence over the terms of the contract becomes essential to mutuality . . . why I am now studying idiosyncratic deals, where workers bargain for themselves as individuals. This works mostly for very skilled or very valued people, but can also be the case in a responsible company that balances standardized practices and individual flexibility. (Rousseau, 2005, personal communication)

---

[12]Upon learning that in the 1880s her Canadian great-grandfather was a telephone company supervisor, her father was aghast because he believed there was no mutual agreement on what organizations and employees owe one another. Rousseau's (1995) book on psychological contracts, dedicated to her dad, won the best book award from the Academy of Management in 1996.

Ironically, however, some supervisors just can't win. Jones and Skarlicki (2005) found that having a reputation of being fair can be a drawback because it sets up employees' expectations for fairness that are easily violated.

[13]Recall Milton Blood's research on job enrichment with Charles Hulin discussed in Part I.

[14]Recall the powerful effects of modeling posited by social cognitive theory.

Rousseau (2005a) defined a psychological contract as a distinctive aspect of such commonly studied concepts as reputations and beliefs regarding an exchange relationship. Specifically, a psychological contract comprises beliefs "largely based upon promises implied or explicit, which over time take the form of a relatively stable mental model or schema. A major feature of a psychological contract is the individual's belief that an agreement exists that is mutual; in effect, his or her beliefs in the existence of a common understanding with another binds that party to a particular course of action. Since individuals rely upon their understanding of this agreement in subsequent choices and efforts they take, they anticipate benefits from fulfilled commitments and incur losses if another fails to live up to theirs, whatever the individual interprets another's commitments to be" (Rousseau, 2005a, p. 193).

Among the distinctive dimensions of a psychological contract is incompleteness and perceived mutuality. The full array of reciprocal obligations inherent in an exchange are usually not known at the outset of a relationship. Perceived mutuality occurs when a person believes that the other person has agreed to these implied or explicit commitments. It is this belief that allows for cooperation and trust under conditions of uncertainty.

Over time, a psychological contract develops from a set of beliefs to a cognitive schema or mental model (Rousseau, 2001). This progression is based on a person's actual experience within an organization rather than on expectations of an employee's objectives.

A key boundary condition of a psychological contract is choice at the level of the individual. No generalizations are made to the level of groups or organizations.[15] There is substantial within-group variation, hence Rousseau's (2005b) concept of "idiosyncratic deals" where one negotiates terms and conditions that differ from one's peers. The result of an idiosyncratic deal for both the employee and the employer can be mutually supportive, constructive, and productive interactions. A danger of idiosyncratic contracts is that they, too, can foster perceptions of injustice when one person learns that a colleague has negotiated a better deal. Ongoing work on psychological contracts is likely to prove useful for practitioners as an intervention for fostering feelings of justice in the workplace and minimizing feelings of injustice.

Recent research suggests that a psychological contract is similar to, yet different from, the concept of perceived organizational support.

---

[15]In non-Western societies, psychological contracts may very well be at the group level (Rousseau, 2005a).

Both concepts are based on the norm of reciprocity (Coyle-Shapiro & Convey, 2005). The two concepts differ in that perceived organizational support captures an employee's belief regarding an organization's commitment; whereas as a psychological contract captures an employee's belief regarding perceived mutual obligations and the extent to which those obligations are fulfilled in the employer-employee exchange relationship. Moreover, perceived organizational support is one sided in that it focuses on the employer side of the exchange as perceived by an employee. In a study involving employees of a local government in the southeast of England, Coyle-Shapiro and Convey found that the measures of these two concepts differentially predicted an employee's organizational citizenship behavior. Perceived organizational support (i.e., level of the organization's commitment to the employee) appears to be an antecedent and outcome of the components of psychological contract fulfillment (i.e., mutual obligations and the extent to which those obligations are fulfilled in the employee-employer exchange relationship that is implicitly or explicitly promised). In relationships characterized by increasing levels of organizational support, the importance of a psychological contract in terms of felt obligations recedes into the background, whereas in relationships characterized by decreasing organizational support, employees are more likely to invoke the psychological contract, possibly as a means of regulating a deteriorating relationship. The motivating mechanism for organizational citizenship behavior, the authors concluded, is not the fulfillment of the psychological contract but rather what employees receive or what they anticipate receiving in the future.

In closing, the importance of justice principles on motivation in the workplace cannot be over-emphasized. Feelings that one's organization is fair leads to employee commitment to and support for organizational policies and procedures. Feelings of injustice usually lead to a host of counterproductive behaviors. Negative feelings over a perceived act of injustice can last for decades (Gilliland, Benson, & Scheppers, 1998; Gilliland & Chan, 2001).

Concluding Comments

The conclusions drawn by Craig Pinder and I (Latham & Pinder, 2005) from our review of the motivation literature in the present century are tenfold. First, at least three theories now dominate the motivation literature: goal setting, social cognitive, and organizational justice.

Behaviorism and expectancy theory have been overwhelmed by goal-setting and social cognitive theories, while equity theory has given way to conceptualizations of justice.

Second, whereas theory and research in the third quarter of the 20th century focused almost exclusively on cognition, this is no longer true. Today there is recognition of the importance of affect and behavior as well as the reciprocal interactions among cognition, affect and behavior. Research on affect is blossoming in HRM, I/O, and OB.

Third, the ability to predict, understand, and influence motivation in the workplace has increased significantly as a result of the attention that has been given to all rather than only a few aspects of an employee's motivation. There is now ongoing research on needs, values, cognition (particularly goals), affect (particularly emotions), and behavior.

Fourth, whereas the dependent variables historically studied were limited to traditional measures of job performance and satisfaction, today's dependent variables range from citizenship to counterproductive behavior in the workplace.

Fifth, Cronbach's (1957) plea a half century ago for experimental and correlational psychology to combine forces has been heeded. Researchers have done a creditable job of explaining the mechanisms, particularly individual differences (personality traits), that mediate between independent and dependent variables.

Sixth, the importance of context to motivation has been recognized much more in recent years than in the past. Significant advances have been made in understanding how societal culture, characteristics of the job itself, and the fit between the person and the organization, particularly with regard to values, influence motivation.

Seventh, these advances in the study of motivation may reflect the fact that this subject is no longer restricted to the research findings of North Americans. Today, motivation is studied empirically by scholars worldwide (e.g., Africa, Asia, Australia, and Europe).

Eighth, behavioral scientists in the latter half of the 20th century responded positively to William James' exhortation to systematically study consciousness; in the present century they are poised to expand their domain to the study of the preconscious or subconscious.

Ninth, the antagonisms among theorists that existed throughout much of the 20th century have either disappeared or have been minimized. Much of the energy expended on theory destruction has been replaced by theory construction aimed at building upon and enhancing what is already known. Relative to the 1960s–1980s, consensus rather than controversy dominates the field.

Tenth, the nomological nets related to work motivation constructs are thicker and tighter than ever before, but the size of the aggregate net (metaphorically speaking) is not growing at a rate commensurate with the energy that scholars and practitioners have invested since 1977. Few fundamentally new models of work motivation have appeared with the ground-breaking impact that Maslow's need theory, Vroom's expectancy theory, Locke and Latham's goal-setting theory, or Bandura's social cognitive theory had when they were initially promulgated.

With regard to the tenth conclusion, Craig Pinder wrote that one solution to remedy it may be to develop fundamentally new models of human functioning such as spirituality. For example, the ancient concept of "callings," as used by Dawis (1996) should be resurrected and examined for its usefulness in explaining a person's attraction to and retention in a variety of unusual and especially demanding occupations. Although traditionally rooted in religion and most commonly associated with theology, callings also have secular connotations. There appears to be a special "something" that attracts some people to certain varieties of work that commits them far beyond any expectations that current theories of work motivation can explain.[16]

Gall et al. (2005) provided a conceptual framework of spirituality and coping that takes into account one's appraisal of personal well-being in terms of emotional, social, and physical factors. They defined spirituality as a multifaceted construct that includes (a) person variables (e.g., dispositions), (b) primary and secondary appraisals (e.g., attributions), and (c) coping behavior that includes "meaning making" (i.e., finding personal significance in an event). For example, hope, defined as a disposition, affects one's cognitive appraisals of ability to initiate and maintain goal directed behavior. Similar to self-efficacy, which is a state, hope affects a person's physical and mental well-being. People who score high on measures of hope tend to find personal meaning or benefit in the context of difficult and traumatic events. At the initial stage of an appraisal process, people make sense of events in relation to their causal attributions (temporary vs. permanent; fate or luck vs. self). Longitudinal studies are needed on the effects of spiritual factors on the coping processes an individual uses when dealing with high stress factors experienced in the workplace.

---

[16]With a 25-page limitation, Craig's suggestion was deleted from our Annual Review chapter. Craig, prior to going to Cornell for his Ph.D. obtained his master's degree at the University of Minnesota where he was influenced by Dawis. Dawis (1996) stated that the word *vocation* has the high-minded meaning of calling and should be viewed as the study of behavior in life choice and the antecedents, concomitants, and consequences of such choice.

Another solution to the tenth conclusion is to develop a boundaryless psychology in which organizational scholars take advantage of the insights being developed in other areas of psychology and the social sciences in general. This subject is addressed in the next chapter.

Part III

Future Directions and
Potential Misdirections

12 Boundaryless Psychology

Introduction

A primary goal of my presidency of the Canadian Psychological Association (1999–2000) was to create a "boundaryless" psychology (Latham, 2003), a word that I borrowed from Jack Welch. As CEO of General Electric (GE), Welch was frustrated over knowledge that was acquired in one division and going unnoticed in other divisions. My goal for a boundaryless psychology was based in part on my observation that discoveries in the biological and neurosciences are shared by scientists who meet at the annual meeting of the Canadian Brain, Behavior, and Cognitive Sciences long before their colleagues who meet annually at CPA's convention learn of them; it was also based in part on my observation that the people in HRM, I/O, and OB are seldom aware of advances in clinical/counseling psychology, despite the fact that we are the four groups who explicitly embrace the scientist-practitioner model. Subsequently, both Eccles and Wigfield (2002) and Locke and I (Locke & Latham, 2004) have called for collaboration and cross-fertilization among the subdisciplines of psychology in the belief that synergies may result with regard to finding "invariants" (Simon, 1990) in human behavior. This recommendation is further discussed here, particularly with regard to social psychology, clinical psychology, life-span research, evolutionary psychology, neuroscience, to the concept of time and teams.[1]

---

[1]Among the duties of the elected president of CPA is to appoint an honorary president. I appointed Bandura. In his honorary address to CPA, Bandura focused on his growing unease regarding the integrity of psychology as a core discipline. "It is ironic," he said, "that an integrative core discipline that deals with the whole person acting in and on environments should consider fractionalizing, farming out subpersonal parts to other disciplines. The field of psychology should be articulating a broad vision of human beings, not a reductive fragmenting one" (Bandura, 2001, p. 13; 2001b). I believe HRM, I/O, and OB scientists and practitioners should heed this advice.

On a related note regarding boundarylessness, I hope you as a reader have grown as tired of reading the abbreviations HRM, I/O, and OB as I have of writing them. Why do we have three distinct

(Continued)

Social Psychology

The fields of HRM, I/O, and OB have long benefited from theory and findings in social psychology (Seijts & B. Latham, 2003). James and Mazerolla (2002) have drawn on the social cognition and achievement motivation literatures to explain how and why the same set of environmental events are framed differently by diverse individuals. Their work on unrecognized biases in conditional reasoning is opening the door to sophisticated measurement systems of personality, and it reveals the importance of need for achievement and fear of failure as determinants for the way people think.

Clinical Psychology

Just as HRM, I/O, and OB have benefited from theory and research in social psychology, they should also benefit from adaptation of theory and particularly methodology in clinical psychology (Latham & Heslin, 2003).[2] For example, Bandura (2001a) noted that when people are confronted by setbacks, they engage in self-enabling or self-debilitating self-talk. Zeeva Millman and I (Millman & Latham, 2001) successfully used Meichenbaum's (1971) methodology to change the dysfunctional

---

(Continued)

groups when the similarities among them overwhelm the differences? Ask 10 people in any one of those three groups to compare and contrast them conceptually and then determine the inter observer reliability. I bet it is low. Ask these 10 people to differentiate these three fields operationally in terms of the subject matter domain. Again, I bet the interobserver reliability is low. In what group will you place careers, emotional intelligence, self-regulation, or organizational justice? With regard to the latter subject matter, keep in mind that Greenberg received the 2005 Herbert Heneman Career Achievement Award from the HRM Division of the Academy of Management. I am the proud 2004 recipient, as is Locke as the 1997 recipient of this award. My proposal regarding boundarylessness is to lock Lyman Porter and Ben Schneider in a room, as they have served as officers in both SIOP and the Academy of Management. I would lock in the room with them all the people who are Fellows of both the Academy and SIOP. I would also lock away with them Michael Frese, the current president of the International Association of Applied Psychology and Miriam Erez, the past president. I would propose that the door not be unlocked until they have developed an effective plan for merging these organizations into one. Think of what this would do to increase our visibility with the public and our effectiveness as advocates of issues of global importance where we have the subject matter expertise to increase knowledge and decision making in the public domain. And, parenthetically, consider the amount of money we might save by belonging to only one organization—an organization that truly has a "high impact" on society. This would be, in my opinion, a truly motivational experience.

[2]Subsequent to getting his Ph.D. in I/O psychology from Cornell University, Locke received training as a psychotherapist. He saw three to eight clients a week, on a part-time basis for 15 years (1973–1985).

self-talk of displaced managers so as to increase their self-efficacy and subsequent re-employment. Similarly, Brown (2003) examined the effectiveness of this verbal self-guidance (VSG) technique with teams who were trained to re-state negative comments about themselves as a group into positive action steps for overcoming a problem. Those in the training condition had higher performance than those in the control group. The team's collective efficacy mediated the training-performance relationship. Brown and I (Brown & Latham, 2006) found that training in VSG increases the team-playing skills of people in an MBA program. Marie Budworth and I (Latham & Budworth, 2006) found that VSG increased the self-efficacy and performance of Native North Americans in a selection interview.

Lucy Morin and I (Morin & Latham, 2000) used Richardson's (1967) methodology regarding mental imagery to increase the self-efficacy and communication skills of supervisors in interactions with their counter-parts in the union. In a study involving accountants, Neck and Manz (1996) combined instruction and practice in VSG with mental imagery and relapse prevention. Although no performance measures were reported, the results showed that self-efficacy, positive affect, and job satisfaction increase significantly relative to the control group.

Ellis' (1999) rational emotive therapy should be investigated with regard to the problem of setting unrealistic goals and as a method for minimizing irrational beliefs regarding outcome expectancies as well as dysfunctional self-talk that is inflexible and perfectionistic. The theory explains the desire on the part of some people for perfectionism that, in turn, may prevent them from completing job assignments in a timely fashion. Ellis found that when the desire for an outcome is expressed as a demand of self, rather than leading people to increase their performance by making themselves more determined to succeed, it tends to predispose them to giving up. Ellis' methodology may prove effective for reframing self-deprecatory demotivating statements. Doing so can have a positive effect on motivation and protect a person's self-efficacy (Bandura, 1997). This methodology might be particularly relevant to motivation in error-management training as well as relapse-prevention training.

There are three forms of cognitive motivation around which different theories of motivation have been formulated. Two have already been described earlier in this book, namely expectancies and goal setting. The third is attribution theory (Weiner, 1985) whereby people make retroactive judgments of the causes of their performance. Seligman's research on learned helplessness/optimism is based on this theory.

Adaptation of Seligman's (1998) work on learned helplessness and the converse, optimism, is highly applicable to organizational settings. Helplessness is an outcome expectancy that effort, performance, and persistence is useless in relation to goal attainment. A perception of lack of control over a situation can lead to a lack of motivation. Helplessness can be predicted, explained, and influenced, argued Seligman, on the basis of attribution theory (globality, stability, locus). Optimists attribute a failure to causes that are temporary and specific to the attainment of a particular goal rather than to all their goals. They see a problem as a result of the environment or setting rather than as an inherent deficiency in themselves. Setbacks, obstacles, and a noncontingent environment are perceived as challenges that provide excitement in their life. Thus, optimists are resilient in the face of failure. Application of Seligman's technique may prove effective in strengthening a person's expectations of attaining challenging goals in organizational settings in the face of repeated setbacks.[3]

Peterson and Seligman (2004) developed a classification of positive characteristics to help clinicians increase the happiness and life satisfaction of their patients. Their methodology is applicable to the workplace, particularly with regard to ways of expressing and inspiring gratitude that can be taught in leadership and management training programs. Emphasis is placed on building a vocabulary for people to talk about and assess positive attributes in others.

Seligman is credited with urging a shift in focus in clinical psychology to what he called *positive psychology*. Walter V. Bingham predates him in our field by 70 or more years. Mrs. Bingham (1962) quoted her husband's dominant purpose as follows:

> To invest my energies in helping the well-adjusted to achieve their fullest usefulness. I have preferred to give a hand to the promising, rather than to the third rate; to the emotionally stable, the strong and vigorous, the very bright, rather than to the weak, the unhappy, the unadjusted, whom we psychologists may wisely leave, whenever we can, to the ministrations of our friends, the psychiatrists and the social workers . . . thereby freeing the psychological profession for the more congenial and, I sincerely believe, more socially useful task of augmenting the productivity and happiness of the mentally well. (p. 341)

---

[3]The effect of causal attributions on performance is mediated almost entirely through changes in perceived self-efficacy (Bandura, 1997).

Bordin's (1994) working alliance model may prove effective in the workplace in that it suggests ways for managers to obtain goal commitment on the part of a recalcitrant employee. In brief, adaptation of this methodology to organizational settings could focus on (a) the quality of the relationship between the manager and the employee, the extent to which there is mutual understanding and agreement on (b) the goals that are set, and (c) the task strategies to be pursued in attaining these goals.

Attachment theory (Bowlby, 1979) explains how a person's attachment style (secure, anxious-ambivalent, avoidant) systematically influences how people seek and process information, interact with and evaluate others, engage in tasks, and regulate their emotions (Lopez & Brennan, 2000). Sumer and Knight (2001) found that dissatisfaction at home is more likely to spill over to the workplace for people who have an anxious ambivalent style than it is for those who have secure or avoidant styles. Kilmann et al. (1999) showed that these styles can be modified by addressing and disputing unrealistic relationship beliefs, and challenging and resolving issues regarding power and control.

With regard to individual difference variables, Spector (e.g., Penney & Spector, 2002) has begun to explore the extent to which counterproductive work behaviors are a function of narcissism.[4] Narcissists have an extreme emotional investment in establishing their superiority, even if they are unsure whether their feelings of superiority are merited. The grandiosity associated with narcissism acts as a defense against having an unfavorable self-image as well as the feelings of failure that accompany it. Because narcissists are vulnerable to ego-threatening information, they are vigilant for opportunities to find ways to maintain their sense of superiority over others. They seek ways to defend their ego against unfavorable evaluative information, particularly against data that are factual and accurate. Threats to their ego quickly elicit their anger and aggression toward the source of the evaluation. They tend to derogate the evaluator and the appraisal instrument as well as innocent third parties. The primary purpose of their aggression is to punish the evaluator and to reaffirm their dominance over the person, thereby achieving an "ego boost" to lessen the impact of the threat to their ego.

---

[4]See A. Brown (1997) for a detailed essay on the effect of employee narcissism in the workplace. The narcissistic personality is described in terms of six broad behavioral predispositions: (1) denial, (2) rationalization, (3) self-aggrandizement, (4) attributional egotism, (5) sense of entitlement, and (6) anxiety.

This is because information that undermines beliefs central to the definition of self is intolerable for highly narcissistic individuals. Complicating the situation, people high in narcissism experience a wide range of events and situations as ego threatening due to their strong desire to be viewed as superior to others.

Penney and Spector's study (2002) showed that highly narcissistic people experience anger more frequently, and are more likely to express their anger by engaging in counterproductive work behavior. Ways of coaching these people to become productive team players in the workplace have yet to be found. The necessity for doing so is the fact that, according to Spector's model (1997), narcissists experience frustration when they interpret an event or situation at work as interfering with goal attainment, including their goal to be seen as better than everyone else. The result is often rage on the part of the narcissist. This finding suggests that emotions have a trait base.

As Latham and Heslin (2003) noted, these suggestions do not imply that the distinction between I/O and clinical psychologists should be ignored. I/O and clinical psychologists deal with different populations of individuals, they work in different settings, and they are trained to predict, understand, and influence very different dependent variables. Nevertheless, there are productive commonalities between I/O and clinical psychology methods and techniques, and perhaps most importantly, theories of behavior.

Life-Span Research

With the repeal of mandatory retirement laws in Canada and the U.S., Kanfer and Ackerman (2004) have stressed the necessity of understanding how age-related changes affect the work motivation of employees. They pointed out that by 2010 nearly half the U.S. workforce will be made up of people age 45 or older. They contended that motivational interventions, such as goal setting, may vary in effectiveness as a function of the age of the workforce. That is, what motivates an employee may change with advancing age as a result of a reorganization of the person's goals around affect. Midlife workers may respond more positively to managerial policies that emphasize cooperation rather than competition. Depending on the demands of the job, and the extent to which a person experiences cognitive decline, Kanfer and Ackerman pointed out that increased effort often entails a cost that can, over time, outweigh the benefits for any increases in a person's performance.

Declining performance, with increasing effort over time, lowers self-efficacy. This, in turn, can lead to goal abandonment and eventually abandonment of the job itself. As workers age, motives for task mastery and openness to new experiences may decline, while motives for promoting positive affect and protecting one's self-concept often increases. Alternative definitions of performance that emphasize such nontechnical functions as organizational citizenship behavior (Organ, 1990), training and helping others may promote motivation in the workplace. In short, work motivation among older employees may be enhanced through tailored reconfiguration of their work roles and by expanding the criteria for performance evaluation to include citizenship behavior.

Carstensen's (Carstensen & Mikels, 2005) socioemotional selectivity theory, a life-span theory regarding the way one's time horizon affects motivation, may provide a useful framework for research and practice in this area. The theory states that self-set goals are always set in temporal contexts. People who see their time horizon as expansive (e.g., younger people) usually set goals that involve the acquisition of information. Those who perceive boundaries on their time typically set goals for emotionally meaningful aspects of their life, such as to feel socially interconnected, and they invest cognitive and social resources to attain them. To the extent that people are motivated to prioritize goal relevant information, their attention to and memory for information that is emotional in nature is said to vary as a function of their age. Older people tend to focus on positive material to the exclusion of the negative. And they rely on feelings (affect) rather than memory (cognition) for details. This can enhance their emotional well-being yet lead to poorly thoughtout decisions. Ways to prevent such decisions await further research.

Evolutionary Psychology

Nigel Nicholson (1997, 2005), a faculty member of the London Business School, introduced the ideas of evolutionary psychology to HRM, I/O, and OB. He argued that the failure to understand the evolutionary origins of behavior is bad science. Similarly, de Waal (2002) has criticized current psychological theories for reducing nearly every motive to either the need or desire to protect and enhance self-identity or to emphasize cognitive rationality. This emphasis, they argued, leads to an unrealistic view of human nature as primarily self-centered and self-interested. They argued further that to focus on proximal motives such as conscious intentions or goals falls short of explanatory power because it ignores the ultimate causal sources stemming from evolution via natural selection. Buss and Reeve (2003) emphasized that although the principles of evolutionary psychology are scarcely more than 15 years old, they have already produced an astonishing array of empirical discoveries ranging from cheater-detection procedures in social exchange to the specificity of social betrayal depending on relationship context, including why men and women have trouble being "just friends." The underlying thesis of evolutionary psychology is that genetic factors predispose people to think, learn, and behave in a particular way. This is because phylogenetic information is encoded in genes. This information unfolds by way of either predetermined maturation or activation by some environmental input.

Evolutionary psychology, Nicholson (2005, pp. 406–407) argued, explains:

> The general absence from women in leadership positions in publicly quoted corporations and their greater frequency in public service organizations is explained by this analysis. On the abundant evidence that men's desire for dominance is greater than women's (Feingold, 1994) and that their preferred leadership behaviours are those that require single-mindedness, competitive striving and political game playing (Browne, 2006), then one might expect organizational designs to look pretty much as they do in the corporate world—pyramidal with linearly divided labour and periodic tournaments for advancement. These will discriminate both directly and indirectly against the accession of women to leadership positions, not least because of the self-selection of women away from them, on the grounds that such positions are unattractive and their demands are felt to be a poor fit with their style. (Eagly & Johnson, 1990)

> One important question that this analysis raises is whether in the 21st century we will see the co-evolutionary process move towards more female-friendly organizational designs and leadership situations. There are grounds for optimism that the new economic realities of decentralization, liberation from monolithic supply chains, more networked structures, and reduced reliance on fixed technologies, could all reduce the competitive advantage of traditional command-and-control hierarchy. However, the sharpening of competition in a globalizing economy continues to reinforce features of organizational design that have an implicit gender-bias. Moreover, there is little reason to be optimistic that men will stop creating systems that are favourable to their motivational orientations. Even in a more female-friendly business environment, should such a world come to pass more generally, there is still to be reckoned the fact that men are more predisposed than women in any circumstances to strive for status and leadership, and to do so with a greater appetite for competitive striving, risk-taking and domination. (Brynes et al., 1999; Geary, 1998)

Lickliter and Honeycutt (2003) responded strongly against beliefs such as this. They stated that it is no longer tenable, in light of empirical findings of contemporary genetics, embryology, and developmental biology to believe that genetic and environmental influences on phenotypic development can be meaningfully separated. Moreover, it is no longer possible to speak of genes as constant and immutable, operating outside the reciprocally interactive developmental system. Converging evidence from these three fields shows that gene activity/inactivity is determined by multiple factors including molecular, cellular, physiological, and behavioral components. External sensory events also activate or inhibit gene expression during an individual's development. In short, to assert that genes alone can make people behave in specific ways ignores well-established findings in both developmental biology and psychology. Lickliter and Honeycutt concluded that in a self-regulated multilevel system of a human being, control of development is not prescribed solely by genes. It is exerted by the regulatory dynamics of the gene-in-a-cell-in-an-organism-in-an-environment system. Although there are many gene-dependent processors, there are no gene-directed ones.

Locke (2005, personal communication) sees this as a very treacherous topic.

A major problem is that one can make up just about any story after the fact regarding why people act the way they do due to evolution, but how do you validate it? Specifically, how do you show that an evolutionary explanation is not only (seemingly) better than some non-evolutionary explanation, but that it is true? What do we know about hereditary so far? We certainly know that capacities (e.g., intelligence) are heritable as are physical characteristics and temperament (e.g., nervous sensitivity, energy level). We know that brain "miswiring" or chemical imbalances or genetic "errors" may make some people susceptible to mental illness including depression and to various physical diseases. But there is no evidence that people inherit actual ideas, moral virtues or vices. Identical twin studies may show statistical trait similarities in some cases, but these studies do not prove that actual ideas are inborn. Ideas have to be acquired through experience and volitional thought.[5]

Neuroscience

Lord, Hanges, and Godfrey (2003) illustrated the potential value of neuropsychologically based models for explaining expectancy theory.

---

[5]See Sewell (2004) for a critical commentary on Nicholson's beliefs on the validity, philosophy, and applicability of evolutionary psychology to organizational behavior.

A major criticism of the theory, they said, is that the computations it hypothesizes that take place are unrealistically time-consuming and often exceed a person's working memory capacity. Using simulation methodology, the authors reinterpreted the theory using neural networks that operate implicitly so that cognitive resources are not exhausted by simple computations.

The value of both the evolutionary and neuropsychological approaches to motivation in the workplace is indeed debatable. HRM, I/O, and OB are concerned with discovering principles on how to design jobs that energize and sustain behavior. This exogenous subject matter has no counterpart in either evolution or neurobiological theory. As Bandura (2001b) noted, knowledge of the locality and brain circuitry subserving motivation yields little or no information on ways to design a work environment that is inherently novel and challenging, let alone ways to provide incentives that will get people to attend to, process, and organize relevant information. Ancestral origin, argued Bandura, "dictates neither current social function, nor a singular socio-structural arrangement . . . I seriously doubt that the genetic makeup of the Nazi Germans . . . differs from the genetic makeup of peaceful Swiss residing in the German canton of Switzerland. People possess the biological potentiality of aggression, but the answer to the cultural variation in aggressiveness lies more in ideology than in biology" (p. 14). In short, human evolution provides bodily structures and biological potentialities rather than behavioral dictates (Bussey & Bandura, 1999). Mental events, Bandura (2001, p. 13) acknowledged, are brain activities, but physicality does not imply the reduction of psychology to biology. "Knowing how the biological machinery works, tells one little about how to orchestrate that machinery for diverse purposes. To use an analogy, the 'psychosocial software' is not reducible to the 'biological hardware.' Thought processes are emergent brain activities that are not ontologically reducible." Thus, the battle is not between nature and nurture, as commonly framed, but whether nature is a determinist that has culture on a "tight leash" or acts as a potentialist that has culture on a loose leash. In his James McKeen Cattell Fellow Award Address to the American Psychological Society, Bandura (2004b) argued that the extant evidence suggests the potentialist view. People have changed little genetically over the past millennium, yet they have changed significantly in recent decades regarding beliefs, mores, social roles, and cohabiting arrangements. They have done so, Bandura argued, through rapid cultural and technological evolution rather than genetic evolution.

Nevertheless, there are preliminary findings in the field of marketing (e.g., Moore, 2005) that suggest that HRM, I/O, and OB researchers may soon be immersed in neuroscience as a way to increase a person's motivation in the workplace. Marketing researchers are already pursuing what they call neuromarketing, that is, the use of brain scans to determine what makes the brain's pleasure centers light up. The purpose of their research is to discover what creates a positive emotional response, and how to boost that feeling so that they can influence a person's emotional visceral responses to sundry stimuli. Future ethical issues around management gaining and using this knowledge to motivate employees are as enormous as are those regarding their use of this knowledge to influence the buying habits of consumers. So far, neuromarketing research is in the infancy stage. The limitations of the current scanning technology means that the information yield from the data is fuzzy. In the distant future, as advances in this scanning technology occur, neuromotivation research may allow managers to know when and how to "push the right buttons" to ensure that a person chooses to exert maximum effort to persist until high goals are attained. Brain scans may reveal ways to design organizational environments that stimulate the left prefrontal cortex, the locus of joy, so as to overwhelm activity in the right prefrontal cortex, the locus of anxiety.

Time

Time appears to be the baby that was thrown out with the bathwater when I/O psychologists in the first half of the 20th century disregarded time and motion study as a methodology for understanding and influencing motivation. There are now both theoretical and practical reasons for retrieving the baby. Knowledge is needed on (1) the time lag between X and Y, (2) the durations of X and Y, (3) the rates of change, if any, in X as well as in Y, and (4) whether there are dynamic changes or (5) reciprocal causation. Both Kozolowski and Klein (2000) and Mitchell and James (2001) explained the pitfalls in measurement, analysis, and influences regarding the strength, order, and direction of causal relationships when there are no theoretical or empirical guidelines regarding when to measure X and Y.

Roe (2005), the first president of the European Association of Work and Organizational Psychology has attributed our failure to study behavioral phenomena without reference to time as the cause of our ignorance regarding answers to such straightforward questions as:

When do employees start feeling dissatisfied with their goals?[6] How can we make sure that quarterly deadlines are met in 80% instead of 50% of the cases? How fast do people respond to a change in a team's composition? Everything people do, Roe stated, involves time: Going to the workplace, meeting deadlines, developing stress, and changing or quitting one's job. Managers and workers alike are preoccupied with time: When do things happen? How fast do they occur? How long do they take? Almost everything they do is framed in terms of time. Despite the practical significance of time for the workplace, Roe's review of research published during the years 2003–2004 in the *European Journal of Work and Organizational Psychology* and the *Journal of Applied Psychology* revealed that time-related referents were rarely used. Similarly, Wright (2002) found that 90% of the research published in OB are non-time based in nature. Also lacking, Roe noted, is research on ways that historic events affect behavior in work settings (e.g., 9/11/2001).

Among the solutions Roe offered to this problem are the use of unobtrusive methods for collecting time-series data (e.g., use of diaries, videos, computer logs, internet surveys). His more provocative solution is to discard the use of the term *variable* because it has led to hypotheses that are almost always devoid of time. A variable expresses variation of the object involved but not dynamic changes in that property. To facilitate understanding of temporality, Roe argued for the replacement of variables with the notion of "phenomenon" defined in terms of onset, offset, duration, and dynamics. The latter refers to the pattern of changing intensity to be characterized by a set of parameters. By identifying the temporal features of phenomena, causal relationships can be established, and the stability and change in a phenomenon can be assessed. For example, we can study when and how people commit to goals and under what conditions goal commitment declines and disappears. As a next step, Roe argued for linking the temporal parameters of two phenomena (e.g., onset, offset, duration, degree of stability, movement of upward or downward change) to each other and to identify both sequential and causal dependencies. To bring this about, Roe advocated that phenomena be cast as verbs rather than nouns. Examples of the former include leading, motivating, committing, and persisting. Consequently,

---

[6]Similar to arguments on the pronunciation of Rensis Likert's last name, there are ongoing bets on the correct pronunciation of Robert "Rob" Roe's (Row vs. Roo) last name. Rob refuses to put an end to the debate. I do know that his Dutch colleagues pronounce his name phonetically as Roo, despite the fact that he asked me at a party in my home to introduce him phonetically as Row. You choose.

phenomena would be viewed as temporarily bound and dynamic, with a beginning, an end, and variation of intensity of one or more attributes during the time interval between these two temporal points.

Fried and Slowik (2004) as well as McGrath and Tschan (2004) have cited evidence and theory that time can be viewed from multiple perspectives and multiple streams; it is cyclical as well as linear, and it is concrete and relational as well as abstract and absolute. As Fried and Slowik pointed out, Asian cultures value the past more so than do Western cultures while the West tends to be more oriented toward the future than are people in Asia. The cyclical subjective experience of time, they said, differs based on meaningful events. Days off from work for most employees feel different for them than do working days. Social time consists of multiple streams. Promising to do something soon is likely to have a different meaning within the work versus non-work setting. Occupational norms also affect what constitutes a quick vs. slow response (e.g., a sales and marketing department vs. research and development). The authors concluded that both subjective (relativistic) and objective (clock) time perspectives are critical for predicting, understanding, and influencing an employee's motivation.

Locke and I (Locke & Latham, 2004) have called for studies on how employees and employers consider and integrate short-term vs. long-term considerations or outcomes. This issue of time perspective is important at both the individual and organizational levels because both have to survive in the short-term, and both have to balance short-term and long-term considerations. Thus, related to a time perspective is the necessity for future studies to examine how people prioritize values and goals and the consequences of different types of priorities.

Johns (2006) stated that time should be viewed as a contextual variable. This is because time is a surrogate for the environmental stimuli that are occurring when the research is conducted. In addition, time, he said, affects the web of social and economic relationships that surround organizational behavior. Those contextual conditions underlying the effects of time include secular trends, changing institutional patterns, evolving technology, organizational change, and accrued feedback as a course of action unfolds.

Computer Models

Computer models can be used to assess interactions among variables over time that would be difficult, if not impossible, to assess empirically in organizational settings (Ilgen & Hulin, 2000). Hulin and Ilgen (2000) have already developed a model for predicting and understanding employee withdrawal in and from the workplace.

Teams

Locke and I (Locke & Latham, 2004) recommended the study of motivation on team effectiveness. This is because in the present millennium the individual is frequently a member of a team within an organization. There are processes affecting teams that do not arise when the focus is limited to the motivation of the individual. These include the way team members motivate/demotivate one another. We suggested that extending research into this domain would lead to the exploration of such issues as team conflicts involving personalities, values, and goals.[7]

Ellemers, deGilder, and Haslam (2004) drew upon self-categorization and self-identity processes to explain how individual and group processes interact to determine work motivation. As noted earlier, Seijts and I (Seijts & Latham, 2000b) had found that in a social dilemma, people behave in ways that are rewarding from an individual's point of view regarding goal attainment and monetary incentives. Social identity theory helps specify the circumstances where an employee is likely to see the self as a separate entity as opposed to part of a team or part of the organization, and how individual behavioral preferences may be aligned with a group's and/or an organization's goals. The cognitive process of social categorization and the evaluative implication of social comparison processes can elicit emotional involvement with a particular group. When a person's definition of self shifts from "I" to "we," social identity theory posits that exactly the same motivational processes that apply to the individual self apply to the collective self.

Based on the work of Tajfel (1978), Ellemers et al. (2004) stated that three intrapsychological processes underlie identification with a group, namely, social categorization, social comparisons, and social identification. Social categorization occurs when group membership is relatively stable over time and people perceive they are excluded on the basis of their group membership (e.g., a person's race).

What determines the group with which a person identifies is a dynamic outcome dependent upon situational factors. Group saliency

---

[7]Borman et al. (2003) have explained from a research perspective the levels of analysis issue (e.g., individual vs. group) in terms of conceptual and measurement issues.

between, for example, manufacturing and marketing people who are working together to increase customer satisfaction will likely increase as conflict occurs due to the two groups having different work experiences (social comparative fit) as well as differences in the problems that they regularly encounter as a function of their day to day work (social normative fit). However, when these two groups are working on an affirmative action plan, for example, the authors pointed out that a categorization of ethnic or gender identity will provide a better comparative fit and hence will determine the social category with which an employee will likely identify.

In short, social identification is the process by which a person sees characteristics of a group as similar to oneself and as enhancing one's status or power. Among the authors' propositions are the following.

1. People identify more with a group to the extent that the group meaningfully distinguishes them from others.

2. Thus, this is more likely to occur with smaller rather than larger groups that are, by definition, more inclusive. In larger groups, one's conception of self in relation to others is less informative since this is an identity that "everyone" shares.

3. People who identify with a specific group are energized to act in terms of group membership rather than in terms of what is rewarding solely to them.

Levels of Analysis

As Erez, Kleinbeck, and Thierry (2001) noted correctly, understanding that the effects of the organization and the groups within them is critical to understanding an employee's performance in a global economy. Nevertheless, while writing our "Annual Review of Psychology" chapter, Craig Pinder pointed out that there is a potential danger here. More than 80 years ago, William McDougall wrote a book to " . . . [sketch] the principles of the mental life of groups" and "make a rough attempt to apply these principles to the understanding of the life of nations" (see McDougall, 1939, p. vii). Since then, individual-level constructs have been ascribed to entities at higher levels of analysis in common parlance, managerial jargon, as well as in scientific discourse. Examples include organizational memory, organizational values, and group equity. It can be easy to interpret calls for more collectivistic mentalities in motivation research pertaining to groups, organizations, and entire economies as implying a recognition of motivation constructs at those higher levels of analysis. Too frequently, importing concepts across levels of analysis is little more than engaging in metaphor and subjecting analysis to serious risks of misspecification. Hence, consistent with Kozlowski and Klein (2000), caution should be exercised in extending individually based constructs to units of analysis higher than the individual (see Stackman, Pinder, & Connor, 2000, regarding "organizational values"). Groups, organizations, and nation states have their own legitimate constructs (such as cohesiveness, formalization, and cultural norms, respectively), most of which are more than simple "compositions" of individual-level properties. It is one thing to build models of *individual motivation* that will increase team effectiveness (e.g., Ilgen & Sheppard, 2001); it is another to anthropomorphize groups, organizations, and nation states for the sake of economy in theory building (i.e., groups, organizations, and nations, per se, are not and cannot be motivated). These are false economies, resulting in part from the metaphorical and misleading use of figurative language in theory construction (Pinder & Bourgeois, 1982) and the imputation of nomological nets that do not cross readily from one level of analysis to others.[8]

Integration

Research and theories seldom if ever suggest smooth, logical transitions from one to the other. There is currently no integrative overarching conceptual framework that ties them all together. Nevertheless, the current theories of work motivation do not so much contradict one another as they focus on different aspects of the motivation process. The task that remains, as Locke and I see it (Locke & Latham, 2004), is to tie them together into an overall comprehensible framework. This framework could be expanded as subsequent discoveries are made. This

---

[8]These larger units of theory and analysis consist of individuals. As Bandura (2005b) noted, there is no group mind. Perceived collective efficacy resides in the minds of the group's members as beliefs regarding their group's capability. Nevertheless, when individuals work together in a group, an outcome is behavior that is appropriately described as group behavior. Thus, when the U.S. basketball team lost to Puerto Rico in the Olympics, the loss can be explained at more than one level of analysis. These different levels of explanation contribute to the understanding of behavior. Goals, for example, have been found to affect performance at the individual, group, organizational unit, and organizational levels (Baum, Locke & Smith, 2001; Latham & Locke, 1975; Locke & Latham, 2002; O'Leary-Kelly, Martocchio, & Frink, 1994; Rodgers & Hunter, 1991).

is particularly true regarding macro-organization theories. Centralization and decentralization undoubtedly have motivational consequences. Motivational issues are particularly salient in the field of strategic management. Motivational issues in accelerating the internalization and implementation of the organization's strategy on the part of the individual and team are not directly included in current motivation theories. At best, they are addressed by implication (e.g., goal setting, self/collective efficacy, outcome expectancies). These issues need to be studied explicitly.

Figure 12.1 presents a model where Locke has integrated current theories of motivation in the workplace (Locke, 1997; Locke & Latham, 2004). The model begins with a person's needs, moves to acquired values and motives, which include personality, then to goal choice, the goal itself, and self-efficacy. Goals and self-efficacy were labeled by Locke as the "motivational hub" because they are, in most instances, the direct, conscious, motivational determinants of an employee's performance. Performance is followed by outcomes that are emotionally appraised. Job characteristics affect a person's job satisfaction. The applicability of a particular theory is shown by the dotted boxes. The next step is to conduct a "mega-analysis" relevant to each path in the model, as well as calculating mediation and moderator effects. The result, as he and I noted (Locke & Latham, 2004), would be the first motivation theory derived from combining different meta-analyses.

Finally, and arguably most importantly, a theory of social diffusion is very much needed. Too many motivation theories and empirical research go unnoticed by managers. As Bandura (2005b) stated, the value of a theory should be judged not only on the basis of its predictive and explanatory power but on its operative power in society.

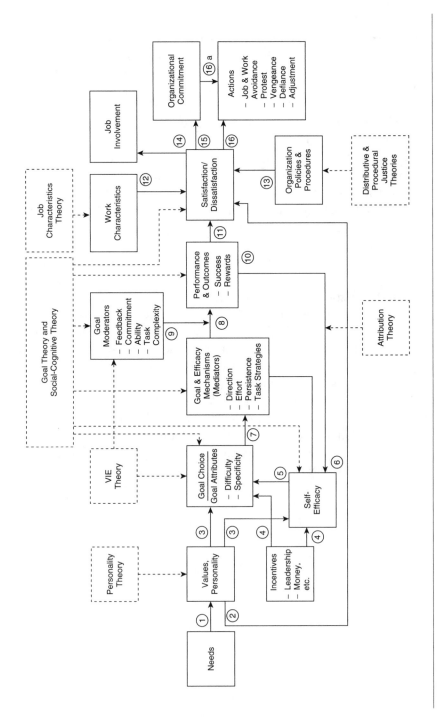

Figure 12.1 An Integrated Model of Work Motivation

1. Needs to values. This is the least empirically researched of the causal connections. Although motivation must start with needs, that is, the objective requirements of the organism's survival and well-being, how work values grow out of needs has not yet been studied. Although Maslow was partly correct in claiming that people value what they need, there are numerous exceptions to this claim. These exceptions, of course, are one of the reasons why we need both a science of mental health and a code of ethics.

2. Values and personality to satisfaction. This pertains to the relation of self-esteem and neuroticism to job perceptions and job satisfaction.

3. Values and personality to goals and self-efficacy. Values and personality affect goals and self-efficacy and their effects on performance are mediated by goals and efficacy.

4. Incentives to goals and self-efficacy. Like personality, incentives affect goals and self-efficacy which in turn mediate the effects of incentives.

5. Self-efficacy to goals. Efficacy affects goal choice and especially goal difficulty.

6. and 7. Self-efficacy and goals to mechanisms. Goals and efficacy affect performance through their effects on direction, effort, persistence, and task strategies or tactics.

8. Goals, that is, goal mechanisms, to performance. Goals, especially goal difficulty, affect performance and performance, depending on the organization's policies, affect rewards.

9. Goal moderators. Goal effects are enhanced by feedback, commitment, ability, and (low) task complexity.

10. Performance to efficacy. Performance, including the attributions one makes for performance, affects self-efficacy.

11. Performance to satisfaction. Success and rewards produce satisfaction.

12. Work characteristics to satisfaction. Mental challenge and related job attributes enhance satisfaction.

13. Organizational policies to satisfaction. The perceived fairness of the organization's policies, procedural justice, and the perceived fairness of the results of these policies, distributive justice, affect satisfaction.

14. Satisfaction to involvement. Job satisfaction enhances job involvement.

15. Satisfaction to organizational commitment. Satisfaction enhances organizational commitment.

16. and 16a. Satisfaction and commitment to action. Satisfaction and commitment, along with other factors, affect action, especially approach and avoidance of the job or work. Several limitations of this model should be noted:

- To limit cognitive-perceptual overload some causal arrows are omitted. For example, self-efficacy affects commitment and presumably choices among alternatives in the face of dissatisfaction. Personality and values can also affect action taken in response to job dissatisfaction. Perceived injustice undoubtedly affects goal commitment.
- The values theories, aside from goal theory, are not fully elaborated. For example, there are many complexities involved in procedural justice and a number of competing subtheories.
- Recursive effects are not shows, except in the case of self-efficacy to performance. In the real world, almost any output can become an input over time.
- The model is static, not dynamic. Mone (1994) has done dynamic analyses of the goal-efficacy-performance relationship and found the basic static model to hold.
- Ability, knowledge, and skill are critical to performance but, with one exception, are not shown in the motivation model. Self-efficacy, of course, reflects how people assess their skills and abilities.
- The model focuses on conscious motivation and omits the subconscious, except insofar as it is acknowledged as being involved in emotions.
- The model does not include theories with dubious or highly limited support (e.g., Maslow, Deci).

Figure 12.1 (Continued)

Source: Reprinted from Locke, E. (1997). *The Motivation to Work: What We Know. Advances in Motivation and Achievement, 10,* 375–412. Reprinted with permission from Elsevier.

261

Part IV

Epilogue

13 The Art of Practice

A practitioner-scientist journal where the emphasis is on the practice of science would likely be value-adding to both science and practice. It would likely provide answers to such questions as why one intervention was chosen over another and how or why organizational decision makers agreed to the implementation of an intervention. It would likely yield clues as to the art of applying behavioral science principles successfully.

I believe that the product of *science* × *art* is what enables people to make a significant contribution to the fields of human resource management, industrial-organizational psychology, and organizational behavior. Science is the bedrock in that it provides the frameworks for predicting, explaining, and influencing a person's behavior. As I said in the Foreword, I have found few things that are more exciting to do. Art is what distinguishes the great from the not so great practitioner in "making a difference," in "making it happen" in organizations through the application of science. I have found few things more worthwhile. The combination of the two—science and art—is exhilarating for a practitioner: "Wow, this works!" "Wow, this flopped!"

The crux of my presidential address to the Canadian Psychological Association (CPA) is that science and practice are interdependent (Latham, 2001a). They are not dichotomous.[1] Scientific theories provide the guidelines or blueprints for practice. The theories facilitate the development of effective methodologies as well as facilitate a basis for understanding the reasons for the success or failure of an intervention. Practice provides evidence for the external validity of a theory. Practice also facilitates the abandonment, modification, or improvement of a theory through subsequent hypothesis testing in both the field and in laboratory settings. In short, practice suggests refinements to theory,

---

[1]Nevertheless, many scientists in CPA believe that this organization exists largely to cater to the practitioners and many practitioners feel that CPA is interested only in the needs of the scientists. I hear similar comments from scientists and practitioners regarding the Society of Industrial/ Organizational Psychology.

and the refined theory provides an improvement in guidelines for effective practice in our field.

That science and practice are on a continuum explains in part the career-long partnership I have had with Ed Locke. On the scientist-practitioner continuum, Locke places himself more toward the scientific end, although he has had a practice in clinical psychology and has worked to a limited extent as a consultant to organizations. I, on the other hand, view myself more on the practitioner side of the continuum, although I conduct research in the field and in laboratory settings, and I hold a full-time position in an academic institution. My consulting practice is incorporated in Canada and the United States, and, as I explained earlier, I was the first staff psychologist for the American Pulpwood Association and the Weyerhaeuser Company. I devour our scholarly journals for ways to shift a dependent variable in a positive direction. Art comes into play in my choosing an appropriate theory, adapting its methodology to the organizational context, and implementing an intervention so as to bring about a relatively permanent change in the behavior of one or more people.

Whereas a scientist-practitioner such as Locke enjoys the freedom to focus on the independent variable of his choice, not to mention the theoretical framework that interests him, I, as a scientist-practitioner have enjoyed the excitement of being confronted by "problem" dependent variables in the workplace (e.g., low job performance, low job attendance, high voluntary turnover, little or no trust among people) and then making a judgment call as to "What intervention is most appropriate when?" "What is likely to prove effective in this particular setting?" "How will I define and measure effectiveness?" Thus, for me as a scientist-practitioner, the first order of business is choosing the dependent variable or criterion. How do I define it/them conceptually? How do I do so in terms of validity (content/construct) and reliability (inter-observer, test-retest, internal consistency)?

The second order of business is to select an independent variable or a predictor and in doing so considering possible moderator variables. In the art of making such decisions, theory and research in our journal articles, without exception, have been invaluable to me. Never have I been concerned about lack of generalizability from laboratory findings to the field setting where I was working. I have found that issue to be much ado about nothing. Always I worried about the art of implementation of my educated guess as to the appropriate performance criteria, the theoretical framework for an intervention, and my adaptation of the methodology in a journal article for influencing the dependent variables or criteria of interest to the organization. Art is the ability to choose theories and measures to one's advantage. In agreement with John Campbell's (1982) outgoing editorial in the *Journal of Applied Psychology*, I have never wanted to pit one theory against another. Rather, I have relied on different theories as heuristics for suggesting answers to questions of importance in the workplace, as frameworks for developing an appropriate intervention.

For example, when I was doing a job analysis of the critical behaviors of loggers, I discovered through casual conversation with the employees that they had no idea of what constituted a good day versus a bad day regarding their performance. None of them kept track of how many trees the crew as a whole or the individuals who made up the crew cut down. I suddenly realized there was no way for them to establish a sense of personal effectiveness.[2] Hence it was not surprising

---

[2]Chris Argyris, now in his 80s is, in my opinion, the dean of the field of organizational development. In February 2004, my wife and I flew to Pasadena to attend the Division 13 (consulting) meeting of the American Psychological Association. Seeing this elder statesman and knowing my wife is a lifelong fan of him, I started to introduce her to Chris. Before I could do so, he greeted me with a request: "Young man, may I speak with you after my presentation?" "Sure," I replied, having no idea as to the nature of our pending discussion. Following his presentation, he immediately led my wife and me to a quiet corner in the lobby of the hotel. "Young man," he began (I was beginning to glow in his use of this phrase, not knowing what lay ahead). "Last night at a dinner with colleagues I remarked that not much of anything useful has emerged from I/O psychology." I began to sniff trouble, recalling my graduate school days when I had read a scathing critique Chris had written on the use of experimental designs to answer meaningful organizational questions (Argyris, 1968). "My colleagues," he went on to say, "responded, what about Gary Latham's field research on goal setting? Now I have read and admired your work with Ed, but I don't recall either of you explaining why goal setting is effective. Would you please enlighten me?" he gently asked. "Oh, that is easy," I naïvely exclaimed. Now I had seen Chris, only three or so years earlier, stop both Michael Porter and Michael Jensen dead in their tracks during a small group meeting that my dean, Roger Martin, chaired on unlocking the keys to change. But on this warm sunny day, in the quiet ambiance of the hotel, I was caught blinking in Chris's headlights. "Goal setting affects a person's choices, it gives direction to one's pursuits. Moreover, a goal increases a person's effort, prolongs persistence, it even cues people to search for strategies to attain it." I was in role and on a roll. "And that's not all," I added for good measure: "A goal is a regulatory mechanism for monitoring, evaluating, and adjusting one's behavior." "Hmmm," said Chris quietly. "What else might explain it?" I was now wishing I had saved one or more of my answers that I had just given him. "Goals can provide meaning to otherwise meaningless tasks. For example with loggers . . ." "Let's think about that," Chris replied firmly and thoughtfully. "There are meaningful tasks for which a goal can be set." "Yes, that's true," I said, thinking erroneously we might now be on the same track. "For example, in my study with engineers and scientists goals provided strong cues as to expected behavior . . ." I could see immediately that citing Mischel on strong vs. weak situations was not going to put me in Chris's good graces. The ol' man continued to grill me with questions like no others since the day of my oral comprehensive examination with Wexley and Yukl in graduate

(Continued)

to me that the loggers had low job attendance even though they were paid on a piece rate basis.[3]

Three factors led me to choose goal-setting theory as a framework for developing an intervention. First, I was very much aware of the number of people who derive pride in their performance knocking down pins with a ball in a bowling alley, as well as the number of people who count the number of swings with a club to get a little ball to go into, what is for me, a ridiculously small hole in the ground. Second, as I stated at the outset of this book, a factor analysis of a survey we had conducted suggested the importance of an item that had been serendipitously included—goal setting (Ronan, Latham, & Kinne, 1973). Third, I had read Locke's laboratory experiments in the journals. So, drawing upon this knowledge, I spent a Saturday afternoon on an air mattress at Lake Spivey, just outside of Atlanta, dreaming up ways I could turn

---

(Continued)

school. "Goal attainment gives people a sense of accomplishment," I finally blurted out. I don't recall how I worked that response into the conversation, but I do recall that it was at that moment that Chris's eyes lit up. The answer seemed to be marginally acceptable to him. As an hour or so had elapsed, Chris took mercy on me by giving me HIS answer: "Could it possibly be that goals increase a person's effectiveness, which is a universal need?" "YES, YES!" I exclaimed. He then effectively charmed my wife by turning to her and saying: "My dear, your husband and I owe you an apology for not including you in our conversation." "Not at all, Dr. Argyris," she replied, "I don't think I've ever seen nor have I ever enjoyed seeing my husband squirm as much as I did today."

I noted from this that the examinations we are subjected to in graduate school never end. On June 13, 2006, Chris received an honorary doctorate from the University of Toronto. I was given the honor of hooding him.

[3]In *The House of the Dead,* the Russian novelist Fyodor Dostoevsky (1911) wrote that if one wants to utterly crush a human being, just give the person completely senseless, irrational work. In describing his own 10 years in Russian prisons, Dostoyevsky reported that if a convict had to move a heap of earth from one place to another and back again, he would hang himself, preferring death to such humiliation. Deprived of meaningful work-related goals, men and women lose their reason for existence. Similarly, Frank (1983) described an event that occurred in 1944 when Allied aircraft began their air strikes in Germany. After a factory was hit by bombs, the Germans ordered prisoners to one end of the building remains, commanding them to shovel the debris into carts and drag it to the other end of the compound. The next day, the prisoners were ordered to move the high pile of the debris back to the other end of the compound. Day after day the prisoners hauled the same mountain of rubble back and forth from one end of the camp to the other. After several weeks of this meaningless drudgery, one man began sobbing uncontrollably and was led away by guards. Another screamed until his captors beat him into silence. Then another man, who had survived 3 years in prison, darted away from the group and raced toward an electrified fence. This activity continued until dozens of prisoners went mad and ran from their work, only to be shot by the guards or electrocuted by the fence. Why did the Germans require this activity? The commandant of the camp later explained that this was an experiment in mental health to see what would happen when people are given what they perceive to be meaningless work.

tree-cutting into a game not unlike bowling or golf. When Syd Kinne, a newly minted Ph.D. in forestry with a high-level job in Georgia Kraft, and I explained our plan to management (assign goals, give people tally meters to keep track of number of trees cut down), we were greeted with good-natured laughter and lots of skepticism. Because the financial cost of our proposed intervention was so small, and the proposal was so straightforward, we were given the green light. Even the two of us were astonished to see the dramatic results in productivity and attendance at the end of the very first week (Latham & Kinne, 1974).

Would another theoretical framework have been as, if not more, effective than goal setting? I ruled out job enrichment/job characteristics theories because there was no way that I knew of to increase the loggers' autonomy, task variety, or opportunities for advancement. Because they were paid on a piece-rate basis, I did not believe that I would be allowed by them or the sponsoring forest product companies of the American Pulpwood Association to switch the payment from a continuous reinforcement schedule to a variable ratio. My belief was and is that a tally meter for counting the trees a person cuts down is not only more easy to implement, it is arguably more effective than teaching a logging supervisor to shout "good," or words to that effect, on a variable ratio schedule when a tree hits the ground. In addition, I could find no evidence in my conversations with the loggers that low productivity was a problem due to their concerns over inequity. And it seemed obvious that all of them could see that their effort leads directly to the number of trees they cut down, the number of trees cut down leads directly to money, and that these people value money as much as I do—hence my ruling out an intervention based on expectancy theory. In short, I did not choose goal setting as an intervention because I was wedded to the theory, I chose it because I believed that in that context it was the most appropriate framework for developing a path forward.

In science as well as practice, it is wise to surround oneself with smart people.[4] Shortly after joining Weyerhaeuser, my self-set goal was to turn

---

[4]For reasons that neither a personality test nor introspection has revealed to me, I have always sought out people who are more intelligent than I. At the age of 6, I formed lifelong relationships with a boy in Massachusetts and another in Nova Scotia, both 2 years my senior. In my senior year of high school, many of my friends were National Merit Scholars. Bob Ford was even a better clarinet player back then than I was of the baritone and cornet. Years later, he would become the editor of the *Academy of Management Executive*. Perhaps the reason can be traced to the fact that Eisenhower was president of the United States when I was in grades 2–10. I can still recall his response to a reporter who asked him

(Continued)

Terry Mitchell, then an assistant professor, into my collaborator.[5] Subsequently, the two of us were called upon when the senior vice president of R&D proclaimed to the company that Weyerhaeuser's scientists and engineers would attain excellence within one year in the eyes of George Weyerhaeuser and the company's line managers. Terry and I had no idea as to how this was to take place.

Gary Johns, a faculty member at Concordia University in Montreal, is fond of saying that a secret to passing the comprehensive examinations at the doctoral level is to include the words job analysis as step 1 for the answer to any question. Terry and I implemented this advice as our initial step for defining excellence in R&D (Latham & Mitchell, 1976).

(Continued)

how he could find so much time to play golf. He said it is easy when you surround yourself with intelligent people. Recalling the research of Bargh and Shah on subconscious goals, perhaps the explanation for my behavior is that I was primed. Regardless of the reason, doing so has paid large dividends for me both personally and professionally. Thus, I strongly urge you, the reader, to emulate Milt Hakel, who as a young assistant professor formed the Summit Group in 1968 (see Foreword). My criteria in doing so would be fourfold. (1) Invite senior level assistant professors who have a proven track record. These individuals by definition are creative. How else can they publish in top tier journals where there is a 85–100% rejection rate. The latter actually occurred one year when I served on Jan Bayer's editorial board for the *Academy of Management Journal*. (2) Similarly, invite HRM, I/O, and OB practitioners from industry who have shown evidence of having a "high impact" in their respective organizations. Keep the number in the group small so as to allow free flowing discussions. (3) Invite people who have different skill sets. (4) Invite people who laugh a lot. My experience is that it is difficult to lose one's motivation, let alone go in the wrong direction, when you are surrounded by people who are high on ability and motivation, and who take an interest in your success. Among the current people in the Summit Group are: Mike Beer (professor emeritus, Harvard, formerly Corning Glass, SIOP and Academy Fellow), Milt Hakel (endowed chair, SIOP past president and Fellow), Tim Hall (Boston University, Academy and SIOP Fellow), David Campbell (Center for Creative Leadership, SIOP Fellow), John Hinrichs (retired, formerly IBM, President of his own consulting firm, SIOP Fellow), George Hollenbeck (retired, Merrill Lynch, SIOP Fellow), Allen Kraut (formerly IBM, currently Baruch University, SIOP Fellow), Edward Lawler (Director, Center for Effective Organizations, University of Southern California, Academy and SIOP Fellow), Simi Ronen (retired, University of Tel Aviv, SIOP Fellow), Cindy McCauley (Center for Creative Leadership, SIOP Fellow), Douglas McKenna (retired from Microsoft, in his 40s, very rich), Morgan McCall (University of Southern California, SIOP Fellow), Bob Morrison (formerly University of Toronto, U.S. Naval Research, retired, SIOP, Fellow), Joel Moses (formerly AT&T, president of his own consulting firm, SIOP Fellow), Lyman Porter (past president of the Academy and SIOP, Fellow in both), Lise Saari (IBM, SIOP Fellow), Ben Schneider (past president of SIOP and OB of the Academy, Fellow in both), Mel Sorcher (retired GE, and Richardson-Merrill, SIOP Fellow), Nancy Tippens (consulting, past president and Fellow of SIOP), and Ellie Weldon (Hong Kong University of Science and Technology). I list these people to demonstrate the diversity of strengths and interests of this phenomenal group of colleagues. What is the probability that I can be confronted by an issue in our field that none of these people can be of considerable help?

[5]After shaking hands, he said, "I bet you thought I would be taller." A tad embarrassed because he was correct, I asked, "Why is that?" "Because I have published so much," he responded laughingly.

(Continued)

Step 2 occurred in a meeting where I reviewed the results of our job analysis with Weyerhaeuser's four R&D Directors. When I finished, a discussion occurred among them as to how the engineers/scientists could be motivated to engage in the newly defined behavioral indices of excellence. One director recommended they be given assigned goals just as the four of them were assigned goals by George Weyerhaeuser and the senior management team. A second director, an avid reader of the *Harvard Business Review*, talked about the necessity of involving the engineers/scientists in the goal-setting process. As a facilitator, I said nothing as they were well aware of the results I had achieved with both the company's logging operations and word processors by implementing goal setting. I did, however, write the words "assigned goals" and "participative goals" on a flip chart.

A third director, who did not hold psychology or me in high regard, argued that goal setting is insulting for already highly motivated scientists and engineers. I recall his glare when I wrote "do your best" on the flip chart. His comment was as follows: "While psychologists are figuring out what motivates people, let's go with what we already know that works—money." I wrote $ on the flip chart. The other directors disagreed with him. Still, I said nothing.

The silence on my part was contrary to my behavior in graduate school. I had received ongoing praise from my professors, Drs. Yukl and Wexley, for being among the first to speak in a doctoral seminar, for

---

(Continued)

Again, he was correct. I have known no one who has managed to become a leader in our field in part by staying abreast of the literature in another field, namely social psychology, than Terry. Terry's Ph.D. was in social psychology where he did his dissertation under the supervision of Fred Fiedler. Fred, who was training as a clinical psychologist, switched to social-industrial psychology early in his career where he devoted his life to the study of leadership in the military and in the private and public sectors. An avid researcher, he told me: "When I started to view my patients as subjects, I knew it was time to get out of the clinic" (Fiedler, 1976, personal communication). When Fred left the University of Illinois in 1969 to come to the University of Washington, he brought his newly minted Ph.D. protégé, Terry, with him. Their lifelong relationship had an amusing start. "Dr. Fiedler," Terry, the entering graduate student began, "I am a great admirer of your work." "Really," Fred replied. "Which one of my articles did you like the most?" Terry had no answer. He had never read a single one. Fred's solution: "Here is my vita; read everything on it this week and then come see me with the answer to my question." The inter-observer reliability of this story is .90. Fred, however, did not always get the upper hand with an incoming doctoral student. To motivate people, he was fond of saying that students who come from your undergraduate institution often do poorly in the doctoral program. Fred had not refreshed his memory when Milt Blood entered his office for the first time. Milt had attended several undergraduate programs: "Young man," Fred said, "People from your undergraduate school typically do not do well in our doctoral program." "Really, sir?" replied Milt. "Which one is that?" Fred was speechless as he rapidly searched his desk for Milt's file.

doing so forcefully, and for doing so argumentatively based on my knowledge of theory and research.[6] I was stunned to find that this behavior did not transfer positively to Weyerhaeuser. As a result of hearing my recommendations on several occasions, within 15 minutes of any meeting that I attended, my boss, the VP of Human Resources, invited me to his office. The essence of his insight was as follows: "When a 28-year-old Ph.D. immediately discovers solutions, albeit good ones, to issues that much older, highly experienced managers are finding difficult, the 28-year-old is likely to engender resentment rather than gratitude. When you enter a meeting, I want you to look at your watch. Do not speak until you have listened attentively to, and can summarize succinctly, what has been said. Now, look at your watch. You should not offer your ideas or suggestions until at least 45 minutes have passed. If you do not follow this advice, your telephone may stop ringing and you will no longer be invited to attend important meetings."

This last sentence in particular caught my attention. There was a maxim in Weyerhaeuser that had been shared with me on my first week on the job by another wise senior VP. "We evaluate the worth of our staff by how often their phone rings." I remain grateful to these two vice presidents for their sage advice on the art of gaining respect, being heard, and ultimately being seen as a team player in an organizational setting.

Applying this wisdom to the R&D directors, I wrote the words "public recognition" after listening to a director argue against the use of monetary bonuses. I did so after I listened to a director stress the pride he had observed among his direct reports when they had a paper published in a scientific journal or accepted for presentation to an academic conference.

Another maxim in the folklore of Weyerhaeuser in that time period was as follows: "If you mess up, you will hear from us. If you don't mess up, assume you are doing well." A fourth director cogently stated why he believed it would be beneficial to reverse the maxim: "If you hear from

---

[6]In 1973 I attended my first APA convention. While listening to psychologists from industry speak in a symposium, I muttered under my breath, "Who put them on the program?" Enchanted by science, and not yet fully appreciative of the art of practice, I was critical of their presentation. Overhearing my comment, the person next to me whispered, "I am Mike Beer, who are you?" I said, "I am Gary Latham, I am a doctoral student," Beer smiled knowingly as he responded: "That is what I guessed." Years later I would be successful in nominating Mike for the award of Fellow in the Academy of Management. I did so not only because of his impact on our field, but because of his impact on me in becoming open to different viewpoints in our field. In 2006, he received the Distinguished Contributions to Psychology as a Profession from the Society of Industrial and Organizational Psychology.

us, you can assume you are doing well, if you don't hear from us, get nervous." I considered writing "instill paranoia," instead I recorded the word "praise."

When it became apparent that the R&D directors were not going to gain consensus, I spoke: "What if we put our ideas to a test? Since this is R&D, let's have fun doing an experiment." I showed them a 3 × 3 factorial design that had emerged from my note-taking on the flipchart: Assigned goals, participative goals, do your best-money, public recognition, and praise. Intrigued, the directors immediately made bets as to who among them was right. At that point, Terry raised the concern that because the engineers/scientists would know everyone who would be in each of the 9 conditions, and since everyone worked relatively close to one another, gossip among the engineers/scientists might bias or contaminate the results.[7] The directors quickly agreed to include a group in Oklahoma/Arkansas who would be kept in the dark as to our experiment (Latham, Mitchell, & Dossett, 1978). The bets were paid off based on the performance of the people in the 9 conditions versus this tenth one.

A scientist-practitioner is unlikely to be effective if the person becomes wedded to one theoretical framework. I did not introduce a schedule of reinforcement intervention to Weyerhaeuser's tree planters and mountain beaver trappers as a way of administering monetary bonuses because of my belief in the philosophy of behaviorism. I was never a behaviorist—at least not consciously. I consciously chose to do so for only two reasons. First, voluminous laboratory experiments showed the effectiveness of operant methodology. Second, I judged that goal setting, which had proven so effective with loggers, word processors, and engineers/scientists, might not prove to be effective with tree planters (Yukl & Latham, 1975; Yukl, Latham & Pursell, 1976) or mountain beaver trappers (Latham & Dossett, 1978). The tree planters carried bags each containing 1,000 seedlings. They would often hide one or more bags under a stump with the hope that a hidden bag would not be found by a supervisor. Rightly or wrongly, I did not believe there would be commitment on the part of these workers to a specific high goal regarding the number of bags of trees to be planted in a given day or

---

[7]In truth, I have never found that results among conditions were contaminated in a field setting because people in one condition were aware of what people were experiencing in another condition. Life would be arguably wonderful if "demand effects" in long-term field settings were effective. Even if employees in a field experiment were as cooperative with an experimenter as their counterparts in a laboratory setting, it would be short-lived. The employees have to do their respective jobs. They do not have the luxury of figuring out ways to please a researcher.

week. I also did not see how the job could be enriched to increase their motivation. No task variety was possible; no increase in job skills was possible, and these employees have maximum job autonomy. There was minimum supervision, hence the temptation by employees to hide a bag of trees. Planting a tree or trapping a rodent is boring tedious work for these people. These are jobs that require little or no skill. If you remember "green up, brown down," you can become a highly proficient tree planter. And as I reported earlier, a trap does not even have to be baited to catch a dimwitted mountain beaver. When I came up with the idea of flipping coins, throwing dice, or guessing the color of a marble in a bag in order to obtain a monetary bonus, management and the union were incredulous. Once again, organizational decision makers laughed good-naturedly at the simplicity of my plan. Their only concern was the need to get a ruling from the company's legal department that this was not gambling. I was given the green light to proceed when the decision came that it was okay to go forward because the employees would not be using their own money. As I noted earlier, subsequent interviews with the employees revealed that they themselves set goals as a result of this intervention. As goal-setting theory states, money is especially effective if it leads to the setting of and commitment to a specific high goal.

Also noted earlier in this book, I had considered applying schedules of reinforcement to increase job attendance. But, at Norpac, a newsprint facility owned in part by Weyerhaeuser and a company in Japan, I subsequently observed that the reason why people were not coming to work was because the obstacles that prevented them from doing so seemed insurmountable to them. As I knew these people quite well, I knew they were telling me the truth as they understood it. Their issues did not seem difficult to me (e.g., not getting along with a supervisor; caring for a sick child). Hence, I concluded the problem was low self-efficacy rather than the necessity for an incentive administered on one or more reinforcement schedules.

Two events led to Collette Frayne's award-winning doctoral dissertation on ways to increase a person's self-efficacy to come to work. First, Paul Goodman asked me to make a presentation to a conference at Carnegie Mellon University on effective interventions for overcoming low job attendance. Each presenter was assigned what Paul called a provocateur. Mine was a good friend, Gary Johns. After I had spoken, Johns told me and the other conference attendees how disappointed he was with my presentation (Latham & Napier, 1984) because, in his words, I had provided a shotgun approach rather than a rifle shot to the problem of absenteeism. Although I continue to believe that I did what Goodman had asked me to do, Johns' criticism gnawed at me during my flight back to Seattle. Recalling the employees at Norpac, I became increasingly convinced that the reason for low job attendance is often due to low self-efficacy for coming to work. There was no evidence of what Johns often refers to as a culture that supports absenteeism. Low job attendance was an issue for only a small subset of people on different paper-making crews in Norpac.

The second event was the discovery that the University of Washington's unionized maintenance workers had high absenteeism.[8] Both the union and management were concerned about the number of people who would soon be terminated in accordance with the negotiated union contract due to their low job attendance. When these people were present, they performed their jobs well. Again, there was nothing to suggest that there was a culture that supports employee absenteeism.

How does one increase self-efficacy of a state-government-unionized employee for coming to work? Enactive mastery and modeling seemed nonsensical in this instance (e.g., "let me model for you how to come to work"). Persuasion from significant others had already proved to be ineffective since union leaders and organizational leaders had been unsuccessful in increasing the job attendance of these employees.

The academic literature gave us an answer. Frayne and I discovered the methodology of Fred Kanfer, a clinical psychologist who specialized in self-management techniques (Frayne & Latham, 1986; Latham & Frayne, 1989). The union leadership immediately gave their support for our proposal as the intervention she and I proposed was employee directed. Management gave a sigh of relief; not so Collette.

The first week of the self-management intervention there was a fist fight among employees due to one employee calling another individual pejorative names. Collette, a phenomenal teacher in the classroom, became visibly distraught: "You are going to ruin my dissertation." This is the only instance where I am aware of demand effects affecting the field work where I have been involved. Chagrined, the two employees not only stopped fighting, they surprised her the following week with a

---

[8]My ability to "sell" an intervention is usually easy because of my long-term relationship with clients. In this instance, I was going to Norpac on a weekly basis. To my amazement, the mill manager, a good friend, with a Ph.D. in pulp and paper making, told me I was naïve to believe my proposal would be effective. It was the first and only time he greeted my idea with an emphatic "no!"

flower box the two of them had made for her—on company time with company material. At least they were now coming to work.

Subsequent to this research, my grandmother's saying that we are often our own worst enemy became salient for me. Friends who were laid off from work talked to me about how difficult it is for someone at their age to once again obtain employment. I concluded that a way needed to be found to challenge their dysfunctional self-talk regarding goal attainment. Using goal setting and social cognitive theories as frameworks, and discovering Meichenbaum's work in the clinical psychology literature, Zeeva Millman and I concluded that a person's self-talk can indeed be changed regarding overcoming perceived obstacles in one's environment to the goal of re-employment (Millman & Latham, 2001).

Goal setting, self-talk, or reinforcement schedules are unlikely, in my opinion, to increase the likelihood that people in a union will increase their union organizational citizenship behavior (e.g., "set a goal for how many union meetings you will attend"; "union members, repeat after me, I will actively support my union"; "union leaders, show appreciation every time a member volunteers for a committee, then switch to doing so after every fourth committee a member chooses to join, now after every tenth committee," etc.). After observing the acrimony and cynicism that many union members display toward their union leaders, Dan Skarlicki and I decided that few things hurt goal commitment in particular and union commitment in general faster than feelings among the workforce of favoritism and injustice. Hence, we turned to Jerry Greenberg and Rob Folger's conceptualizations of organizational justice for guidance in developing an effective intervention for union leaders in their interactions with the union membership (Skarlicki & Latham, 2005).

With regard to field settings, the number of questions I receive as to how to gain access to organizational sites in order to conduct research puzzles me. It puzzles me only because it is invariably asked by doctoral students who are standing in the middle of one as they are asking me the question. A university is an organization. Among a university's employees are engineers, scientists, medical doctors, dentists, medical and dental clinicians, lawyers, administrative staff, electricians, machinists, maintenance workers, and groundskeepers. There are usually unions, and there is always management. And there is invariably a beleaguered HRM department. Unlike many organizations in the private sector, many universities are operating on very limited financial budgets. Hence, they have always welcomed highly educated experts who are willing to work pro-bono, namely, my doctoral students.

Frayne's work with unionized employees at the University of Washington has already been described. Having read her work, Nina Cole visited the HRM department at the University of Toronto. As she anticipated, there was a high degree of conflict among management and employees as well as their union officers over the implementation of the negotiated disciplinary process. Would a goal-setting intervention be appropriate in this context? An intervention on ways to increase self-actualization? We didn't think so. In our judgment, the solution begged for an intervention based on the principles of organizational justice (Cole & Latham, 1997).

At the Rotman Faculty of Management, my dean is very receptive to ways of increasing our Business School's ratings in the *Financial Times*, where schools in Asia, Australia, Europe, and North America are rated.[9] Ute Klehe's idea for a predictive validation study of the situational interview and the patterned behavior interview for selecting MBA students was immediately welcomed, as was Dan Skarlicki's proposal for an assessment of the ability of those two interview methods for predicting the organizational citizenship behavior of business school faculty (Klehe & Latham, 2005; Latham & Skarlicki, 1995). Christina Sue-Chan received full cooperation from the MBA office when she proposed different ways of coaching MBA students (Sue-Chan & Latham, 2004), as did Travor Brown when he suggested examining the benefit of learning versus performance goals as a way to increase MBA student satisfaction with their classes (Latham & Brown, in press), as well as the use of verbal self guidance for increasing their interpersonal effectiveness in their respective study groups (Brown & Latham, 2006).

What is the source of art in the application of behavioral science theory and research findings in the workplace? I believe a primary source is our journals and scholarly conferences.[10] I heard Bob Guion, an icon

---

[9]In 1993 *Macleans* magazine ranked us number 1 in Canada; our present dean's specific high goal is to be ranked within the top 10 in the world. We are currently ranked number 20.

[10]I am disappointed by the number of people who only go to SIOP, Canadian SIOP, or the Academy of Management. Financial considerations aside, why not go to all of them? Why not go to the European Work and Organization Psychology (EWOP) too? The conferences allow face-to-face dialogue: "How did you do that?" The conferences also increase one's visibility. A large number of my invited colloquiua presentations and presentations in symposia occurred because of earlier conversations I had with someone at a conference: "I didn't know you were doing that. Would you be interested in making a presentation?" And that request occurred when "so and so" introduced me to "so and so." "So, Gary, what are you working on these days?" For me, giving an address in a city in Asia, Australia, or Europe is not only educational in itself, it helps in building an international reputation which, in turn, helps in getting a favorable tenure and promotion decision.

in our field, state and then subsequently write in his commentary as the incoming editor of the *Journal of Applied Psychology* (Guion, 1983) that it is possible but unlikely that important insights will come from research that has no history or from people who are not well acquainted with the literature relevant to the problem they wish to solve. Contributions, he stated, grow logically out of prior research and theory and offer findings that lead logically to new levels of thought.

I also believe that art comes from what my dean, Roger Martin, calls integrative thinking. This involves the ability to consider/embrace the tension between opposing viewpoints (e.g., cognitive vs. operant camps), and generating/creating new solutions. This is where I believe Bandura, a former behaviorist, excels. I encourage my doctoral students to "steal" ideas from one seminar (e.g., decision making) and apply them to another (e.g., HRM). In doing so, Dan Skarlicki, then a doctoral student, asked me if utility analysis (HRM) wasn't in essence a decision-making process. He had reached this conclusion in Glen Whyte's seminar on decision making. At that point in time, Glen, who publishes primarily in decision-making journals had not heard of utility analysis. The result of Skarlicki's question was three publications (Latham & Whyte, 1994; Skarlicki, Latham, & Whyte, 1996; Whyte & Latham, 1997).

Art also comes into play in formulating the question for which one or more answers are sought. Ways of doing this can be gleaned from the journals and conference presentations. As John Campbell (1982) warned, there are certain forms of questions that should be avoided because they often lead to answers that are not very useful, or they yield at best a small return of information. An example is the tendency to pose a general question with the hope that a general answer is possible: "Are the employees in the organization motivated?" What tends to come out from such a question, he said, is a rather bland set of mixed results. Another kind of question that Campbell warned should be avoided is of the form, is variable A or variable B a more important influence on variable C? Is money or feedback a more powerful motivator? Unless the scientist/practitioner "has a reasonably good idea of the relevant population variances and can interpret the sample variances accordingly, the results can be misleading. Beware of two-factor designs with biased or haphazard selection treatment level effects that are interpreted as if they were either fixed or random" (Campbell, 1982, pp. 697–698).

I continue to be in agreement with another observation by Campbell (1982).[11] The most interesting and valuable questions that we behavioral scientists investigate rarely come from merely reading the literature. Rather, they come from the scientist-practitioner's observations, experiences, and hunches.[12] The literature provides us with ideas for how to go forward as well as what to do next. It is my sincere hope that this book has advanced your thinking on the practice of science with regard to predicting, understanding, and influencing the motivation of people in organizational settings.

---

[11]For me, John Campbell is among the most insightful people in our field. He epitomizes the word pithy by his one-sentence observations. A past president of SIOP and a former editor of the *Journal of Applied Psychology*, he is also a founding member of the Summit Group. At a Summit meeting not long after I received my Ph.D., I engaged him in a discussion of the pros and cons of various selection tests. His one-sentence answer: "A predictor only takes on significance in relation to a criterion." His one-sentence response to another problem I presented to him in considerable detail was: "You need to find an appropriate dependent variable with sufficient reliability to allow you to test the effectiveness of your intervention." A one-sentence reply from John is followed by long periods of silence. This always allows me the time necessary to formulate a well-thought-out response: "Yes."

[12]Campbell used the word "conviction" rather than "hunch." I confess that I often feel my heart pumping as to whether the intervention I am implementing in an organizational setting is going be effective. Hence, the thrill I derive from the practice of science.

References

Adair, J. G. (1984). The Hawthorne effect: A reconsideration of the methodological artifact. *Journal of Applied Psychology, 69,* 334–345.

Adams, J. S. (1963). Toward an understanding of inequity. *Journal of Abnormal and Social Psychology, 67,* 422–436.

Adams, J. S. (1965). Inequity in social exchange. In L. Berkowitz (Ed.), *Advances in experimental psychology* (Vol. 2, pp. 267–299). San Diego: Academic Press.

Adams, J. S. (1968). Effects of overpayment: Two comments to Lawler's paper. *Journal of Personality and Social Psychology, 10,* 315–316.

Adler, A. (1930). Individual psychology. In C. Murchinson (Ed.), *Psychologies of 1930* (pp. 395–405). Worcester, MA: Clark University Press.

Adler, S. (1986). *Toward a role for personality in goal setting research.* Paper presented at the International Congress of Applied Psychology, Jerusalem.

Adler, S. & Weiss, H. M. (1988). Recent developments in the study of personality and organizational behavior. In C. L. Cooper & I. T. Robertson (Eds.), *International review of industrial and organizational psychology* (pp. 307–330). Oxford, UK: John Wiley & Sons.

Aguinis, H., & Henle, C. A. (2003). The search for universals in cross-cultural organizational behavior. In J. Greenberg (Ed.), *Organizational behavior: The state of science* (pp. 373–419). Mahwah, NJ: Erlbaum.

Ajila, C. O. (1997). Maslow's hierarchy of needs theory: Applicability to the Nigerian industrial setting. *IFE Psychologia: An International Journal, 5,* 162–174.

Ajzen, I. (2001). Nature and operation of attitudes. *Annual Review of Psychology, 10,* 27–58.

Alderfer, C. P. (1972). *Existence, relatedness, and growth: Human needs in organizational settings.* New York: Free Press.

Allport, G. W. (1951). Basic principles in improving human relations. In K. W. Bigelow (Ed.), *Cultural groups and human relations* (pp. 8–28). Oxford, UK: Bureau of Publications.

Allscheid, S. P., & Cellar, D. F. (1996). An interactive approach to work motivation: The effects of competition, rewards, and goal difficulty on task performance. *Journal of Business and Psychology, 11,* 219–237.

Alnajjar, A. A. (1996). Relationship between job satisfaction and organizational commitment among employees in the United Arab Emirates. *Psychological Reports, 79,* 315–321.

Alpander, G. G., & Carter, K. D. (1991). Strategic multinational intra-company differences in employee motivation. *Journal of Managerial Psychology, 6,* 25–32.

Amabile, T. M., Hadley, C. N., & Kramer, S. J. (2002). Creativity under the gun. *Harvard Business Review, 80,* 52–61.

Ambrose, M. L. (2002). Contemporary justice research: A new look at familiar questions. *Organizational Behavior and Human Decision Processes, 89,* 803–812.

Ambrose, M. L., & Kulik, C. T. (1999). Old friends, new faces: Motivation research in the 1990s. *Journal of Management, 25,* 231–292.

Ambrose, M. L., Seabright, M. A., & Schminke, M. (2002). Sabotage in the workplace: The role of organizational justice. *Organizational Behavior and Human Decision Processes, 89,* 947–965.

Anshel, M. H., Weinberg, R. S., & Jackson, A. (1992). The effect of goal difficulty and task complexity on intrinsic motivation and motor performance. *Journal of Sport Behaviour, 15,* 159–176.

Argyle, M. (1953). The relay test room in retrospect. *Occupational Psychology, 27,* 98–103.

Argyris, C. (1957). *Personality and organization.* New York: Harper.

Argyris, C. (1960). *Understanding organizational behavior.* Homewood, IL: Dorsey Press.

Argyris, C. (1964). *Integrating the individual and the organization.* New York: Wiley.

Argyris, C. (1968). Some unintended consequences of rigorous research. *Psychological Bulletin, 70,* 185–197.

Argyris, C. (1973). Personality and organization theory revisited. *Administrative Science Quarterly, 18,* 141–167.

Ashford, S. J., & Black, J. S. (1996). Proactivity during organizational entry: The role of desire for control. *Journal of Applied Psychology, 81,* 199–214.

Ashford, S. J., Blatt, R., & VandeWalle, D. M. (2003). Reflections on the looking glass: A review of research on feedback-seeking behavior in organizations. *Journal of Management, 29,* 773–799.

Ashford, S. J., & Tsui, A. S. (1991). Self-regulation for managerial effectiveness: The role of active feedback seeking. *Academy of Management Journal, 34,* 251–280.

Atkinson, J. W. (Ed.). (1958). *Motives in fantasy, action, and society.* Princeton: Van Nostrand.

Audia, G., Kristof, B., Brown, K., & Locke, E. A. (1996). Relationship of goals and microlevel work processes to performance on a mulitipath manual task. *Journal of Applied Psychology, 81,* 483–497.

Audia, P. G., Locke, E. A., & Smith, K. G. (2000). The paradox of success: An archival and a laboratory study of strategic persistence following radical environmental change. *Academy of Management Journal, 43,* 837–853.

Austin, J. T., & Vancouver, J. B. (1996). Goal constructs in psychology: Structure, process, and content. *Psychological Bulletin, 120,* 338–375.

Azrin, N. H. (1977). A strategy for applied research: Learning based but outcome oriented. *American Psychologist, 33,* 140–149.

Baer, M., & Frese, M. (2003). Innovation is not enough: Climates for initiative and psychological safety, process innovation and firm performance. *Journal of Organizational Behavior, 24,* 45–68.

Bagozzi, R. P., & Warshaw, P. R. (1990). Trying to consume. *Journal of Consumer Research, 17,* 127–140.

Bagozzi, R. P., Verbeke, W., & Gavino, J. C. (2003). Culture moderates the self-regulation of shame and its effects on performance: The case of salespersons in the Netherlands and the Philippines. *Journal of Applied Psychology, 88,* 219–233.

Bailey, J. B., Chen, C. C., & Don, S. G. (1997) Conceptions of self and performance-related feedback in the US, Japan, and China. *Journal of International Business Studies, 28,* 605–625.

Bandura, A. (1969). *Principles of behavior modification.* New York: Holt, Rinehart and Winston.

Bandura, A. (1974). Behavior theory and the models of man. *American Psychologist, 29,* 859–869.

Bandura, A. (1977a). Self-efficacy: Toward a unifying theory of behavioral change. *Psychological Review, 84,* 191–215.

Bandura, A. (1977b). *Social learning theory.* Englewood Cliffs, NJ: Prentice Hall.

Bandura, A. (1982). Self-efficacy mechanism in human agency. *American Psychologist, 37,* 122–147.

Bandura, A. (1986). *Social foundations of thought and action: A social cognitive theory.* Englewood Cliffs, New Jersey: Prentice Hall.

Bandura, A. (1989). Self-regulation of motivation and action through internal standards and external goal systems. In L. A. Pervin (Ed.), *Goal concepts in personality and social psychology* (pp.19–85). Hillsdale, NJ: Lawrence Erlbaum.

Bandura, A. (1991). Social cognitive theory of self-regulation. *Organizational Behavior and Human Decision Processes, 50,* 248–287.

Bandura, A. (1997). *Self-efficacy: The exercise of control.* Stanford: W. H. Freeman.

Bandura, A. (2000). Cultivate self-efficacy for personal and organizational effectiveness. In E. A. Locke (Ed.), *The Blackwell handbook of principles of organizational behavior* (pp. 120–136). Oxford, UK: Blackwell.

Bandura, A. (2001a). Social cognitive theory: An agentic perspective. *Annual Review of Psychology, 52*, 1–26.

Bandura, A. (2001b). The changing face of psychology at the dawning of a globalization era. *Canadian Psychology, 42*, 12–23.

Bandura, A. (2002). Social cognitive theory in cultural context. *Applied Psychology: An International Review, 51*, 269–290.

Bandura, A. (2004a). Swimming against the mainstream: The early years from chilly tributary to transformation mainstream. *Behavior Research and Therapy, 42*, 613–630.

Bandura, A. (2004b). *Toward a psychology of human agency*. James McKeen Cattell Fellow Award Address. American Psychological Society, Chicago.

Bandura, A. (2005a). The primacy of self regulation in health promotion. *Applied Psychology: An International Review, 54*, 245–254.

Bandura, A. (2005b). The evolution of social cognitive theory. In K. G. Smith & M. A. Hitt (Eds.). *Great minds in management: The process of theory development* (pp. 9–35). Oxford, UK: Oxford University Press.

Bandura, A., & Adams, N. E. (1977). Analysis of self-efficacy theory of behavioral change. *Cognitive Therapy and Research, 1*, 287–310.

Bandura, A., Adams, N. E., & Beyer, J. (1977). Cognitive processes mediating behavioral change. *Journal of Personality and Social Psychology, 35*, 125–139.

Bandura, A., Caprara, G. V., & Zsolnai, L. (2002). Corporate transgressions. In L. Zsolnai (Ed.), *Ethics in the economy: Handbook of business ethics* (pp. 151–164). Oxford, UK: Peter Lang Publishers.

Bandura, A., & Cervone, D. (1983). Self-evaluative and self-efficacy mechanisms governing the motivational effects of goal systems. *Journal of Personality and Social Psychology, 45*, 1017–1028.

Banduras, A., & Cervone, D. (1986). Differential engagement of self-reactive influences in cognitive motivation. *Organizational Behavior and Human Decision Processes, 38*, 92–113.

Bandura, A., Gian-Vittorio, C., & Laszlo, Z. (2000). Corporate transgressions through moral disengagement. *Journal of Human Values, 6*, 57–64.

Bandura, A., & Locke, E. A. (2003). Negative self-efficacy and goal effects revisited. *Journal of Applied Psychology, 88*, 87–99.

Bandura, A., & Schunk, D. H. (1981). Cultivating competence, self-efficacy and intrinsic interest through proximal self-motivation. *Journal of Personality and Social Psychology, 41*, 586–598.

Barber, A. E. & Bretz, R. D., Jr. (2000). Compensation, attrition and retention. In S. L. Rynes and B. Gerhart (Eds.), *Compensation in organizations: Current research and practice* (pp. 32–60). San Francisco, Jossey-Boss.

Bar-Eli, M., Levy-Kolker, N., Tenenbaum, G., & Weinberg, R. S. (1993). Effect of goal difficulty on performance of aerobic, anaerobic and power tasks in laboratory and field settings. *Journal of Sport Behaviour, 16*, 17–32.

Bargh, J. A. (1994). The four horseman of automaticity: Awareness, efficiency, intention, and control in social cognition. In R. S. Wyer, Jr. & T. K. Srull (Eds.), *Handbook of social cognition* (pp. 1–40). Hillsdale, NJ: Erlbaum.

Bargh, J., & Ferguson, M. J. (2000). Beyond behaviorism: On the automaticity of higher mental processes. *Psychological Bulletin, 126*, 925–945.

Bargh, J. A., Gollwitzer, P. M., Lee-Chai, A., Barndollar, K. & Tröetschel, R. (2001). The automated will: Nonconscious activation and pursuit of behavioral goals. *Journal of Personality and Social Psychology, 81*, 1014–1027.

Barlay, L. J., Skarlicki, D. P., & Pugh, S. D. (2005). Exploring the role of emotions in injustice perceptions and retaliation. *Journal of Applied Psychology, 90*, 629–643.

Barrick, M. R., Mount, M. K., & Judge, T. A. (2001). Personality and performance at the beginning of the new millennium: What do we know and where do we go next? *International Journal of Selection and Assessment, 9*, 9–30.

Barrick, M. R., Parks, L., Mount, M. K. (2005). Self-monitoring as a moderator of the relationship between personality traits and performance. *Personnel Psychology, 58,* 745–767.

Barrick, M. R., Stewart, G. L., Newbert, M. J., & Mant, M. K. (1998). Relating member ability and personality to work team processes and team effectiveness. *Journal of Applied Psychology, 83,* 377–391.

Barrick, M. R., Stewart, G. L., & Piotrowski, M. (2002). Personality and job performance: Test of the mediating effects of motivation among sales representatives. *Journal of Applied Psychology, 87,* 43–51.

Barsade, S. G., Brief, A. P., & Spataro, S. E. (2003). The affective revolution in organizational behavior: The emergence of a paradigm. In J. Greenberg (Ed.), *Organizaitonal behavior: The state of the science* (2nd ed., pp. 3–51). Hillsdale, NJ: Erlbaum.

Barsalou, L. W., Simmons, W. K., Barbey, A. K., & Wilson, C. D. (2003). Grounding conceptual knowledge in modality-specific systems. *Trends in Cognitive Sciences, 7,* 84–91.

Bartle, S. A., & Hayes, B. C. (1999, April). *Organizational justice and work outcomes: A meta-analysis.* Paper presented at the Annual Meeting of the Society for Industrial and Organizational Psychology, Atlanta.

Bateman, T. S., & Crant, J. M. (1993). The proactive component of organizational behavior: A measure and correlates. *Journal of Organizational Behavior, 14,* 103–118.

Baum, J. R., & Locke, E. A. (2004). The relationship of entrepreneurial traits, skill and motivation to subsequent venture. *Journal of Applied Psychology, 89,* 587–598.

Baum, J. R., Locke, E. A., & Smith, K. G. (2001). A multidimensional model of venture growth. *Academy of Management Journal, 44,* 292–303.

Bavelas, J., & Lee, E. S. (1978). Effect of goal level on performance: A trade-off of quantity and quality. *Canadian Journal of Psychology, 32,* 219–240.

Bennis, W. (1985). Foreword: In *The human side of the enterprise: 25th anniversary printing.* New York: McGraw-Hill.

Bernichon, T., Cook, K. E., & Brown, J. D. (2003). Seeking self-evaluative feedback: The interactive role of global self-esteem and specific self-views. *Journal of Personality and Social Psychology, 84,* 194–204.

Berry, J. M., & West, R. L. (1993). Cognitive self-efficacy in relation to personal mastery and goal setting across the life span. *International Journal of Behavioural Development, 16,* 351–379.

Bies, R. J., & Moag, J. F. (1986). Interactional justice: Communication criteria of fairness. In R. J. Lewicki, B. H. Sheppard & M. H. Bazerman (Eds.), *Research on negotiations in organizations* (Vol. 1, pp. 43–55). Greenwich, CT: JAI Press.

Bingham, W. (1962). Remarks. In B. V. H. Gilmer (Ed.), *Walter VanDyke Bingham* (pp. 33–35). Pittsburgh, PA: Carnegie Institute of Technology.

Blader, S. L., & Tyler, T.R. (2005). How can theories of organizational justice explain the effects of fairness? In J. Greenberg & J. A. Colquitt (Eds.), *Handbook of organizational justice* (pp. 329–354). Mahwah, NJ: Lawrence Erlbaum.

Blood, M. R., & Hulin, C. L. (1967). Alienation, environmental characteristics, and worker responses. *Journal of Applied Psychology, 51,* 284–290.

Blum, M. L., & Naylor, J. C. (1968). *Industrial Psychology: Its theoretical and social foundations.* New York: Harper & Row.

Bobocel, D. R., & Holmvall, C. M. (2001). Are interactional and procedural justice different? Framing the debate. In S. Gilliland, D. Steiner & D. Skarlicki (Eds.), *Theoretical and cultural perspectives on organizational justice* (pp. 85–110). Greenwich, CT: Information Age Publishing.

Boekaerts, M., Maes, S., & Karoly, P. (2005). Self-regulation across domains of applied psychology: Is there an emerging consensus? *Applied Psychology: An International Review, 54,* 149–154.

Bond, F. W., & Bunce, D. (2003). The role of acceptance and job control in mental health, job satisfaction, and work performance. *Journal of Applied Psychology, 88,* 1057–1067.

Boone, J., & Bowen, W. (1987). *The great writings in management and organizational behavior* (2nd ed.). New York: Random House.

Bordin, E. S. (1994). Theory and research on the therapeutic working alliance: New directions. In A. O. Horvath & L. S. Greenberg (Eds.), *The working alliance: Theory, research, and practice. Wiley series on personality processes* (pp. 13–37). New York: John Wiley & Sons.

Borg, I. (1990). Multiple facetisations of work values. *Applied Psychology: An International Review. Special Issue: Facet Theory, 39,* 401–412.

Boring, E. G. (1950). *A history of experimental psychology* (2nd ed.). East Norwalk, CT: Appleton-Century-Crofts.

Borman, W. C., Klimoski, R. J., & Ilgen, D. R. (2003). Stability and change in industrial and organizational psychology. In W. C. Borman, D. R. Ilgen, & R. J. Klimoski (Eds.), *Handbook of psychology* (Vol. 12, pp. 1–17). New York: John Wiley and Sons.

Bowlby, J. (1979). *The making & breaking of affectional bonds.* London: Tavistock.

Boyce, B. A., & Wayda, V. K. (1994). The effects of assigned and self-set goals on task performance. *Journal of Sport and Exercise Psychology, 16,* 258–26.

Brandstadtter, V., Lengfelder, A., & Gollwitzer, P. M. (2001). Implementation intentions and efficient action intitiation. *Journal of Personality and Psychology, 81*(5), 946–960.

Brandstätter, V., Heimbeck, D., Malzacher, J. T., & Frese, M. (2003). Goals need implementation intentions: The model of action phases tested in the applied setting of continuing education. *European Journal of Work and Organizational Psychology, 12,* 37–59.

Bray, D. W., & Grant, D. L. (1966). The assessment center in the measurement of potential for business management. *Psychological Monographs, 80* (17, Whole No. 625).

Brayfield, A. H. & Crockett, W. H. (1955). Employee attitudes and employee performance. *Psychological Bulletin, 52,* 396–424.

Brett, J. (2000). *Negotiating globally: How to negotiate deals, resolve disputes, and make decisions across cultural boundaries.* San Francisco, CA: Jossey-Bass.

Brett, J. F., & VandeWalle, D. M. (1999). Goal orientation and goal content as predictors of performance in a training program. *Journal of Applied Psychology, 84,* 863–873.

Brief, A. P., & Dukerich, J. M. (1991). Theory in organizational behavior: Can it be useful? In B. M. Staw & L. L. Cummings (Eds.), *Research in organizational behavior* (Vol. 13, pp. 327–352). Greenwich, CT: JAI Press.

Brief, A. P., & Roberson, L. (1989). Job attitude organization: An exploratory study. *Journal of Applied Social Psychology, 19*(9), 717–727.

Brief, A. P., & Schneider, B. (1986). Foreword. In E. A. Locke (Ed.), *Generalizing from laboratory to field settings.* Lexington, MA: Lexington Books.

Brief, A. P., & Weiss, H. M. (2002). Organizational behavior: Affect in the workplace. *Annual Review of Psychology, 53,* 279–307.

Brockner, J., Ackerman, G., Greenberg, J., Gelfand, M. J., Francesco, A. M, Chen, Z. X., Leung, K., Bierbauer, G., Gomez, C., Kirkman, B. L., & Shapiro, D. (2001). Culture and procedural justice: The influence of power distance on reactions to voice. *Journal of Experimental Social Psychology, 37,* 300–315.

Brockner, J., & Wiesenfeld, B. M. (1996). An integrative framework for explaining reactions to decisions: Interactive effects of outcomes and procedures. *Psychological Bulletin, 120,* 189–208.

Brown, A. (1997). Narcissism, identity, and legitimacy. *Academy of Management Review, 22,* 648–686.

Brown, R. (1968). *Social psychology.* New York: Free Press.

Brown, S. P., Ganesan, S., & Challagalla, G. (2001). Self-efficacy as a moderator of information-seeking effectiveness. *Journal of Applied Psychology, 86,* 1043–1051.

Brown, S. P., Jones, E., & Leigh, T. W. (2005). The attenuating effect of role overload on relationships linking self-efficacy and goal level to work performance. *Journal of Applied Psychology, 90,* 972–979.

Brown, T. C. (2003). The effect of verbal self-guidance training on collective efficacy and team performance. *Personnel Psychology, 56,* 935–964.

Brown, T. C., & Latham, G. P. (2002). The effects of behavioral outcome goals, learning goals, and urging people to do their best on an individual's teamwork behavior in a group problem solving task. *Canadian Journal of Behavioural Science, 34,* 276–285.

Brown, T. C., & Latham, G. P. (2006). The effect of training in verbal self guidance on performance effectiveness in a MBA program. *Canadian Journal of Behavioural Science, 38*, 1–11.

Browne, K. R. (2006). Evolved sex differences and occupational segregation. *Journal of Organizational Behavior, 27*(2), 143–162.

Burtt, H. E. (1926). *Principles of employment psychology.* Boston: Houghton Mifflin.

Buss, D. M., & Reeve, H. K. (2003). Evolutionary psychology and developmental dynamics: comment on Lickliter and Honeycutt (2003). *Psychological Bulletin, 129*(6), 8480853.

Bussey, K., & Bandura, A. (1999). Social cognitive theory of gender development and differentiation. *Psychological Review, 106*, 676–713.

Button, S. B., Mathieu, J. E., & Aikin, K. J. (1996). An examination of the relative impact of assigned goals and self-efficacy on personal goals and performance over time. *Journal of Applied Social Psychology, 26*, 1084–1103.

Button, S. B., Mathieu, J. E., & Zajac, D. M. (1996). Goal orientation in organizational research: A conceptual and empirical foundation. *Organizational Behavior and Human Decision Processes, 67*, 26–48.

Byrne, Z. S., & Cropanzano, R. (2001). History of organizational justice: The founders speak. In R. Cropanzano (Ed.), *Justice in the workplace: From theory to practice* (Vol. 2, pp. 3–26). Mahwah, NJ: Erlbaum.

Cable, D. M., & Edwards, J. R. (2004). Complementary and supplementary fit: A theoretical and empirical integeration. *Journal of Applied Psychology, 89*(5), 822–834.

Cable, D. M, & Parsons, C. K. (2001). Socialization tactics and person-organization fit. *Personnel Psychology, 54*, 1–23.

Cable, J. P., & DeRue, D. S. (2002). The convergent and discriminant validity of subjective fit perceptions. *Journal of Applied Psychology, 87*, 875–884.

Cameron, J., & Pierce, W. D. (1994). Reinforcement, reward, and intrinsic motivation: A meta-analysis. *Review of Educational Research, 64*, 363-423.

Campbell, D. (2005). Globalization: A trendy cosmetic managerial distraction: The basic principles of leadership are universal and timeless. In W. H. Mobley & E. Weldon (Eds.), *Advances in global leadership.* Oxford: Elsevier/JAI Press.

Campbell, D. T., & Stanley, J. C. (1972). *Experimental and quasi-experimental designs for research.* Chicago: Rand McNally.

Campbell, J. P. (1971). Personnel training and development. *Annual Review of Psychology, 22*, 565–602.

Campbell, J. P. (1982, August). I/O psychology and the enhancement of productivity. Paper presented at the meeting of the *American Psychological Association*, Washington, DC.

Campbell, J. P. (1982). Editorial: Some remarks from the outgoing editor. *Journal of Applied Psychology, 67*, 691–700.

Campbell, J. P. (1986). Labs, fields and straw issues. In E. A. Locke (Ed.), *Generalizing from laboratory to field settings* (pp. 269–279). Lexington, MA: Lexington Books.

Campbell, J. P. (1992). Experiments as reforms. In P. Frost & R. Stablein (Eds.), *Doing exemplary research* (pp. 173–176). Newbury Park, CA: Sage.

Campbell, J. P., Dunnette, M. D., Lawler, E. E., & Weick, K. E. (1970). *Managerial behavior, performance, and effectiveness.* New York: McGraw-Hill.

Campbell, J. P., & Pritchard, R. D. (1976). Motivation theory in industrial and organizational psychology. In M. D. Dunnette (Ed.), *Handbook of industrial-organizational psychology* (pp. 63–130). Chicago: Rand McNally.

Campion, M. A. (1996). *Reinventing work: A new era of I/O research and practice.* Presidential address to the annual meeting of The Society of Industrial and Organizational Psychology, San Diego, CA.

Campion, M. A., & Lord, R. G. (1982). A control-systems conceptualization of the goal-setting and changing process. *Organizational Behavior and Human Performance, 30*, 265–287.

Campion, M. A., & Thayer, P. W. (1985). Development and field evaluation of an interdisciplinary measure of job design. *Journal of Applied Psychology, 70*, 29–43.

Cappelli, P., & Scherer, P. D. (1991). The missing role of context in OB. The need for a meso-level approach. *Research in Organizational Behavior, 13,* 55-110.

Carson, K. D., & Carson, P. P. (1993a). The moderating effects of students' negative affectivity on goal-setting. *College Students Journal, 27,* 65–74.

Carstensen, L. L., & Mikels, J. A. (2005). At the intersection of emotion and cognition. Aging and the positivity effect. *Current Directions in Psychological Science, 14,* 117–121.

Carver, C. S., & Scheier, M.F. (1981). *Attention and self-regulation: A control-theory approach to human behavior.* New York: Springer-Verlag.

Carver, C. S., & Scheier, M. F. (1998). *On the self-regulation of behavior.* New York: Cambridge University Press.

Carver, C. S., Sutton, S. K., & Scheier, M. F. (2000). Action, emotion, and personality: Emerging conceptual integration. *Personality and Social Psychology Bulletin, 26,* 741–751.

Cellar, D. F., Degrendel, D., Sidle, S., & Lavine, K. (1996). Effects of goal type on performance, task interest, and affect over time. *Journal of Applied Social Psychology, 26,* 804–824.

Cervone, D., Jiwani, N., & Wood, R. (1991) Goal setting and the differential influence of self regulatory processes on complex decision-making performance. *Journal of Personality and Social Psychology, 61,* 257–266.

Cervone, D., Shadel, W. G., Smith, R. E., & Fiori, M. (in press). Self-regulation: Reminders and suggestions from personality science. *Applied Psychology: An International Review.*

Chacko, T., Stone, T., & Brief, A. P. Participation and feedback in goal setting programs: An attributional analysis. (1979). *Academy of Management Review, 4,* 433–438.

Chang, G.S., & Lorenzi, P. (1983). The effects of participative versus assigned goal setting on intrinsic motivation. *Journal of Management, 9,* 55–64.

Chartrand, T. L., & Bargh, J. A. (2002). Nonconscious motivations: Their activation, operation and consciousness. In A. Tesser, D. A. Stapel & J. V. Woods (Eds.), *Self and motivation* (pp. 13–41). Washington, DC: American Psychological Association.

Chatman, J. A. (1989). Improving interactional organizational research: A model of person-organization fit. *Academy of Management Review, 14,* 333–349.

Chatman, J. A. (1991). Matching people and organizations: Selection and socialization in public accounting firms. *Administrative Science Quarterly, 36,* 459–484.

Chen, G., Gully, S. M., & Eden, D. (2001). Validation of a new general self-efficacy scale. *Organizational Research Methods, 4,* 62–83.

Chen, G., Gully, S. M., & Eden, D. (2004). General self-efficacy and self-esteem: Toward theoretical and empirical distinction between correlated self-evaluations. *Journal of Organizational Behavior, 25,* 375–395.

Chesney, A. A., & Locke, E. A. (1991). Relationships among goal difficulty, business strategies, and performance on a complex management simulation task. *Academy of Management Journal, 34,* 400–424.

Ciske, P. (2004). All labs great and small: A look at the history of psychology laboratories. *Observer, 14,* 11–12.

Cleeton, G. U. (1962). A tribute to pioneering leadership in industrial psychology. In B. V. H. Gilmer, (Ed.), *Walter VanDyke Bingham* (pp. 31–35). Pittsburgh, PA: Carnegie Institute for Technology.

Coch, L., & French, J. R. P. (1948). Overcoming resistance to change. *Human Relations, 1,* 512–532.

Cohen, A., & Lowenberg, G. (1990). A reexamination of the side-bet theory as applied to organizational commitment: A meta-analysis. *Human Relations, 43,* 1015–1050.

Cole, N., & Latham, G. P. (1997). The effects of training in procedural justice on perceptions of disciplinary fairness by unionized employees and disciplinary subject matter experts. *Journal of Applied Psychology, 82,* 699–705.

Colquitt, J. A., Conlon, D. E., Wesson, M. J., Porter, C. O., & Ng, K. Y. (2001). Justice at the millennium: A meta-analysis of 25 years of organizational justice research. *Journal of Applied Psychology, 86,* 425–445.

Colquitt, J. A., & Greenberg, J. (2003). Organizational justice: A fair assessment of the literature. In J. Greenberg (Ed.), *Organizational Behavior: The State of the Science*. Mahwah, NJ: Lawrence Erlbaum.

Colquitt, J. A., LePine, J. A., & Noe, R. A. (2000). Toward an integrative theory of training motivation: A meta-analytic path analysis of 20 years of research. *Journal of Applied Psychology, 85*, 678–707.

Cooper, C. L., & Robertson, I. T. (1986). Editorial foreword. In *International review of industrial and organizational psychology* (pp. ix–xi). Chichester, UK: John Wiley & Sons.

Cooper-Hakim, A., & Viswesvaran, C. (2005). The construct of work commitment: Testing an integrative framework. *Psychological Bulletin, 131*, 241–259.

Cordery, J. L. (1996). Autonomous work groups and quality circles. In M. West (Ed.), *Handbook of work and group psychology* (pp. 225–240). Chichester, UK: John Wiley & Sons.

Cordery, J. L. (1997). Reinventing work design theory and practice. *Australian Psychologist, 32*, 185–189.

Cote, S. & Moskowitz, D. S. (1998). On the dynamic covariation between interpersonal behavior and affect: Prediction from neuroticism, extraversion, and agreeableness. *Journal of Personality and Social Psychology, 75*, 1032–1046.

Coyle-Shapiro, J., & Conway, N. (2005). Exchange relationships: Examining psychological contracts and perceived organizational support. *Journal of Applied Psychology, 90*, 774–781.

Cron, W. L., Slocum, J. W., VandeWalle, D. M., & Fu, Q. (2005). The role of goal orientation on negative emotions on goal setting when initial performance falls short of one's performance goal. *Human Performance. 18*(1), 55–8.

Cronbach, L. J. (1957). The two disciplines of scientific psychology. *American Psychologist, 12*, 671–684.

Cronbach, L.J. (1958). Proposals leading to analytic treatment of social perception scores. In R. Tagiuri & L. Petrullo (Eds.), *Person perception and interpersonal behavior* (pp. 353–379). Stanford, CA: Stanford University Press.

Cronbach, L. J., & Meehl, P. E. (1955). Construct validity in psychological tests. *Psychological Bulletin, 52*, 581–602.

Cropanzano, R., Byrne, Z. S., Bobocel, D. R., & Rupp, D. E. (2001). Moral virtues, fairness heuristics, social entities, and other denizens of organizational justice. *Journal of Vocational Behavior, 58*, 164–209.

Cropanzano, R., & Greenberg, J. (1997). Progress in organizational justice: Tunneling through the maze. In C. L. Cooper & I. T. Roberson (Eds.), *International Review of Industrial and Organizational Psychology* (Vol. 12, pp. 317–372). Chichester, UK: John Wiley & Sons.

Crown, D. F., & Rosse, J. G. (1995). Yours, mine, and ours: Facilitating group productivity through the integration of individual and group goals. *Organizational Behavior and Human Decision Processes, 64*, 138–150.

Cummings, L. L. (1982). Organizational behavior. *Annual Review of Psychology, 33*, 541–579.

Cummings, L. L., & Earley, P. C. (1992). Comments on the Latham/Erez/Locke study. In P. Frost & R. Stablein (Eds.), *Doing exemplary research* (pp. 167–172). Newbury Park, CA: Sage.

Cureton, E. E. (1950). Validity, reliability, and baloney. *Educational and Psychological Measurement, 10*, 94–96.

d'Ailly, H. (2004). The role of choice in children's learning: A distinctive cultural and gender difference in efficacy, interest and effort. *Canadian Journal of Behavioural Science, 36*, 17–29.

Dawis, R. V. (1992). The individual differences tradition in counseling psychology. *Journal of Counseling Psychology, 39*, 7–19.

Dawis, R. V. (1996). Vocational psychology, vocational adjustment, and the workforce. *Psychology, Public Policy and Law, 2*, 229–248.

Dawis, R. V., & Lofquist, L. H. (1984). *A psychological theory of work adjustment*. Minneapolis: University of Minnesota Press.

Day, D. V., & Schleicher, D. J. (2006). Self-monitoring at work: A motive based perspective. *Journal of Personality. Journal of Personality, 74*, 685–714.

Day, D. V., Schleicher, D. J., Unckless, A. L., & Hiller, N. J. (2002). Self-monitoring personality at work: A meta-analytic investigation of construct validity. *Journal of Applied Psychology, 87,* 390–401.

de Waal, F. B. M. (2002). Evolutionary psychology: The wheat and the chaff. *Current Directions in Psychological Science, 11,* 187–191.

Debowski, S., Wood, R. E., & Bandura, A. (2001). Impact of guided exploration on self-regulatory mechanisms and information acquisition through electronic search. *Journal of Applied Psychology, 86,* 1129–1141.

Deci, E. L. (1975). *Intrinsic motivation.* New York: Plenum.

Deci, E. L., & Ryan, R. M. (1985). The general causality orientation scale: Self-determination in personality. *Journal of Research in Personality, 19,* 109–137.

Deci, E. L., & Ryan, R. M. (1990). A motivational approach to self: Integration in personality. In R. Dienstbier (Ed.), *Nebraska symposium on motivation* (Vol. 38, pp. 237–288). Lincoln: University of Nebraska Press.

Dennis, A. R., & Valacich, J. S. (1999). Rethinking media richness: Towards a theory of mean synchronicity. *Proceedings of the 32nd Hawaii International Conference of System Sciences* (pp. 170).

DeShon, R. P., & Landis, R. S. (1997). The dimensionality of the Hollenbeck, Williams, and Klein (1989) measure of goal commitment on complex tasks. *Organizational Behavior and Human Decision Processes, 70,* 105–116.

Deutsch, M. (1973). *The resolution of conflict.* New Haven, CT: Yale University Press.

Dirks, K. T., & McLean Parks, J. (2003). Conflicting stories: The state of the science of conflict. In J. Greenberg (Ed.), *Organizational behavior: The state of the science* (pp. 283–324). Mahwah, NJ: Lawrence Erlbaum.

Doherty, E. M. (1998). Emotional and outcome responses to experiences of negative rewards. *Psychological Reports, 82,* 997–998.

Donovan, J. J., & Radosevich, D. J. (1998). The moderating role of goal commitment on the goal difficulty-performance relationship: A meta-analytic review and critical reanalysis. *Journal of Applied Psychology, 83,* 308–315.

Donovan, J. S., & Williams, K. J. (2003). Minding the mark: Effects of time and causal attributions on goal revision in response to goal performance descriptions. *Journal of Applied Psychology, 88,* 379–390.

Dorner, D. (1991). The investigation of action regulation in uncertain and complex situations. In J. Rasmussen & B. Brehmer (Eds.), *Distributed decision making: Cognitive models for cooperative work* (pp. 349–354). Chichester, UK: John Wiley & Sons.

Dossett, D. L., Cella, A., Greenberg, C. L., & Adrian, N. (1983). Goal setting, participation and leader supportiveness effects on performance. Paper presented at the annual meeting of the American Psychological Association, Anaheim, CA.

Dossett, D. L., Latham, G. P., & Mitchell, T. R. (1979). Effects of assigned vs. participatively set goals, knowledge of results, and individual differences on employee behavior when goal difficulty is held constant. *Journal of Applied Psychology, 64,* 291–298.

Dostoevsky, F. (1911). *The house of the dead.* London: JM Dent.

Drach-Zahavy, A., & Erez, M. (2002). Challenge versus threat effects on the goal-performance relationship. *Organizational Behavior and Human Performance, 88,* 667–682.

Drucker, P. C. (1973). *Management: Tasks, responsibilities and practices.* New York: Harper & Row.

Dulany, D. E. (1968). Awareness, rules and propositional control: A confrontation with S-R behavior theory. In D. Horton & T. Dixon (Eds.), *Verbal behavior and S-R behavior theory* (pp. 340–387). New York: Prentice Hall.

Duncan, J. (1995). Attention, intelligence, and the frontal lobes. In M. Gazzaniga (Ed.), *The cognitive neurosciences* (pp. 721–733). Cambridge, MA: Bradford.

Dunnette, M. D. (1962). Personnel management. *Annual Review of Psychology, 13,* 285–314.

Dunnette, M. D. (1976). Aptitudes, abilities, and skills. In M. D. Dunnette (Ed.), *Handbook of industrial and organizational psychology* (pp. 473–520). New York: John Wiley & Sons.

Dunnette, M. D., & Kirchner, W. R. (1965). *Psychology applied to industry.* Oxford: Appleton-Century Crofts.

Durham, C. C., Knight, D., & Locke, E. A. (1997). Effects of leader role, team-set goal difficulty, efficacy, and tactics on team effectiveness. *Organizational Behavior and Human Decision Processes, 72,* 203–231.

Dweck, C. S. (1986). Motivational processes affecting learning. *American Psychologist, 41,* 1040–1048.

Dweck, C. S. (1999). Self-theories: Their role in motivation, personality, and development. In *Essays in social psychology* (p. 195). Philadelphia, PA: Psychology Press.

Dyer, L., & Parker, D. F. (1975). Classifying outcomes in work motivation research: An examination of the intrinsic-extrinsic dichotomy. *Journal of Applied Psychology, 60,* 455–458.

Eagly, A. H. (1992). Uneven progress: Social psychology and the study of attitudes. *Journal of Personality and Social Psychology, 63,* 693–710.

Eagly, A. H., & Johnson, B. T. (1990). Gender and leadership style: A meta-analysis. *Psychological Bulletin, 108,* 233–256.

Earley, P. C. (2002). Redefining interactions across cultures and organizations: Moving forward with cultural intelligence. In B. M. Staw & R. M. Kramer (Eds.), *Research in organizational behavior: An annual series of analytical essays and critical reviews* (pp. 271–299). Philadelphia, PA: Elsevier.

Earley, P. C., & Kanfer, R. (1985). The influence of component participation and role models on goal acceptance, goal satisfaction, and performance. *Organizational Behavior and Human Decision Processes, 36,* 378–390.

Earley, P. C., Lee, C., & Hanson, L. A. (1990). Joint moderating effects of job experience and task component complexity: Relations among goal setting, task strategies, and performance. *Journal of Organizational Behavior, 11,* 3–15.

Earley, P. C., & Lituchy, T. R. (1991). Delineating goal and efficacy effects: A test of three models. *Journal of Applied Psychology, 76,* 81–98.

Eby, L. T., Freeman, D. M., Rush, M. C., & Lance, C. E. (1999). Motivational bases of affective organizational commitment: A partial test of an integrative theoretical model. *Journal of Occupational and Organizational Psychology, 72,* 463–483.

Eccles, J. S., & Wigfield, A. (2002). Motivational beliefs, values, and goals. *Annual Review of Psychology, 53,* 109–132.

Eden, D. (1990). *Pygmalion in management: Productivity as a self fulfilling prophecy.* Lexington, MA: Lexington Books.

Eden, D. (2001). Means efficacy: External sources of general and specific efficacy. In M. Erez & U. Kleinbeck (Eds.), *Work motivation in the context of a globalizing economy* (pp. 73–85). Mahwah, NJ: Lawrence Erlbaum.

Eden, D. (2003). Self-fulfilling prophecies in organizations. In J. Greenberg (Ed.), *Organizational behavior: The state of the science* (pp. 91–124). Mahwah, NJ: Lawrence Erlbaum.

Eden, D., & Sulimani, R. (2002). Pygmalion training made effective: Greater mastery through augmentation of self-efficacy and means efficacy. In B. J. Avolio & F. J. Yammarino (Eds.), *Transformational and charismatic leadership: The road ahead* (pp. 287–308). Oxford, UK: Elsevier.

Edminster, R. O., & Locke, E. A. (1987). The effects of differential goal weights on the performance of a complex financial task. *Personnel Psychology, 40,* 505–517.

Edwards, J. R. (1993). Problems with the use of profile similarity indices in the study of congruence in organizational research. *Personnel Psychology, 46,* 641–665.

Edwards, J. R., & Rothbard, N. P. (1999). Work and family stress and well-being: An examination of person-environment fit in the work and family domains. *Organizational Behavior and Human Decision Processes, 77,* 85–129.

Edwards, J. R., Scully, J. A., & Brtek, M. D. (1999). The measurement of work: Hierarchical representation of the Multimethod Job Design Questionnaire. *Personnel Psychology, 52,* 305–334.

Edwards, J. R., Scully, J. A., & Brtek, M. D. (2000). The nature and outcomes of work: A replication and extension of interdisciplinary work-design research. *Journal of Applied Psychology, 85,* 860–868.

Egeth, H. (1967). Selective attention. *Psychological Bulletin, 67,* 41–57.

Eisenberg, N., Fabes, R. A., Guthrie, I. K., & Reiser, M. (2000). Dispositional emotionality and regulation: Their role in predicting quality of social functioning. *Journal of Personality and Social Psychology, 78,* 136–157.

Eisenberger, R., & Cameron, J. (1996). Detrimental effects of reward: Reality or myth. *American Psychologist, 51,* 1153–1166.

Ellemers, N., deGilder, D., & Haslam, S. A. (2004). Motivating individuals and groups at work: A social identity perspective on leadership and group performance. *Academy of Management Review, 29,* 459–478.

Elliot, A. J., & Harackiewicz, J. M. (1996). Approach and avoidance achievement goals and intrinsic motivation: A mediational analysis. *Journal of Personality and Social Psychology, 70,* 461–475.

Elliott, E. S., & Dweck, C. S. (1986). Goals: An approach to motivation and achievement. *Journal of Personality and Social Psychology, 54,* 5–12.

Ellis, A. (1999). Early theories and practices of rational emotive behavior therapy and how they have been augmented and revised during the last three decades. *Journal of Rational-Emotive & Cognitive Behavior Therapy, 17,* 69–93.

Emery, F. E., & Trist, E. L. (1965). The causal texture of organizational environments. *Human Relations, 18,* 21–32.

Endler, N. S., & Magnusson, D. (Eds.), (1976). *Interactional psychology and personality.* New York: Hemisphere.

Erez, A., & Judge, T. A. (2001). Relationship of core self-evaluations to goal setting, motivation and performance. *Journal of Applied Psychology, 86,* 1270–1279.

Erez, M. (1977). Feedback: A necessary condition for the goal setting-performance relationship. *Journal of Applied Psychology, 62,* 624–627.

Erez, M. (1986). The congruence of goal-setting strategies with socio-cultural values and its effect on performance. *Journal of Management, 12,* 585–592.

Erez, M. (1992). Reflections on the Latham/Erez/Locke study. In P. Frost & R. Stablein (Eds.), *Doing exemplary research* (pp. 155–166). Newbury Park, CA: Sage.

Erez, M. (1997). A culture-based model of work motivation. In C. P. Earley, & M. Erez (Eds.), *New perspectives on international industrial/organizational psychology* (pp. 193–242). San Francisco, CA: Jossey-Bass.

Erez, M. (2000). Make management practice fit the national culture. In E. A. Locke (Ed.), *Handbook of principles of organizational behavior* (pp. 418–434). Oxford, UK: Blackwell.

Erez, M., & Earley, P. C. (1993). *Culture, self-identity, and work.* New York: Oxford University Press.

Erez, M., Earley, P. C., and Hulin, C. (1985). The impact of participation upon goal acceptance and performance: A two-step model. *Academy of Management Journal, 28,* 50–66.

Erez, M., & Kanfer, F. H. (1983). The role of goal congruence in goal setting and task performance. *Academy of Management Review, 8,* 454–463.

Erez, M., Kleinbeck, U., & Thierry, H. (Eds.) (2001). *Work motivation in the context of a globalizing economy.* Hillsdale, NJ: Lawrence Erlbaum.

Ericksen, C. W. (1960). Discrimination and learning without awareness: A methodological survey and evaluation. *Psychological Review, 67,* 279–300.

Farh, J., Griffeth, R. W., & Balkin, D. B. (1991). Effects of choice of pay plans on satisfaction, goal setting, and performance. *Journal of Organizational Behavior, 12,* 55–62.

Farkas, A. J., & Tetrick, L. E. (1989). A three-wave longitudinal analysis of the causal ordering of satisfaction and commitment on turnover decisions. *Journal of Applied Psychology, 74,* 855–868.

Farr, J. L., Hoffman, D. A., & Ringenbach, K. L. (1993). Goal orientation and action control theory: Implications for industrial and organizational psychology. *International Review of Industrial and Organizational Psychology, 8,* 193–232.

Faucheux, C., Amado, G., & Laurent, A. (1982). Organizational development and change. *Annual Review of Psychology, 33,* 343–370.

Fay, D., & Frese, M. (2000). Self-starting behavior at work: Toward a theory of personal initiative. In J. Heckhausen (Ed.), *Motivational psychology of human development* (pp. 307–324). Amsterdam, The Netherlands: Elsevier.

Fay, D., & Frese, M. (2001). The concept of personal initiative: An overview of validity studies. *Human Performance, 14*, 97–124.

Feeney, E. J. (1973). *Behavioral engineering systems training.* Redding, CT: Edward J. Feeney & Associates.

Feingold, A. (1994). Gender differences in personality. *Psychological Bulletin, 116*, 429–456.

Ferguson, L. W. (1962). Industrial psychology and labor. In B. V. H. Gilmer (Ed.), *Walter VanDyke Bingham* (pp. 7–22). Pittsburgh, PA: Carnegie Institute of Technology.

Ferster, C. B., & Skinner, B. F. (1957). *Schedules of reinforcement.* East Norwalk, CT: Appleton Century Crofts.

Festinger, L. (1957). *A theory of cognitive dissonance.* Evanston, IL: Row Peterson.

Fisher, V. E., & Hanna, J. V. (1931). *The dissatisfied worker.* New York: McMillan.

Flanagan, J. C. (1954). The critical incident technique. *Psychological Bulletin, 51*, 327–358.

Flood, P. C., Turner, T., Ramamoorthy, N., & Pearson, J. (2001). Causes and consequences of psychological contracts among knowledge workers in the high technology and financial services industries. *International Journal of Human Resource Management, 12*, 1152–1165.

Folger, R., & Cropanzano, R. (1998). *Organizational justice and human resource management.* Thousand Oaks, CA: Sage.

Ford, J. K., Smith, E. M., Weissbein, D. A., Gully, S. M., & Salas, E. (1998). Relationships of goal orientation, metacognitive activity, and practice strategies with learning outcomes and transfer. *Journal of Applied Psychology, 83*, 218–233.

Ford, M. E. (1992). *Motivating humans.* Newbury Park, CA: Sage.

Forgas, J. P., & George, J. M. (2001). Affective influences on judgments and behavior in organizations: An information processing perspective. *Organizational Behavior and Human Decision Processes, 86*, 3–34.

Franco, L. M., Bennett, S., & Kanfer, R. (2002). Health sector reform and public sector health work motivation: A conceptual framework. *Social Science and Medicine, 54*, 1255–1266.

Frank, J. (1983). *Dostoevsky: The years of ordeal.* Princeton, NJ: Princeton University Press.

Franke, R. H., & Kaul, J. D. (1978). The Hawthorne experiments: First statistical interpretation. *American Sociological Review, 43*, 623–643.

Frayne, C. A., & Geringer, J. M. (2000). Self-management training for improving job performance: A field experiment involving salespeople. *Journal of Applied Psychology, 85*, 361–372.

Frayne, C. A., & Latham, G. P. (1987). The application of social learning theory to employee self-management of attendance. *Journal of Applied Psychology, 72*, 387–392.

Frederiksen, L. W. (1982). *Organizational behavior management.* New York: Wiley.

French, J. R. P., Jr., Caplan, R. D., & Harrison, R. V. (1982). *The mechanisms of job stress and strain.* London: Wiley.

French, J.R.P., Jr., Rodgers, W.L., & Cobb, S. (1974). Adjustment as person-environment fit. In G. Coelho, D. Hamburg, & J. Adams (Eds.), *Coping and adaptation* (pp. 316–333). New York: Basic Books.

Frese, M. (2000). *Success and failure of micro business owners in Africa: A psychological approach.* Westport, CT: Quorum Books.

Frese, M. (2005). Grand theories and midrange theories. Cultural effects on theorizing and the attempt to understand active approaches to work. In K. G. Smith and M. Hitt (Eds.), *The Oxford handbook of management theory: The process of theory development.* New York: Oxford University Press.

Frese, M., & Fay, D. (2001). Personal Initiative (PI): The theoretical concept and empirical findings. In B. M. Staw & R. M. Sutton (Eds.), *Research in organizational behavior* (Vol. 23, pp. 133–187). Amsterdam, The Netherlands: Elsevier Science.

Frese, M., Garst, H., & Fay, D. (2000). Control and complexity in work and the development of personal initiative (PI): A four-wave longitudinal structural equation model of occupational socialization. Giessen, Germany: University of Giessen.

Frese, M., Kring, W., Soose, A., & Zempel, J. (1996). Personal initiative at work: Differences between East and West Germany. *Academy of Management Journal, 39*, 37–63.

Frese, M., & Zapf, D. (1994). Action as the core of work psychology: A German approach. In H. C. Triandis, M. D. Dunnette & L. Hough (Eds.), *Handbook of industrial and organizational psychology* (Vol. 4, pp. 271–340). Palo Alto, CA: Consulting Psychologists Press.

Freud, S. (1913). *The interpretation of dreams.* (A. A. Brill, Trans.). New York: Macmillan. (Original work published 1900).

Fried, Y., & Ferris, G. R. (1987). The validity of job characteristics model: A review and meta-analysis. *Personnel Psychology, 40*, 287–332.

Fried, Y., & Slowik, L. H. (2004). Enriching goal setting theory with time: An integrated approach. *Academy of Management Review, 29*, 404–422.

Frinke, D. D., & Klimoski, R. J. (1998). Toward a theory of accountability in organization and human resources management. *Research in Personnel and Human Resources Management, 16*, 1–51.

Fulmer, I. S., Gerhart, B., & Scott, K. S. (2003). Are the 100 best better? An empirical investigation of the relationship between being a "great place to work" and firm performance. *Personnel Psychology, 56*, 965–993

Furnham, A., Forde, L., & Ferrari, K. (1999). Personality and work motivation. *Personality and Individual Differences, 26*, 1035–1043.

Gall, T. L., Charbonneau, C., Clarke, N. H., Grant, K., Joseph, A., & Shouldice, L. (2005). Understanding the nature and role of spirituality in relation to coping and health: A conceptual framework. *Canadian Psychology, 46*, 88–104.

Garland, H. (1984). Relation of effort-performance expectancy to performance in goal setting experiments. *Journal of Applied Psychology, 69*, 79–84.

Gauggel, S. (1999). *Goal setting and its influence on the performance of brain-damaged patients.* Unpublished doctoral dissertation, Philipps University of Marburg, Germany.

Geary, D. C. (1998). *Male, female.* Washington, DC: American Psychological Association.

Gellatly, I. R., & Meyer, J. P. (1992). The effects of goal difficulty on physiological arousal, cognition, and task performance. *Journal of Applied Psychology, 77*, 694–704.

George, J. M. (2000). Emotions and leadership: The role of emotional intelligence. *Human Relations, 53*, 1027–1055.

Ghiselli, E. E. (1966). The validity of the personnel interview. *Personnel Psychology, 19*, 389–394.

Ghiselli, E. E., & Brown, C. W. (1948). *Personnel and industrial psychology.* New York: McGraw Hill.

Gilbreth, F. B. (1914). *Motion study, a method for increasing the efficiency of the workman.* London: Constable and Robinson.

Gilbreth, F. B. (1920). *Fatigue study: The elimination of humanity's greatest unnecessary waste. A first step in motion study.* London: Rutledge.

Gilbreth, F .B., & Gilbreth, L. M. (1923). Scale cage in motion study for finding the factor of the one best way to do work. *Journal of Personnel Research, 2*, 65–69.

Gilliland, S. W., Benson, L., & Schepers, D. H. (1998). A rejection threshold in justice evaluation: Effects in judgment and decision-making. *Organizational Behavior and Human Decision Processes, 76*, 113–131.

Gilliland, S. W., & Chan, D. (2001). Justice in organizations. In N. Anderson, D. Ones, H. Sinangil & C. Viswesvaran (Eds.), *Handbook of industrial, work and organizational psychology* (Vol. 2, pp. 143–165). London: Sage.

Gilmer, B. V. H. (1962). Introduction. In B. V. H. Gilmer (Ed.), *Walter VanDyke Bingham* (pp. vii–viii). Pittsburgh, PA: Carnegie Institute of Technology.

Gist, M. E., & Mitchell, T. R. (1992). Self-efficacy: A theoretical analysis of its determinants and malleability. *Academy of Management Review, 17*, 183–211.

Glomb, T. M., & Welsh, E. T. (2005). Can opposites attract? Personality heterogeneity in supervi-
sor-subordinate dyads as a predictor of subordinate outcomes. *Journal of Applied Psychology,*
90, 749–757.

Godat, L. M., & Brigham, T. A. (1999). The effect of self-management training on employees of a
mid-sized organization. *Journal of Organizational Behavior Management, 19,* 65–83.

Gollwitzer, P. M. (1999). Implementation intentions and effective goal pursuit: Strong effects of
simple plans. *American Psychologist, 54,* 493–503.

Gollwitzer, P. M., & Bayer, U. (1999). Deliberative versus implemental mindsets in the control
of action. In S. Chaiken & Y. Trope (Eds.), *Dual-process theories in social psychology*
(pp. 403–422). New York: Guilford Press.

Goodman, J. S., Wood, R. E., & Hendrickx, M. (2004). Feedback specificity, exploration, and learning. *Journal of Applied Psychology, 89,* 248–262.

Grandey, A. A. (2003). When "the show must go on": Surface acting and deep acting as determinants of emotional exhaustion and peer-rated service delivery. *Academy of Management*
Journal, 46, 86–96.

Grant, H., & Dweck, C. S. (2003). Clarifying achievement goals and their impact. *Journal of*
Personality and Social Psychology, 85, 541–553.

Gray, J. A. (1994). Personality dimensions and emotion systems. In P. Ekman & R. J. Davidson (Eds.),
The nature of emotion: Fundamental questions (pp. 329–331). New York: Oxford University Press.

Greenberg, J. (1987). A taxonomy of organizational justice theories. *Academy of Management*
Review, 12, 9–22.

Greenberg, J. (1990a). Looking fair vs. being fair: Managing impressions of organizational justice.
In B. M. Staw & L. L. Cummings (Eds.), *Research in organizational behavior* (Vol. 12,
pp. 111–158). Greenwich: JAI Press.

Greenberg, J. (1990b). Employee theft as a reaction to underpayment inequity: The hidden costs
of pay cuts. *Journal of Applied Psychology, 72,* 55–61.

Greenberg, J. (1993). The social side of fairness. Interpersonal and informational classes of organizational justice. In R. Cropanzano (Ed.), *Justice in the workplace: Approaching fairness in*
human resources management (pp. 79–103). Hillsdale, NJ: Lawrence Erlbaum.

Greenberg, J. (1994). Using socially fair treatment to promote acceptance of a work site smoking
ban. *Journal of Applied Psychology, 79,* 288–297.

Greenberg, J. (1999). *Managing behavior in organizations* (2nd ed). Upper Saddle River, NJ:
Prentice Hall.

Greenberg, J. (2000). Promote procedural justice to enhance the acceptance of work outcomes.
In E. A. Locke (Ed.), *A handbook of principles of organizational behavior.* Oxford, UK:
Blackwell.

Greenberg, J., Bies, R. J., & Eskew, D. E. (1991). Establishing fairness in the eye of the beholder:
Managing impressions of organizational justice. In R. A. Giacalone & P. Rosenfeld
(Eds.), *Applied impression management: How image-making affects managerial decisions*
(pp. 111–132). Thousand Oaks, CA: Sage.

Greenberg, J., & Folger, R. (1983). Procedural justice, participation and the fairness process effect
in groups and organizations. In P. B. Paulus (Ed.), *Basic group processes* (pp. 236–256). New
York: Springer-Verlag.

Guest, D., Michie, J., Conway, N., & Sheehan, M. (2003). Human resource management and
corporate performance in the UK. *British Journal of Industrial Relations, 41,* 291–314.

Guion, R. M. (1958). Industrial morale: The problem of terminology. *Personnel Psychology, 11,* 59–64.

Guion, R. M. (1983). Editorial: Comments from the new editor. *Journal of Applied Psychology, 68,*
547–551.

Guion, R. M., & Gottier, R. F. (1965). Validity of personality measures in personnel selection.
Personnel Psychology, 18, 49–65.

Gustafson, S. B., & Mumford, M. D. (1995). Personal style and person environment fit: A pattern
approach. *Journal of Vocational Behavior, 46,* 163-188.

Guzzo, R. A., Yost, P. R., Campbell, R. J., & Shea, G. P. (1993). Potency in groups: Articulating a construct. *British Journal of Social Psychology, 32,* 987–106.

Hackman, J. R., & Lawler, E. E. (1971). Employee reactions to job characteristics. *Journal of Applied Psychology, 55,* 259–286.

Hackman, J. R., & Oldman, G. R. (1975). Development of the job diagnostic survey. *Journal of Applied Psychology, 60,* 159–170.

Hackman, J. R., & Oldman, G. R. (1976). Motivation through the design of work: Test of a theory. *Organizational Behavior and Human Performance, 16,* 250–279.

Hackman, J. R., & Oldham, G. R. (1980). *Work redesign.* Reading, MA: Addison-Wesley.

Haire, M. (1960). Business is too important to be studied only by economists. *American Psychologist, 15,* 271–272.

Hall, D. T., & Nougaim, K. E. (1968). An examination of Maslow's need hierarchy in an organizational setting. *Organizational Behavior & Human Performance, 3,* 12–35.

Harlos, K. P., & Pinder, C. C. (2000). Emotion and injustice in the workplace. In S. Fineman (Ed.), *Emotion in organizations* (2nd ed., pp. 255–276). Thousand Oaks, CA: Sage.

Harrell, T. W. (1949). *Industrial Psychology.* Oxford, UK: Rinehart.

Haslam, S. A., Powell, C., & Turner, J. C. (2000). Social identity, self-categorization, and work motivation: Rethinking the contribution of the group to positive and sustainable organizational outcomes. *Applied Psychology: An International Review, 49,* 319–339.

Hawkley, L. C., Bernston, G. G., Engeland, C. G., Marucha, P. T., Maji, C. M., & Cacioppo, J. T. (2005). Stress, ageing and resilience: Can accrued wear and tear be slowed? *Canadian Psychology, 46,* 115–125.

Hebb, D. O. (1949). *The organization of behavior: A neuropsychological theory.* Oxford: Wiley.

Hebb, D. O. (1969). Hebb on hocus-pocus: A conversation with Elizabeth Hall. *Psychology Today, 6,* 20–21.

Heckhausen, J., & Schulz, R. (1999). The primacy of primary control is a human universal: A reply to Gould's (1999) critique of the life-span theory of control. *Psychological Review, 106,* 605–609.

Heggestad, E. D., & Kanfer, R. (2001). Individual differences in trait motivation: Development of the Motivational Trait Questionnaire (MTQ). *International Journal of Educational Research, 33,* 751–776.

Heimbeck, D., Frese, M., Sonnentag, S., & Keith, N. (2003). Integrating errors in the training process: The function of error management instructions and the role of goal orientation. *Personnel Psychology, 56,* 333–361.

Heine, S. J., Kitayama, S., Lehaman, D. R., Takata, T., Ide, E., Leung, C., & Mtsumoto, H. (2001). Divergent consequences of success and failure in Japan and North America: An investigation of self-improving motivators and malleable selves. *Journal of Personality and Social Psychology, 81,* 599–615.

Heneman, H. G., & Schwab, D. P. (1972). Evaluation of research on expectancy theory predictions of employee performance. *Psychological Bulletin, 78,* 1–9.

Heron, A. (1954). Industrial psychology. *Annual Review of Psychology, 5,* 203–228.

Herzberg, F. (1966). *Work and the nature of man.* New York: The Word Publishing Company.

Herzberg, F. (1968). One more time: How do you motivate employees? *Harvard Business Review, 46,* 53–62.

Herzberg, F., Mausner, B., & Snyderman, B. B. (1959). *The motivation to work.* New York: Wiley.

Heslin, P., & Latham, G. P. (2004). The effect of upward feedback on managerial behavior. *Applied Psychology: An International Review, 53,* 23–37.

Higgins, E. T. (2000). Making a good decision: Value from fit. *American Psychologist, 13,* 141–154.

Hinrichs, J. R. (1970). Psychology of men at work. *Annual Review of Psychology, 21,* 519–554.

Hinsz, V. B. (1991). Individual versus group goal decision making: Social comparison in goals for individual task performance. *Journal of Applied Social Psychology, 22,* 1296–1317.

Hinsz, V. B. (1995). Goal setting by groups performing an additive task: A comparison with individual goal setting. *Journal of Applied Social Psychology, 25,* 965–990.

Hinsz, V. B., & Matz, D. C. (1997). Self-evaluations involved in goal setting and task performance. *Social Behavior and Personality, 25,* 177–182.

Hinsz, V. B., & Ployhart, R. E. (1998). Trying, intentions, and the processes by which goals influence performance: An empirical test of the theory of goal pursuit. *Journal of Applied Social Psychology, 28,* 1051–1066.

Hofstede, G. (1979). Value systems in forty countries: Interpretation, validation, and consequences for theory. In L. H. Eckensberger, W. J. Lonner & Y. H. Poortinga (Eds.), *Cross-cultural contributions to psychology* (pp. 398–407). Lisse, The Netherlands: Swets & Zeitlinger.

Hofstede, G. (1980). *Culture's consequences: International differences in work-related values.* Beverly Hills, CA: Sage.

Hofstede, G. (1984). The cultural relativity of the quality of life concept. *Academy of Management Review, 9,* 389–398.

Hofstede, G. (2001). *Culture's consequences.* Thousand Oaks, CA: Sage.

Hogan, J., & Holland, B. (2003). Using theory to evaluate personality and job-performance relations: A socioanalytic perspective. *Journal of Applied Psychology, 88,* 100–112.

Hogan, R. (2004). Personality psychology for organizational research. In B. Schneider & D. Brent Smith (Eds.), *Personality and organizations,* (pp. 3–24). Mahwah, NJ: Lawrence Erlbaum.

Hogan, R., & Shelton, D. (1998). A socioanalytic perspective of job performance. *Human Performance, 11,* 129–144.

Hogan, R.,. & Warremfeltz, R. (2003). Educating the modern manager. *Academy of Management Journal, 2,* 74–84.

Holland, J. L. (1973). *Making vocational choices.* Englewood Cliff, NJ: Prentice Hall.

Hollenbeck, J. R., Klein, H. J., O'Leary-Kelly, A. M., & Wright, P. M. (1989). Investigation of the construct validity of a self-report measure of goal commitment. *Journal of Applied Psychology, 74,* 951–956.

Hollenbeck, J. R., Moon, H., Ellis, A. P. J., West, B. J., Ilgen, D. R., Sheppard, L., Porter, C. O., & Wagner, J. A., III. (2002). Structural contingency theory and individual differences: Examination of external and internal person-team fit. *Journal of Applied Psychology, 87,* 599–606.

Homans, G. C. (1941/1977). The Western Electric researches. In M. T. Matteson & J. M. Ivancevich (Eds.), *Management classics.* Santa Monica: Goodyear.

Hoppock, R. (1935). *Job satisfaction.* New York: Harper.

Hothersall, D. (1984). *A history of psychology.* Philadelphia: Temple University Press.

Hough, L. M., & Schneider, R. J. (1996). Personality traits, taxonomies, and applications in organizations. In K. R. Murphy (Ed.), *Individual differences and behavior in organizations* (pp. 31–99). San Francisco: Jossey-Bass.

Houkes, I., Janssen, P. P. M., de Jonge, J., & Nijhuis, F. J. N. (2001). Specific relationships between work characteristics and intrinsic work motivation, burnout and turnover intention: A multi-sample analysis. *European Journal of Work and Organization, 10,* 1–23.

House, R. J., Shapiro, H. J., & Wahba, M. A. (1974). Expectancy theory as a predictor of work behavior and attitude: A reevaluation of empirical evidence. *Decision Sciences, 5,* 481–506.

Houser, J. D. (1938). Measurement of the vital products of business. *Journal of Marketing, 2,* 181–189.

Howard, A. (2005). Subconscious and conscious motives in long-term managerial success. In G. P. Latham (Chair), *Into the lion's den: The effects of subconscious trait and state motivation on performance.* Symposium at the annual meeting of the Society for Industrial and Organizational Psychology, Los Angeles.

Howard, A. & Bray, D. W. (1988). Managerial lives in transition: Advancing age and changing times. *Adult development and aging.* New York: Guilford Press.

Hulin, C. L., & Ilgen, D. R. (2000). Introduction to computational modeling in organizations: The good that modeling does. In D. R. Ilgen & C. L. Hulin (Eds.), *Computational modeling of behavior in organizations: The third scientific discipline* (pp. 3–18). Washington, DC: American Psychological Association.

Hulin, C. L., & Judge, T. A. (2003). Job attitudes. In W. C. Borman, D. R. Ilgen, & R. J. Klimoski (Eds.), *Handbook of psychology* (pp. 255–276). New York: John Wiley.

Hull, C. L. (1928). *Aptitude testing.* New York: World.

Hull, C. L. (1943). *Principles of behavior.* New York: Appleton-Century-Crofts.

Huselid, M. A., & Becker, B. E. (1996). Methodological issues in cross-sectional and panel estimates of the human resource-firm performance link. *Industrial Relations, 35,* 400–422.

Ilgen, D. R., & Hulin, C. L. (2000). Lessons learned and insights gained. In D. R. Ilgen & C. L. Hulin (Ed.), *Computational modeling of behavior in organizations: The third scientific discipline* (pp. 275–289). Washington, DC: American Psychological Association.

Ilgen, D. R., & Sheppard, L. (2001). Motivation in work teams. In M. Erez, U. Kleinbeck & H. Thierry (Eds.), *Work motivation in the context of a globalizing economy* (pp.169–179). Mahwah, NJ: Lawrence Erlbaum.

Ilies, R., & Judge, T. A. (2005). Goal regulation across time: The effects of feedback and affect. *Journal of Applied Psychology, 90,* 453–467.

Inness, M., Barling, J., & Turner, N. (2005). Understanding supervisor-targeted aggression: A within-person, between-jobs design. *Journal of Applied Psychology, 90,* 731–739.

Ivancevich, J. M. (1976). Effects of goal setting on performance and job satisfaction. *Journal of Applied Psychology, 61,* 605–612.

Ivancevich, J. M. (1977). Different goal setting treatments and their effects on performance and job satisfaction. *Academy of Management Journal, 20,* 406–419.

James, K. (1993). The social context of organizational justice: Cultural, intergroup, and structural effects on justice behaviors and perceptions. In R. Cropanzano (Ed.), *Justice in the workplace: Approaching fairness in human resource management* (pp. 21–50). Hillsdale, NJ: Lawrence Erlbaum.

James, L. R., & Mazerolle, M. (2002). *Personality at work.* Thousand Oaks, CA: Sage.

James, W. (1890). *The principles of psychology.* New York: H. Holt.

James, W. (1892). *Psychology.* New York: H. Holt.

Jensen, M. C. (2001). Corporate budgeting is broken—let's fix it. *Harvard Business Review, 79,* 94–101.

Johns, G. (2006, April). The essential impact of context on organizational behavior. *Academy of Management Review, 31,* 386–408.

Johnson, R. E., Rosen, C. C., & Levy, P. E. (2006, May). *Getting to the core of self-evaluations: A critical review.* Paper presented at the 21st Annual meeting of the Society for Industrial and Organizational Psychology, Dallas.

Jones, D. A., & Skarlicki, D. P. (2005). The effects of overhearing peers discuss an authority's reputation for fairness on reactions to subsequent treatment. *Journal of Applied Psychology, 90,* 363–372.

Jones, G., & Cale, A. (1997). Goal difficulty, anxiety and performance. *Ergonomics, 40,* 319–333.

Jones, J. M., & Pettigrew, T. F. (2005). Kenneth B. Clark (1914–2005). *American Psychologist, 60,* 649–65.

Judge, T. A., & Bono, J. E. (2001). Relationship of core self-evaluations traits—self-esteem, generalized self-efficacy, locus of control, and emotional stability—with job satisfaction and job performance: A meta-analysis. *Journal of Applied Psychology, 86,* 80–92.

Judge, T. A., & Colquitt, J. A. (2004). Organizational justice and stress: The mediating role of work family conflict. *Journal of Applied Psychology, 89,* 395–404.

Judge, T. A., Erez, A., Bono, J. E., & Thoresen, C. J. (2003). The core self-evaluations scale: Development of a measure. *Personnel Psychology, 56*(2), 303–331.

Judge, T. A., Locke, E. A., & Durham, C. C. (1997). The dispositional causes of job satisfaction: A core self-evaluation approach. *Research in Organizational Behavior, 19,* 151–188.

Judge, T. A., Locke, E. A., Durham, C. C., & Kluger, A. N. (1998). Dispositional effects on job and life satisfaction: The role of core evaluations. *Journal of Applied Psychology, 83,* 17–31.

Judge, T. A., Thoresen, C. J., Bono, J. E., & Patton, G. K. (2001). The job satisfaction-job performance relationship: A qualitative and quantitative review. *Psychological Bulletin, 127,* 376–407.

Kahneman, D. (2003). Experiences of collaborative research. *American Psychologist, 58,* 723–730.

Kamalanabhan, T. J., Uma, J., & Vasanthi, M. (1999). A dephi study of motivational profile of scientists in research and development organizations. *Psychological Reports, 85,* 743–749.

Kanfer, F. H. (1980). Self management methods. In F. H. Kanfer & A. P. Goldstein (Eds.), *Helping people change: A textbook of methods* (2nd ed., pp. 334–389). New York: Pergamon.

Kanfer, R. (1990). Motivation theory and industrial and organizational psychology. In M. D. Dunnette (Ed.), *Handbook of industrial and organizational psychology* (pp. 75–170). Palo Alto, CA: Consulting Psychologists Press.

Kanfer, R. (2005). Self regulation in work and I/O psychology. *Applied Psychology: An International Review, 54,* 186–191.

Kanfer, R., & Ackerman, P. L. (1989). Motivation and cognitive abilities: An integrative/aptitude-treatment interaction approach to skill acquisition. *Journal of Applied Psychology, 74,* 657–690.

Kanfer, R., & Ackerman, P. L. (2000). Individual differences in work motivation: Further explorations of a trait framework. *Applied Psychology: An International Review, 49,* 470–482.

Kanfer, R., & Ackerman, P. L. (2004). Ageing, adult development, and work motivation. *Academy of Management Review, 29,* 440–458.

Kanfer, R., Ackerman, P. L., Murtha, T. C., Dugdale, B., & Nelson, L. (1994). Goal setting, conditions of practice, and task performance: A resource allocation perspective. *Journal of Applied Psychology, 79,* 826–835.

Kanfer, R., & Heggestad, E. D. (1997). Motivational traits and skills: A person-centered approach to work motivation. *Research in Organizational Behavior, 19,* 1–56.

Kanfer, R., & Heggestad, E. D. (1999). Individual differences in motivation: Traits and self-regulatory skills. In P. Ackerman & P. C. Roberts (Eds.)., *Learning and individual differences: Process, trait, and content determinants* (pp. 293–313). Washington, DC: American Psychological Association.

Kanfer, R., & Kantrowitz, T. M. (2002). Emotion regulation: Command and control of emotion in work life. In R. G. Lord, R. J. Klimoski & R. Kanfer (Eds.), *Emotions in the workplace: Understanding the structure and role of emotions in organizational behavior* (pp. 433–472). San Francisco, CA: Jossey-Bass.

Kanfer, R., Wanberg, C. R., & Kantrowitz, T. M. (2001). Job search and employment: A personality-motivational analysis and meta-analytic review. *Journal of Applied Psychology, 86,* 837–855.

Kaplan, A. (1964). *The conduct of inquiry: Methodology for behavioral science.* Scranton, PA: Chandler.

Kaplan, E., Erez, M., & Van-Dijk, D. (2004, April). Reconciling potential differences between the goal setting and the self regulation theories. In M. Erez (Chair), *Goal setting, goal orientation, and self-regulation focus—An integration.* Symposium presented at the 19th annual meeting of the Society for Industrial and Organizational Psychology, Chicago, IL.

Karoly, P. (1993). Mechanisms of self-regulation: A systems view. *Annual Review of Psychology, 44,* 23–52.

Katzell, R. A., & Austin, J. T. (1992). From then to now: The development of industrial-organizational psychology in the United States. *Journal of Applied Psychology, 77,* 803–835.

Kaufman, A., Baron, A., & Kopp, R. E. (1966). Some effects of instructions on human operant behavior. *Psychonomic Monograph Supplements, 1,* 243–250.

Kehr, H. M. (2004). Integrating implicit motives, explicit motives, and perceived abilities: The compensatory model of work motivation and volition. *Academy of Management Review, 29,* 479–499.

Keith, N., & Frese, M. (2005). Self-regulation in error management training: Emotion control and metacognition as mediators of performance effects. *Journal of Applied Psychology, 90,* 677–691.

Kelloway, E. K., & Day, A. L. (2005). Building healthy workplaces: What we know so far. *Canadian Journal of Behavioural Science, 37,* 223–235.

Kelloway, E. K., Francis, L., & Montgomery, J. (2005). *Management of occupational health and safety.* Toronto, ON: Thomson Nelson.

Kernan, M. C., & Hanges, P. J. (2002). Survivor reactions to reorganization: Antecedents and consequences of procedural, interpersonal, and informational justice. *Journal of Applied Psychology, 87,* 916–928.

Kernan, M. C., & Lord, R. G. (1988). Effects of participative vs assigned goals and feedback in a multitrial task. *Motivation and Emotion, 12,* 75-86.

Kernan, M. C., & Lord, R. G. (1990). Effects of valence, expectancies, and goal-performance discrepancies in single and multiple environments. *Journal of Applied Psychology, 75,* 194–203.

Kernan, M. C., & Lord, R. G. (1991). An application of control theory to understanding the relationship between performance and satisfaction. *Human Performance, 4,* 173–185.

Kiesler, C. A. (1971). *The psychology of commitment.* New York: Academic Press.

Kihlstrom, J. F., Mulvaney, S., Tobias, B. A., & Tobis, I. P. (2000). The emotional unconscious. In E. Eich, J. F. Kihlstrom, G. H. Bower, J. P. Forgas, & P. M. Miedenthal (Eds.), *Cognition and emotion* (pp. 30–86). New York: Oxford University Press.

Kilmann, P. R., Laughlin, J. E., Carranza, L. V., Downer, J. T., Major, S., & Parnell, M. M. (1999). Effects of an attachment-focused group preventive intervention on insecure women. *Group Dynamics: Theory, Research, and Practice, 3,* 138–147.

Kim, W. C., & Mauborgne, R. A. (1993). Procedural justice, attitudes, and subsidiary top management compliance with multinationals' corporate strategic decision. *Academy of Management Journal, 36,* 502–526.

King, N. (1970). Clarification and evaluation of the two-factor theory of job satisfaction. *Psychological Bulletin, 74,* 18–31.

Kirkpatrick, S. (1992). The effect of psychological variables on the job characteristics-work outcome relations. Paper presented at the Eastern Academy of Management.

Kirkpatrick, S., & Locke, E. A. (1996). Direct and indirect effects of three core charismatic leadership components on performance and attitudes. *Journal of Applied Psychology, 81,* 36–51.

Klehe, U. C., & Latham, G. P. (2005). The predictive and incremental validity of the situational and patterned behavior description interviews for teamplaying behavior. *International Journal of Selection and Assessment, 13,* 108–115.

Klein, H. (1989). An integrated control theory model of work motivation. *Academy of Management Review, 14,* 150–172.

Klein, H. J. (1991). Further evidence on the relationship between goal setting and expectancy theories. *Organizational Behavior and Human Decision Processes, 49,* 230–257.

Klein, H. J., & Kim, J. S. (1998). A field study of the influence of situational constraints, leader-member exchange, and goal commitment on performance. *Academy of Management Journal, 41,* 88–95.

Klein, H. J., & Mulvey, P. W. (1995). Two investigations of the relationship among group goals, goal commitment, cohesion, and performance. *Organizational Behavior and Human Decision Processes, 61,* 44–53.

Klein, H. J., Wesson, M. J., Hollenbeck, J. R., & Alge, B. J. (1999). Goal commitment and the goal-setting process: Conceptual clarification and empirical synthesis. *Journal of Applied Psychology, 84,* 885–896.

Klein, H. J., Wesson, M. J., Hollenbeck, J. R., Wright, P. M., & DeShon, R. P. (2001). The assessment of goal commitment: A measurement model meta-analysis. *Organizational Behavior and Human Decision Processes, 85,* 32–55.

Klein, K. J., & Zedeck, S. (2004). Introduction of the special section on theoretical methods and conceptual analysis. Theory in applied psychology: Lessons (re)learned. *Journal of Applied Psychology, 89,* 931–933.

Kluger, A.V., & DeNisi, A. (1996). The effects of feedback interventions on performance: A historical review, a meta-analysis, and a preliminary feedback intervention theory. *Psychological Bulletin, 119,* 254–284.

Kluger, A. N., & Tikochinsky, J. (2001). The error of accepting the "theoretical" null hypothesis: The rise, fall, and resurrection of commonsense hypotheses in psychology. *Psychological Bulletin, 127,* 408–423.

Knight, D., Durham, C. C., & Locke, E. A. (2000). The relationship of team goals, incentives, and efficacy to strategic risk, tactical implementation, and performance. *Academy of Management Journal, 44,* 623–339.

Koestner, R., Lekes, N., Powers, T. A., & Chicoine, E. (2002). Attaining personal goals: Self-concordance plus implementation intentions equals success. *Journal of Personality and Social Psychology, 83*, 231–244.

Kolb, B. (2003). The impact of Hebbian learning rule on research in behavioral neuroscience. *Canadian Psychology, 44*, 14–16.

Kolstad, A. (1938). Employees in a department store. *Journal of Applied Psychology, 22*, 470–479.

Komaki, J. L. (1977). Alternative evaluation strategies in work settings: Reversal and multiple-baseline designs. *Journal of Organization Behavior Management, 1*, 53–77.

Komaki, J. L. (1981). A behavioral view of paradigm debates: Let the data speak. *Journal of Applied Psychology, 66*, 111–112.

Komaki, J. L. (1998). When performance improvement is the goal: A new set of criteria for criteria. *Journal of Applied Behavior Analysis, 31*, 263–280.

Komaki, J. L. (2003). Reinforcement theory at work: Enhancing and explaining what employees do. In L. W. Porter, G. A. Bigley & R. M. Steers (Eds.), *Motivation and work behavior* (7th ed., pp. 95–113). Burr Ridge, IL: Irwin/McGraw Hill.

Komaki, J. L., Coombs, T., Redding, Jr., T. P., & Schepman, S. (2000). A rich and rigorous examination of applied behavior analysis research in the world of work. In C. L. Cooper & I. T. Robertson (Eds.), *International review of industrial and organizational psychology* (pp. 265–367). Sussex, England: John Wiley.

Konovsky, M. A. (2000). Understanding procedural justice and its impact on business organizations. *Journal of Management, 26*, 489–511.

Konovsky, M. A., & Cropanzano, R. (1993). Justice considerations in employee drug testing. In R. Cropanzano (Ed.), *Justice in the workplace: Approaching fairness in human resource management* (pp. 171–192). Hillsdale, NJ: Lawrence Erlbaum.

Koppes, L. L. (2003). Industrial-organizational psychology. In I. B. Weiner (General Ed.) and D. K. Freedheim (Volume Ed.), *Comprehensive handbook of psychology: History of psychology* (Vol. 1, pp. 367–389). New York: Wiley.

Korman, A. K., Greenhaus, J. H., & Badin, I. J. (1977). Personnel attitudes and motivation. *Annual Review of Psychology, 28*, 5–196.

Kornhauser, A. W. (1965). *Mental health of the industrial worker*. New York: Wiley.

Kornhauser, A. W., & Sharp, A. A. (1932). Employee attitudes: Suggestions from a study in factory. *Personnel Journal, 10*, 393–404.

Kozlowski, S. W. J., & Klein, K. J. (2000). A multi-level approach to theory and research in organizations: Contextual, temporal, and emergent properties. In K. J. Klein & S. W. J. Kozlowski (Eds.), *Multi-level theory, research, and methods in organizations* (pp. 3–90). San Francisco: Jossey-Bass.

Kristof-Brown, A. L., Jansen, K. J., & Colbert, A. E. (2002). A policy-capturing study of simultaneous effects of fit with jobs, groups, and organizations. *Journal of Applied Psychology, 97*, 985–993.

Kristof-Brown, A. L., Zimmerman, R. D., & Johnson, E. C. (2005). Consequences of individual's fit at work: A meta-analysis of person-job, person-organization, person-group, and person-supervisor fit. *Personnel Psychology, 58*, 281–342.

Lambert, S. H., Moore, D. W., & Dixon, R. S. (1999). Gymnasts in training: The differential effects of self- and coach-set goals as a function of locus of control. *Journal of Applied Sport Psychology, 11*, 72–82.

Landy, F. (2005). Postmodernism and applied psychology: A long road. *The Industrial-Organizational Psychologist, 43*, 16–22.

Lane, A. M., & Karageorghis, C. I. (1997). Goal confidence and difficulty as predictors of goal attainment in junior high school cross-country runners. *Perceptual and Motor Skills, 84*, 747–752.

Langfred, C. W., & Moye, N. A. (2004). Effects of task autonomy on performance: An extended model considering motivational, informational, and structural mechanisms. *Journal of Applied Psychology, 89*, 934–945.

Latham, G. P. (1989). Behavioral approaches to the training and learning process in organizations. In I. L. Goldstein (Ed.), *Training and career development in work organizations: Frontiers of industrial and organizational psychology* (pp. 256–295). San Francisco, CA: Jossey-Bass.

Latham, G. P. (1992). Resolving a scientific dispute with Dr. Miriam Erez: Genesis, process, outcome, and reflection. In P. Frost & R. Stablein (Eds.), *Doing Exemplary Research* (pp. 146–154). Newbury Park, CA: Sage.

Latham, G. P. (2001a). The reciprocal effects of science on practice: Insights from the practice and science of goal setting. *Canadian Psychology, 42*, 1–11.

Latham, G. P. (2001b). The importance of understanding and changing employee outcome expectancies for gaining commitment to an organizational goal. *Personnel Psychology, 54*, 707–716.

Latham, G. P. (2003a). Toward a boundaryless psychology. *Canadian Psychology, 44*, 216–217.

Latham, G. P. (2003b). Goal setting: A five step approach to behavior change. *Organization Dynamics, 32*, 309–318.

Latham, G. P. (2004). The motivational benefits of goal setting. *Academy of Management Executive, 18*, 126–129.

Latham, G. P., & Baldes, J. J. (1975). The "practical significance" of Locke's theory of goal setting. *Journal of Applied Psychology, 60*, 122–124.

Latham, G. P., & Beach, H. D. (1974). Awareness in the conditioning and extinction of the galvanic skin response. *The Psychological Record, 24*, 497–505.

Latham, G. P., & Brown, T.C. (in press). The effect of learning, distal, and proximal goals on MBA self-efficacy and satisfaction. *Applied Psychology: An International Review.*

Latham, G. P., & Budworth, M. H. (2006). The effect of training in verbal self guidance on the self efficacy and performance of Native North Americans in the selection interview. *Journal of Vocational Behavior.*

Latham, G. P., & Budworth, M. H. (2006). The study of employee motivation in the 20th century. In L. Koppes (Ed.), *Historical perspectives in industrial-organizational psychology: The first hundred years* (353–381). Mahwah, NJ: Lawrence Erlbaum.

Latham, G. P., & Dossett, D. L. (1978). Designing incentive plans for unionized employees: A comparison of continuous and variable ratio reinforcement schedules. *Personnel Psychology, 31*, 47–61.

Latham, G. P., Erez, M., & Locke, E. A. (1988). Resolving scientific disputes by the joint design of crucial experiments by the antagonists: Application of the Erez-Latham dispute regarding participation in goal setting. *Journal of Applied Psychology Monograph, 73*, 753–772.

Latham, G. P., & Frayne, C. A. (1989). Self management training for increasing job attendance: A follow-up and a replication. *Journal of Applied Psychology, 74*, 411–416.

Latham, G. P., & Heslin, P.A. (2003). Training the trainee as well as the trainer: Lessons learned from clinical psychology. *Canadian Psychology, 44*, 218–231.

Latham, G. P., & Kinne, S. B. (1974). Improving job performance through training in goal setting. *Journal of Applied Psychology, 59*, 187–191.

Latham, G. P., & Latham, S. D. (2003). Facilitators and inhibitors of the transfer of knowledge between scientists and practitioners in human resource management: Leveraging cultural, individual, and institutional variables. *European Journal of Work and Organizational Psychology, 12*, 245–256.

Latham, G. P., & Lee, T. W. (1986). Goal setting. In E. A. Locke (Ed.), *Generalizing from laboratory to field settings*. Lexington, MA: Heath.

Latham, G. P., & Locke, E. A. (1975). Increasing productivity with decreasing time limits: A field replication of Parkinson's law. *Journal of Applied Psychology, 60*, 524–526.

Latham, G. P., & Locke, E. A. (1979). Goal setting: A motivational technique that works. *Organizational Dynamics, 8*, 68–80.

Latham, G. P., & Locke, E. A. (1991). Self regulation through goal setting. *Organizational Behavior and Human Decision Processes, 50*, 212–247.

Latham, G. P., Locke, E. A., & Fassina, N. E. (2002). The high performance cycle: Standing the test of time. In S. Sonnentag (Ed.), *The psychological management of individual performance. A handbook in the psychology of management in organizations* (pp. 201–228). Chichester, UK: John Wiley & Sons.

Latham, G. P. & Mann, S. (2006). Advances in the science of performance appraisal: Implications for practice. In G. P. Hodgkinson & J. K. Ford (Eds.), *International Review of Organizational and Industrial Psychology* (pp. 295–337). Chichester, UK: John Wiley & Sons.

Latham, G. P., & Marshall, H. A. (1982). The effects of self-set, participatively set, and assigned goals on the performance of government employees. *Personnel Psychology, 35*, 399–404.

Latham, G. P., & Mitchell, T. R. (1976). Behavioral criteria and potential reinforcers for the engineer/scientist in an industrial setting. *JSAS Catalog of Selected Documents in Psychology, 6*, 38, 1, 316.

Latham, G. P., Mitchell, T. R., & Dossett, D. L. (1978). The importance of participative goal setting and anticipated rewards on goal difficulty and job performance. *Journal of Applied Psychology, 63*, 163–171.

Latham, G. P., & Napier, N. K. (1984). Practical ways to increase employee attendance. In P. S. Goodman & R. S. Atkin (Eds.), *Absenteeism: New approaches to understanding, measuring, and managing employee absence* (pp. 322–359). San Francisco, CA: Jossey Bass.

Latham, G. P., & Pinder, C. C. (2005). Work motivation theory and research at the dawn of the twenty-first century. *Annual Review of Psychology, 56*, 485–516.

Latham, G. P., & Pursell, E. D. (1975). Measuring absenteeism from the opposite side of the coin. *Journal of Applied Psychology, 60*, 369–371.

Latham, G. P., & Saari, L. M. (1979a). The application of social learning theory to training supervisors through behavioral modeling. *Journal of Applied Psychology, 64*, 239–246.

Latham, G. P., & Saari, L. M. (1979b). The effects of holding goal difficulty constant on assigned and participatively set goals. *Academy of Management Journal, 22*, 163–168.

Latham, G. P., & Saari, L. M. (1979c). The importance of supportive relationships in goal setting. *Journal of Applied Psychology, 64*, 151–156.

Latham, G. P., & Seijts, G. H. (1997). The effect of appraisal instrument on management perceptions of fairness and satisfaction with appraisals from their peers. *Canadian Journal of Behavioural Science, 29*, 275–282.

Latham, G. P., & Seijts, G. H. (1999). The effects of proximal and distal goals on performance on a moderately complex task. *Journal of Organizational Behavior, 20*, 421–429.

Latham, G. P., & Skarlicki, D. (1995). Criterion related validity of the situational and patterned behavior description interviews with organizational citizenship behavior. *Human Performance, 8*, 67–80.

Latham, G. P., & Steele, T. P. (1983). The motivational effects of participation versus assigned goal setting on performance. *Academy of Management Journal, 26*, 406–417.

Latham, G. P., Steele, T. P., & Saari, L. M. (1982). The effects of participation and goal difficulty on performance. *Personnel Psychology, 35*, 677–686.

Latham, G. P., & Sue-Chan, C. (1999). A meta-analysis of the situational interview: An enumerative review of reasons for its validity. *Canadian Psychology, 40*, 56–67.

Latham, G. P., & Wexley, K. N. (1977). Behavioral observation scales for performance appraisal purposes. *Personnel Psychology, 30*, 255–268.

Latham, G. P., & Wexley, K. N. (1994). *Increasing productivity through performance appraisal.* Reading, MA: Addison Wesley.

Latham, G. P., & Whyte, G. (1994). The futility of utility analysis. *Personnel Psychology, 47*, 31–46.

Latham, G. P., Winters, D. C., & Locke, E. A. (1994). Cognitive and motivational effects of participation: A mediator study. *Journal of Organizational Behavior, 15*, 49–63.

Latham, G. P., & Yukl, G. A. (1975). A review of research on the application of goal setting in organizations. *Academy of Management Journal, 18*, 824–845.

Latham, G. P., & Yukl, G. A. (1976). Effects of assigned and participative goal setting on performance and job satisfaction. *Journal of Applied Psychology, 61*, 166–171.

Lauver, K. J., & Kristof-Brown, A. (2001). Distinguishing between employees' perception of person-job person-organization fit. *Journal of Vocational Behavior, 59*, 454–470.

Lawler, E. E. (1965). Managers' perceptions of their subordinates' pay and their superiors' pay. *Personnel Psychology, 18*, 413–422.

Lawler, E. E. (1969). Job design and employee motivation. *Personnel Psychology, 22*, 426–435.

Lawler, E. E. (1971). *Pay and organizational effectiveness: A psychological view*. New York: McGraw-Hill.

Lawler, E. E., Mohrman, S. A., & Ledford, G. E. (1995). *Creating high performance organizations: Practices and results of employee involvement and total quality management in Fortune 1000 companies*. San Francisco, CA: Jossey-Bass.

Lawler, E. E., & Porter, L. W. (1967). The effect of performance on job satisfaction. *Industrial Relations, 7*, 20–28.

Lazarus, R. S. (1991). *Emotion and adaptation*. New York: Oxford University.

Leavitt, H. S. (1962). Toward organizational psychology. In B. V. H. Gilmer (Ed.) *Walter VanDyke Bingham* (pp. 23–30). Pittsburgh, PA: Carnegie Institute of Technology.

Lee, C., & Bobko, P. (1992). Exploring the meaning and usefulness of measures of subjective goal difficulty. *Journal of Applied Social Psychology, 22*, 1417–1428.

Lee, C., & Bobko, P. (1994). Self-efficacy beliefs: Comparison of five measures. *Journal of Applied Psychology, 79*, 364–369.

Lee, C., & Earley, P. C. (1992). Comparative peer evaluations of organizational behavior theories. *Organization Development Journal, 10*, 37–42.

Lee, T. W., Locke, E. A., & Latham, G. P. (1989). Goal setting theory and job performance. In L. A. Pervin (Ed.), *Goal concepts in personality and social psychology* (pp. 291–328). Hillsdale, NJ: Lawrence Erlbaum.

Lee, T. W., Locke, E. A., & Phan, S. H. (1997). Explaining the assigned goal-incentive interaction: The role of self-efficacy and personal goals. *Journal of Management, 23*, 541–559.

Leifer, R. & McGannon, K. (1986). Goal acceptance and goal commitment: Their differential impact on goal setting theory. Paper presented at the annual meeting of the Academy of Management, Chicago, IL.

Lerner, B. S., & Locke, E. A. (1995). The effect of goal setting, self-efficacy, competition, and personal traits on the performance of an endurance task. *Journal of Sport and Exercise Psychology, 17*, 138–152.

Leung, K. (2001). Different carrots for different rabbits: Effects of individualism-collectivism and power distance on work motivation. In M. Erez & U. Kleinbeck (Eds.), *Work motivation in the context of a globalizing economy* (pp. 329–339). Mahwah, NJ: Lawrence Erlbaum.

Leung, K. (2004). Negotiation and reward allocations across cultures. In P. C. Earley & M. Erez (Eds.), *New perspectives on international industrial/organizational psychology* (pp. 640–675). San Francisco: Jossey-Bass.

Leventhal, G. S. (1980). What should be done with equity theory? In K. J. Gergen, M. S. Greenberg & R. H. Willis (Eds.), *Social exchange: Advances in theory and research* (pp. 27–55). New York: Plenum.

Lewin, K. (1945). The research center for group dynamics at Massachusetts Institute for Technology. *Sociometry, 8*, 126–135.

Lewin, K., Lippitt, R., & White, R. K. (1939). Patterns of aggressive behavior in experimentally created "social climates." *Journal of Social Psychology, 10*, 271–299.

Lickliter, R., & Honeycutt, H. (2003). Developmental dynamics: Toward a biologically plausible evolutionary psychology. *Psychological Bulletin, 129*, 819–835.

Likert, R. (1932). A technique for the measurement of attitudes. *Archives of Psychology, 140*, 55.

Likert, R. (1967). *The human organization: Its management and values*. New York: McGraw-Hill.

Lind, E. A. (2001). Fairness heuristic theory: Justice judgments as pivotal cognitions in organizational relations. In J. Greenberg & R. Cropanzano (Eds.), *Advances in organizational justice* (pp. 56–88). Stanford, CA: Stanford University Press.

Lind, E. A., Greenberg, J., Scott, K. S., & Welchans, T. D. (2000). The winding road from employee to complainant: Situational psychological determinants of wrongful termination claims. *Administrative Science Quarterly, 45,* 557–590.

Lind, E. A., & Tyler, T. R. (1988). *The social psychology of procedural justice.* New York: Plenum.

Locke, E. A. (1964). *The relationship of intentions to motivation and affect.* Unpublished doctoral dissertation.

Locke, E. A. (1965). The relationship of task success to task liking and satisfaction. *Journal of Applied Psychology, 49,* 379–385.

Locke, E. A. (1967). Further data on the relationship of task success to liking and satisfaction. *Psychological Reports, 20,* 246.

Locke, E. A. (1968). Toward a theory of task motivation and incentives. *Organizational Behavior & Human Performance, 3,* 157–189.

Locke, E. A. (1970). Job satisfaction and job performance: A theoretical analysis. *Organizational Behavior and Human Performance, 5,* 484–500.

Locke, E. A. (1975). Personnel attitudes and motivation. *Annual Review of Psychology, 26,* 457–480.

Locke, E. A. (1976). Nature and causes of job satisfaction. In M. D. Dunnette (Ed.), *Handbook of industrial and organizational psychology* (pp. 1297–1349). Chicago: Rand McNally.

Locke, E. A. (1977). The myths of behavior mod in organizations. *Academy of Management Review, 2,* 543–553.

Locke, E. A. (1978). The ubiquity of the technique of goal setting in theories of and approaches to employee motivation. *Academy of Management Review, 3,* 594–601.

Locke, E. A. (1980). Latham versus Komaki: A tale of two paradigms. *Journal of Applied Psychology, 65,* 16–23.

Locke, E. A. (1982a). The ideas of a short work period and multiple goal levels. *Journal of Applied Psychology, 67,* 512–514.

Locke, E. A. (1982b). Relation of goal level to performance with Frederick W. Taylor: An evolution. *Academy of Management, 7,* 14–24.

Locke, E. A. (1986). Generalizing from laboratory to field: Ecological validity or abstraction of essential elements. In E. A. Locke (Ed.), *Generalizing from laboratory to field settings* (pp. 3–9). Lexington, MA: Lexington Books.

Locke, E. A. (1991). The motivation sequence, the motivation hub, and the motivation core. *Organizational Behavior and Human Decision Processes, 50,* 288–299.

Locke, E. A. (1992). Reflections on the Latham/Erez/Locke study. In P. Frost & R. Stablein (Eds.), *Doing exemplary research* (pp. 165–172). Newbury Park, CA: Sage.

Locke, E. A. (2000). Motivation, cognition, and action: An analysis of studies of task goals and knowledge. *Applied Psychology: An International Review, 49,* 408–429.

Locke, E. A. (2001). Self-set goals and self-efficacy as mediators of incentives and personality. In M. Erez & U. Kleinbeck (Eds.), *Work motivation in the context of a globalizing economy* (pp. 13–26). Mahwah, NJ: Lawrence Erlbaum.

Locke, E. A. (2003). Foundations for a theory of leadership. In S. E. Murphy & R. E. Riggio (Eds.), *The future of leadership development* (pp. 29–46). Mahwah, NJ: Lawrence Erlbaum.

Locke, E. A. (2004). Comment: "Promise and peril in implementing pay-for-performance" by Michael Beer and Mark D. Cannon. *Human Resources Management, 43*(1), 41–43.

Locke, E. A. (2005). Linking goals to monetary incentives. *Academy of Management Executive, 18,* 130–133.

Locke, E. A., Alavi, M., & Wagner, J. (1997). Participation in decision making: An information exchange perspective. In G. Ferris (Ed.), *Research in personnel and human resources management* (Vol. 15, pp. 293–331). Greenwich, CT: JAI Press.

Locke, E. A., Cartledge, N., & Koeppel, J. (1968). Motivation effects of knowledge of results: A goal setting phenomenon? *Psychological Bulletin, 70,* 474–485.

Locke, E. A., Feren, D. B., McCaleb, V. M., Shaw, K. N., & Denny, A. T. (1980). The relative effectiveness of four methods of motivating employee performance. In K. D. Duncan,

M. M. Greenberg & D. Wallis (Eds.), *Changes in working life* (pp. 363–388). London: John Wiley & Sons.

Locke, E. A., Frederick, E., Buckner, E., & Bobko, P. 91984). Effects of previously assigned goals on self-set goals and performance. *Journal of Applied Psychology, 69,* 694–699.

Locke, E. A., Frederick, E., Lee, C., & Bobko, P. (1984). Effect of self-efficacy, goals, and task strategies on task performance. *Journal of Applied Psychology, 69,* 241–251.

Locke, E. A., & Henne, D. (1986). Work motivation theories. In C. L. Cooper & I. Robertson (Eds.), *International review of industrial and organizational psychology* (pp. 1–36). New York: Wiley.

Locke, E. A., & Kirkpatrick, S. A. (1990). The use of qualitative goals to promote task revision. Unpublished manuscript.

Locke, E. A., & Latham, G. P. (1984). *Goal setting: A motivational technique that works.* Englewood Cliffs, NJ: Prentice Hall.

Locke, E. A., & Latham, G. P. (1985). The application of goal setting to sports. *Journal of Sports Psychology, 7,* 205–222.

Locke, E. A., & Latham, G. P. (1990a). *A theory of goal setting and task performance.* Englewood Cliffs, NJ: Prentice Hall.

Locke, E. A., & Latham, G. P. (1990b). Work motivation and satisfaction: Light at the end of the tunnel. *Psychological Science, 1,* 240–246.

Locke, E. A., & Latham, G. P. (2002). Building a practically useful theory of goal setting and task motivation: A 35-year odyssey. *American Psychologist, 57,* 705–717.

Locke, E. A., & Latham, G. P. (2004). What should we do about motivation theory? Six recommendations for the 21st century. *Academy of Management Review, 29,* 379–387.

Locke, E. A., & Latham, G. P. (2005). Goal setting theory: Theory by induction. In K. Smith & M. Hitt (Eds.), *Great minds in management: The process of theory development* (pp. 128–150). Oxford University Press.

Locke, E. A., McClear, K., & Knight, D. (1996). Self esteem and work. In C. Cooper & I. Robertson (Eds.), *International review of industrial & organizational psychology.* Chichester, UK: John Wiley & Sons.

Locke, E. A., Motowidlo, S. J., & Bobko, P. (1986). Using self efficacy theory to resolve the conflict between goal setting theory and expectancy theory in organizational behavioral and industrial/organizational psychology. *Journal of Social and Clinical Psychology, 4,* 328–338.

Locke, E. A., Shaw, K. M., Saari, L. M., & Latham, G. P. (1981). Goal setting and task performance: 1969–1980. *Psychological Bulletin, 90,* 125–152.

Locke, E. A., Smith, K. G., Erez, M., Chah, D. O., & Schaffer, A. (1994). The effects of intra-individual goal conflict on performance. *Journal of Management, 20,* 67–91.

Lopez, F. G., & Brennan, K. A. (2000). Dynamic processes underlying adult attachment organization: Toward an attachment theoretical perspective on the healthy and effective self. *Journal of Counseling Psychology, 47,* 283–300.

Lord, R. G., & Harvey, J. L. (2002). An information processing framework for emotional regulation. In R. G. Lord, R. J. Klimoski, & R. Kanfer, (Eds.), *Emotions in the workplace: Understanding the structure and role of emotions in organizational behavior* (pp. 115–146). San Francisco, CA: Jossey-Bass.

Lord, R. G., Hanges, P. J., & Godfrey, E. G. (2003). Integrating neural networks into decision-making and motivational theory: Rethinking VIE theory. *Canadian Psychology, 44,* 21–38.

Lord, R. G., & Kanfer, R. (2002). Emotions and organizational behavior. In R. G. Lord, R. J. Klimoski, & R. Kanfer *Emotions in the workplace: Understanding the structure and role of emotions in organizational behavior* (pp. 5–19). San Francisco, CA: Jossey-Bass.

Lord, R. G., Klimoski, R. J., & Kanfer, R. (2002). *Emotions in the workplace: Understanding the structure and role of emotions in organizational behavior.* San Francisco: Jossey-Bass.

Lord, R. G., & Levy, P. E. (1994). Moving from cognition to action: A control theory perspective. *Applied Psychology: An International Review, 43,* 335–367.

Luthans, F., & Kreitner, R. (1975). *Organizational behavior modification.* Glenview: Scott, Foresman.

Mace, C. A. (1935). *Incentives: Some experimental studies.* Industrial Health Research Board Report (Great Britain), No. 72.

MacKenzie, S. B., Podsakoff, P. M., & Jarvis, C. B. (2005). The problem of measurement model mis-specification in behavioral and organizational research and some recommended solutions. *Journal of Applied Psychology, 90,* 710–730.

Magnusson, D., & Endler, N. S., (Eds.). (1977). *Personality at the crossroads: Current issues in inter-actional psychology.* Hillsdale, NJ: Lawrence Erlbaum.

Maier, N. R. F. (1946). *Psychology in industry.* Boston: Houghton Mifflin.

Maier, N. R. F. (1955). *Psychology in industry* (2nd ed.). Boston: Houghton Mifflin.

Mainemelis, C. (2001). When the muse takes it all: A model for the experience of timelessness in organizations. *Academy of Management Review, 26,* 548–565.

Malka, A., & Chatman, J. A. (2003). Intrinsic and extrinsic orientations as moderators of the effect of annual income on subjective well-being: A longitudinal study. *Personality and Social Psychology Bulletin, 29,* 737–746.

Markman, A. B., & Brendl, C. M. (2000). The influence of goals on value and choice. *Psychology of Learning and Motivation, 39,* 97–128.

Marrow, A. J. (1969). *The Practical theorist: The life and work of Kurt Lewin.* New York: Basic Books.

Maruping, L. M., & Agarwal, R. (2004). Managing team interpersonal process through technology: A task-technology fit perspective. *Journal of Applied Psychology, 89,* 975–990.

Maslow, A. H. (1943). A theory of human motivation. *Psychological Review, 50,* 370–396.

Maslow, A. H. (1954). *Motivation and personality.* New York: Harper.

Maslow, A. H. (1965) *Eupsychian management: A journal.* Homewood, IL: Irwin.

Masterson, S. S. (2001). A trickle-down model of organizational justice: Relating employees' and customers' perceptions and reactions to fairness. *Journal of Applied Psychology, 86,* 594–604.

Mathews, J. A. (1997). Introduction to the special issue. *Human Relations, 50,* 487–496.

Mathieu, J. E., & Button, S. B. (1992). An examination of the relative impact of normative infor-mation and self-efficacy on personal goals and performance over time. *Journal of Applied Social Psychology, 22,* 1758–1775.

Mathieu, J. E., & Hamel, K. (1989). A causal model of the antecedents of organizational commit-ment among professionals and non-professionals. *Journal of Vocational Behavior, 34,* 299–317.

Mathieu, J. E., & Zajac, D. M. (1990). A review and meta-analysis of the antecedents, correlates and consequences of organizational commitment. *Psychological Bulletin, 108,* 171–194.

Matsui, T., Okada, A., & Kakuyama, T. (1982). Influence of achievement need on goal setting, performance, and feedback effectiveness. *Journal of Applied Psychology, 67,* 645–648.

Matsui, T., Okada, A., & Mizuguchi, R. (1981). Expectancy theory prediction of the goal theory postulate "the harder the goals, the higher the performance." *Journal of Applied Psychology, 66,* 54–58.

Mayo, E. (1933). *The human problems of an industrialized civilization.* Illinois: Scott, Foresman.

McClelland, D. C. (1961). *The achieving society.* Princeton, NJ: Van Nostrand.

McClelland, D. C. & Winter, D. G. (1969). *Motivating economic achievement.* New York: Free Press.

McDougall, W. (1908). *An introduction to social psychology.* London: Methuen.

McDougall, W. (1930). Autobiography. In C. Murchinson (Ed.), *A history of psychology in auto-biography.* Worcester, MA: Clark University Press.

McDougall, W. (1939). *The group mind.* New York: Cambridge University Press.

McGrath, J. E. & Tschan, F. (2004). *Temporal matters in social psychology.* Washington, DC: American Psychological Association.

McGregor, D. M. (1957). The human side of the enterprise. *Management Review, 46,* 22–28.

McGregor, D. M. (1960). *The human side of the enterprise.* New York: McGraw-Hill.

McLean Parks, J. (1997). The fourth arm of justice: The art and science of revenge. In R. J. Lewicki & R. J. Bies, *Research on negotiations in organizations* (pp. 113–144). Grennwich, CT: Elsevier Science/JAI.

McNatt, D. B. (2000). Ancient Pygmalion joins contemporary management: A meta-analysis of the result. *Journal of Applied Psychology, 85,* 314–322.

McNatt, D. B., & Judge, T. A. (2004). Boundary conditions of the Galatea effect: A field experiment and a constructive replication. *Academy of Management Journal, 47,* 550–565.

Meichenbaum, D. H. (1971). Examination of model characteristics in reducing avoidance behavior. *Journal of Personality and Social Psychology, 17,* 298–307.

Mento, A. J., Cartledge, N. D., & Locke, E. A. (1980). Maryland vs. Michigan, vs Minnesota: Another look at the relationship of expectancy and goal difficulty to task performance. *Organizational Behavior and Human Performance, 25,* 419–440.

Mento, A. J., Locke, E. A., & Klein, H. J. (1992). Relationship of goal level to valence and instrumentality. *Journal of Applied Psychology, 77,* 395–405.

Merton, R. K. (1948). The self-fulfilling prophecy. *Antioch Review, 8,* 193–210.

Metcalfe, J., & Mischel, W. (1999). A hot/cool-system analysis of delay of gratification: Dynamics of willpower. *Psychological Review, 106,* 3–19.

Meyer, G. J. (1996). The Rorschach and MMPI: Toward a more scientifically differentiated understanding of cross-method assessment. *Journal of Personality Assessment, 67,* 558–578.

Meyer, J. P., & Allen, N. J. (1991). A three component conceptualization of organizational commitment. *Human Resource Management Review, 1,* 61–89.

Meyer, J. P., Becker, T. E., & Vandenberghe, C. (2004). Employee commitment and motivation: A conceptual analysis and interpretative model. *Journal of Applied Psychology, 89,* 991–1007.

Meyer, J. P., & Herscovitch, L. (2001). Commitment in the workplace: Toward a general model. *Human Resource Management Review, 11,* 299–326.

Millman, Z., & Latham, G. P. (2001). Increasing re-employment through training in verbal self-guidance. In M. Erez, U. Kleinbeck, & H. K. Thierry (Eds.), *Work motivation in the context of a globalizing economy* (pp. 87–98). Hillsdale, NJ: Lawrence Erlbaum.

Miner, J. B. (1960). The effect of a course in psychology on the attitudes of research and development supervisors. *Journal of Applied Psychology, 44,* 224–232.

Miner, J. B. (1984). The validity and usefulness of theories in emerging organizational science. *Academy of Management Review, 9,* 296–306.

Miner, J. B. (2003). The rated importance, scientific validity, and practical usefulness of organizational behavior theories: A quantitative review. *Academy of Management: Learning and Education, 2,* 250–268.

Miner, J. B. (2005). Role motivation theories. In J. C. Thomas & D. L. Segal (Eds.), *Comprehensive handbook of personality and psychopathology: Personality and everyday functioning* (pp. 233–250; Vol. 1). Hoboken, NJ: John Wiley.

Miner, J. B., & Dachler, H. P. (1973). Personnel attitudes and motivation. *Annual Review of Psychology,* 379–402.

Miner, J. B., & Raju, N. S. (2004). Risk propensity differences between managers and entrepreneurs and between low- and high-growth entrepreneurs: A reply in a more conservative vein. *Journal of Applied Psychology, 89,* 3–13.

Mischel, W. (1968). *Personality and assessment.* New York: Wiley.

Mischel, W. (1973). Toward a cognitive social learning reconceptualization of personality. *Psychological Review, 80,* 252–283.

Mischel, W. (1977). The interaction of person and situation. In D. Magnusson & N. S. Endler (Eds.), *Personality at the crossroads: Current issues in interactional psychology.* Hillsdale, NJ: Lawrence Erlbaum.

Mitchell, T. R. (1975). Cognitions and Skinner: Some questions about behavioral determinism. *Organization and Administrative Sciences, 6,* 63–72.

Mitchell, T. R. (1979). Organizational behavior. *Annual Review of Psychology, 30,* 243–81.

Mitchell, T. R., & Biglan, A. (1971). Instrumentality theories: Current uses in psychology. *Psychological Bulletin, 76,* 432–454.

Mitchell, T. R., & Daniels, D. (2003). Motivation. In W. C. Borman, D. R. Ilgen, & R. J. Klimoski (Eds.), *Comprehensive handbook of psychology: Industrial organizational psychology* (Vol. 12, pp. 225–254). New York: Wiley & Sons.

Mitchell, T. R., & James, L. R. (2001). Building a better theory: Time and the specification of when things happen. *Academy of Management Review, 26,* 530–548.

Mitchell, T. R., Lee, T. W., Lee, D. Y., & Harman, W. (2004). Attributions and the cycle of work. In M. Martinko (Ed.), *Attribution theory in organizational sciences: Theoretical and empirical contributions* (pp. 25–40). Greenwich, CT: Information Age.

Mone, M. A., & Shalley, C. E. (1995). Effects of task complexity and goal specificity on change in strategy and performance over time. *Human Performance, 8,* 243–262.

Moore, B. (1962). Some beginnings of industrial psychology. (1962). Industrial psychology and labor. In B. V. H. Gilmer (Ed.), *Walter VanDyke Bingham* (pp. 1–5). Pittsburgh, PA: Carnegie Institute of Technology.

Moore, K. (2005). Maybe it is like brain surgery. *Marketing, 110,* 12.

Morgeson, F. P., & Campion, M. A. (2002). Minimizing tradeoffs when redesigning work: Evidence from a longitudinal quasi-experiment. *Personnel Psychology, 55,* 589–612.

Morin, L., & Latham, G. P. (2000). Effect of mental practice and goal setting as a transfer of training intervention on supervisors' self-efficacy and communication skills: An exploratory study. *Applied Psychology: An International Review, 49,* 566–578.

Morrison, E. W., & Robinson, S. L. (1997). When employees feel betrayed: A model of how psychological contract violation develops. *The Academy of Management Review, 22,* 226–256.

Moskowitz, D. S., & Cote S. (1995). Do interpersonal traits predict affect? A comparison of three models. *Journal of Personality and Social Psychology, 69,* 915–924.

Mount, M. K., & Barrick, M. R. (1995). The Big Five personality dimensions: Implications for research and practice in human resources management. *Research in Personnel and Human Resources, 13,* 153–200.

Mowday, R. T. (1991). Equity theory predictions of behavior in organizations. In R. M. Steers & L. W. Porter, (Eds.), *Motivation and work behavior* (5th ed., pp. 111–130). New York: McGraw-Hill.

Mowday, R. T., & Colwell, K. A. (2003). Employee reactions to unfair outcomes in the workplace: The contributions of Adams's equity theory to understanding work motivation. In L. W. Porter, G. A. Bigley & R. M. Steers (Eds.), *Motivation and work behavior* (7th ed., pp. 65–87). Burr Ridge, IL: McGraw-Hill/Irwin.

Mowday, R., & Sutton, R. I. (1993). Organizational behavior: Linking individuals and groups to organizational contexts. *Annual Review of Psychology, 44,* 195–229.

Muchinsky, P. M., & Monahan, C. J. (1987). What is person-environment congruence? Supplementary versus complementary models of fit. *Journal of Vocational Behavior, 31,* 268–277.

Multon, K. D., Brown, S. D., & Lent, R. W. (1991). Relation of self-efficacy beliefs to academic outcomes: A meta-analytic investigation. *Journal of Counselling Psychology, 38,* 30–38.

Mulvey, P. W., & Klein, H. J. (1998). The impact of perceived loafing and collective efficacy in group goal processes and group performance. *Organizational Behavior and Human Decision Processes, 74,* 62–87.

Munsterberg, H. (1913). *Psychology and industrial efficiency.* Boston: Houghton Mifflin.

Murphy, J. E. (2001). Feeling without thinking: Affective primacy and the unconscious processing of emotion. In J. A. Bargn & D. K. Apsley (Eds.), *Unraveling the complexities of social life: A festschrift in honor of Robert B. Zajonc* (pp. 39–53). Washington, DC: American Psychological Association.

Murray, H. (1938). *Explorations in personality.* New York: Oxford University Press.

Nagle, E. (1961). *The structure of science.* New York: Harcourt, Brace, and World.

Naylor, J. C., Pritchard, R. D., & Ilgen, D. R. (1980). *A theory of behavior in organizations.* New York: Academic Press.

Nease, A. A., Mudgett, B. O., & Quinones, M. A. (1999). Relationships among feedback sign, self-efficacy, and acceptance of performance feedback. *Journal of Applied Psychology, 84,* 806–814.

Neck, C., & Manz, C. C. (1996). Thought self-leadership: The impact of mental strategies on training on employee cognition, behavior and affect. *Journal of Organizational Behavior, 17,* 445–476.

Neubert, M. J. (1998). The value of feedback and goal setting over goal setting alone and potential moderators of this effect: A meta-analysis. *Human Performance, 11,* 321–335.

Newell, A., Shaw, J., & Simon, H. (1958). Elements of a theory of human problem solving. *Psychological Review, 65,* 151–166.

Newman, R. S. (1998). Students' help seeking during problem solving: Influences of personal and contextual achievement goals. *Journal of Educational Psychology, 90,* 644–658.

Nicholson, N. (1997). Evolutionary psychology: Toward a new view of human nature and organizational society. *Human Relations, 50,* 1053–1078.

Nicholson, N. (2005). Objections to evolutionary psychology: Reflections, implications and the leadership exemplar. *Human Relations, 58,* 393–409.

Nicholson, N., & Johns, G. (1985). The absence culture and the psychological contract: Who's in control of absence? *Academy of Management Review, 10,* 397–407.

Niepce, W., & Molleman, E. (1998). Work design issues in lean production from a sociotechnical systems perspective: Neo-Taylorism or the next step in sociotechnical design? *Human Relations, 51,* 259–287.

Nisbett, R. E. (2003). *The geography of thought: How Asians and Westerners think differently and why.* New York: The Free Press.

Nord, W. R. (1969). Beyond the teaching machine: The neglected area of operant conditioning in the theory and practice of management. *Organizational Behavior & Human Performance, 4,* 375–401.

Nord, W. R., Brief, A. P., Atieh, J. M., & Doherty, E. M. (1988). Work values and the conduct of organizational behavior. In B. M. Staw & L. L. Cummings (Eds.), *Research in organizational behavior* (Vol. 10, pp. 1–42). Greenwich, CT: JAI Press.

Nord, W. R., & Fox, S. (1996). The individual in organizational studies: The great disappearing act? In S. T. Clegg & C. Hardy (Eds.), *Handbook of organization studies* (pp. 148–174). Thousand Oaks, CA: Sage.

Oettingen, G., & Mayer, D. (2002). The motivating function of thinking about the future: Expectations versus fantasies. *Journal of Personality and Social Psychology, 83,* 1198–1212.

O'Driscoll, M. P., & Randall, D. M. (1999). Perceived organisational support, satisfaction with rewards, and employee job involvement and organizational commitment. *Applied Psychology: An International Review, 48,* 197–209.

O'Leary-Kelly, A. M., Martocchio, J. J., & Frink, D. D. (1994). A review of the influence of group goals on performance. *Academy of Management Journal, 37,* 1285–1301.

O'Reilly, C. A. (1991). Organizational behavior: Where we've been, where we're going. *Annual Review of Psychology, 42,* 427–458.

O'Reilly, C.A., Chatman, J., & Caldwell, D. F. (1991) People and organizational culture: A profile comparison approach to assessing person-organization fit. *Academy of Management Journal, 34,* 489–516.

Oldham, G. R. (1976). Job characteristics and internal motivation: The moderating effect of interpersonal and individual variables. *Human Relations, 29,* 559–569.

Organ, D. W. (1977). A reappraisal and reinterpretation of the satisfaction-causes-performance hypothesis. *Academy of Management Review, 2,* 46–53.

Organ, D. W. (1990). The motivational basis of organizational citizenship behavior. In B. M. Staw & L. L. Cummings (Eds.), *Research in organizational behavior* (Vol. 12, pp. 43–72). Greenwich, CT: JAI Press.

Organ, D. W., & Near, J. P. (1985). Cognitive vs. affective measures of job satisfaction. *International Journal of Psychology, 20,* 241–254.

Ostroff, C. (1992). The relationship between satisfaction, attitudes, and performance: An organizational level analysis. *Journal of Applied Psychology, 77*, 963–974.

Ottaway, D., & Stevens, J. (2001, October 29). Diplomats meet with Taliban on Bin Laden: Some contend U.S. missed its chance. *The Washington Post*, p. A01.

Parker, S. K. (2003). Longitudinal effects of lean production on employee outcomes and mediating role of work characteristics. *Journal of Applied Psychology, 88*, 620–634.

Parker, S. K., & Wall, T. D. (1998). *Job and work design: Organizing work to promote well-being and effectiveness.* Thousand Oaks, CA: Sage.

Penney, L. M., & Spector, P. E. (2002). Narcissism and counterproductive work behavior: Do bigger egos mean bigger problems? *International Journal of Selection and Placement, 10*, 126–133.

Perrewé, P. L., & Spector, P. E. (2002). Personality research in the organizational sciences. *Research in Personnel and Human Resources Management, 21*, 1–63.

Pervin, L. A. (1989). Goal concepts in personality and social psychology: A historical introduction. In L. A. Pervin (Ed.), *Goal concepts in personality and social psychology* (pp. 1–17). Hillsdale, NJ: Lawrence Erlbaum.

Peters, T. J., & Waterman, R. H. (1982). *In search of excellence.* New York: Harper & Row.

Peterson, C., & Seligman, M. E. P. (2004). *Character strengths and virtues: A handbook and classification.* Oxford University Press.

Peterson, R. S., Owens, P. D., & Martorana, P. V. (2000). *How does leadership affect organizational performance? Top management team dynamics moderate the relationship between CEO personality and organization performance.* Unpublished manuscript, Cornell University.

Pfeffer, J. (1982). *Organizations and organization theory.* Boston: Pitman Press.

Pfeffer, J., & Salancik, G. R. (1978). *The external control of organizations: A resource dependence perspective.* New York: Harper & Row.

Philips, D.C. (1987). *Philosophy, science, and social inquiry: Contemporary methodological controversies in social science and related fields of research.* New York: Pergamon.

Phillips, J. M., & Gully, S. M. (1997). Role of goal orientation, ability, need for achievement, and locus of control in the self-efficacy and goal setting process. *Journal of Applied Psychology, 82*, 792–802.

Phillips, J. M., Hollenbeck, J. R., & Ilgen, D. R. (1996). Prevalence and prediction of positive discrepancy creation: Examining a discrepancy between two self-regulation theories. *Journal of Applied Psychology, 81*, 498–511.

Pierce, C. S., & Jastrow, J. (1885). On small differences of sensation. *Memoirs of the National Academy of Sciences, 3*, 73–93.

Pinder, C. C. (1984). *Work motivation: Theory, issues, and applications.* Glenview, IL: Scott Foresman.

Pinder, C. C. (1998). *Work motivation: Theory, issues, and applications.* Upper-Saddle River, NJ: Prentice Hall.

Pinder, C. C., & Bourgeois, V. W. (1982). Controlling tropes in administrative science. *Administrative Science Quarterly, 27*, 641–652.

Pinder, C. C., & Harlos, K. P. (2002). Employee silence: Quiescence and acquiescence as responses to perceived injustice. In G. R. Ferris (Ed.), *Research in personnel and human resource management* (Vol. 20, pp. 331–369). Stratford, CT: JAI Press.

Platt, J. R. (1964). Strong inference. *Science, 146*, 347–353.

Polzer, J. T., & Neale, M. A. (1995). Constraints or catalysts? Reexamining goal setting with in the context of negotiation. *Human Performance, 8*, 3–26.

Pomaki, G., & Maes, S. (2005). *Beneficial and detrimental effects of goal attainment and goal disengagement on nurses well being.* Paper presented at the annual meeting of the Society of Industrial and Organizational Psychology, Los Angeles.

Popp, G. E., Davis, H. J., & Herbert, T. T. (1986). Those things yonder are no giants, but decision makers in international teams. In P. C. Earley & M. Erez (Eds.), *New perspectives on international industrial/organizational psychology* (pp. 410–455). San Francisco: Josey-Bass.

Porter, L. W. (1961). A study of perceived need satisfaction in bottom and middle management jobs. *Journal of Applied Psychology, 45,* 1–10.

Porter, L. W. (1962). Job attitudes in management: I. Perceived deficiencies in need fulfillment as a function of job level. *Journal of Applied Psychology, 46,* 375–384.

Porter, L. W. (1963a). Job attitudes in management: II. Perceived importance of needs as a function of job level. *Journal of Applied Psychology, 46,* 375–384.

Porter, L. W. (1963b). Job attitudes in management: III. Perceived deficiencies in need fulfillment as a function of line versus type of job. *Journal of Applied Psychology, 47,* 267–275.

Porter, L. W. (1963c). Job attitudes in management: IV. Perceived deficiencies in need fulfillment as a function of size of company. *Journal of Applied Psychology, 47,* 386–397.

Porter, L. W. (1965). Personnel management. *Annual Review of Psychology, 14,* 395–422.

Porter, L. W., & Lawler, E. E. (1968). *Managerial attitudes and performance.* Homewood, IL: Irwin.

Powell, D. M, & Meyer, J. P. (2004). Side-bet theory and the three-component model of organizational commitment. *Journal of Vocational Behavior, 65,* 157–177.

Prince-Gibson, E., & Schwartz, S. H. (1998). Value priorities and gender. *Social Psychology Quarterly, 61,* 49–67.

Pritchard, R. D. (1969). Equity theory: A review and critique. *Organizational Behavior & Human Performance, 4,* 176–211.

Pritchard, R. D. (1995). *Productivity measurement and improvement: Organizational case studies.* New York: Praeger.

Pritchard, R. D., Paquin, A. R., DeCuir, A. D., McCormick, M. J., & Bly, P. R. (2002). The measurement and improvement of organizational productivity: An overview of ProMES, the productivity measurement and enhancement system. In R. D. Pritchard, H. Holling, F. Lammers, & B. D. Clark (Eds.), *Improving organizational performance with the Productivity Measurement and Enhancement System: An international collaboration* (pp. 3–49). Huntington, NY: Nova Science.

Pugh, S. D. (2002). Emotion regulation in individuals and dyads: Causes, costs, and consequences. In R. Lord, R. J. Klimoski & R. Kanfer (Eds). *Emotions in the workplace* (pp. 147–182). San Francisco: Jossey-Bass.

Quick, J. C., Quick, J. D., Nelson, D. L., & Hurrell, J. J., Jr. (1997). *Preventive stress management in organizations.* Washington, DC: American Psychological Association.

Rao, P. U. B., & Kulkarni, A.V. (1998). Perceived importance of needs in relation to job level and personality make-up. *Journal of Indian Academy of Applied Psychology, 24,* 37–42.

Rasch, R. H., & Tosi, H. L. (1992). Factors affecting software developers' performance: An integrated approach. *MIS Quarterly, 16,* 395–413.

Renn, R. W. (1998). Participation's effect on task performance: Mediating roles of goal acceptance and procedural justice. *Journal of Business Research, 41,* 115–125.

Renn, R. W., & Fedor, D. B. (2001). Development and field test of a feedback seeking, self-efficacy, and goal setting model of work performance. *Journal of Management, 27,* 563–583.

Richardson, A. (1967). Mental practice: A review and discussion, Part I. *Research Quarterly, 38,* 95–97.

Richins, M. L., Dawson, S. (1992). A consumer values orientation for materialism and its measurement: Scale development and validation. *Journal of Consumer Research, 19,* 303–316.

Roberson, L., Deitch, E. A., Brief, A. P., & Block, C. J. (2003). Stereotype threat and feedback seeking in the workplace. *Journal of Vocational Behavior, 62,* 176–188.

Roberson, L., Korsgaard, A. M., & Diddams, M. (1990). Goal characteristics and satisfaction: Personal goals as mediators of situational effects on task satisfaction. *Journal of Applied Social Psychology, 20,* 920–941.

Roberson-Bennett, P.A. (1983). *The relationship between need for achievement and goal setting and their joint effect on task performance.* College of Business and Management, University of Maryland, unpublished doctoral dissertation.

Roberts, K. H., & Glick, W. (1981). The job characteristics approach to task design: A critical review. *Journal of Applied Psychology, 66,* 193–217.

Robinson, S. L. (1996). Trust and breach of the psychological contract. *Administrative Science Quarterly, 41,* 574–599.

Robinson, S. L., & Morrison, E. W. (2000). The development of psychological contract breach and violation: A longitudinal study. *Journal of Organizational Behavior, 21,* 525–546.

Rodgers, R., & Hunter, J. E. (1991). Impact of management by objectives on organizational productivity. *Journal of Applied Psychology, 76,* 322–336.

Roe, R. A. (1999). Work performance: A multiple regulation perspective. In C. L. Cooper & I. T. Robertson (Eds.), *International review of industrial and organizational psychology* (pp. 231–335). New York: John Wiley & Sons.

Roe, R.A. (2005). No more variables, please! Giving time a place in work and organizational psychology. In F. Avalone, S. Kepir Sinanagil, & A. Caetano (Eds.), *Convivence in organizations* (pp. 11–20). Milano: Guerini.

Roe, R. A., Zinovieva, I. L., Diebes, E., & Ten Horn, L.A. (2000). A comparison of work motivation in Bulgaria, Hungary, and the Netherlands: Test of a model. *Applied Psychology: An International Review, 49,* 658–687.

Roethlisberger, F. J. (1941). *Management and morale.* Cambridge, MA: Harvard University Press.

Roethlisberger, F. J. (1977). *The elusive phenomena.* Cambridge, MA: Harvard University Press.

Roethlisberger, F. J., & Dickson, W. J. (1939). *Management and the worker.* Cambridge, MA: Harvard University Press.

Rokeach, M. (1973). *The nature of human values.* NY: Free Press.

Ronan, W. W., Latham, G. P., & Kinne, S. B. (1973). The effects of goal setting and supervision on worker behavior in an industrial situation. *Journal of Applied Psychology, 58,* 302–307.

Ronen, S. (2001). Self-actualization versus collectualization: Implications for motivation theories. In M. Erez, U. Klenbeck & H. K. Thierry (Eds.), *Work motivation in the context of a globalizing economy* (pp. 341–368). Hillsdale, NJ: Lawrence Erlbaum.

Roney, C. J. R., Grigg, M., & Shanks, B. (2003). *The mediation and moderation of general motivational variables by specific goals that are negatively framed.* Unpublished manuscript.

Rosenthal, R. (2002). Covert communications in classrooms, clinics, courtrooms, and cubicles. *American Psychologist, 57,* 839–849.

Rosenthal, R., & Jacobson, L. (1966). Teachers' expectancies: Determinants of pupils' IQ gains. *Psychological Reports, 19,* 115–118.

Rounds, J. B. (1995). Vocational interests: Evaluating structural hypotheses. In O. Lubinski & R. V. Davis (Eds.), *Assessing individual differences in human behavior* (pp. 177–232). Palo Alto, CA: Davies-Black.

Rousseau, D. M. (1995). *Psychological contracts in organizations: Understanding written and unwritten agreements.* Thousand Oaks, CA: Sage.

Rousseau, D. M. (1997). Organizational behavior in the new organizational era. *Annual Review of Psychology, 48,* 515–546.

Rousseau, D. M. (2001). Schema, promise and mutuality: The building blocks of the psychological contract. *Journal of Occupational and Organizational Psychology, 74,* 511–541.

Rousseau, D. M. (2005a). Developing psychological contract theory. In M. Smith & M. Hitt (Eds.), *Great minds in management: The process of theory development* (pp. 190–214). Oxford, UK: Oxford University Press.

Rousseau, D. M. (2005b). *Idiosyncratic deals: When workers bargain for themselves.* New York: W. E. Sharp.

Rousseau, D. M., & Fried, Y. (2001). Location, location, location: Contextualizing organizational research. *Journal of Organizational Behavior, 22,* 1–13.

Rotter, J. B. (1966). Generalized expectancies for internal versus external control of reinforcement. *Psychological Monographs, 33,* 300–303.

Ruttenberg, H. (1941). Self-expression and labor unions. In National Research Council. *Fatigue of Workers.* New York: Reinhold Press.

Ryan, A. Sacco, J. M., McFarland, L. A., & Kriska, S. D. (2000). Applicant self-selection: Correlates of withdrawal from a multiple hurdle process. *Journal of Applied Psychology, 85*(2), 163–179.

Ryan, A. M., Sacco, J. M., McFarland, L. A., & Kriska, S. D. (2000). Applicant self-selection: Correlates of withdrawal from a multiple hurdle process. *Journal of Applied Psychology, 85,* 163–179.

Ryan, R. M., & Deci, E. L. (2000). Self-determination theory and the facilitation of intrinsic motivation, social development, and well-being. *American Psychologist, 55,* 68–78.

Ryan, T. A. (1947). *Work and Effort: The psychology of production.* New York: Ronald Press.

Ryan, T. A. (1970). *Intentional behavior.* New York: Ronald Press.

Ryan, T. A. & Smith, P. C. (1954). *Principles of industrial psychology* (pp. 353–427). New York: Ronald Press.

Saari, L. M., & Latham, G. P. (1982). Employee reactions to continuous and variable ratio reinforcement schedules involving a monetary incentive. *Journal of Applied Psychology, 67,* 506–508.

Sadri, G., & Robertson, I. T. (1993). Self-efficacy and work-related behavior: A review and meta-analysis. *Applied Psychology: An international review, 42,* 139–152.

Salancik, G. R. (1977). Commitment and the control of organizational behavior and belief. In B. M. Staw & G. R. Salancik (Eds.), *New directions in organizational behavior* (pp. 1–54). Chicago, IL: St. Claire Press.

Salancik, G. R., & Pfeffer, J. (1977). An examination of need-satisfaction models of job attitudes. *Administrative Science Quarterly, 22,* 427-456.

Saskin, M. (1984). Participative management is an ethical imperative. *Organization Dynamics, 12,* 4–22.

Schaubroeck, J., Ganster, D. C., & Jones, J. R. (1998). Organization and occupation influences in the attraction-selection-attrition process. *Journal of Applied Psychology, 83,* 869–891.

Schein, E. H. (1992). *Organizational culture and leadership* (2nd ed.). San Francisco: Jossey-Bass.

Schmidt, A. M., & Ford, J. K. (2003). Learning within a learner control training environment: The interactive effects of goal orientation and metacognitive instruction on learning outcomes. *Personnel Psychology, 56,* 405–429.

Schmidt, F. L. (1973). Implications of a measurement problem for expectancy theory research. *Organizational Behavior & Human Performance, 10,* 243–251.

Schminke, M., Cropanzano, R., & Rupp, D. E. (2002). Organization structure and fairness perceptions: The moderating effects of organizational level. *Organizational Behavior and Human Decision Processes, 89,* 881–905.

Schmitt, N., Cortina, J. M., Ingerick, M. J., & Weichmann, D. (2003). Personnel selection and employee performance. In W. C. Borman, D. R. Ilgen, R. J. Klimoski, & I. B. Weiner (Eds.), *Handbook of Psychology* (Vol. 12, pp. 77–106). New York: John Wiley and Sons.

Schneider, B. (1985). Organizational behavior. *Annual Review of Psychology, 36,* 573–611.

Schneider, B., Smith, B. D., & Paul, M. C. (2001). P-E fit and the attraction-selection-attrition model of organizational functioning: Introduction and overview. In M. Erez & U. Kleinbeck (Eds.), *Work motivation in the context of a globalizing economy* (pp. 231–246). Mahwah, NJ: Lawrence Erlbaum.

Schneider, B., Smith, D. B., Taylor, S., & Fleenor, J. (1998). Personality and organization: A test of the homogeneity of personality hypothesis. *Journal of Applied Psychology, 83,* 462–470.

Schneider, J., & Locke, E. A. (1971). A critique of Herzberg's incident classification system and a suggested revision. *Organizational behavior and human performance, 6,* 441–457.

Scholz, U., Dona, B., Sud, S., & Schwarzer, R. (2002). Is general self-efficacy a universal construct? Psychometric findings from 25 countries. *European Journal of Psychological Assessment, 18,* 242–251.

Schraw, G., Flowerday, T., & Reisetter, M. F. (1998). The role of choice in reader engagement. *Journal of Educational Psychology, 90,* 705–714.

Schwartz, S. H., & Sagie, G. (2000). Value consensus and importance: A cross-national study. *Journal of Cross Cultural Psychology, 31,* 465–497.

Schweitzer, M. E., Ordóñez, L., & Douma, B. (2004). The role of goal setting in motivating unethical behavior. *Academy of Management Journal, 47,* 422–432.

Seijts, G. H., & Latham, G. P. (2000a). The concept of goal commitment: Measurement and relationships with task performance. In R. Goffin & E. Helmes (Eds.), *Problems and solutions in human assessment: Honoring Douglas N. Jackson at seventy* (pp. 315–332). Dordrecht, The Netherlands: Kluwer Academic Publishers.

Seijts, G. H., & Latham, G. P. (2000b). The effects of goal setting and group size on performance in a social dilemma. *Canadian Journal of Behavioural Science, 32*, 104–116.

Seijts, G. H., & Latham, G. P. (2001). The effect of learning, outcome, and proximal goals on a moderately complex task. *Journal of Organizational Behavior, 22*, 291–307.

Seijts, G. H., & Latham, B. W. (2003). Creativity through applying ideas from fields other than one's own: Transferring knowledge from social psychology to industrial/organizational Psychology. *Canadian Psychology, 44*, 232–239.

Seijts, G. H., Latham, G. P., Tasa, K., & Latham, B. W. (2004). Goal setting and goal orientation: An integration of two different yet related literatures. *Academy of Management Journal, 47*, 227–239.

Seijts, G. H., Meertens, R. M., & Kok, G. (1997). The effects of task importance and publicness on the relation between goal difficulty and performance. *Canadian Journal of Behavioural Science, 29*, 54–62.

Seligman, M. E. P. (1998). *Learned Optimism: How to change your mind and your life.* New York: Pocket Books.

Seligman, E. P., & Czikszentmihalyi, M. (2000). Positive psychology: An introduction. *American Psychologist, 55*, 5–14.

Seo, M., Feldman Barrett, L. F., & Bartunek, J. M. (2004). The role of affective experience in work motivation. *Academy of Management Review, 29*, 423–439.

Sewell, G. (2004). Yabba-dabba-doo! Evolutionary psychology and the rise of Flintstone psychological thinking in organization and management studies. *Human Relations, 57*, 923–955.

Shaffer, R. H. (1953). Job satisfaction as related to need satisfactions in work. *Psychological Monographs: General and Applied, 67*, 364.

Shah, J. (2003a). The motivational looking glass: How significant others implicitly affect goal appraisals. *Journal of Personality and Social Psychology, 85*, 424–439.

Shah, J. (2003b). Automatic for the people: How representations of significant others implicitly affect goal pursuit. *Journal of Personality and Social Psychology, 84*, 661–681.

Shah, J. Y. (2005). The automatic pursuit and management of goals. *Current Directions in Psychological Science, 14*, 10–13.

Shalley, C., Oldham, G. , & Porac, J. (1987). Effects of goal difficulty, goal-setting method, and expected external evaluation on intrinsic motivation. *Academy of Management Journal, 30*, 553–563.

Shaw, J. D., & Gupta, N. (2004). Job complexity, performance, and well-being: When does supplies-values fit matter? *Personnel Psychology, 57*, 847–879.

Shoenfelt, E. (1996). Goal setting and feedback as a posttraining strategy to increase the transfer of training. *Perceptual and Motor Skills, 83*, 176–178.

Siero, F. W., Bakker, A. B., Dekker, G. B., & van den Burg, M. T. C. (1996). Changing organizational energy consumption behaviour through comparative feedback. *Journal of Environmental Psychology, 16*, 235–246.

Silver, W. S., & Bufanio, K. M. (1996). The impact of group efficacy and group goals on group task performance. *Small Group Research, 27*, 347–359.

Silverthorne, C. D. (1992). Motivation and management styles in the public and private sectors in Taiwan and a comparison with the United States. *Journal of Applied Social Psychology, 26*, 1827–1837.

Simmering, M. J., Colquitt, J. A., Noe, R. A., & Porter, C. (2003). Conscientiousness, autonomy fit, and development: A longitudinal study. *Journal of Applied Psychology, 88*, 954–963.

Simon, H. A. (1990). Invariants of human behavior. *Annual Review of Psychology, 41*, 1–19.

Skarlicki, D. P., Ellard, J. H., & Kelln, B. R. C. (1998). Third-party perceptions of a layoff: Procedural, derogation and retributive aspects of justice. *Journal of Applied Psychology, 83*, 119–127.

Skarlicki, D. P., & Latham, G. P. (1996). Increasing citizenship behavior within a labor union: A test of organizational justice theory. *Journal of Applied Psychology, 81*, 161–169.

Skarlicki, D. P., & Latham, G. P. (1997). Leadership training in organizational justice to increase citizenship behavior within a labor union: A replication. *Personnel Psychology, 50,* 617–633.

Skarlicki, D. & Latham, G. P. (2005). Training leaders in principles of organizational justice. In J. Greenberg & J. Colquitt (Eds). *Handbook of organizational justice* (pp. 499–522). Hillsdale, NJ: Lawrence Erlbaum.

Skarlicki, D. P., Latham, G. P., & Whyte, G. (1996). Utility analysis: Its evolution and tenuous role in human resource management decision making. *Canadian Journal of Administrative Sciences, 12,* 13–21.

Skinner, B. F. (1953). *Science and human behavior.* New York: Macmillan.

Skinner, B. F. (1974). *About behaviorism.* Oxford, UK: Knopf.

Smith, P. C., & Cranny, C. J. (1968). Psychology of men. *Annual Review of Psychology, 19,* 467–496.

Smith, P. C., Kendall, L. M., & Hulin, C. L. (1969). *The measurement of satisfaction in work and retirement: A strategy for the study of attitudes.* Skokie, IL: Rand McNally.

Sonnentag, S. (2002). Performance, well-being and self-regulation. In S. Sonnentag (Ed.), *Psychological management of individual performance* (pp. 405–424). New York: John Wiley & Sons.

Spangler, W. D., House, R. J., & Palrecha, R. (2004). Personality and leadership. In R. Schneider & D. B. Smith (Eds.), *Personality and organization* (pp. 251–291). Mahwah, NJ: Lawrence Erlbaum.

Spector, P. E. (1997). The role of frustration in antisocial behavior at work. In R. A. Giacalone & J. Greenberg (Eds.), *Antisocial behavior in organizations* (pp. 1–17). London: Sage.

Spence, K. W. (1948). The postulates and methods of "behaviorism." *Psychological Review, 55,* 67–78.

Spence, K. W. (1966). Cognitive and drive functions in the extinction of the conditioned eye-blink in human subjects. *Psychological Review, 73,* 445–457.

Srivastava, A., Locke, E. A., & Bartol, K. M. (2001). Money and subjective well-being: It's not the money, it's the motives. *Journal of Personality and Social Psychology, 80,* 959–971.

Stackman, R. W., Pinder, C. C., & Connor, P. R. (2000). Values lost: Redirecting research on values in the workplace. In N. M. Ashkanasy, C. P. M. Wilderom & M. F. Peterson (Eds.), *Handbook of organizational culture and climate* (pp. 37–54). Thousand Oaks, CA: Sage.

Stagner, R. (1950). Psychological aspects of industrial conflict. II. Motivation. *Personnel Psychology, 3,* 1–15.

Stagner, R. (1958). Industrial morale: II. Motivational aspects of industrial morale. *Personnel Psychology, 11,* 64–70.

Stajkovic, A. D., Locke, E. A. B., & Blair E. S. (in press). A first examination of the relationship between primed subconscious goals, assigned conscious goals, and task performance. *Journal of Applied Psychology.*

Stajkovic, A. D., & Luthans, F. (1998). Self-efficacy and work-related performance: A meta-analysis. *Psychological Bulletin, 124,* 240–261.

Stanne, M. B., Johnson, D. W., & Johnson, R. T. (1999). Does competition enhance or inhibit motor performance: A meta-analysis. *Psychological Bulletin, 125,* 133–154.

Staw, B. M. (2004). The dispositional approach to job attitudes: An empirical and conceptual review. In B. Schneider & D. B. Smith (Eds.), *Personality and organization* (pp. 163–191). Mahwah, NJ: Lawrence Erlbaum.

Staw, B. M., & Boettger, R. D. (1990). Task revision: A neglected form of work performance. *Academy of Management Journal, 33,* 534–559.

Steers, R. M. (2001). Call for papers. AMR Special Topic Forum—The Future of Work Motivation Theory. *Academy of Management Review, 26,* 686–687.

Steers, R. M., Mowday, R. T., & Shapiro, D. (2004). The future of work motivation. *Academy of Management Review, 29,* 379–387.

Steers, R. M., & Porter, L. W. (1974). The role of task-goal attributes in employee performance. *Psychological Bulletin, 81,* 434–452.

Steers, R. M., & Sanchez-Runde, C. J. (2002). Culture, motivation, and work behavior. In M. J. Gannon & K. L. Newman (Eds.), *The Blackwell handbook of cross-cultural management* (pp. 190–216). Oxford, UK: Blackwell Ltd.

Stevens, C. K., & Kristof, A. L. (1995). Making the right impression: A field study of applicant impression management during job interviews. *Journal of Applied Psychology, 80,* 587–606.

Stewart, G. L., & Barrick, M. R. (2004). Four lessons learned from the person-situation debate: A review and research agenda. In B. Schneider & D. B. Smith (Eds.), *Personality and organization* (pp. 61–86). Mahwah, NJ: Lawrence Erlbaum.

Sue-Chan, C., & Latham, G. P. (2004) The relative effectiveness of external, peer, and self-coaches for improving MBA teamplaying and EMBA academic performance. *Applied Psychology: An International Review, 53,* 260–278.

Sue-Chan, C., & Ong, M. (2002). Goal assignment and performance: Assessing the mediating role of goal commitment and self-efficacy and the moderating role of power distance. *Organizational Behavior and Human Decision Processes, 89,* 1140–1161.

Sumer, H. C., & Knight, P. A. (2001). How do people with different attachment styles balance work and family? A personality perspective on work-family linkage. *Journal of Applied Psychology, 86,* 653–663.

Summers, T. P., & Hendrix, W. H. (1991). Modelling the role of pay equity perceptions: A field study. *Journal of Occupational Psychology, 64,* 145–157.

Survey Research Center, University of Michigan (1948). Selected findings from a study of clerical workers in the Prudential Insurance Company of America. *Survey Research Center Study #6,* University of Michigan, Ann Arbor.

Swann, W. B. (1990). To be adored or known? The interplay of self-enhancement and self verification. In R. M. Sorrento & E. J. Higgins (Eds.), *Motivation and cognition* (pp. 408–448). New York: Guilford Publications.

Tabernero, C., & Wood, R. E. (1999). Implicit theories versus the social construal of ability in self-regulation and performance on a complex task. *Organizational Behavior and Human Decision Processes, 78,* 104–127.

Tajfel, H. (Ed.). (1978). *Differentiation between social groups: Studies in the social psychology of intergroup relations.* London: Academic Press.

Tan, V., Cheatle, M. D., Mackin, S., Moberg, P. J., & Esterhai, J. L. (1997). Goal setting as a predictor of return to work in a population of chronic musculoskeletal pain patients. *International Journal of Neuroscience, 92,* 161–170.

Tang, T. L. P., & Reynolds, D. B. (1993). Effects of self-esteem and perceived goal difficulty on goal setting, certainty, task performance, and attributions. *Human Resource Development Quarterly, 4,* 153–170.

Taylor, F. W. (1911). *Principles of scientific management.* New York: Harper.

Tekleab, A. G., Takeuchi, R., & Taylor, M. S. (2005). Extending the chain of relationships among organizational justice, social exchange, and employee reactions: The role of contract violations. *Academy of Management Journal, 48,* 146–157.

Tepper, B. J. (2000). Consequences of abusive supervision. *Academy of Management Journal, 43,* 176–190.

Tett, R. P., & Burnett, D. D. (2003). A personality trait-based interactionist model of job performance. *Journal of Applied Psychology, 88,* 500–517.

Tett, R. P., Jackson, D. N., Rothstein, M., & Reddon, J. R. (1994). Meta-analysis of personality-job performance relations: A reply to Ones, Mount, Barrick, and Hunter (1994). *Personnel Psychology, 47,* 147–156.

Tett, R. P., & Meyer, J. P. (1993). Job satisfaction, organizational commitment, turnover intention, and turnover: Path analysis based on meta-analytic findings. *Personnel Psychology, 46,* 259–293.

Theodorakis, Y., Laparidis, K., Kioumourtzoglou, E., & Goudas, M. (1998). Combined effects of goal setting and performance feedback on performance and physiological response on a maximum effort task. *Perceptual and Motor Skills, 86,* 1035–1041.

Theorell, T., & Karasek, R. A. (1996). Current issues to the psychosocial job strain and cardiovascular disease research. *Journal of Occupational Health Psychology, 1,* 9–26.

Thorensen, C. J., Kaplan, S. A., Barsky, A. P., Warren, C. R., & de Chermont, K. (2003). The affective underpinnings of job perceptions and attitudes: A meta-analytic review and integration. *Psychological Bulletin, 129,* 914–945.

Thorndike, E. L. (1911). *Animal intelligence.* New York: Macmillan.

Thorndike, E. L. (1917). The curve of work and the curve of satisfyingness. *Journal of Applied Psychology, 1,* 265–267.

Thurstone, L. L. (1929). Theory of attitude measurement. *Psychological Review, 36,* 222–241.

Tiffin, J. (1952). *Industrial psychology.* New York: Prentice Hall.

Tjosvold, D., Leung, K., & Johnson, D. (2000). Cooperative and competitive conflict in China. In M. Deutsch & P. T. Coleman (Eds.), *The handbook of conflict resolution: Theory and practice* (pp. 475–495). San Francisco: Jossey-Bass.

Tolman, E. C. (1932). *Purposive behavior in animals and men.* New York: Appleton-Century-Crofts.

Triandis, H. C. & Suh, E. M. (2002). Cultural influences on personality. *Annual Review of Psychology, 53,* 133–160.

Trip, T. M., Bies, R. J., & Aquino, K. (2002). Poetic justice or petty jealousy? The aesthetics of revenge. *Organizational Behavior and Human Decision Processes, 89,* 966–984.

Trist, E. L. (1981). *The evolution of socio-technical systems: A conceptual framework and an action research program.* Ontario: Ministry of Labour.

Trist, E. L., & Bamforth, K. W. (1951). Some social and psychological consequences of the Longwall method of coal-getting. *Human Relations, 4,* 3–38.

Trompenaars, F., & Hampden-Turner, C. (1998). *Riding the waves of culture: Understanding diversity in global business.* New York: McGraw-Hill.

Tubbs, M. E. (1993). Commitment as a moderator of the goal performance relation: A case for clearer concept definition. *Journal of Applied Psychology, 78,* 86–97.

Tubbs, M. E. (1994). Commitment and the role of ability in motivation: Comment on Wright, O'Leary-Kelly, Cortina, Klein, and Hollenbeck (1994). *Journal of Applied Psychology, 79,* 804–811.

Tubbs, M. E., & Dahl, J. G. (1992). An examination of individuals' information processing in the formation of goal commitment judgements. *Journal of Psychology, 126,* 181–188.

Tubbs, M. E., & Ekerberg, S. E. (1991). The role of intentions in work motivation: Implications for goal setting theory and research. *Academy of Management Review, 16,* 188–199.

Tuckey, M., Brewer, N., & Williamson, P. (2002). The influence of motives and goal orientation on feedback seeking. *Journal of Occupational and Organizational Psychology, 75,* 195–216.

Turillo, C. J., Folger, R., Lavelle, J. J., Umphress, E. E., & Gee, J. O. (2002). Is virtue its own reward? Self-sacrificial decisions for the sake of fairness. *Organizational Behavior and Human Decision Processes, 89,* 839–865.

Uhrbrock, R. S. (1934). Attitudes of 4430 employees. *Journal of Social Psychology, 5,* 365–377.

Umstot, D. D., Bell, C. H., & Mitchell, T. R. (1976). Effects of job enrichment and task goals on satisfaction and productivity: Implications for job design. *Journal of Applied Psychology, 61,* 379–394.

Van den Bos, K. (2002). Assimilation and contrast in organizational justice: The role of primed mindsets in the psychology of the fair process effect. *Organizational Behavior and Human Decision Processes, 89,* 866.

Van den Bos, K., Wilke, H. A. M., & Lind, E. A. (1998). When do we need procedural fairness? The role of trust in authority. *Journal of Personality and Social Psychology, 75,* 1449–1458.

Van Eerde, W., & Thierry, H. (1996). Vroom's expectancy models and work-related criteria: A meta-analysis. *Journal of Applied Psychology, 81,* 575–586.

Van Vianen, A. E. M. (2000). Person-organization fit: The match between newcomers' and recruiters' preferences for organizational cultures. *Personnel Psychology, 53,* 113–149.

Vance, R. J., & Colella, A. (1990). Effects of two types of feedback on goal acceptance and personal goals. *Journal of Applied Psychology, 75,* 68–76.

Vancouver, J. B., & Day, D. V. (2005). Industrial and organizational research on self-regulation: From constructs to applications. *Applied Psychology: An International Review, 54,* 155–185.

Vancouver, J. B., Thompson, C. M. & Williams, A. A. (2001). The changing signs in the relationships among self-efficacy, personal goals, and performance. *Journal of Applied Psychology, 86,* 605–620.

Vanderslice, V. J., Rice, R. W., & Julian, J. W. (1987). The effects of participation in decision-making on worker satisfaction and productivity: An organizational simulation. *Journal of Applied Social Psychology, 17,* 158-170.

VandeWalle, D. M. (1996). *Are our students trying to prove or improve their ability? Development and validation of an instrument to measure academic goal orientation.* Paper presented at the 56th annual meeting of the Academy of Management, Cincinnati, OH, August.

VandeWalle, D. M. (1997). Development and validation of a work domain goal orientation instrument. *Educational and Psychological Measurement, 57,* 995–1015.

VandeWalle, D. M. (1999). *Goal orientation comes of age for adults: A literature review.* Paper presented at the annual meeting of the Academy of Management, Chicago, IL.

VandeWalle, D. M. (2003). A goal orientation model of feedback-seeking behavior. *Human Resource Management Review,* 13, 581–604.

VandeWalle, D. M., Brown, S. P., Cron, W. L., & Slocum, J. W. (1999). The influence of goal orientation and self-regulation tactics on sales performance: A longitudinal field test. *Journal of Applied Psychology, 84,* 249–259.

VandeWalle, D. M., Cron, W. L., & Slocum, J. W. (2001). The role of goal orientation following performance feedback. *Journal of Applied Psychology, 86,* 629–640.

VandeWalle, D. M., & Cummings, L. L. (1997). A test of the influence of goal orientation on the feedback-seeking process. *Journal of Applied Psychology, 82,* 390–400.

Van-Dijk, D., & Kluger, A. N. (2004). Feedback sign effect on motivation: Is it moderated by regulatory focus? *Applied Psychology: An International Review, 53,* 113–135.

Vermunt, R., & Steensma, H. (2001). Stress and justice in organizations: An exploration into justice processes with the aim to find mechanisms to reduce stress. In R. Cropanzano (Ed.), *Justice in the workplace: From theory to practice* (Vol. 2, pp. 27–48). Mahwah, NJ: Lawrence Erlbaum.

Verplanken, B., & Holland, R.W. (2002). Motivated decision making: Effects of activation and self-centrality of values on choices and behavior. *Journal of Personality and Social Psychology, 82,* 434–447.

Viteles, M. S. (1932). *Industrial psychology.* New York: WW. Norton.

Viteles, M. S. (1953). *Motivation and morale in industry.* New York: WW Norton.

Von Bergen, C. W., Soper, B., & Rosenthal, G. T. (1996). The moderating effects of self-esteem and goal difficulty level on performance. *College Student Journal, 30,* 22–267.

Vroom, V. H. (1959). Some personality determinants of the effects of participation. *Journal of Abnormal Social Psychology, 59,* 322–327.

Vroom, V. H. (1960). *Some personality determinants of the effects of participation.* Englewood Cliffs, NJ: Prentice Hall.

Vroom, V. H. (1964). *Work motivation.* New York: John Wiley & Sons.

Vroom, V. H. (1967). *Some observations on Herzberg's two-factor theory.* Paper presented at the meeting of American Psychological Association, Washington.

Vroom, V. H. (2005). On the origins of expectancy theory. In K. Smith & M. Hitt (Eds.), *Great minds in management: The process of theory development* (pp. 239–258). New York: Oxford University Press.

Vroom, V. H., & Maier, N. R. (1961). Industrial psychology. *Annual Review of Psychology, 12,* 413–441.

Wagner, J. A., III. (1994). Participation's effect on performance and satisfaction: A reconsideration of research evidence. *Academy of Management Journal, 19,* 312–330.

Wahba, M. A., & Bridwell, L.G. (1976). Maslow reconsidered: A review of research on the need hierarchy theory. *Organizational Behavior and Human Performance, 15,* 212–240.

Wall, T. D., & Jackson, P. R. (1995). New manufacturing initiatives and shop floor job design. In A. Howard (Ed.), *The changing nature of work* (pp. 139–174). San Francisco, CA: Jossey-Bass.

Wanous, J. P. (1973). Effects of realistic job previews on job acceptance, job attitudes and job survival. *Journal of Applied Psychology, 58,* 327–332.

Watson, J. B. (1913). Psychology as the behaviorist views it. *Psychological Review, 20,* 158–177.

Watson, J. B. (1925). *Behaviorism.* New York: WW Norton.

Watson, J. B., & McDougall, W. (1928). *The battle of behaviorism.* London: Kegan Paul.

Wanberg, C. R., Glomb, T. M., Song, Z., & Sorenson, S. (2005). Job-search persistence during unemployment: A 10 wave longitudinal study. *Journal of Applied Psychology, 90,* 411–430.

Wanberg, C. R., Kanfer, R., & Rotundo, M. (1999). Unemployed individuals: Motives, job-search competencies, and job-search constraints as predictors of job seeking and reemployment. *Journal of Applied Psychology, 84,* 897–910.

Wathne, K. H., & Heide, J. B. (2000). Opportunism in interfirm relationships: Forms, outcomes, and solution. *Journal of Marketing, 64,* 35–51.

Watson Wyatt Worldwide (2002). Human capital index: Human capital as a lead indicator of shareholder value, Washington, DC.

Weinberg, R. S., Fowler, C., Jackson, A., Bagnall, J., & Bruya, L. (1991). Effect of goal difficulty on motor performance: A replication across tasks and subjects. *Journal of Sport and Exercise Psychology, 13,* 160–173.

Weiner, B., & Graham, S. (1999). Attribution in personality psychology. In L. Pervin & O. Johns (Eds.), *Handbook of personality: Theory and research* (pp. 605–628). New York: Guilford Press.

Weiss, H. M., & Brief, A. P. (2001). Affect at work: A historical perspective. In R. L. Payne and C. L. Cooper (Eds.), *Emotions at work: Theory, research, and applications for management* (pp. 133–172). Chichester, UK: John Wiley & Sons.

Weiss, H. M., & Cropanzano, R. (1996). Affective events theory: A theoretical discussion of the structure, causes, and consequences of affective experiences at work. In B. M. Staw and L. L. Cummings (Eds.), *Research in Organizational Behavior, 18,* 1–74. Greenwich, CT: JAI Press.

Weldon, E., Jehn, K. A., & Pradham, P. (1991). Processes that mediate the relationship between group goal and improved group performance. *Journal of Personality and Social Psychology, 61,* 555– 569.

Wernimont, P. F., & Campbell, J. P. (1968). Signs, samples, and criteria. *Journal of Applied Psychology, 52,* 372–376.

Wexley, K. M., & Baldwin, T. T. (1986). Posttraining strategies for facilitating positive transfer: An empirical exploration. *Academy of Management Journal, 29,* 503-520.

Wexley, K. M., & Latham, G. P. (2002). *Developing and training human resources in organizations* (3rd ed.). New York: Harper Collins.

White, J. (1982). *Rejection.* Reading, MA: Addison-Wesley.

Whyte, G., & Latham, G. P. (1997). The futility of utility analysis revisited: When even an expert fails. *Personnel Psychology, 50,* 601–610.

Whyte, G., Saks, A., & Hook, S. (1997). When success breeds failure: The role of self-efficacy in escalating commitment to a losing course of action. *Journal of Organizational Behavior, 18,* 415–433.

Wicker, F. W., Brown, G., Wiehe, J. A., Hagen, A. S., & Reed, J. L. (1993). On reconsidering Maslow: An examination of the deprivation/domination proposition. *Journal of Research in Personality, 27,* 118–199.

Wiese, B. S., & Freund, A. M. (2005). Goal progress makes one happy, or does it? Longitudinal findings from the work domain. *Journal of Occupational and Organizational Psychology, 78,* 1–19.

Wiggins, J. S. (Ed.). (1996). *The five factor model of personality.* New York: Guilford Press.

Williams, J. R., Miller, C. E., Steelman, L. A., & Levy, P. E. (1999). Increasing feedback seeking in public contexts: It takes two (or more) to tango. *Journal of Applied Psychology, 84,* 969–976.

Wilson, E. O. (1999). *Consilience: The unity of knowledge.* New York: Vintage.

Winters, D., & Latham, G. P. (1996). The effect of learning versus outcome goals on a simple versus a complex task. *Group and Organization Management, 21,* 236–250.

Witt, L. A., & Ferris, G. R. (2003). Social skill as a moderator of the conscientiousness-performance relationship: Convergent results across four studies. *Journal of Applied Psychology, 88,* 809–821.

Witt, L. A., Burke, L. A. Barrick, M. R., & Mount, M. K. (2002). The interactive effective of consciousness and agreeableness on job performance. *Journal of Applied Psychology, 87*, 164–189.

Wofford, J. C., Goodwin, V. L., & Premarck, S. (1992). Meta-analysis of the antecedents of personal goal level and of the antecedents and consequences of goal commitment. *Journal of Management, 18*, 595–615.

Wong, A., Tjosvold, D., & Zi-Ya. (2005). Organizational partnerships in China: Self-interest, goal interdependence, and opportunism. *Journal of Applied Psychology, 90*, 782–791.

Wood, R. E. (2005). New frontiers for self regulation research in I/O psychology. *Applied Psychology: An International Review, 54*, 192–198.

Wood, R. E., & Bandura, A. (1989). Social-cognitive theory of organizational management. *Academy of Management Review, 14*, 361–384.

Wright, P. M., & Cordery, J. L. (1999). Production uncertainty as a contextual moderator of employee reactions to job design. *Journal of Applied Psychology, 84*, 456–463.

Wright, P. M., Gardner, T. M., Moynihan, K. N., & Allen, M. R. (2005). The relationship between HR practices and firm performance: Examining causal order. *Personnel Psychology, 58*, 409–446.

Wright, P. M., George, J. M., Farnsworth, S. A., & McMahan, G. C. (1993). Productivity and extra-role behavior: The effects of goals and incentives on spontaneous helping. *Journal of Applied Psychology, 78*, 374–381.

Wright, P. M., Kacmar, K. M., McMahan, G. C., & Deleeuw, K. (1995). P=f(M x A): Cognitive ability as a moderator of the relationship between personality and job performance. *Journal of Management, 21*, 1129–1139.

Wright, P. M., O'Leary-Kelly, A. M., Cortina, J. M., Klein, H. J., & Hollenbeck, J. R. (1994). On the meaning and measurement of goal commitment. *Journal of Applied Psychology, 79*, 795–803.

Wright, T. A. (2002). Dialogue: The importance of time in organizational research. *Academy of Management Journal, 45*, 343–345.

Wyatt, S., Fraser, J. A., & Stock, F. G. L. (1929). The effects of monotony in work. A preliminary inquiry. *Industrial Health Research Board Report, 56*, 47.

Wyatt, S., Frost, L., & Stock, F. G. L. (1934). *Incentives in repetitive work.* Industrial Health Research Board (Great Britain), Report No. 69.

Yankelovich, D. (1974). Turbulence in the working world: Angry workers, happy grads. *Psychology Today, 8*, 80–87.

Yukl, G. A., & Latham, G. P. (1975). Consequences of reinforcement schedules and incentive magnitudes for employee performance: Problems encountered in an industrial setting. *Journal of Applied Psychology, 60*, 294–298.

Yukl, G. A., & Latham, G. P. (1978). Interrelationships among employee participation, individual differences, goal difficulty, goal acceptance, goal instrumentality and performance. *Personnel Psychology, 31*, 305–324.

Yukl, G. A., Latham, G. P., & Pursell, E. D. (1976). The effectiveness of performance incentives under continuous and variable ratio schedules of reinforcement. *Personnel Psychology, 29*, 221–231.

Yukl, G., Wexley, K. N., & Seymore, J. D. (1972). Effectiveness of pay incentives under variable ratio and continuous reinforcement schedules. *Journal of Applied Psychology, 56*, 13–23.

Zetik, D. C., & Stuhlmacher, A. F. (2002). Goal setting and negotiation performance: A meta-analysis. *Group Processes & Intergroup Relations, 5*, 35–52.

Zimmerman, B. J., Bandura, A., & Martinez-Pons, M. (1992). Self-motivation for academic attainment: The role of self-efficacy beliefs and personal goal setting. *American Educational Research Journal, 29*, 663–676.

Index

Ability, 177
Academy of Management, xiv, xv
Academy of Management Journal, 219, xv
Achievement theory, 64
Ackerman, P. L., 17, 67, 68, 138, 152,
    155, 183, 248
Action theory, 63, 217–219
Adair, J. G., 19
Adams, J. S., 43, 44n, 95, 99
Adams, N. E., 72
Adler, A., 28n, 84, 177
AET (affective events theory), 223–224
Affect/emotion, emphasis on
    conclusions, 237–239
    introduction, 221–222
    moods and, 222–229
    organizational justice principles,
        229–233
    psychological contracts, 233–237
    spirituality factors, 239–240
Affect infusion model (AIM), 224
Affective events theory (AET), 223–224
Agarwal, R., 166
Age-related changes, 248
Aguinis, H., 154, 160
Aikin, 83
AIM (affect infusion model), 224
Ajila, C. O., 130
Ajzen, I., 15n
Albee, G., 37
Alderfer, C. P., 36, 40, 118
Allen, M. R., 4n
Allen, N. J., 179
Allport, G. W., 32
Alnaijar, A. A., 94
Alpander, G. G., 160
Alvi, M., 116
Amabile, T. M., 187
Amado, G., 157n

Ambrose, M. L., 60, 83, 162, 232
American Institutes for Research
    (AIR), xxvi
American Psychological Association
    (APA), xiii, xv
American Pulpwood Association
    (AP), xv, xxv, xxvi
Analysis, levels of, 257–258
Appraisal systems, 96, 233
Aquino, K., 232
Argyle, M., 20
Argyris, C., 233, 267n
Argyris, H., 38n, 40, 111
Arnold, H., xv, xvii, xviii
ASA (attraction, selection, attrition)
    model, 167–168
Ashford, S. J., 198, 199
Atieh, J. M., 118
Atkinson, J., 46, 56, 64
Attachment theory, 247
Attitudes, 224, xx
Attitude surveys, 15–16, 27, 53, 122
Attraction, selection, attrition
    (ASA) model, 167–168
Attribution theory, 53, 185, 186,
    245, 246
Audia, G., 183, 208
Austin, J. T., 11, 113
Automatic/non-conscious goals,
    190–198
Azrin, N. H., 78

Badin, I. J., 41
Bagnall, J., 82
Bagozzi, R. P., 85, 154, 155
Bailey, J. B., 199
Baldes, J. J., 62
Baldwin, T. T., 113
Bamworth, K. W., 42

Bandura, A., 7, 14n, 56, 64n, 66, 67, 70, 71, 72, 73n, 74, 75, 82, 101, 102, 103, 106, 119, 120, 122, 127, 128, 130, 147, 155, 159, 169, 172n, 183, 184, 200, 202n, 203, 205, 207, 208, 209, 213, 214, 216, 219, 243n, 244, 245, 252, 258n, 259, xi
Barber, A. E., 99
Barbey, 67
Bar-Eli, M., 82
Bargh, J. A., 192, 193
Barlay, I. J., 233
Barling, J., 232
Baron, A., 51
Barrett, L. F., 221, 225, 226, 227
Barrick, M. R., 133, 135, 136, 145
Barsade, S. G., 191, 222, 227
Barsalou, 67
Barsky, A. P., 222, 224
Bartlett, J., 167n
Bartol, K. M., 150
Bartunek, J. M., 221, 225, 226.227
Baum, J. R., 146
Bavelas, J., 22, 63
Bayer, U., 203
Beach, H. D., 194, xxiv, xxix
Beach, L., xv
Beacker, B. E., 4n
Becker, T. E., 178
Beer, M., xxxiii
Behavioral observation scales (BOS), xxvi
Behaviorism, 9–11, 27, 48–52, 175, 238, xx
Behavior modification, 48–52
    See also Behaviorism
Bell, C. H., 62, 84, xv, xvii, xxx
Belluschi, P., xvii, xxxii
Bennett, S., 16n, 162
Bennis, W., 32
Benson, L., 237
Berdahl, J., xv
Bernichon, T., 199
Bernston, G. G., 229
Berry, J. M., 82
Beyer, J., 72
Bierbauer, G., 152, 155
Bies, R. J., 96, 232
Biglan, A., 47
Billingual, xxiii, xxxii
Bingham, W. V., 246

Biological determinants, 6–9, 27, 251
Black, J. S., 199
Blader, S. L., 233
Blair, E. S., 194, 195
Blatt, R., 198
Block, C. J., 199
Blood, M. R., 40, 41n, 235n, xxix
Blum, M. L., 21
Bly, P. R., 206
Bobko, P., 73n, 74n, 82
Bobocel, D. R., 230, 231, 232
Boekaerts, M., 203
Boettger, R. D., 70
Bono, J. E., 106, 140
Boone, J., 32, 60
Borden, E. S., 247
Borman, W. C., 169, 256n
Boundaryless psychology
    clinical psychology and, 244–248
    computer models, 255–256
    evolutionary psychology and, 249–251
    integration and, 258–261
    introduction, 228n, 243
    levels of analysis, 257–258
    life span research, 248–249
    social psychology and, 244
    teams and, 256–257
    time factors, 253–255
Bourgeois, V. W., 258
Bowen, W., 32, 60
Bowlby, J., 247
Brandstätter, V., 191, 203
Bray, D. W., 56, 112
Brayfield, A. H., 28, 105, 106, xxiv
Brendl, C. M., 15n
Brennan, K. A., 247
Brett, J. F., 142, 152
Brewer, N., 199
Bridwell, L. G., 35, 121
Brief, A. P., 110n, 113, 118, 127, 191, 199, 222, 223, 227
Brigham, T. A., 204
Britz, R. D., Jr., 99
Brockner, J., 97, 152, 155
Brown, A., 247n
Brown, C. W., 22
Brown, G., 128, 129
Brown, J. D., 199
Brown, S. P., 142, 202
Brown, T. C., 184, 245, 277, xvi

Brtek, M. D., 159
Bruya, L., 82
Brynes, J. P., 250n
Budworth, M. H., 116, 245, xiv, xvi
Bufanio, K. M., 83
Burke, L. A., 136
Burnett, D. D., 145
Burtt, H. E., 11, 13
Business strategy, ix
Buss, 250
Bussey, 252
Butler, B., xxxii
Button, S. B., 142, 201
Byrne, Z. S., 231, 232

Cable, J. P., 162, 163, 167, 171n
Cacioppo, J. T., 229
Caldwell, D. F., 168
Cale, A., 82
Cameron, J., 102, 103, 104
Campbell, D., 221n
Campbell, D. T., 43, 62
Campbell, J. P., 49, 50, 68, 70, 78, 84n,
    108, 111n, 113, 115, 267, 278,
    279n, xxvii
Campbell, R, xivn
Campion, M. A., 65n, 79, 83, 159, 160
Canadian Psychological Association
    (CPA), xix, xxx
Canadian Society of Industrial and
    Organizational Psychology, xiv
Caplan, R. D., 162
Cappelli, P., 43n
Caprara, G. V., 213
Carranza, L. V., 247
Carson, K. D., 82
Carson, P. P., 82
Carstensen, L. L., 249
Carter, K. D., 160
Cartledge, N. D., 65, 198
Carver, C. S., 65, 66n, 67, 200
Cella, A., 113
Cervone, D., 64n, 66, 106
Chacko, T., 113
Chah, 63
Challagalla, G., 202
Chan, D., 237
Chang, G. S., 113
Charbonneau, C., 239
Chartrand, T. L., 193
Chatman, J. A., 149n, 150, 157, 168

Cheatle, M. D., 81
Chen, C. C., 199
Chen, G., 209
Chen, Z. X., 152, 155
Chicoine, E., 227
Ciske, P., 8(f)
Clark, K. B., 232n
Clarke, N. H., 239
Classical conditioning, 224
Cleeton, G. U., 7n, 8n
Clinical psychology, 244–248
Coch, L., 22, 108
Cognition, relevance of
    goal-setting theory, 176–198
    introduction, 175–176
    seeking feedback, 198–203
    self-regulation processes, 203–206
Cognitive dissonance theory, 43
Cognitive theory, 71, 130, 200
Cohen, A., 94
Cole, N., 97, 231, 277, xvi, xxxii
Collectivist cultures, 154
Colquitt, J. A., 168, 207, 230, 231, 232
Competition, 181
Complacency, 208
Complementary needs-supplies fit
    model, 163
Computer models, 255–256
Conflicting goals, 180
Conlon, D. E., 230, 232
Conscious goals, 177–180
Contractual agreements, 233–237
Control theory, 65–67, 130, 200, 208
Conway, N., 4n, 237
Conway, S., xvii
Cook, K. E., 199
Cooper, C. L., xix
Cooperative goal setting, 181
Cooper-Hakim, A., 94
Coping efforts, 221
Cordery, J. L., 84, 157, 158
Core self-evaluations, 139–141
Correlational psychology, 41n
Cortina, J. M., 135
Cote, S., 133, 134, xv
Coyle-Shapiro, J., 237
Cranny, C. J., 39
Critical incident technique (CIT),
    37n, 38
Crockett, W. H., 28, 105, 106, xxiv
Cron, W. L., 142, 201, 202

Cronbach, L. J., 51n, 171n, 238
Cropanzano, R., 96, 223, 229, 231, 232
Crown, D. F., 82n
Csikszentmihalyi, M., 204
Cultural self-representation model, 152
Cummings, L. L., 42, 114

D
Dachler, H. P., 59
D'Ailly, H., 144
Dalhousie University, xxiii
Daniels, D., 56, 119, 133, 176, xix
Davis, H. J., 160
Dawis, R. V., 41n, 133n, 162, 228n, 239
Dawson, S., 150
Day, A. L., 7, 139, 205
Deadline goals, 185
Debowski, S., 200
Deception, 216
De Chermont, K., 222, 224
Deci, E. L., 22, 101, 102, 103, 104, 142,
    143, 144
Decision making, participative, 108–116
DeCuir, A. D., 206
DeGilder, D., 256
Deitch, E. A., 199
De Jonge, J., 159
Deleeuw, K., 21n
DeNisi, A., 199
Dennis, A. R., 166
Denny, A. T., 102
Depression, 230
DeRue, D. S., 162
Determinism, 51
Developmental theory, 137
De Waal, F. B. M., 249
Dickson, W. J., 18
Diddams, M., 83
Diebes, E., 160
Differential clinical psychology,
    41n, xxiii
Direction mediators, 85
Dirks, K. T., 153
Discontent, 29, 37n
Distributive justice, 95, 97, 230
Dixon, R. S., 85
Doherty, E. M., 118
Don, S. G., 199
Dona, B., 155
Donovan, J. S., 204

Dorner, D., 183
Dossett, D. L., 50, 78, 110, 113, 122, 273,
    xvi, xxxii
Dostoyevsky, F., 268n
Douma, B., 189
Downer, J. T., 247
Drach-Zahavy, A., 182
Drucker, P. C., 5
Drug screening policy, 96
Dukerich, J. M., 118
Dulaney, D. E., 51
Dunnette, M. D., 17, 20, 21, 39, 43, 50,
    59n, 108, 115, xxv, xxvii
Durham, C. C., 139, 184, 210
Dust-bowl empiricism. See Motivation
    psychology (1925-1950)
Dweck, C. S., 141, 202, 204
Dyer, L., 104
Dysfunctional persistence, 208

Eagly, A. H., 15n, 250n
Earley, P. C., 63, 82, 112, 113, 114, 152
Eccles, J. S., 127, 243
Eden, D., 209, 214, 215, 216
Edminster, R. O., 63
Edwards, J. R., 159, 162, 163, 164n, 171
Efficacy beliefs. See Self-efficacy
Egeth, H., 194n
Eisenberger, R., 102, 103, 227
Ellard, J. H., 232
Ellemers, N., 256
Elliot, A. J., 201
Ellis, A. P. J., 165, 218, 245
Emery, F. E., 42
Emotional control, 228–229
Emotional exhaustion, 230
Emotional maladjustment, 222–223
    See also Affect/emotion,
        emphasis on
Emotional stability, 136, 166
Emotional unconscious, 225
Emotion appraisals, 226
Emotion regulation, 226
Empathy box, 210f, 211, 212
Employee-attitude survey, 15
    See also Attitude surveys
Employee environment. See
    Person-environment fit model
Employee narcissism, 247–248
Employee performance, 28–29

Endler, N. S., 161
Engeland, C. G., 229
Environmental events/influences, 224, 251
Epiphenomenalism, 51
Equity theory, 42–44, 95, 123
Erez, M., 22n, 63, 64n, 67n, 74, 78, 113, 114, 133, 140, 152, 178, 182, 257
Ericksen, C. W., 194
Error management, 182–183, 200, 201
Eskew, D. E., 96
Esteem needs, 31, 34
Esterhai, J. L., 81
Evolutionary psychology, 249–251
Expectancy theory, 44–48, 60, 64, 65, 71n, 74, 75, 149, 238
Explicit motives, 187
Exploitation, prevalence of, 180
Extrinsic motivation, 102–105, 142, 179, 187–188
Extroverts, 135

Fabes, R. A., 227
Fairness feelings, 231–232
Farkas, A. J., 94n
Farnsworth, S. A., 63
Farr, J. L., 141
Farris, G. R., 79
Fassina, N. E., 80, 101, xix, xvi
Faucheux, C., 157n
Fay, D., 143, 144, 203, 218n, xvi
Fedor, D. B., 198
Feedback, processing of, 52, 62, 63, 66, 177, 192, 198–203, 204
Feeney, E. J., 51
Feingold, A., 250n
Feldman, 221
Feminine cultures, 151
Feren, D. B., 102n
Ferguson, L. W., 8n, 161
Ferguson, M. J., 192
Ferrari, K., 135
Ferris, G. R., 41, 135
Ferster, C. B., 49
Festinger, L., 43
Fiedler, F., 71n, 271n, xv
Field experiments, 17–18
Fisher, 222, 223
Fitzsimons, G. M., 193
Five Factor Model (FFM), 134, 135–137

Flanagan, J. C., 37, xxv, xxvi
Fleishman, E., xxix, xxvi
Flood, P. C., 233
Flowerday, T., 144
Folger, R., 59, 95, 96, 120, 122, 231, 232
Ford, J. K., 104, 120, 182
Ford, R., 269
Forde, L., 135
Forgas, J. P., 224
FOS (Foundations for Organizational Science). *See* Organizational science, foundations for
Fowler, C., 82
Francesco, A. M., 152, 155
Francis, L., 7n
Franco, L. M., 16n, 162
Franke, R. H., 20
Fraser, J. A., 17
Frayne, C. A., 75, 76, 204, 218n, 275, xvi, xxxii
Frederiksen, L. W., 50
French, J. R. P., 22, 108, 162
French, W., xv
Frese, M., 14n, 63, 69, 79, 111n, 143, 144, 182, 183, 191, 200, 203, 217, 218, 228
Freud, S., 6, 7, 14, 27, 191
Freund, A. M., 228
Fried, Y., 41, 78, 79, 151n, 186, 219, 255
Frinke, D. D., 185
Frost, P., ix
Furnham, A., 135

Galatea effect, 214–216
Gall, T. L., 239
Ganesan, S., 202
Ganster, D. C., 167
Gardner, T. M., 4n
Garland, H., 65
Gauggel, S., 81
Gavino, J. C., 154, 155
Geary, D. C., 250n
Gee, J. O., 232
Gelfand, J., 152, 155
General Causality Orientation Scale, 143
General self-efficacy (GSE) measure, 209–210
George, J. M., 63, 223n, 224
Georgia Tech, xxv, xxvi

Gerhart, F., 4n
Geringer, J. M., 204
Ghiselli, E. E., 22, 33, 34, 84n, xxv
Gilbreth, F. B., 11
Gilbreth, L. M., 11
Gilliland, S. W., 237
Gilmer, B. V. H., 8n
Gist, M., 74, xv
Glick, W., 41, 59, 121
Global village, 166
Glomb, T. M., 134, 140
Goal attainment. *See* Goal-setting theory
Goal commitment, 177
Goal limitations, 63–70
Goal orientation theory, 141–142,
     178, 201, 202, 204
Goal regulation, 179
Goal-setting theory
   action theory and, 217–218
   conscious goals and, 177–180
   contextual conditions of, 180–190
   emergence of, 54–58
   emotional control and, 227–229
   empirical studies on, 60–63, 73, 75,
        80, 95, 176–177
   implementation intentions and
        subconscious goals, 190–198
Godat, L. M., 204
Godfrey, E. G., 251
Gollwitzer, P. M., 191, 192, 203
Gomez, C., 152, 155
Goodman, J. S., 200
Goodman, P., 200, 274-275
Goodness-of-fit model, 169
Gottier, R. F., 84n
Graham, S., 185
Grant, D. L., 112, 2021
Grant, K., 239
Gray, J. A., 135
Great Depression, 13, 30, 117
Greenberg, J., 22, 59, 95, 96, 97, 98,
        113, 120, 122, 152, 155, 229, 230,
        232, 244n
Greenhaus, J. H., 41
The Greening of America, xxviii
Growth facilitating tasks, 83–84
Guest, D., 4n
Guion, R. M., 28n, 84n, 107n,
        110n, 278
Gully, S. M., 85, 142, 182, 209
Gunz, H., xv

Gupta, N., 163, 164
Gustafson, S. B., 165
Guthrie, I. K, 227
Guzzo, R. A., 210n

Hackman, J. R., 40, 41, 53, 59, 79, 121,
     157, 159, 160
Hadley, C. N., 187
Hagen, A. S., 129
Haire, M., 19n, 34n
Hakel, M., xivn, 270
Hall, D. T., 35
Hall, G. S., 8n
Hamel, K., 94
Hampden-Turner, C., 156
*Handbook of Organizational Behavior
     Management* (Frederiksen), 50
Hanges, P. J., 230, 251
Hannah, 222, 223
Harackiewicz, J. M., 201
Harlos, K. P., 231
Harmon, W., 185, 186
Harpell, 182
Harrell, J. J., Jr., 7n, 23, 24n
Harrell, T. W., 6
Harrison, R. V., 162
Harvey, J. L., 128
Haslam, S. A., 130, 256
Hawkley, L. C., 229
Hawthorne studies, 18–21, 28
Hebb, D. O., 8, 36
Heckhausen, J., 226
Heggestad, E. D., 56, 137, 138
Heide, J. B., 180
Heimbeck, D., 191, 200, 203
Heine, S. J., 199
Hendrickx, M., 200
Heneman, H. G., 47, 57, 60
Henle, C. A., 154, 160
Henne, D., 127n, 149
Herbert, T. T., 160
Heron, A., 29, 30
Herzberg, F., 16, 33n, 37, 38, 39, 40, 41,
     99, 118, 157, 158
Heslin, P., 202, 244, 248, xvi
Higgins, E. T., 141
High Performance Cycle, 79, 80–95,
     101, 107
Hiller, N. J., 139
Hinrichs, J. R., 57, 121
Hinsz, V. B., 81, 82

Hired hands, 23
Historical perspectives in industrial organizational psychology: The first hundred years (Budworth), xix
Hoffman, D. A., 141
Hofstede, G., 24n, 151, 152, 156, 157
Hogan, J., 131
Hogan, R., 7n, 131, 133, 134, 135n, 136
Hoke, B., xxx, xxxii, xxxiii
Holland, B., 131
Holland, J., 133n
Holland, R. W., 150
Hollenbeck, J. R., 165, 167n
Holmvall, C. M., 230
Homans, G. C., 18, 19
Honeycutt, H., 251
Hook, S., 208
Hopelessness feelings, 221, 231, 239
Hoppock, 16
Hothersall, D., 8
Hough, L. M., 133, 136, 137n, xi
Houkes, I., 159
House, R. J., 47, 135, xxx
Houser, J. D., 16
Howard, A., 56, 197, 198
Huber, V., xv
Huff, A., ix
Hulin, C. L., 40, 41n, 55n, 113, 138n, 169, 256
Hull, C. L., 23, 27, 72
Human Relations Movement, 18
Human Resource Management (HRM), 3, ix
Huselid, M. A., 4n

Ide, E., 199
Ilgen, D. R., 165, 169, 256, 258
Ilies, R., 204, 205, 224
Implementation intentions, 190–198
Implicit knowledge, 191
Implicit memory, 225n
Implicit motives, 187, 197
Individual differences, 84–85, 199
Individualistic cultures, 154
Individual motivation, 258
Industrial and Organization Psychology (I/O), 3
The Industrial/Organizational Psychologist (TIP), xxi
Ingerick, M. J., 135
Inness, M., 232

Integration model, of work motivation, 258–262
Interactional justice, 97, 230, 231
International Paper Company, xxx
Intrapsychological processes, 256
Intrinsic motivation, 102–105, 142, 179, 187
Ivancevich, J. M., 113

Jackson, A., 82
Jackson, D. N., 134, 165
Jacob, N., xvii
James, K., 153
James, L. R., 253
James, W., 7, 8, 127, 196, 238
Janssen. P. P. M., 159
Jarvis, C. B., 77n
Jensen, M. C., 188
Jiwani, 106
Job characteristics, effects of, 36–42, 53, 54, 79–80, 119, 157–161
Job choice literature, 99
Job depression, 158
Job Descriptive Index (JDI), 55n
Job Diagnostic Survey, 159
Job enrichment theory, 37, 40, 41, 42, 84
Job satisfaction, moods and, 222–229
Job satisfaction, performance and, 105–108
See also Goal-setting theory
Job satisfaction theory, 16, 24, 28–29, 37n, 57, 59
Johns, G., 151, 234, 255
Johnson, B. T., 250n
Johnson, D. W., 181
Johnson, E. C., 163
Johnson, R. E., 140
Johnson, R. T., 181
Jones, G., 82
Jones, J. M., 232n, 235n
Jones, J. R., 167
Joseph, A., 239
Journal of Applied Psychology, 219, xxix
Journal of Organizational Behavior Management, 50
Judge, T. A., 106, 133, 139, 140, 169, 204, 205, 210, 216, 224, 231, xi
Julian, J. W., 113
Justice theory, organizational, 95–98, 229–233

Kacmar, K. M., 21n
Kahneman, D., 113n
Kamalanabhan, T. J., 130
Kanfer, F., 76
Kanfer, R., 16n, 17, 56, 67, 68, 76n, 113,
    128, 137, 138, 139, 147n, 162, 183,
    208, 221, 224, 226, 227, 248, xi, xix
Kantrowitz, T. M., 128, 139, 221,
    226, 227
Kaplan, E., 52n, 178
Kaplan, S. A., 222, 224
Karasek, R. A., 158
Karoly, P., 76, 203
Katzell, R. A., 11
Kaufman, A., 51
Kaul, J. D., 20
Kehr, H. M., 187, 188, 219
Keith, N., 183, 200, 228
Kelloway, E. K., 7
Kendall, L. M., 55n
Keppel, G., 33, 34n
Kernan, M. C., 113, 114, 230
Kihlstrom, J. F., 225
Kilmann, P. R., 247
Kim, W. C., 96
King, N., 39, 112
King George III, xxiii
Kinne, S. B., 17, 57, 61, 108, 178,
    268, 269
Kirchner, W. R., 17, 20, 21
Kirkman, B. L., 152, 155
Kirkpatrick, S. A., 70, 76n, 83
Kitayama, S., 199
Klehe, U. C., 277, xvi
Klein, K. J., 30n, 60, 66n, 82n, 177, 219,
    253, 258
Kleinbeck, U., 257
Klimoski, R. J., 169, 185, 224, 256n
Klinger, 225
Kluger, A.V., 129, 199, 200, 210
Knight, D., 150, 184
Knight, P. A., 247
Knowledge, 176, 177, 191, 253
Koeppel, J., 198
Koestner, R., 227
Kolb, B., 8
Kolstad, A., 16
Komaki, J. L., 9, 51
Konovsky, M. A., 96, 232
Kopp, R. E., 51

Koppes, L. L., 13
Korman, A. K., 41, xxviii
Kornhauser, A. W., 7n, 24n
Korsgaard, A. M., 83
Kozolowski, S. W. J., 253, 258
Kramer, S. J., 187
Kraut, A., 151n
Kreitner, R., 50
Kring, W., 79, 218
Kristof-Brown, A. L., 162, 163, 168, 169,
    172n, xi
Kukuyama, T., 56
Kulik, C. T., 60, 83, 162
Kulkarni, A. V., 130

Laboratory experiments, 16–17
Lambert, S. H., 85
Landy, F., 9
Langfred, C. W., 160
Latham, B. W., 127, 177, 200, 202, xxxi
Latham, G. P., 4, 8n, 17, 21n, 50, 52, 55,
    56, 57, 58, 60, 61, 62, 63, 64, 66, 67,
    69, 72, 74n, 75, 76, 77n, 78, 80, 83,
    94, 97, 101, 102n, 103, 106, 107,
    108, 109, 110, 111, 112, 113, 114,
    115, 116, 122, 145, 146, 172, 176,
    177, 178, 180, 181, 182, 183, 184,
    185, 187, 188, 190, 194, 198, 200,
    202, 203, 204, 209, 211, 218n, 231,
    237, 243, 244, 245, 248, 255, 256,
    258, 259, 268, 269, 270, 273, 274,
    275, 276, 277, 278, xix, xxxi,
    xxxii, xxxiii
Laughlin, J., 247
Laurent, A., 157n
Lauver, K. J., 168
Lavelle, J. J., 232
Lawler, E. E., 12, 16, 17, 40, 43, 44n, 46,
    52n, 53, 57, 100, 101, 106, 107, 108,
    115, 120, 121, 160, xi, xxvii
Lazarus, R. S., 226, 232
Leadership theory, 108
Learned helplessness, 204, 245–246
Learning goal orientation, 178, 201
Learning objectives, to FOS authors,
    ix–x
Learning theory, xxviii
Ledford, G. E., 160
Lee, C., 63, 73n, 82
Lee, D. Y., 185, 186

Lee, E. S., 63
Lee, T. W., 56, 122, 185, 186, 188, xv
Lehman, D. R., 199
Leifer, R., 113
Lekes, N., 227
Lengfelder, 191
Leonardelli, G., xv
LePine, J. A., 207
Lerner, B. S., 82
Leung, C., 199
Leung, K., 152, 153, 154, 155
Leventhal, G. S., 122
Levitt, H., 25
Levy, P. E., 66n, 140, 199
Levy-Kolker, N., 82
Lewin, K., 22n, 29, 48, 71n, 108
Lickliter, R., 251
Life span research, 248–249
Likert, R., 15, 108, 111, 114, 117
Lind, E. A., 96, 97, 231, 233
Lippitt, R., 22n, 108
Lituchy, T. R., 82
Locke, E. A., 8n, 17n, 28n, 39, 47, 52, 54,
    55, 56, 57, 58, 60, 61, 62, 63, 64, 65,
    66, 67, 69n, 70, 74, 75, 76, 80, 82,
    94, 101, 102n, 103, 106, 107, 111n,
    113, 114, 116, 118, 121, 122, 127n,
    128, 129, 130, 139, 145, 146, 147,
    149, 150, 157n, 172, 176, 183, 188,
    189, 190, 194, 195, 198, 200, 208,
    209, 210, 216n, 226n, 230n, 243,
    251, 255, 256, 258, 259, xi, xix, xv
Lofquist, L. H., 162, 228n
Logic, 97
Lopez, F. G., 247
Lord, R. G., 65n, 66n, 113, 114, 128,
    221, 224, 251
Lorenzi, P., 113
Lovenberg, G., 94
Love needs, 31, 34
Luthans, F., 50, 74, 207

Mace, C. A., 16, 17
MacKenzie, S. B., 77n
Mackin, S., 81
Maes, S., 203
Magnusson, D., 161
Maier, N. R. F., 3, 21, 37, 44
Mainemelis, C., 186, 219
Maji, C. M., 229

Major, S., 247
Maladjustments, employee, 222–223
Malka, A., 150
Malzacher, J. T., 191, 203
Manahin, C. J., 162
Mann, S., 4
Mant, M. K., 135
Manz, C. C., 245
Markman, A. B., 15n
Marrow, A. J., 22n
Marshall, H. A., 111, 115
Martin, R., 278
Martinez-Pons, M., 82
Martocchio, J. J., 82n
Martorana, P. V., 135
Marucha, P. T., 229
Maruping, L. M., 166
Masculine cultures, 151
Maslow, A. H., 13, 25, 30, 31, 32, 33, 35,
    118, 128, 130
Masterson, S. S., 230
Mathieu, J. E., 83, 94, 142, 201
Matsui, T., 56, 144n
Matz, D. C., 82
Mauborgne, R. A., 96
Mausner, B., 16, 38
Mayer, D., 217
Mayo, E., 18, 21, 99
McCaleb, V., 102n
McCarthy, J., xv
McClear, K., 150
McClelland, D. C., 56, 57, 197
McCormick, M. J., 206
McDougall, W., 9, 11n, 257
McGannon, K., 113
McGrath, J. E., 255
McGregor, D. M., 25, 30, 32, 33, 35n, 36,
    96n, 117, 130
McLean Parks, J., 153, 232
McLuhan, M., 166
McMahan, G. C., 21n, 63
McNatt, D. B., 210, 215, 216
Mediators, 85–86
Meehl, P. E., 51n
Meichenbaum, D. H., 244
Mental health, 159
Mental imagery, 245
Mento, A. J., 65, 69n
Merton, R. K., 214
Metacognition ability, 228

Metacognition training, 182
Metcalfe, J., 225n
Meyer, J. P., 94n, 178, 179, 197, 219, xi
Michie, J., 4n
Mid life workers, 248
Mikels, J. A., 249
Miller, C. E., 199
Miller, D. C., 250n
Millman, Z, 244, 276, xvi
Miner, J. B., 59, 60, 127, 196, 197
Miner Sentence Competition Scale
    (MSCS), 197
Minnesota Satisfaction Questionnaire
    (MSQ), 39n
Mischel, W., 70, 84n, 146n, 161, 225n
Misdirection, potential. See Work
    motivation, future directions
Mitchell, T. R., 41, 47, 51, 56, 59, 62, 74,
    78, 84, 95, 109, 110, 119, 122, 133,
    145, 162n, 176, 185, 186, 219, 253,
    270, 273, xix, xv, xvii, xxx, xxxii
Mizuguchi, R., 144n
Moag, J. F., 96
Moberg, P. J., 81
Moderators concept, 41n
Mohrman, S. A., 160
Mone, M. A., 68
Monetary incentives, 99–102, 150,
    187–189
Money theories, in work motivation,
    11–12
Montgomery, J., 7n
Moods, job satisfaction and, 222–229
Moon, H., 165
Moore, B., 8n
Moore, D. W., 85
Moore, K., 253
Moral disengagement, 212–214
Morale, 28
Morgeson, F. P., 159, 160
Morin, L., 245, xvi
Morrison, E. W., 234
Moskowitz, D. S., 133, 134
Motion-study, 11
Motivation and Morale (Viteles), 29
Motivation-hygiene theory, 37, 38, 39
Motivation predictors. See Personality
    traits, appraisal of
Motivation psychology (1900-1925)
    behavior theories, 9–11

biology theories, 6–9
introduction, 3–6
money theories, 11–12
Motivation psychology (1925-1950)
    attitude surveys, 15–16
    field experiments, 17–18
    Hawthorne studies, 18–21
    introduction, 13–15
    laboratory experiments, 16–17
    summary, 24–25
    World War II, 21–24
Motivation psychology (1950-1975)
    behavior modification, 48–52
    equity theory, 42–44
    expectancy theory, 44–48
    goal-setting theory, 54–58
    introduction, 27–28
    job characteristics, 36–42
    job satisfaction and performance,
        28–29
    motivation theory, 29–30, xx
    need hierarchy theory, 30–32
    summary, 52–54
    theory-driven empirical research,
        33–36
    Theory X and Theory Y, 32–33
Motivation psychology (1975-2000)
    goal limitations, 63–70
    goal-setting theory, 60–63
    high-performance cycle, 80–95
    introduction, 59–60
    job characteristics, 79–80
    organizational justice theory, 95–98
    self-regulation, 76–79
    social cognitive theory, 70–76
Motivation psychology controversies
    intrinsic vs. extrinsic motivation,
        102–105
    introduction, 99, xxi
    monetary incentives, 99–102
    participative decision making,
        108–116
    performance and job satisfaction,
        105–108
    practitioner's viewpoint, 121–124
    scientist's viewpoint, 116–121
Motivation theory, 29–30, 60, xx
Motowidlo, S. J., 74n
Mount, M. K., 133, 135, 136
Mowday, R. T., 3, 44n, 46, 221, ix

Moye, N. A., 160
Moynihan, K. N., 4n
Mtsumoto, H., 199
Muchinsky, P. M., 162
Mudgett, B. O., 202
Multimethod Job Design Questionnaire
    (MJDQ), 159
Mulvaney, S., 225
Mulvey, P. W., 82n
Mumford, M. D., 165
Munsterberg, H., 8n, 72
Murphy, J. E., 225

Nagle, E., 51
Napier, N. K., 274
Narcissistic personality, 247–248
National cultures, 154
Naylor, J. C., 21, xxx
Near, J. P., 223
Nease, A. A., 202
Neck, C., 245
Need deficiency scale, 34
Need hierarchy theory, 30–32,
    53, 128–130
    See also Motivation psychology
        (1950-1975)
Need satisfaction theory. *See* Need
    hierarchy theory
Negative feedback. *See* Feedback,
    processing of
Nelson, D. L., 7n
Neurophysiological states, 225
Neurorehabilitation, 81
Neuroscience models, 251–253
Newbert, M. J., 135
Newell, A., 43n
Ng, K. Y., 230, 232
Nicholson, N., 234, 249, 250
Nijhuis, F. J. N., 159
Nisbett, R. E., 156
Noe, R. A., 168, 207
Nord, W. R., 49, 118
Nougaim, K. E., 35

Occupational norms, 255
O'Driscoll, M. P., 94
Oettingen, G., 217
Okada, A., 56, 144n
Oldham, G. R., 40, 41, 53, 59, 79, 113,
    121, 157, 159, 160

O'Leary-Kelly, A. M., 82n
Ong, M., 155
Operant conditioning, 48, 49, 50
Opportunism, prevalence of, 180
Optimism. *See* Learned helplessness
Ordóñez, L., 189
O'Reilly, C. A., 95, 168, 171n, xix
Organ, D. W., 106, 223, 249
Organizational Behavior (OB), 3
Organizational Behavior Series,
    contributions of, xi–xii
Organizational commitment, 179, 237
Organizational justice theory, 95–98,
    229–233
Organizational science, foundations
    for, ix–x
Organziational theory, ix
Ostroff, 106
Outcome expectancies, 186, 210–212
Owens, P. D., 135

Palrechar, R., 135
Paquin, A. R., 206
Parker, D. F., 104, 106
Parker, S. K., 157, 158, 159, 164
Parkinson's Law, 62
Parks, L., 136
Parnell, M. M., 247
Parsons, C. K., 167, 171n
Participative decision making, 108–116
Paul, M. C., 168
Pay incentives, 99–102, 150, 187–189
Pearson, J., 233
Penney, L. M., 247, 248
Perceived injustice, 231
Performance, job satisfaction and,
    105–108
    See also Goal-setting theory
Performance contingent rewards, 101
Performance goals, 187
Perrewé, P. L., 136, 210
Personal assessments, xiii
Personal initiative, 203, 217, 218
Personality traits, appraisal of
    context affects of, 150–151
    core self-evaluations, 139–141
    Five Factor Model (FFM), 135–137
    goal orientation theory, 141–142
    introduction, 133–135
    self-determination theory, 142–144

self-regulatory/self-monitoring
    personality, 137–139
summary, 145–147
Person-environment fit model, 161–172
Person-group fit model, 171
Person-job fit model, 171
Person-organization fit model, 171
Person-supervisor fit model, 171, xvi
Pervin, L. A., 56
Peters, T. J., 220
Peterson, C., 246
Peterson, D., 188n
Peterson, R. S., 135
Pettigrew, T. F., 232n
Pfeffer, J., 36, 52, 53, 54, 121, 223n
Phan, S. H., 188
Philips, D. C., 59n
Phillips, J. M., 85, 142
Physiological drives, 24
Physiological needs, 31
Pierce, W. D., 103, 104
Pinder, C. C., 59n, 60, 104, 105,
    120, 121, 127n, 231, 237, 239,
    257, 258, xi, xix
Piotrowski, M., 136
Platt, J. R., 47
Podsakoff, P. M., 77n
Popp, G. E., 160
Porac, J., 113
Porter, C., 168
Porter, C. O., 165, 230, 232
Porter, L. W., 12, 16, 33, 34, 35, 46, 57,
    60, 106, 109, 118, 120, 196n
Positive psychology, 246
Powell, C., 130
Powell, D. M., 94n
Powers, T. A., 227
Practitioner principles, xxx–xxxiii
Practitioner-scientist model, 265–279,
    xiv, xxiii–xxxiii
Prevention focus, 179, 200n
Prince-Gibson, E., 149
Priorities, 255
Pritchard, R. D., 43, 68, 175, 206
Procedural justice. See Organizational
    justice theory
Productivity, defining, 206
Promotion focus, 179, 200n
Proximal goals, 183–184, 204
Psychiatry, xxiii
Psychological Abstracts, xxvi

Psychological contracts, 233–237
Pugh, S. D., 226, 232, 233
Pursell, E. D., 77n, 273
Pursuit *vs.* abandonment, 229
Pygmalion effect, 214–216

Quick, J., 7n
Quinones, M. A., 202

Rabble hypothesis, 23
Ramamoorthy, N., 233
Randall, D. M., 94
Rao, P. U. B., 130
Rational emotive therapy, 245
Reddon, J. R., 134, 165
Reed, J. L., 128, 129
Reeve, 250
Reiser, M., 227
Reisetter, M. F., 144
Relapse-prevention training, 245
Renn, R. W., 198
Research process, xxxii
Resilience, 229
Resource allocation time, 185
Reward systems. *See* Monetary
    incentives
Reynolds, D. B., 82
Rice, R. W., 113
Richardson, A., 245
Richins, M. L., 150
Ringenbach, K. L., 141
Roberson, L., 83, 199, 223
Roberson-Bennett, P. A., 56
Roberts, K. H., 41, 59, 121
Robertson, I. T., 74, 207, xix
Robinson, S. L., 234
Roe, R. A., 160, 203, 253, 254
Roethlisberger, F. J., 18, 19, 20
Rokeach, M., 149n
Ronan, W. W., 37, 38, 57, 61, 108, 115,
    268, xxv, xxvii
Ronen, S., 129
Roney, C. J. R., 182
Rosen, C. C., 140
Rosenthal, G. T., 81
Rosenthal, R., 214
Rosse, J. G., 82n
Rothbard, N. P., 164n
Rothstein, M., 134, 165
Rotman, J., xviii
Rotter, 71n

Rotundo, M., 139
Rounds, J. B., 133n
Rousseau, D. M., 78n, 151n, 234, 235n, 236, xi
Routundo, M., xv
Rupp, D. E., 231, 232
Ruttenberg, H., 21
Ryan, T. A., 21, 23, 27, 28, 54, 55, 65, 104, 119, 142, 143

Saari, L. M., 50, 55, 72, 110n, 111, 112, 115, 145, 151n, xvi
Sadri, G., 74, 207
Safety needs, 31
Sagie, G., 149, 155n
Saks, A., 208, xv
Salancik, G. R., 52, 53, 54, 116, 121, 223n
Salas, E., 182
Sanchez-Runde, 154
Sashkin, M., 108
Satisfaction. *See* Job satisfaction theory
Schafer, W. D., 250n
Schaubroeck, J., 167
Scheier, M. F., 65, 66n, 67, 200
Schein, E. H., 215n
Schepers, D. H., 237
Scherer, P. D., 43n
Schleicher, D. J., 139
Schmidt, F. L., 47, 121, 182
Schminke, M., 232
Schmitt, N., 135
Schneider, B., 19n, 39, 40, 42, 52, 57, 59, 60, 106, 110n, 129n, 133, 167, 168, 215n, ix, xv, xxi
Scholz, U., 155
Schraw, G., 144
Schully, J. A., 159
Schunk, D. H., 184
Schwab, D. P., 47, 57, 60
Schwartz, S. H., 149, 155n
Schwarzer, R., 155
Schweitzer, M. E., 189
Scientific management, principles of, 12, 16, 21
Scientist-practitioner, art of, 265–279
Scott, B., xv
Scott, K. S., 97
Scott, W. D., 4n, 8n, 161
Seabright, M. A., 232

Seijts, G. H., 69, 83, 127, 177, 180, 183, 184, 185, 200, 202, 209, 256, xxxiii
Self-actualization, 31, 34, 37n
Self-determination theory, 101, 103, 142–144
Self-efficacy
  effects of, 65, 71n, 207–210
  emotional control and, 229
  goal-setting theory and, 72, 73, 74, 75, 76, 184
  high-performance cycle and, 82–83
  self-regulation and, 79
  values and, 155, 159
Self-esteem, 209
Self-expectations, 214
Self-fulfilling prophecy (SFP), 214
Self-management, 75, 77, 204, 205
Self-motivation, 66, 137–139
Self-regulation, of behavior, 63, 67, 72, 76–79, 137, 177, 203–206, 225
Self-talk, 244-245, 276
Seligman, M. E. P., 204, 245, 246
Sempel, J., 79, 218
Seo, M., 225, 226, 227
Sewell, G., 251n
Seymore, J. D., 49
Shaffer, R. H., 63
Shah, J., 192, 193
Shalley, C. E., 68, 113
Shapiro, D., 3, 46, 152, 155
Shapiro, H. J., 47
Sharp, A. A., 24n
Shaw, J., 43n, 55
Shaw, J. D., 163, 164
Shaw, K. M., 102n, 145
Sheehan, M., 4n
Shelton, D., 135n
Sheppard, L., 165, 258
Shouldice, L., 239
Shultz, R., 226
Siegel, D., xvii
Silver, W. S., 83
Silverthorthorne, C. D., 160
Simmering, M. J., 168
Simmons, 67
Simon, H., 43n, 243
Sincerity, 97
Sirota, D., 151n
Skarlicki, D. P., 97, 231, 232, 233, 235n, 276, 277, 278, xvi
Skinner, B. F., 27, 48, 49

Slocum, J. W., 142, 201, 202
Slowik, L. H., 186, 219, 255
Smith, B. D., 168
Smith, E. M., 182, 183
Smith, K. G., 146, 208
Smith, P. C., 21, 23, 27, 28, 39, 54, 55, 63
Snyderman, B. B., 16, 38
Social cognitive theory
    action theory, 217–219
    goal-setting theory and, 70–76, 185
    introduction, 207
    moral disengagement, 212–214
    need hierarchy theory and, 129
    outcome expectancies, 210–212
    personality traits and, 145
    Pygmalion effect, 214–216
    self efficacy and, 207–210
    self-regulation and, 205
    summary, 219–220
    20th century controversies, 120
    values and, 159
Social comparative fit, 257
Social diffusion theory, 259
Social identity theory, 130, 256, 257
Social learning, 71
Social normative fit, 257
Social psychology, 244
Social Sciences and Humanities
    Research Council, xix
Societal culture, effects of, 151–157
Society for the Promotion of the Science
    of Management, 11
Society of Industrial and Organization
    Psychology (SIOP), xiv, xxx
Socioanalytic theory, 131, 135n
Socioemotional selectivity theory, 249
Socio-technical systems theory, 42
Song, Z., 140
Sonnentag, S., 200, 205
Soose, A., 79, 218
Soper, B., 81
Sorenson, S., 140
Spangler, W. D., 135
Spatero, S. E., 191, 222, 227
Spector, P. E., 136, 210, 247, 248
Spence, K. W., 23, 27, 70, 194n
Spirituality factors, 239–240
Srivastava, A., 150
Stackman, 258
Stagna, 182

Stagner, R., 23, 28n, 107n
Stajkovic, A. D., 74, 194, 195, 207
Stanley, J. C., 62, 113
Stanne, M. B., 181
Staw, B. M., 70, 201
Steele, T. P., 112, 115
Steelman, L. A., 199
Steensma, 231
Steers, R. M., 3, 46, 60, 154, 219
Stewart, G., 135, 136, 145
Stock, F. G. L., 17
Stone, T., 113
Strategic management, 259
Strategic plan, 96
Stress, appraisal of, 158, 182, 229, 231
Stuart, C., xvi
Stuhlmacher, A. F., 180
Subconscious goals, 190–198
Successful performance. See
    Performance, job satisfaction and
Sud, S., 155
Sue-Chan, C., 155, 203, 277, xvi
Suh, E. M., 136
Sulimani, R., 214, 215, 216
Sumer, H. C., 247
Summit Group of the Society of
    Organizational Behavior (SOB), xiv
Superordinate goals, 181
Supplementary fit model, 162–163
Supplies-value fit model, 163
Sutton, S. K., 200, 221
Swann, W. B., 199n
Synchronicity theory, 166
Systemic injustice, 231

Tabernero, C., 83, 201
Taijfel, H., 256
Takata, T., 199
Takeuchi, R., 233
Tan, V., 81
Tang, T. L. P., 82
Tasa, K., 177, 200, 202
Taylor, F. W., 12, 14, 17n, 25, 99, 158n
Taylor, M. S., 233
Taylor, S., ix
Team effectiveness, 256–257
Tekleab, A. G., 233
Tenenbaum, G., 82
Ten Horn, L. A., 160
Tepper, B. J., 230

Tetrick, L. E., 94(f)
Tett, R. P., 134, 145, 165
Thayer, P., 15n, 65n, 79, 159
Thematic Apperception Test (TAT),
    56, 197
Theorell, T., 158
Theory-driven empirical research.
    See Motivation psychology
    (1950-1975)
Theory X, 32–33, 35n, 130, 215n
Theory Y, 33, 117, 130, 215n
Thierry, H., 47, 257
Thompson, C. M., 207
Thorensen, C. J., 222, 224
Thorndike, E., 10, 24n, 30, 48, 105, 117
Thurstone, L. L., 15
Tiffin, J., 23
Tikochinsky, J., 129
Time factors, 253–255
Time-study, 11
Tjosvold, D., 181
Tobis, B. A., 225
Toh, S. M., xv
Tolman, E. C., 45
Tosi, H., xxix
Traits. *See* Personality traits, appraisal of
Trans-situational goals. *See* Values, as
    trans-situational goals
Triandis, H. C., 29n, 136
Trip, T. M., 232
Trist, E. L., 42
Trompenaars, F., 156
Tschan, F., 255
Tsui, A. S., 199
Tuckey, M., 199
Turillo, C. J., 232
Turner, J. C., 130
Turner, N., 232
Two factor theory, 37, 38, 39
Tyler, T. R., 96, 233

Uhrbrock, R. S., 15
Uma, J., 130
Umphress, E. E., 232
Umstot, D. D., 62, 84
Unckless, A. L., 139
Universalism-particularism, 156
University of Maryland, xxvi
University of Toronto, xv, xvi
University of Washington, xv, xvi

Valacich, J. S., 166
Values, as trans-situational goals
    context affects of, 150–151
    effect of job characteristics,
        157–161
    effect of person-environment fit,
        161–172
    effect of societal culture, 151–157
    introduction, 149–150
    summary, 172–173
Vancouver, J. B., 66n, 205, 207
Vandenberghe, C, 178
Van den Bos, K., 97, 233
Vanderslice, V. J., 113
Van de Ven, A., ix
VandeWalle, D. M., 141, 142, 178n, 198,
    201, 202
Van-Dijk, D., 129, 178, 200
Van Eerde, W., 47
Van Vianen, A. E. M., 163
Vasnathi, M., 130
Verbal self-guidance (VSG), 245
Verbeke, W., 154, 155
Verma, A., xv
Vermut, R., 231
Verplanken, B., 150
VIE theory (valence, instrumentality,
    expectancy), 45
Virtual teams, 166
Viswesvaran, C., 94
Viteles, M. S., 13, 14, 24n, 28, 29, 99,
    105, 117, 223
Vocational maladjustment, 222
Von Bergen, C. W., 81
Vroom, V. H., 28, 29n, 37, 39, 44, 45, 46,
    47, 48, 71n, 73, 105, 106, 108, 117,
    118, 121, xi, xvii
VSG (verbal self-guidance), 245

Wagner, J. A., III, 22n, 116, 165
Wahba, M. A., 35, 47, 121
Walbridge, T., xvii
Wall, T. D., 158
Wanberg, C. R., 139, 140
Wanous, J. P., 123
Warremfeltz, R., 131
Warren, C. R., 222, 224
Waterman, R. H., 220
Wathne, K. H., 180
Watson, J. B., 9, 10, 27, 30, 48

Weber, M., xv
Webster, E., 29n, xxv
Weichmann, D., 135
Weick, K. E., 43, 108, 115, xxvii
Weinberg, R. S., 82
Weiner, B., 185, 245
Weiss, H. M., 84, 127, 177, 222,
    223, 224n
Weissbein, D. A., 182
Welch, J., 134n, 214n
Welchans, T. D., 97
Well-being, 227n, 239
Welsh, E. T., 134
Wernimont, P. F., 84n
Wesson, M. J., 230, 232
West, B. J., 165
West, R. L., 82
Wexley, K. M., 21n, 49, 102n, 109, 113,
    xxix, xxvii, xxxi
White, J., 209n
White, R. K., 22n, 108, xiii
Whyte, G., 83, 208, 234n, 278, xv
Wicker, F. W., 128, 129
Wiehe, J. A., 128, 129
Wiese, B. S., 228
Wigfield, A., 127, 243
Wiggins, J. S., 134
Wilke, H. A. M., 97
Williams, A. A., 207
Williams, J. R., 199
Williams, K. J., 204
Williamson, P., 199
Wilson, E. O., 67, 234
Winters, D., 69, 115, 182, 184,
    187, xvi
Wisenfeld, B. M., 97
Witt, L. A., 135, 136
Wolff, R., xvii
Wong, A., 181
Wood, R. E., 69n, 74, 83, 106, 120,
    200, 206
Working alliance model, 247
Work motivation, examining the
    present
    emphasis on affect/emotion, 221–240
    need hierarchy theory, 127–131
    personality traits, 133–147
    relevance of cognition, 175–206
    social cognitive theory, 207–220
    values as trans-situational goals,
        149–173

Work motivation, future directions
    clinical psychology and, 244–248
    computer models, 255–256
    evolutionary psychology and,
        249–251
    integration and, 258–261
    introduction, 228n, 243
    levels of analysis, 257–258
    life span research, 248–249
    social psychology and, 244
    teams and, 256–257
    time factors, 253–255
Work motivation, integration model
    of, 258–262
Work motivation, practitioner-scientist,
    265–279, xiv
Work motivation, understanding
    the past
    applicability of organizational justice
        (1975-2000), 59–98
    biology, behavior, and money
        (1900-1925), 3–12
    dust bowl empiricism (1925-1950),
        13–25
    emergence of theory (1950-1975),
        27–58
    20th century controversies,
        99–124, xxi
Work-related stress, 158, 182, 229, 231
World War I, 11
World War II, 21, xxv
Wright, P. M., 4n, 21n, 63, 158, 254
Wyatt, S., 4n, 17
Wyerhaeuser Company, xv, xxviii

Xie, J. L., xv

Yanar, B., xvi
Yankelovich, 42
Yukl, G. A., 49, 56, 58, 60, 74n, 106,
    109, 273, xxvii, xxviii

Zajac, D. M., 83, 94, 142, 201
Zapf, D., 63, 69, 183
Zedeck, S., 30n, 219
Zetik, D. C., 180
Zimmerman, B. J., 82, 163
Zinovieva, I. L., 160
Zi-Ya, 181
Zsolnal, I., 213
Zweig, D., xv

About the Author

Gary Latham is Secretary of State Professor of Organizational Effectiveness in the Rotman School of Management at the University of Toronto, with cross-appointments in the Departments of Psychology and Industrial Relations, and in the School of Nursing. He is Past President of the Canadian Psychological Association, a Fellow of the Academy of Management, the American Psychological Association, Association for Psychological Science, Canadian Psychological Association, and the Royal Society of Canada. He is the only person to receive both the awards for Distinguished Contributions to Psychology as a Profession and as a Science from the Society for Industrial/ Organizational Psychology. He is also the recipient of the Scholarly Practitioner award from the Academy of Management and the Heneman Career Achievement Award from the Academy of Management Human Resource Division. In 2006 he was awarded the prestigious Michael R. Losey prize from the Society for Human Resource Management. He is the coauthor of *A Theory of Goal Setting and Task Performance* (1990) with Edwin A. Locke, and *Increasing Productivity Through Performance Appraisal* (1994) and *Developing and Training Human Resources* (2002), both with K. N. Wexley.